Contents at a Glance

SAMS Teach Yourself

Network Troubleshooting

24 Hours

Jonathan Feldman

SECOND EDITION

SAMS   *201 West 103rd St., Indianapolis, Indiana, 46290 USA*

Sams Teach Yourself Network Troubleshooting in 24 Hours, Second Edition

Copyright © 2003 by Sams Publishing

International Standard Book Number: 0-672-32373-7

Library of Congress Catalog Card Number: 2001099343

Printed in the United States of America

First Printing: October 2002

05   04   03   02   4   3   2   1

Trademarks

Warning and Disclaimer

ACQUISITIONS EDITORS
Jenny L. Watson
Dayna Isley

DEVELOPMENT EDITOR
Maryann Steinhart

MANAGING EDITOR
Charlotte Clapp

PROJECT EDITOR
Matthew Purcell

COPY EDITOR
Rhonda Tinch-Mize

INDEXER
Sandy Henselmeier

PROOFREADER
Abby Vanhuss

TECHNICAL EDITOR
Bill Wagner
Marc Charney

TEAM COORDINATOR
Amy Patton

INTERIOR DESIGNER
Gary Adair

COVER DESIGNER
Aren Howell

PAGE LAYOUT
D&G Limitted, LLC

GRAPHICS
Oliver Jackson
Tammy Graham
Steve Adams
Laura Robbins

Contents

About the Author

JONATHAN FELDMAN is a hands-on network troubleshooting professional who is also a columnist and contributing editor for *Network Computing* magazine.

He is the author of *Network+ Exam Guide*, and a contributor to *Maximum Security, Third Edition*. A multi-disciplinary troubleshooting expert, Jonathan has given networking workshops throughout the United States, at venues such as PC Expo/TECHXNY and Certification Expo. Network tools that he's developed have been used by large organizations including American Express, the State of Virginia, the State of Montana, Novell, and NASA.

He currently lives and works in Savannah, Georgia as Chatham County's chief technical manager. In his copious spare time, he enjoys running, cooking, and playing the guitar, but not all at the same time. He can be reached at jf@feldman.org.

Dedication

This is still for Jim Reich because he's still a rocket scientist, GM, best man, friend, partner-in-crime, and fellow hacker. —IHTFP, Mofo.

Acknowledgments

Once again, I could not have finished this book without the encouragement, intelligent advice, friendship, and love of my partner and best friend, Stacy Feldman. I am more fortunate than I deserve to be married to such a level-headed and giving person.

My Pop is largely responsible for attempting to beat good, diagnostic techniques into my head at an early age; my hat is off to him. He is one of the best diagnosticians I have ever met. In particular, I thank him for teaching me how to write SOAP notes, and I thank both of my folks for teaching all seven of us to think and fend for ourselves at an early age—both of which come in handy when troubleshooting anything.

I'm grateful to the entire Reich family, notably Jim and his mom Mary, for allowing me to be a teenage computer (and cookie) parasite decades ago. I probably wouldn't be in this profession today but for the hours I spent in their home hacking away on the Trash-80 and the good old Apple. (Not to mention the fact that I probably owe them thousands of dollars for groceries.)

Wade Rockett and Tony "Sergeant" Clark deserve mention here as two buddies who provided inspiration to keep me on track on this project. (Beatings will continue until morale improves!) I also thank Logan Johnson for providing much-needed groovy tunes to help me through my last marathon weekend; and Brian Groff for the curbside rant sessions. Live for the swarm!

Pat Segal, of course, is the woman who likely made the second edition of this book possible—Bookstore owners beware.

Network Computing has been a big part of my life for many years, both personally and professionally. Judy Biener, Kevin Cooke, Amy Lipton, Brad Shimmin, and a "cast of thousands," including all the behind-the-scenes folks and readers writing in to praise or flame—all have helped me grow and learn as a network professional. Similar kudos goes to Neohapsis' Greg Shipley and the varied denizens of the "neo-tech" mailing list. Thanks, folks.

I don't think I would have gotten through this project without the help and professional-ism of several folks associated with Sams Publishing: Jenny Watson and Maryann Steinhart in particular showed enough tough love that I actually finished this edition rather than stretching it into a ten-year project. A tip of my hat also goes to Mark Taber, Rhonda Tinch-Mize, and Matt Purcell for taking care of business and keeping their sense of humor while I was cranking through this.

Leo, Moshe, and Avi: Yes, we can go camping now. Thanks for keeping me smiling!

Jonathan Feldman
August 4, 2002, Savannah, Georgia

Tell Us What You Think!

As the reader of this book, *you* are our most important critic and commentator. We value your opinion and want to know what we're doing right, what we could do better, what areas you'd like to see us publish in, and any other words of wisdom you're willing to pass our way.

You can email or write me directly to let me know what you did or didn't like about this book—as well as what we can do to make our books stronger.

Please note that I cannot help you with technical problems related to the topic of this book, and that due to the high volume of mail I receive, I might not be able to reply to every message.

When you write, please be sure to include this book's title and author as well as your name and phone or email address. I will carefully review your comments and share them with the author and editors who worked on the book.

Email: networking@samspublishing.com

Mail: Mark Taber
          Associate Publisher
          Sams Publishing
          201 West 103rd Street
          Indianapolis, IN 46290 USA

Reader Services

For more information about this book or others from Sams Publishing, visit our Web site at www.samspublishing.com. Type the ISBN (excluding hyphens) or the title of the book in the Search box to find the book you're looking for.

Introduction: Getting Ready to Troubleshoot

Welcome.

Four years ago, I wrote what I thought was a guide for the network perplexed; a fairly concise and practical book, a brain dump of everything I knew about network troubleshooting. (Make of that what you will.) I specifically wrote it for people who were reasonably smart, but didn't know anything about computing, and thought that it would be largely ignored by those who did.

I was wrong.

In fact, there were two groups of folks who jumped on that book so darn hard that it gave me a concussion: folks who didn't know anything about computing, sure; but also, new-on-the-job system administrators who had gotten various "paper" certifications and yearned for more real-world troubleshooting tips that would help them do their jobs more effectively.

I've gotten feedback from both groups, both saying embarrassingly nice things about that book and suggesting things to cover in future editions; this feedback is what largely encouraged me to tackle this project again, and I thank you all more than you know. I welcome further feedback at `tynt@feldman.org`.

That said, this edition of *Sams Teach Yourself Network Troubleshooting in 24 Hours* retains all the crunchy wholesome taste of the first one, slightly reorganized so that I could also cover the latest gee-whiz technology. Accordingly, you will find coverage of the latest gadgets herein.

Troubleshooters-R-Us

Like surgeons about to embark on a heart transplant, network professionals with years of training and experience gear up to tackle a complex network problem. They might tote complex and costly tools and speak network protocols as a second language. Pretty scary!

Yet, most network problems don't require a degree in rocket science to solve. In fact, just as you are the person who clears the paper jam or changes your toner cartridge on your own photocopier without having to call Mr. Xerox, you can also be the person who unclogs your office's email when it snarls up. Why not? You have a brain, and with a basic understanding of how this stuff works, you can come to logical conclusions just like the next person. You might annoy your dependency-oriented consultant by calling him less frequently, but such is the price of success.

Do network professionals really need expensive toys to solve most of your network problems? Not really. The reality is that network folks who rely on network toys rather than their brains, gumption, and common sense do not tend to be very good troubleshooters at all. They tend to concentrate on the accumulation of cool toys rather than solutions that address your business needs.

Most really good networking professionals are able to make these expensive network toys work for them only because of their keen observation abilities and plain old common sense. And much of the time, they don't even need the expensive toy to troubleshoot the problem. Why? Because they understand the fundamentals of "black box" troubleshooting, principles that you can learn in Part II, "Black Box Troubleshooting." Of course, they also understand the underlying principles of computer networking, but those principles are actually pretty simple. This is great news because it means that you don't have to spend $10,000 on a network analyzer to get similar results most of the time. If you operate a small business, breathe a sigh of relief; if you are a computing professional for a large business, prepare to get patted on the back for saving the company large amounts of money.

Black Box Troubleshooting

Black box troubleshooting is how I refer to treating a complex system as a series of simpler systems. Each piece is a "mysterious little black box," a box with hidden stuff in it that makes it do what it does. (Black boxing is used in all sorts of scientific endeavors, including software development, and it's really useful in troubleshooting.) From a troubleshooting perspective, the hidden stuff doesn't matter while you do your "high level" troubleshooting.

That is, you don't care why one of the pieces of the system is doing what it is doing; the important thing is that it is doing it. Much like object-oriented programming, black box troubleshooting allows you do more work in less time because you're not worried about the picky little details!

For example, although you might know nothing about the internals of a fuel pump (and don't really care to know), you still might suspect it as a potential cause of your car's random stalling. (This is a true story, by the way, from yours truly, who really does not know all that much about automobile repair.) As a matter of fact, if you decided to learn all about the internal workings of fuel pumps, you would quickly burn up all the spare time that you had to actually do work on your car; why bother? Learning about fuel pumps is a nonessential item to handling this problem, and merely wastes time. Avoiding time wasters like this by only considering information that is pertinent to the problem at hand is called information hiding, and is essential to black box troubleshooting.

Because you treat the fuel pump as a black box, you rule it out or rule it in as a cause by replacing it with a known good fuel pump to see if the system (your car) starts behaving properly. After a day or so of a trouble-free car, you know that the fuel pump was in fact the cause—all without having to know how a fuel pump works on the inside. Black box troubleshooting is a way for a busy person to troubleshoot just about any problem that you care to think of.

On a computing front, this book will teach you to categorize and classify various systems, sub-systems, and equipment into different "boxes;" this will enable you to quickly and effectively rule in or rule out a given "box" as a source of network or computing trouble.

Even if you rely on a vendor (and you will; even pros do!), knowing what you are doing can only help speed up the resolution of your problems. Think of it as going into a limited partnership with your professional network installers and troubleshooters—your *vendor*. You solve the simple stuff and look like a hero, and you can hand off the really annoying stuff to them.

The ratio of users to network professionals is rather low, and a lot of times a person (you, perhaps) gets roped into being an unofficial, unsung, and (of course!) unpaid network troubleshooter. As long as you are in this capacity, you might as well not be miserable doing it, so it makes sense to get comfortable with the technology and techniques.

Of course, even if you're lucky enough not to have been roped into being an unofficial network troubleshooter, it's likely that your job depends heavily on your network ability. Whether your job is obviously related to the network (like system administration, programming, or help desk management) or your job simply depends on your access to data (like engineering or medicine), the fact is that you need to be able to share data to get your work done. If you can get past most network bugaboos by yourself, you'll not only be able to pat yourself on the back and allow yourself a congratulatory smile, but you'll also work faster than the guy in the next office who has to wait for the hard-core network geek to show up.

Do you have to become a geek yourself to be any good at this? Definitely not; some of the best troubleshooters I know are people who actually have a life.

On the other hand, there are topics and levels of detail not covered by this book that are absolutely essential to being a professional network engineer, designer, or manager. (See `http://feldman.org/books` for some recommendations.)

Still, the nitpicky details themselves are not essential to somebody employing black box troubleshooting, where it is axiomatic that the nonessential details remain hidden. However, you'll learn enough in this book to have a competent conversation with a high-level network support person about your more complex network issues.

You're also about to learn a lot of the simple-but-powerful concepts that professionals rely on. In addition to network fundamentals, even the best troubleshooting professional needs

- Product documentation
- Site documentation
- Additional books and materials
- Observation and common sense
- Note-taking and record-keeping skills
- Black box troubleshooting skills
- Other support people

How to Use This Book

If you are a total network newcomer, I recommend that you start with Hour 1, "Understanding Networking: The Telephone Analogy." This will help you get up to speed on network terms and the framework in which networks live. After you get through that, you'll feel pretty comfortable with the rest of the book; more importantly, you'll understand a lot of the main terms and principles of networking as well as the way a network conversation flows from start to finish, and you'll start to understand why your network might be broken. You can skip this if you feel comfortable with networking terms and principles and want to dive right into the troubleshooting methods.

Whether or not you are familiar with networking, if you are not familiar with the OSI model of networking, you might want to check out Hour 2, "The OSI Model of Networking: Understanding the Old School." The OSI model breaks networking down into seven "layers," which are useful concepts when applying black box troubleshooting to a problem.

Although a basic understanding of networking is necessary to figure out some specific problems, troubleshooting a network actually doesn't require a deep and highly geeky understanding of networking. Troubleshooting a network, particularly a large network, is very much like figuring out a puzzle. If you've got a basic idea about how the network should work, and if you know which piece depends on which (much like how you always place the edge pieces on a jigsaw puzzle before delving into the middle ones) and the way information should flow, pointing the finger at the general problem area usually isn't much of a challenge. After you figure out the general area of the problem, you can then use basic troubleshooting techniques to figure out which specific piece of the puzzle is causing your grief. After all, you don't need to be a Rembrandt expert to do a jigsaw puzzle of a Rembrandt painting, do you?

Troubleshooting with No Technical Knowledge?

Well, sure. Let's take a real-life puzzle that you'd probably be pretty good at troubleshooting. Say that you're a teacher; your problem is that you have three boys who tend to cause trouble in your classroom. You will probably engage in two of the most powerful black box troubleshooting techniques, "divide and conquer" and the "delta method."

You'll realize that one of the boys is new in town, and thus is the only factor that has changed recently in your classroom, which up until now has been serene. You separate him from the group, reasoning that he is almost certainly the cause. By dividing him from the other two boys and watching the problem move to another section of the classroom, you rule him in as a cause, and rule out the other two boys. Easy, right? So, right away, before even reading the rest of this book, you've got some ammunition to use against network problems.

Let's consider a similar problem to your classroom problem. Because skilled labor is hard to come by, your retailer has hired some gorillas to come in and install a new PC in your office. They come in, install it, and everything seems fine. The next day, nobody can send email! One of the gorillas decides that it's time to rebuild your email server, but you cleverly realize that the only change since yesterday is the new PC. You insist that the gorillas disconnect it from the network, and voila! The problem miraculously goes away. Upon inspection, the new PC's network cable has visible damage to it, which has caused a network problem affecting the email server. One of the gorillas replaces the network cable and walks away muttering something about "still need to rebuild that server." You're a hero, you have avoided the risks of having a gorilla rebuild a perfectly fine mail server, and you haven't broken a sweat.

Of course, it's not always that easy. A lot of times, it's tough to know what has changed, or even who's changed it. (This is the Nobody Admits Anything principle in action, a principle that you will come to know and love.) Or, something might legitimately break without a new element even entering the picture. Unfortunately, because networks are what tie everything together, pretty much anything in the mix, soup to nuts, can be a source of trouble. And because everything is tied into the network, it's easy to blame the network. Actually, a lot of times, you simply have to figure out that the trouble is NOT the network!

The bottom line is you only have to know a little bit about everything in order to start troubleshooting a problem, and then adapt and learn as necessary in order to solve a given problem. And you will!

PART I

Basic Networking Concepts

Hour

HOUR **1**

Understanding Networking: The Telephone Analogy

Every man is a damned fool for at least five minutes every day. Wisdom consists in not exceeding the limit.

—Elbert Hubbard

Nobody's born knowing how anything works; and trying to understand the pieces and parts that make up a computer network can be pretty daunting, even to folks who are fairly computer literate in other areas. If you're already familiar with basic network terms and concepts (like *switch* or *protocol*), you can skip this hour and move on to bigger and better things; if you're not, this hour's a good way to get comfortable with the basics of network technology. (The next hour lays out a more structured and formal model called the OSI model, which is also helpful.)

Getting a handle on something foreign to you by using terms and concepts you already know is a good way to learn it faster. Learning the lingo helps a lot, but even getting good at the jargon does you no good if you don't have something familiar with which to compare the new terms. Accordingly, what follows is a comparison of networking terms to something familiar to most of us: telephone terms.

> The following term comparisons are analogies. They are *not* identical; be careful not to assume that they are.

Comparing the public telephone system to computer networks can help newcomers bring their network understanding up to speed pretty fast. Although *many* differences exist under the hood, there are enough similarities on the surface to allow you to grasp the concept of how a network really works. In theory, network calls act very much like telephone calls. Figure 1.1 shows a rough comparison of a data network to the telephone system. Here's a quick reference list:

Network Buzzword	Telephone Equivalent
NIC (network interface card)	The telephone in your house.
Network media (cabling)	The phone wire.
Address	The telephone number.
Router or gateway	The telephone company's central office equipment that connects different "area codes."
Switch	A telephone PBX that can offer private lines and connect party lines to the main system.
Hub or concentrator	A shared line used by folks in a common area.
Protocol	The language. You can communicate with someone only if you both understand the language being used. Any language can be used for any kind of conversation, but as in real life, some people (in the case of networks,

Network Buzzword	Telephone Equivalent
	programs rather than people) don't understand more than one language, and certain languages are more dominant than others.
Packet or frame	A sentence of a conversation (not the entire conversation, but one part of it).
Port or socket number	The extension. Suppose you want to speak to Ms. Jones, who works at Company XYZ. Typically, you'll call Company XYZ's main phone number and ask for Ms. Jones's extension.
Socket pair	The unique combination of both callers' information, combining both network address (telephone number) and port numbers (extensions). In the telephone world, if Jonny, at 912-555-1212, extension 585 is talking to Joey at 516-555-1212, extension 852, the socket pair might be expressed as 912-555-1212:585/ 516-555-1212:852.
Program or service	The entity on the other end of the line that can provide information, or a service that you get during a conversation. Once you get Ms. Jones on the line by asking for her extension, you can then ask her how much a particular gadget costs, or you can ask her to send a technician out to install your gadget. Not all services can handle more than one protocol—just as not all people speak more than one language.
Name resolution and directory services	The electronic phone book. Instead of having to remember that Ms. Jones's number is 1-212-888-5555, x205, you can simply perform an automatic lookup-and-dial on "Ms. Jones."

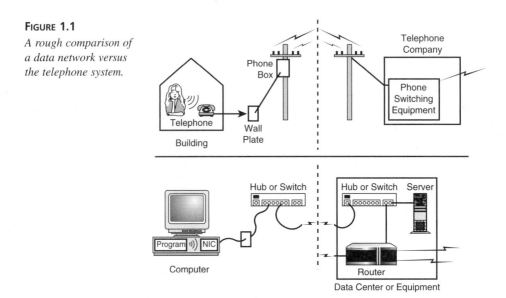

FIGURE 1.1

A rough comparison of a data network versus the telephone system.

Network Interface Cards

Your telephone is very much like the network interface card (NIC) in your computer. Both of them help an individual entity (you, in the case of your telephone, and your computer, in the case of the NIC) talk to others. Also, both the telephone and the network card are oblivious to who is being communicated with and what kind of business is being transacted.

Your telephone is a physical piece of hardware that enables you to connect through telephone company equipment to talk to folks next door or halfway around the world. This is also true of your NIC. It can talk to other NICs on the same line as well as NICs on different lines by using switching equipment that's connected to the line.

MAC Attack

Just as each residence has a unique telephone number, your computer's NIC also has a unique number. However, unlike a telephone, each NIC has a unique number built (or burned) into it at the factory; this is referred to as its burned-in address, or BIA. The BIA is also referred to as the *MAC (media access control)* address. This address is long enough so that trillions and trillions of addresses are possible. For convenience, the address has a compact form, represented by six hexadecimal bytes.

> We'll talk more about MAC in Hour 10, "Ethernet and Switching."

Yikes! Hexadecimal sounds like a witch trial and a math contest rolled up into one. Really, though, it's just a different method of counting—instead of having digits 0–9 (decimal), you use digits 0–F (hex). Because you have more options for digits (16 rather than 10), you can express numbers more compactly. Don't worry about it, though. All you really need to know is that a byte consists of two of these hex digits and that a MAC address is expressed using six bytes. Actually, 00-00-10-2B-5C-8D isn't too much more intimidating than 1-800-555-1212, is it? (For what it's worth, hexadecimal values are *not case sensitive*; that is, 2b-5c-8d is the same as 2B-5C-8D. Using caps or lowercase in a text is merely a preference or a style convention.)

IEEE and OUI

The Institute of Electronic and Electrical Engineers (or IEEE, pronounced "*eye triple-E*") is the organization that, among other things, acts as a standards body for various electronic standards. One of the IEEE's roles is to act as a clearinghouse for MAC addresses.

> How come a clearinghouse is needed for MAC addresses? Many network manufacturers exist, so it's really important that MAC addresses be tracked. Otherwise, two different manufacturers might accidentally make network cards with the same address, which causes network problems if two of these network cards end up on the same network. This could happen even though there are many, many possible MAC addresses. A MAC address's six-hex-digit format (or 48-bit address, if you want to sound geeky by talking in binary terms) turns into 281 trillion possible addresses—281,474,976,710,656 (minus a couple of special, reserved addresses) to be precise! That's a heck of a lot of combinations. Compare this to the phone system in the United States, where only nine billion phone numbers are available.

The IEEE hands out *ranges* of MAC addresses rather than the addresses themselves (for instance, Xircom has all numbers that start with 00-10-A4). This means you can tell who made a network card by looking at the MAC address's first three hex bytes. This is called the *OUI (organizational unique identifier)* and can be useful if you're troubleshooting certain kinds of problems.

OUI ou Non?

Knowing the OUI came in handy for me once when I was experiencing intermittent problems with a new application. The application vendor pointed the finger at one of my network card vendors, who, in turn, told me to get the latest and greatest drivers for its network cards to eliminate the problems I was experiencing with the application. Fortunately, I rolled out only a small set of those drivers, which turned out not to be the greatest. I started to have major network problems and noticed (from the OUIs listed by the network analyzer) that I was only experiencing problems with the cards I had just updated. I undid the update, the network problems went away, and I leaned on the application vendor to solve the original problem. The OUI can really be a useful concept to know. Here's one caution: the OUI list won't always list the manufacturer who made your NIC; the number listed might indicate the *chip* maker. (For example, some Proteon cards use Emulex OUIs.)

If a network configuration option ever asks you whether you want to override the MAC address of a NIC, say no! This option is intended only for experienced network administrators and can wreak havoc if not used correctly.

Routers and Switches

Just as every phone in a corporation might have the same prefix, and allow for in-house, four-digit dialing without hitting the phone company's switching equipment, so too do networks have the concept of local network versus remote network. NICs on a local network can communicate with each other without needing remote-capable equipment. To communicate with a NIC on a remote network, a *router* is required.

To make it easier for routers to differentiate between networks, each network (in modern times, usually referred to as a VLAN, or Virtual Local Area Network) is given a network number. It will come as no surprise, because a router is connected to more than one network, that a router has more than one NIC in it. Its function is to examine incoming "calls" and forward (or route) them to the appropriate destination network.

Routers must understand something about the network protocol they are routing. This is where the analogy breaks down: Although phone switches care nothing about the conversation on the wire, routers do care. It might help to think of routers as friendly neighbors who can pass your message along (that is, if they speak your language). (See Hour 2 for some clarification on this.)

Of course, the phone system needs equipment peppered throughout your neighborhood, and it also needs the high-end equipment at the telephone company. The same goes for your network. Two types of network "glue" tie you and your network neighborhood together:

- Hubs (concentrators)
- Switches

Think of a hub as a shared neighborhood party line (like the one you used to have at Uncle Harry's cabin in the woods). It used to be cost-prohibitive to give each network card its own channel to talk on because more silicon "smarts" were required. Just as its name implies, a *hub* is where all of the NICs on the party line (or *segment*) come together. Each NIC's wire is connected to the hub in a spoke-like fashion, where they all physically share the same wire.

A common physical connection like this is generally referred to as a *bus*, and each participant that tries to use this common connection "gets on" or "gets off" the bus.

Because NICs share a common bus, each NIC can "hear" other NICs. NICs have built-in rules for using this common area, which is discussed further in Hour 10. For the moment, you just need to know that each NIC has been schooled in "netiquette" and has been taught in the factory to play well with others and to share the wire nicely—that is, most of the time. Be aware that if a network card does not obey these rules, this can cause problems on an entire hub, or even an entire VLAN. (See Figure 1.2 for an illustration of shared versus dedicated telephone lines and network segments.)

Computers on older networks were actually connected together on the same wire, much like older Christmas lights used to be. Therefore, a physical break in the wire meant that all the computers on one side of the break went down. A hub-based segment fixes this because each computer has its own physical connection, and the hub ties them all together. The newer method of sharing the wire is called a *star topology* because it looks like a star. The older method is called *bus topology*—the line from PC to PC is the common bus area. (See Hour 10 for some practical tips on wiring.)

A technology called *switching* allows each network card to have its own private line; however, a lot of hub-based shared networks are still in existence, despite the benefits of switching. You'll find switching to be more and more exciting as you get into network troubleshooting. Similar to the way hubs allow users to get away from the "Christmas light bulb" problem, switches allow users to get away from many of the problems of shared networks. Instead of each computer having to compete for the right to talk when it wants to, each computer can transmit pretty much when it needs to—as long as the computer on the other end is available, of course. Others in the network neighborhood no longer compete for the right to talk on the wire because each computer has its own connection.

FIGURE 1.2

Shared versus dedicated lines.

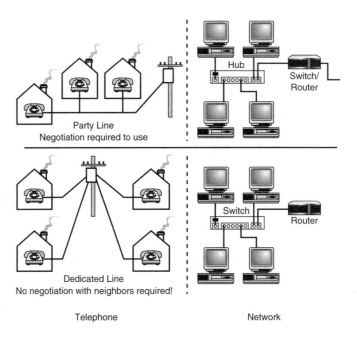

How does this work? In a nutshell, a switch looks at the MAC addresses of two workstations on the network that want to communicate, and it opens up a high-speed private channel for them. A hub has one common channel, but a switch has many, many channels, as well as the intelligence to switch conversations between them. With a switch that does not introduce any propagation delay into the network due to internal processing (called a *wire speed* switch), workstations conversing on the switch are not affected whatsoever by other workstations talking away at full speed.

Although shared hubs have their virtues (for example, it's easy to see the conversations on a shared line, and that's good for troubleshooting), the fact remains that they are more trouble-prone than switched networks (which are much faster and more reliable). As we'll discuss in Hour 10, one of the best things you can do to a hub-based network is replace the hubs with switches.

Protocols

Your computer "talks" through its network card, but, unfortunately, technology has not advanced to the point where it can speak English quite yet. Instead, your computer uses a more primitive language—a protocol with a much more limited vocabulary. This protocol is most likely TCP/IP.

Because of the huge success of the TCP/IP-based Internet, other protocols like AppleTalk, DEC-LAT, IPX/SPX, NetBEUI, and SNA are either niche or obsolete, but you should be aware of them: As much as vendors like to talk about this-or-that being obsolete, real people on real networks can be slow to change, and you just might see these on one job or another.

What's the bottom line? Because you can think of these protocols as languages on a telephone, you simply need to make sure that your computer, your application, your router, as well as the far-end computer, and far-end application are all speaking the same language. For example, if you're trying to use an IPX/SPX application on a workstation to communicate with a remote server, make sure that your workstation has IPX/SPX loaded, and make sure that your router handles IPX/SPX.

Parlez Vous TCP/IP?

The good news is that you don't have to know much about protocols to troubleshoot—most of the time, your problems won't be protocol related because protocols are rather simple and well-defined. For example, TCP/IP has been around for more than 25 years (a huge life span in computer years), and its feature additions have been rather modest. This means that unlike a typical desktop application, TCP/IP has had an opportunity to stabilize.

This, among other factors, makes TCP/IP (Transmission Control Protocol/Internet Protocol) pretty much the universal language of network protocols. Again, the Internet has made TCP/IP a household appliance, which means that you most likely already know something about it. For instance, you probably know that a TCP/IP hostname is something like myhost.mycompany.com, and a TCP/IP address looks something like `167.195.160.6`.

What's with the three-dotted address? After all, didn't I just say that an address is a six-byte hexadecimal number? Well, it is for network cards, but it isn't for protocols. Just as your telephone number sounds a bit different when you say it in French, your network address is represented in another way when you "say" it in TCP/IP. For example, although a TCP/IP address and a MAC address look dissimilar, they perform similar roles: They are both, for their own purposes, the "telephone number" of your network card; it just depends on what language you're speaking at the moment.

TCP/IP addresses are always four numbers between 0 and 254 that are represented in the decimal system you know and love. These addresses are typically allocated by an administrator, who must assign a unique address to each computer on her network.

Why should there be two different addresses? Because the OUI is guaranteed to be unique, why not just represent the TCP/IP address in hexadecimal? Long ago, network cards did not all have unique IEEE-distributed MAC addresses; some were limited to 254 addresses! Because of this, using the MAC address for a TCP/IP address in a large network was not practical, so TCP/IP designers invented a method of translating a MAC address into a larger, more unique value. This obviously isn't necessary with today's MAC addresses, but the translation hangs on to this day.

Duplicate TCP/IP addresses can make your TCP/IP-dependent programs stop functioning. If you assign your own TCP/IP addresses—that is, if you use static numbering rather than a *DHCP (Dynamic Host Configuration Protocol)* server—be sure to document well and keep each unique.

DHCP server programs can dynamically hand out IP numbers and other configuration information to many, many computers. This can be a blessing or a curse—would you like it if your phone number changed every few days? On the other hand, DHCP automates the addressing process, hands out other important configuration information (such as DNS servers, which are discussed more in the "DNS" section later in this hour) and tends to eliminate address-duplication errors. You can find practical troubleshooting information on DHCP in Hour 19, "Internet and Intranet Troubleshooting: TCP/IP at Work."

Like a phone number, TCP/IP has its network number (or "area code") built right into it. Unlike a phone number, though, the "area code" is the longer part of the number. The shorter part of the number (referred to as the *node* or *host number*) is the local phone number, with the first part of the address referring to the "area code," known as the network number. The length of a TCP/IP network number is calculated with a network mask, a number that mathematically separates the network number from the node number.

Fortunately, most small TCP/IP networks have the same network mask, so you can calculate your network numbers just by following an example rather than engaging in horrible binary arithmetic.

> The most common use of a network mask in troubleshooting is during configuration verification. Because an incorrect network mask can cause a workstation to malfunction, making sure that a problem PC's network mask is the same as the others is important.

For a network mask whose numbers are all 255, it's pretty easy. Simply write down the IP number with the network mask beneath it; each number that matches up to a 255 is a network number. The remaining number is the node number. Figure 1.3 shows an example.

So what's the point of figuring out which part of a TCP/IP address is the *node* versus the *network* number? If two workstations have the same network number, they are part of the same *subnet*, which means that they are using the same hub or VLAN. This is essential to know that when you're troubleshooting, two folks who have the same network number are using the same PBX.

FIGURE 1.3

When separating node from network number for a network mask with 255s, the node is under the 0.

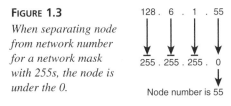

Consider a server whose IP number is 192.168.5.10, with a network mask of 255.255.255.0. The network number you get from this is 192.168.5.0, and the node number is 10. Because simple TCP/IP networks work this way, the binary manipulations for more unusual network masks may be left for those who enjoy pain.

Okay, fine, you don't enjoy pain, but you also need to deal with a workstation that has an address of 192.168.20.50 and a network mask of, say, 255.255.255.224. What's the network number versus the node number? Go grab one of the many IP calculators out on the Internet. Here are two that are pretty good:

- http://www.tactix.com/subnet.html
- http://jodies.de/ipcalc

The one at tactix.com tends to be easier to read if you're just looking to see if two IP numbers fall into the same range, and thus are using the same network number. Figure 1.4 shows the output of this tool using the 255.255.255.224 network mask and 192.168.20.50 IP number. Ignore the ugly looking binary and hexadecimal stuff and jump down to the subnet table. You can see that 192.168.20.50, with the given mask, has a network number of

192.168.20.32 and all numbers that fall between 192.168.20.33 through 192.168.20.62 are in this network. That's all you need to know to effectively troubleshoot.

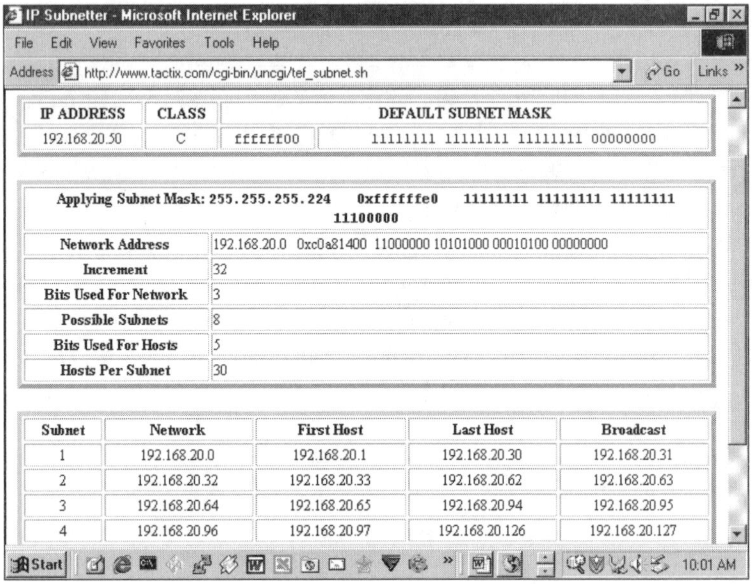

FIGURE 1.4

The IP Subnetter at www.tactix.com is a good way to discover what subnet a given IP address is on.

Although the concept of network masks and network numbers might seem challenging at first, you really do need to know which portion of your TCP/IP address is your network number, so that you can document it and, in turn, troubleshoot it when you need to. These concepts aren't so terrible once you get used to them, so hang in there. (It's the price you pay for being able to "dial out" of your neighborhood.)

Two Dead Protocols

There are many, many obsolete protocols out there, and we definitely don't want to waste time talking about stuff that you'll never run into. Unfortunately, TCP/IP isn't the only protocol out there, and you want to be prepared to deal with existing, as well as newer networks. I still see plenty of older Windows PCs as well as older NetWare networks in use. Accordingly, a quick discussion of two obsolete protocols are in order.

Sprechen Sie DLC?

Some protocols can't dial out of the neighborhood. Have they been bad? Are they being punished? No, they're just not very bright and are largely based on the network card's capability to talk to the local network. These protocols can speak only to other MAC addresses and are known as *DLC (data link control)* protocols. They are not routable,

1

which means that they can talk only to other stations on the same network. You can think of DLC as the "four-digit dialing" we mentioned earlier (without the ability to press 9 to dial out).

Microsoft's NetBEUI is an example of a DLC protocol. NetBEUI stands for *NetBIOS Extended User Interface*, which tells you nothing unless you know what NetBIOS is— Network Basic Input Output System. In a nutshell, NetBEUI is simply an improvement of NetBIOS. NetBIOS is a simple networking protocol that was used by IBM and Microsoft in early DOS-based file-sharing products; NetBEUI is an improvement used in current Windows products.

> Windows 9x users inevitably ask me, "Why can't I see other people's work-groups on the network?" Usually, this is because they're asking Windows 9x to use NetBEUI for file sharing, but they're trying to see workgroups on the other side of a router. You can add a routable protocol such as IPX/SPX or TCP/IP to solve this problem—but you'll need a WINS server if you decide to use TCP/IP. See Hour 12 for details.

Hablas IPX/SPX?

IPX/SPX, in addition to being a routable protocol, is a very easy protocol to work with from a user's perspective. Instead of having to deal with network masks and figuring out network numbers, you need only look at the server (or router) on a network to get the network number, which is an arbitrary and unique hexadecimal number. The node address is simply the MAC address of the network card. The full address, "area code" and all, looks something like this:

```
0000001D: 000093552899
```

This translates to network number 1D, node number 93552899 and involves no figuring at all. Even better, workstations need no address configuration whatsoever because the address is simply lifted from the network card's MAC address. Unfortunately, because IPX/SPX (invented by Novell, the makers of NetWare) used to be a somewhat propri-etary protocol, it never got the market presence that TCP/IP has. Even though Microsoft adopted IPX/SPX as a routable protocol for file and print sharing under Windows NT and 95, the juggernaut-like momentum of the Internet (and as a result, TCP/IP) probably means that IPX/SPX will remain the less dominant player. It isn't going away too soon, though. If you have IPX/SPX in your shop, it's definitely worth being familiar with. See Hour 14, "NDS and NetWare Troubleshooting," for details.

Frames, Packets, and Packet Switching

Two other important building blocks of a network (as important to networking as the cells in your veins are to you) are the protocol packet and the NIC's frame. The frame is the smallest unit of communication for your network card; the packet is the smallest unit of communication for your network protocol—much like a sentence is the smallest whole unit of communication in a conversation. (Although words themselves are even smaller units, they're not complete units of communication. For example, just saying "dinner" to someone doesn't tell him whether you want to invite him to dinner, eat him for dinner, or skip dinner altogether.)

For what it's worth, packets live *in* frames. Why? Well, packets are structured to traverse multiple networks, and frames aren't—they're built for local data transport. However, packets aren't built for local data transport, so they live inside a frame, which is. Don't worry too much about this, we'll get into more detail in the next hour; for the purposes of the following discussion, we'll talk about packets—just bear in mind that when we say "packet," we mean "packet within frame."

Only one packet can be on the wire at a time, which makes it tough when multiple users are on the network attempting to complete multiple tasks. For example, suppose that the following chunks of conversations traveled the wire in this order, without identifiers as to whom is speaking:

"Why don't I pick up some bread for dinner?"

"I'd like you to come home and play."

"Please do pick up some bread on your way home."

"I'll be home soon and would love to play!"

"Will do."

It's tough to follow, huh? Luckily, networks use *packet switching*. The idea of packet switching is simple. Because conversations need to appear to be seamless, each chunk of the conversation contains source and destination information to keep track of who is talking and to whom. Suddenly, what once appeared to be one confused conversation becomes two logical ones:

"Stacy, this is Jonathan. Why don't I pick up some bread for dinner?"

"Jonathan, this is Stacy. Please do pick up some bread on your way home."

"Stacy, this is Jonathan. Will do."

"Jonathan, this is Leo. I'd like you to come home and play."

"Leo, this is Jonathan. I'll be home soon and would love to play!"

Because each packet actually has the address (or "phone number") of the person you need to talk to, and because one computer might have more than one program that wants to talk, there's an additional concept called known as a *socket number* (also called port), which acts very much like a telephone extension. Therefore, just like you might call Frobozz Magic Gadgets and ask to speak to the Wizard at extension 412, when your computer makes a network call, it calls a network address and asks for a port (or socket number).

A socket number is frequently represented by a colon (:) after the address. For example, when you fire up your Web browser to `http://www.co.chatham.ga.us`, you're actually referring to `167.195.160.9:80` (or socket 80 of the TCP/IP address `167.195.160.9`). Socket 80 is the standard socket for Web services, called HTTP (Hypertext Transfer Protocol).

HTTP is the name of the service that is usually offered at socket 80 by the program that lives there. However, HTTP also refers to the set of rules that allow for Web transactions that Web servers and browsers attempt to follow. It's important to understand that there are two definitions of HTTP here: the port name (as in "port 80 is the socket number typically used for HTTP") and the protocol, itself (as in "All Web servers need to follow the HTTP protocol to ensure error-free operation"). Many other protocols and services have this dual reference as well—for example, SMTP, which refers both to socket number 25 (typically used for mail services) as well as the Simple Mail Transfer Protocol's rules of engagement.

Because a port or socket number is the equivalent of a phone extension, the program that picks up the call is the equivalent of the person within the house or company that you want to talk to (see Figure 1.5). The program can do things for you once you "talk"—either give you information or kick off a process that you need accomplished. Some requests can be a combination of both: When you search the Internet, you ask the program on the other end to do a search, and you ask for the answer to your search.

FIGURE 1.5
*A socket number (also
called port) is the
equivalent of a phone
extension.*

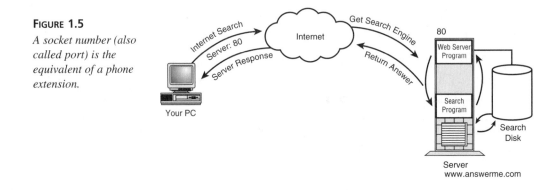

Name Resolution, or What's in a Name?

You've probably asked yourself in one of the preceding paragraphs, "How does
`www.co.chatham.ga.us` get translated into `167.195.160.9`?" Furthermore, why use
names at all? People can deal with phone numbers, why not just use the IP number?
These are good questions. The answer to the latter is that just because people can deal
with a number doesn't mean that they *prefer* to use a number. Which would you rather
remember, 1-800-NETWORK or 1-800-638-9675? Obviously, most people prefer to
remember a name. Actually, names are the better thing to use when networking because
numerical addresses can change during a reconfiguration or a move, whereas symbolic
names typically stay the same.

Name-to-address translation (also known as *name lookup* or *name resolution*) occurs via
name services. Very similar to the speed dial button on your phone, name services are the
networking equivalent of an electronic phone book. They're just as cool and useful as
your cell phone that you can "say the name" to dial with.

DNS

Name resolution services are provided by a server-based program that hands out an
address when you give it a name. Like your speed dial buttons, you must program in a
name entry; entering the correct number for a given name is important.

In particular, TCP/IP name services, although powerful and able to handle millions and
millions of names, isn't exactly plug-and-play. The DNS (Domain Name Service) that
you use when surfing the Web works pretty automatically for you once it's configured

correctly, and it will translate `www.co.chatham.ga.us` to `167.195.160.9`. However, you'll need to know the exact IP address of your DNS server (likely given to you by your system administrator or handed out by a DHCP server). Unlike telephone information, DNS servers all have different addresses; verifying that a workstation's DNS server is correct can be an important troubleshooting step (see Figure 1.6).

FIGURE 1.6

Name resolution on DNS.

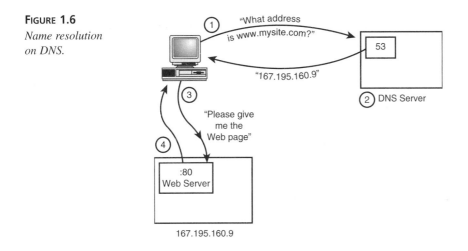

Note that some smaller sites that use TCP/IP might not have a DNS server. (Newer sites will; but some older sites won't.) Instead, each workstation will have a hosts file on the hard drive.

Even worse, some workstations might be using a hosts file, but some might not be. The practical upshot of this, for troubleshooting purposes, is that a hosts file always takes precedence over the DNS. So, if `myserver` gets moved to a new IP address, the DNS gets updated, but a workstation doesn't seem to receive the update, check the hosts file.

A DNS zone (its scope of responsibility for naming) can be huge—for example, `.com` has millions of subzones (`yahoo.com`, `jotto.com`, and so on); on the other hand, it can be small—for example, `feldman.org` lists only a couple of hosts (such as `www.feldman.org` and `mail.feldman.org`) and no subzones.

With DNS servers getting easier to manage and being a mandatory component of Internet access, you can expect to see more of them in smaller shops. It's worth mentioning one buzzword here: When folks refer to a DNS *zone*, it's just a way of referring to the database portion that covers a given DNS name. For example, www.yahoo.com lives in the yahoo.com zone. Simple!

Each DNS server is responsible for its own zone, so if you can't get to one particular address (say, yahoo.com) but can get to another (say, jotto.com), it might be that the name server responsible for that zone is down. On the Internet at large, this rarely happens because the DNS organizers require backup DNS servers for a zone. DNS problems are more likely to happen within a smaller organization's intranet, particularly when all the eggs for that organization are in one basket.

> Remember that you can still dial a number yourself when your speed dial buttons are broken. Similarly, if you cannot get to something by name on your network, try getting to it by number. For example, rather than going to http://www.co.chatham.ga.us, you could try http://167.195.160.9. If this works, you know there's something up with name services.

WINS

Older Microsoft Windows servers, and all Windows *clients* (NT Server 4.0) can use another TCP/IP name resolution service, called *WINS (Windows Internet Name Service)*. WINS is a Windows-specific name service for TCP/IP, and was used to provide name resolution services for Windows networks that spanned more than one VLAN.

Microsoft's new default name resolution service, introduced with Windows 2000, is DNS. Yes, Microsoft ditched out on WINS—it was hard to handle on many levels, and was never as scalable as DNS. However, because WINS is built into all Windows clients, and is a requirement with older Windows servers, you'll still see it around from time to time.

> As I mentioned previously, DHCP can be used to hand out various configuration information, including DNS servers. It can also hand out WINS server information; but some DHCP servers won't call it WINS. Look for something to do with NetBIOS name resolution. That's your WINS server category.

Directory Services

The notion of a directory is similar to the name services concept, but it goes one step further: Instead of simply resolving a name to a number, directory services offer many pieces of vital data on the network. In particular, directory services allow users from all

1

over to log in to the network rather than into a specific server; each server on the network relies on the directory services to assign security rights, and so on.

This is terrific because administrators no longer need to update multiple servers with username and password information; instead, they can administer updates from one point and distribute them throughout the network. The long-term goal has been simplification, which makes troubleshooting easier, but be sure that you understand the amount of ongoing maintenance that is required before you implement. Three notable players and their products in this space are Microsoft's Active Directory, Novell's NDS, and Sun's iPlanet.

Summary

This hour is a reasonably complete introduction to most of the networking concepts you'll run into. However, as they say, the devil's in the details. This hour provides a good foundation on which you can build your troubleshooting knowledge as you read on.

Here are some things to remember:

- A network card acts as your computer's telephone to the outside world. Also, it has its own unique identifier (MAC address) built in to it.

- Some LANs are based on a shared bus (hub) or "party line." As with real party lines, hurt feelings and even major disasters are caused by those who talk out of turn.

- In modern networks, NICs are connected via switches for local communication—these local networks are called VLANs.

- A router is used to route packets (sentences from a network conversation) to and from differing networks; each different network has a different network number that uniquely identifies it.

- Network protocols can be thought of as the different languages humans use. Like humans, programs do not all speak more than one language, so you need to find out what protocol a program uses before you start to troubleshoot it.

- Network naming services, such as DNS and WINS, make it possible for end users to refer to a computer by a symbolic name rather than an address. However, even when the naming service is broken, you should still be able to contact a computer by numerical address.

- Directory services are "naming services on steroids," and they provide more than address-to-name services. They can keep track of any information on a network, including usernames, passwords, and security information.

Q&A

Q **Do Apple Macintosh networks work like a telephone network, too? What about AppleTalk?**

A Modern Macintosh computers use TCP/IP—in fact, Mac OS/X is built on top of UNIX, which is highly TCP/IP-based. There is a certain amount of legacy AppleTalk out there, and I don't talk about it specifically in this book. However, all the general concepts of networking apply. You still have a network interface, shared media, network numbers, name services, and so on—the specifics are just different. AppleTalk is a protocol and has its own rules and regulations, just like TCP/IP or IPX/SPX.

Q **What about IPv6? Do you cover that in this book?**

A No. IPv6 (a shorthand for TCP/IP, version 6) is not in use in most production (versus experimental) networks; most analysts expect that to continue for a good many years. The good news is that most of the changes are "under the hood," and from a troubleshooting perspective, you'll need to learn very little (such as, an IPv6 address is longer than a version 4 address, and is expressed in hexadecimal rather than in decimal).

Q **You mentioned that WINS was meant for Windows networks that spanned more than one VLAN—what's up with that?**

A Although applications like Web browsers rely on the operating system to provide name resolution services, the original Microsoft file-and-print sharing service used NetBIOS, which had its own name resolution service. The primary means of name resolution was through network broadcast (yelling at everyone on the "intercom" and seeing who responds), which only works on a local VLAN. Broadcasts aren't allowed to traverse VLANs because designers and troubleshooters like us think it's a bad thing to create traffic to every node in the network every time someone does a query; it adds up quickly. WINS uses a targeted lookup rather than broadcast, and therefore will work between VLANs.

Q **Shouldn't I learn more about TCP/IP? Don't I need to be a TCP/IP whiz to troubleshoot TCP/IP problems?**

A Learning more is never a waste, but as you'll see in later hours, dealing pragmatically with most TCP/IP problems doesn't really require a deep knowledge of the inner workings of the protocol itself—just a knowledge of workstation configuration and general troubleshooting techniques.

Q My networking buddy says that switches, routers, and bridges are all the same thing. Is that correct?

A It depends on who you ask. Certainly, they all take network conversations (traffic) in on one port and spit them out on another. Switches, by definition, handle NIC traffic (and a bridge is basically a two-port switch, as we'll discuss in Hour 10). Routers, by definition, handle protocol-level conversations.

Innovations in routing and switching technology have created layer 3 switches (which refers to a protocol rather than DLC) that can act as wire-speed routers. In other words, they take in packets of any kind and spit them out as fast as possible. However, the line does tend to blur with hybrid, high-end equipment. We'll talk about layers in the next hour, "The OSI Model of Networking: Understanding the Old School."

Q How does the concept of intranet versus Internet apply to the telephone analogy?

A Just think of an intranet as your internal phone system, and the Internet as the world's phone system.

Workshop

Welcome to workshop time! Here's a brief quiz and a couple activities to help you make the most out of this hour's lesson.

Quiz

1. True or False: Some network cards have name services built in to them.
2. What do all network cards have?
    a. Telephone numbers
    b. Burned-out numbers
    c. Burned-in addresses
    d. Telephone addresses
3. Which of the following is a valid MAC address?
    a. `00-55-D5-AA-D5-AA-D5-AA`
    b. `ad-00-a2-00-ad-30-c0`
    c. `00-00-c9-aa-c5-50`
    d. `c9-aa-50`

4. Which definition aptly describes routers?

    a. Routers are combo woodworking and network diagnostic tools.

    b. Routers forward packets from a local network to a remote network.

    c. Routers listen for packets from a troubled network.

    d. Routers can help connect networks with bad MAC addresses.

5. True or False: A hub creates a shared network segment.

6. A _____ TCP/IP address can make TCP/IP-dependent programs stop functioning.

7. If your PC's TCP/IP address is 200.1.5.26 and your network mask is 255.255.255.0, your node address is _____ and your network number is _____.

8. True or False: A packet must have a source and a destination address.

9. DNS is a _____.

    a. Socket

    b. Service

    c. Server

    d. Slushee

10. If my Web server's address is 208.60.153.82, and my workstation's IP address is 192.168.2.202, what is the socket pair created, given that I am calling out on port 2880 on my workstation, and given that Web services are running on port 80 on the server?

    a. 192.168.2.202:2880—208.60.153.82:80

    b. 208.60.153.82:2880—192.168.2.202:80

    c. 192.168.2.202:80—208.60.153.82:2880

    d. None of the above

Answers to Quiz Questions

1. False

2. C

3. C

4. B

5. True

6. Duplicate

1

7. `26; 200.1.5`

8. True

9. B or C, depending on context. (Although DNS is not a physical server, one does talk about "the DNS server," but one can also refer to "the DNS service running on the server.")

10. A. Pair the server port number with the server address, and the workstation port number with the workstation address. The order doesn't really matter, as long as these are correct.

Activities

1. Pretend that it's your first day on the job. Instead of referring to the netmask in a dotted format, your boss has given you a different format called CIDR, which specifies the number of bits in the subnet mask. You must determine whether servers `128.6.1.5/28` and `128.6.1.55/28` are on the same IP network. Head to `http://jodies.de/ipcalc` to find out.

2. Your MAC address is `00-40-96-40-41-1A`. Use `http://standards.ieee.org/regauth/oui/index.shtml` to determine who manufactured your LAN card.

Hour **2**

The OSI Model of Networking: Understanding the Old School

Simplicity doesn't mean living in misery and poverty. You have what you need, and you don't want to have what you don't need.

—Charan Singh

A seven-layer cake is perhaps one of your best tools for understanding the complex interactions between different networking functions. Oh c'mon, I've got to be kidding, right?

No, really, one of the ways that network architects simplify the incredibly complex world of networking is by dividing it into seven areas of functionality. This model of modern networking looks very much like a layer cake; it is called the OSI (Open Systems Interconnect) model. It was created by the

ISO (the International Standards Organization) earlier this century as a complete model of computer networking. (The ISO also created a network protocol, called GOSIP, which never really caught on.)

One of my colleagues at Network Computing recently wrote a column recommending that we as network professionals ditch the OSI model as an outmoded dinosaur because folks newer to networking can become confused when they see some of the more obscure layers. Although this can definitely be true, it's just as true that being able to encapsulate something as big and scary as networking in just seven layers is a powerful simplification technique, both in network design as well as troubleshooting. The column went on to recommend that folks new to networking just focus on the pertinent layers, and I agree heartily. There's nothing like stuff you don't need to complicate your life, and we'll avoid doing that here!

In that spirit, the first thing you want to remember about OSI is that *it is only a model*. It is only a model. I say that twice because it's really important to remember. The seven OSI layers (shown in Figure 2.1) are Physical, Data Link, Network, Transport, Session, Presentation, and Application.

FIGURE 2.1

The networking world is divided into seven categories, according to the OSI model.

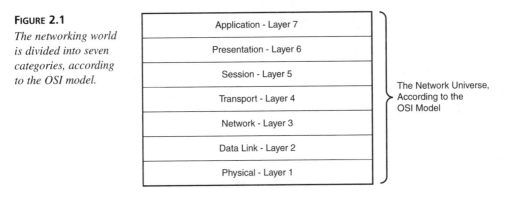

Not everything in real life fits neatly into these categories. Many, many, many people have asked me over the years, "Where does such-and-such fit in the OSI model?" Sometimes the answer is cut-and-dried; but sometimes, the function in question fits a little bit in one layer, and a little bit in another layer. This is perfectly okay. You guessed it: OSI is only a model. (Have I said this enough now?) In a nutshell, if OSI helps you visualize something (and it will), great. Otherwise, ignore it.

You're probably somewhat familiar with the OSI Physical layer troubleshooting technique already. I wager that most of the time you start troubleshooting at the Physical layer—because, as we all know, when a user says, "It's totally broken!" the first question you ask is, "Is it plugged in?"

You can't do without the Physical layer. Once the workstation is on, even if you have a well-configured workstation with a functioning network card, things don't work unless they're plugged in.

Even if the Physical layer is okay, everything comes to a screeching halt if the Data Link layer (layer 2) is not working right. (One example of this is if your hub is physically okay, but malfunctioning.) Every layer builds on the preceding layers. Are you starting to see how this works?

> The key point to remember is that each layer builds on the previous layer—Physical, the first layer, is shown at the *bottom* of the cake. Application, layer 7, is at the top because it rests on all the other layers: Without them, it "falls down" and can't function.

Here's a great sentence mnemonic to help you remember the order of the OSI layers:

Persistent	(1. Physical)
Diligent	(2. Datalink)
Network	(3. Network)
Troubleshooting	(4. Transport)
Solves	(5. Session)
Problems	(6. Presentation)
Accurately	(7. Application)

Do you really have to memorize the layer order? No, you don't *have* to, but I think you should, for two reasons. First, when some technician on the other end of the phone is asking if you've checked for layer 3 problems, you can say yes or no with confidence because you'll know what she's talking about. Confidence and sounding like you know what you're doing are always good things. Second, if you remember the layer order, you'll immediately know which layers you can rule out when looking at a problem.

Layer Definitions

Although you definitely don't want to get caught up in unnecessary details (avoiding that is the point here, after all), it *is* a good idea to discuss each layer so that you can correlate reality back to the model.

I have always agreed with my column-writing colleague; to someone who is not designing network software or hardware, the layers that really matter for troubleshooting purposes are: Physical (1), Data Link (2), Network (3), and Application (7). Read on, and you'll see why.

Physical: Layer 1

The Physical layer includes everything from the power supply of a device to the way that electrons, photons, or radio waves that compose a network signal get from point A to point B, as well as everything that you can touch, from powering the darn thing up to plugging in the network cable to hardware resources. This is one of the easiest layers to think about: Either something is physical, or it's not. (For what it's worth, the radio signals of wireless networking are grouped into the Physical layer.) And it's clearly an important layer to think about when troubleshooting.

Data Link: Layer 2

Somehow, all those electrons, photons, or radio waves need to be encoded to represent information. This is what the Data Link layer is all about. This also includes any type of inter-device communication, for example, the "banshee screaming" negotiation that we all know and love from the modem world. It's worth mentioning here that information traveling at this layer is grouped into units called *frames* (which are generated by your Network Interface Card, as we discussed in Hour 1, "Understanding Networking: The Telephone Analogy"), are Data Link entities. There is a pretty easy one-to-one correlation to this layer, making it an important layer to consider when troubleshooting.

Network: Layer 3

The Network layer is the superstructure that allows information to get from point A to point C—via point B. It's the layer that allows multiple data link domains (or VLANs) to be hooked together (the device that does so is a *router*). Information traveling at this layer is subdivided into units called *packets*.

Devices that occupy the same data link domain can talk to each other on the Network layer. A good example of this is when you ping one local workstation from another local workstation. Sure, you're verifying that the data link is okay; but you're doing so by using a Network-layer tool (ping). Remember, the Network layer (layer 3) won't work unless the layer below it (Data Link, layer 2) works.

When troubleshooting remote networks, make sure to take router concepts into account (for example, routing tables). See Hour 15, "Home and Office Routers" for more details on routing concepts.

Transport: Layer 4

The Transport layer (layer 4) deals with how the data payload is structured, how the data gets there, what kind of feedback can be expected by the sender. It defines connection-less versus connection-oriented. For example, when you throw a crumpled up note to me in class, sailing two rows behind the teacher's back (yahoo!), that's a *connectionless* transport. When you use two tin cans with a string between them, that's *connection-oriented*. Don't worry too much about this, except to know that applications that use TCP (such as the Web, which uses TCP/80) are *connection-oriented*, and applications that use UDP (such as DNS, which uses UDP/53) are *connectionless*.

Session: Layer 5

The Session layer (layer 5) is the place where the traffic lights are—handles flow control, or the stopping and starting of data in a session. Think of this layer as cranky old Madge in the trucker dispatch room. She can delay a cargo if another cargo is more important, and so on. Don't worry too much about this layer; you will rarely, if ever, have to deal with it.

Presentation: Layer 6

The Presentation layer (layer 6), like it sounds, presents the data to the application. But what the heck is "presentation?" Many times, an application wants a special treatment of the data. For example, a Web browser might be expecting data encryption; or a file transfer program might need character conversion from one system to another. (For example, IBM mainframes use a character encoding called EBCDIC, versus everybody else in the world who uses ASCII.) Any kind of data transformation services are handled in this layer. Again, don't worry too much about this, except if considering this layer during a troubleshooting session makes a lightbulb go off in your head.

Application: Layer 7

The whole reason for networking is to be able to use a program that is network-enabled. Properly stated in OSI lingo, the Application layer is the interface between a real, live program, and the network. In fact, in practical use, you can just think of this layer as the application that loads up and runs on your PC.

People get into holy wars saying, "The actual program *isn't* the Application layer," but I say, "Who cares?" We are not ivory tower academes here; we are people trying to solve real-world problems. It is useful as a troubleshooter to consider the program itself in this layer, so I say, go for it. Layer 7 is obviously an extremely important layer: it's where users see the results of the other six layers.

Using the "Important Parts"

You'll never arrive at a final solution by using OSI, but you'll use it as an important targeting mechanism. When you're in the targeting phase of a problem (that is, when you're first figuring out where to focus your efforts), you should start to run through the OSI layers that matter (1, 2, 3, and 7), but instead of running through them in order (from 1 to 7), go from *top to bottom (7 to 1)*.

Because each layer relies on the next, it makes sense to ask, "Does the summation of everything work?" (the Application layer) before moving on to the next thing. See Figure 2.2 for a flowchart of this. Should you *always* ask about layer 7 first? Well, no. There are certainly times when you should jump right to layer 1, like when someone says that his monitor won't turn on. But for more complex problems, starting at the top and going down is usually a good idea.

FIGURE **2.2**

When considering how to tackle a complex problem, consider the "good parts" of OSI from the top down.

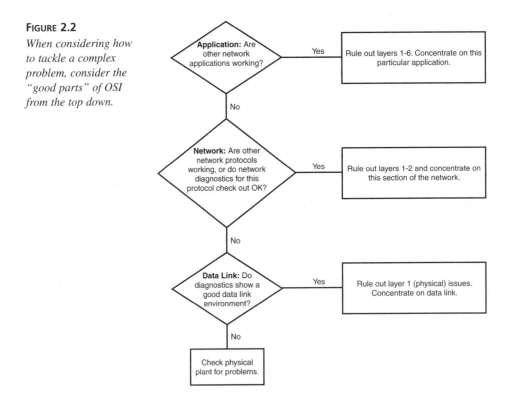

Here are some practical actions you can take to check out the various layers.

Layer	Practical Actions
Application (7)	Are other networked applications working? If no immediate application comes to mind, I suggest Telnet as a good TCP/IP application. If you use Telnet, make sure to put it under load; that is, display a large file. (In the Unix world, I've used `cat /etc/termcap` to display a pretty large file to the screen in order to stress Telnet, for example.)
Network (3)	With TCP/IP, check to see if `ping` works; but also check router logs; firewall logs; operating system logs; IP error counts (`netstat -s` command on Windows; `netstat -i` on Unix), and other sources of network diagnostic information. (When checking error counts, make sure to see if these counts are climbing—you don't care about yesterday's errors.)
Data Link (2)	Run network card diagnostics. Check out the interface characteristics of switches for error rates. (For example, on a Cisco 3500-series switch, you can type `show int f0/14` to check out Fast Ethernet port 14. On Windows, you can type `netstat -e`.) Again, if those error rates are climbing, you have a problem. If they're not, you probably don't. (However, collisions error rates are a normal part of Ethernet, and you're going to get some of those. See Hour 10, "Ethernet and Switching," for details.)
Physical (1)	Is it plugged in? Are associated "ready" lights (such as power, online, and link lights) on? Are there enough physical resources? (See Hour 9, "Overcoming Hardware Phobia" for hardware tips.)

Summary

The OSI model can be your friend if you don't take it too seriously, and just implement the useful parts. The useful parts to a network troubleshooter are Physical (1), Data Link (2), Network (3), and Application (7). The Physical layer includes everything from the physical world; the Data Link layer usually involves the signaling from your Ethernet interface (but could also be the communications from your wide-area link or other network type). The Network layer means TCP/IP (or other protocol) connectivity; and for troubleshooting purposes, you can consider the Application layer as everything else. When troubleshooting a complex problem, you'll want to start with layer 7 and move backward to layer 1.

Q&A

Q I had a problem where Microsoft SQL's Data Transformation Services was hanging on a data import. My data guru said it was because SQL server wasn't handling data from my Unix system that was separated by newlines— rather than the standard carriage-return followed by newline found in the Windows world. Isn't this a layer 6 problem rather than a layer 7 problem?

A Well, sure. But who cares? Ultimately, SQL server's DTS was choking—which was the application you were working on. Considering that the problem from layer 6 might have helped, just because thinking about presentation might have made you think, "Hey! Unix—Windows—Different! Maybe they handle data a bit differently." And you would have been right. But although layer 6 can *help*, forgetting about it usually doesn't *hurt*.

Q Where does the Domain Name System (DNS) fit into the OSI model?

A People disagree about this. (Remember, the only true correlation between OSI and a real, live system was the GOSIP protocol—may it rest in peace.) Many of my technology cronies and I think that DNS is a client-server application, and belongs in layer 7, even though it is built in to the operating system. It's a hard call; after all, many applications rely on the DNS to work, so you would think that it belongs in a lower layer. So, think about DNS as being a crucial part of layer 3 if it makes you happy. Hey, OSI is only a model.

Workshop

It's workshop time again! Wowzer! Here's a brief quiz and an activity to help you make the most out of this hour's lesson.

Quiz

1. How many layers, total, are in the OSI model?

2. The network is which OSI layer?

3. When considering a complex problem, which OSI layer should you consider first?

4. The "good parts" of OSI, in numeric order, are ____, ____, ____, and ____.

5. In Windows, you can check the data link statistics by typing _____

6. TCP is a _____-oriented protocol

7. UDP is a _____-oriented protocol

Answers to Quiz Questions

1. 7
2. 2
3. Application (7)
4. 1 (Physical), 2 (Data link), 3 (Network), 7 (Application)
5. `netstat -e`
6. connection
7. connectionless

Activity

Find someone who works with networks and ask how the OSI model has been useful in his or her troubleshooting work. What about design work?

PART II

Black Box Troubleshooting

Hour

Hour **3**

Documentation: Your Essential Discovery Tool

I am always at a loss to know how much to believe of my own stories.

—Washington Irving, *Tales of a Traveller*

Would you start out on a car trip in a strange country without a map? Would you simply presume that you'll figure it out when you get there? Of course you wouldn't, but this is what people do every day when they fail to document their ever expanding networks.

When it comes time to troubleshoot, those who don't have a map to go by just shrug and shake their heads. Undocumented networks are mostly incomprehensible. You need some method of getting your bearings, and network documentation can be an invaluable compass in what can be a sea of confusion.

This goes for an existing network as well as for one that you are just building. "As you build it, so shall it be," to quote one of my mentors. That is, if you build a network without documenting it for your future self, expect your future self to be befuddled, asking, "What exactly did my past self *do* here?" Networks are complex beasts by nature. And there is no such thing as a network that doesn't grow.

As such, it's absolutely essential that you and others who work on your network have some sort of well accepted rules (standard operating procedure, or SOP, to use the industry term) that dictate how and when you document. Just as no traditional job is finished until the paperwork is done, no network upgrade or addition is complete until the documentation is done. Documentation can include anything from logs and lists to charts and diagrams. It's anything that will make your life easier in the future.

You and your peers are not the only people who document your network, of course. Although you're the only folks who can document the *way* that your network is put together, it's worth your time and effort to *completely* read product documentation before deploying. It's amazing how many misconfigured (and thus malfunctioning) networks you will see with the simple problem that the implementers did not read the product documentation. Some problems are resolved, as they say out on the Net, by "RTFM" (Read The Fabulous Manual). (See Hour 6, "The Sesame Street Method: Using What Works," for more on vendor-supplied information.)

Navigating a Bad Network Neighborhood

Some people will tell you that complete documentation is too much trouble, or that it takes too much time and doesn't buy you all that much. This is utter hogwash. (Although many gray areas exist in network troubleshooting, this is one issue that is definitely black and white.) Folks without documented networks are the ones running around with their hair on fire; those with documented networks have fixed the problem, gone to lunch, done something productive, and gone home to spend time with their kids. This might sound rather judgmental, but too much evidence suggests that either you document once and have a reference during times of trouble or you fail to document at all and end up having to figure out something multiple times: once during each crisis.

For example, let's say that your wiring closet isn't labeled at all. Without documentation, if you are having a problem with a certain PC and want to check the switch port, you'd need to spend anywhere from 5 to 15 minutes tracing the cable from the workstation to the closet switch. Now multiply this by the many potential workstation cable problems that you'll see in your lifetime as a troubleshooter, and the amount of wasted time becomes horrific.

Not only does insufficient documentation waste time when your network is having problems, but it also causes unnecessary fear and confusion during the crisis . You owe it to yourself to have as clear a situation as possible when you start to troubleshoot—believe me, there's enough uncertainty and doubt when you're trying to find your way out of a bad network neighborhood without adding to it due to a lack of a good map.

Documentation Dividends

Enough with the dire warnings and horror stories! Let's set aside all the negatives due to a lack of documentation. On the positive side, you can see tangible benefits to having an acceptable level of documentation. Perhaps the one benefit you'll appreciate most is that a documented network is a network from which you can walk away. You can take a vacation from a documented network without worrying about whether you're going to be called if something goes wrong. Because you're not the only person with access to information about how your network is set up, others can deal with it while you watch the sun rise on your beach vacation without your pager or cellular phone ringing. The work day is already occupied enough without having to drag somebody around to show her all the nuances of the network; your network documentation does this for you, leaving you time to do other work. Table 3.1 describes the major types of network documentation.

TABLE 3.1 Types of Documentation

Type	Purpose
Functional map	The "org chart" of your network, this type of documentation gives an overview of how data flows in general. This is the "black box" part of your documentation. It likely leaves out individual workstations and wire runs and simply shows the important parts of the network (such as critical servers, routers, and network segments), along with how they connect.
Physical documentation	This "nuts and bolts" documentation shows very specific information about the network, including wires, hubs, switches, and workstations. After you have used high-level documentation to aid in troubleshooting the problem flow, and you suspect a physical problem, use this to guide your specific fix.
Logical documentation	Shows the nonphysical, or "virtual" parts of your network, servers, and so on. VLAN documentation is a good example of virtual documentation because VLANs aren't physical entities. (A wireless LAN's SID is another good example because there can be many different SIDs on the radio waves.)

TABLE 3.1   Types of Documentation

Type	Purpose
Device and cable labeling	A type of physical documentation, it deserves its own category because it is *highly* important. Consists of physical labels that identify the devices or cables they're attached to in big, bold letters. This allows someone to *find* the equipment that has been documented.
Descriptive (or detail) documentation	Usually consists of an organized write-up of an application or system, lists, or an everyday log of what's done to a device or system. It includes anything that's not intuitive and not included in the manufacturer's documentation. For example, if you use static IP addresses, you *really* want to make sure that you document them in a list format to make sure that you don't issue duplicates.

Why do you need both functional maps *and* detail documentation? Well, when applying black box techniques to documentation, keep the "encapsulation" principle in mind: It is best, initially, to have the details as hidden as possible, that is, "in the box." So, you don't *always* necessarily need the highest level of detail on each map; sometimes, the 20,000-foot view is the correct view, sometimes you need a street map.

For example, when initially planning a trip from Atlanta to Savannah, it makes sense to have a Georgia map, not a map of the United States because you are doing the "high level" planning: You want to know the approximate distance, the highways you'll use, and so on. Then, assuming that you know how to get to the Atlanta highways, you'd switch to a Savannah street map to see how to get to your final destination. Similarly, when you are documenting something, you want to make sure that you provide "detail" documentation, as well as the "high level" documentation.

Functional Maps

Functional maps are probably the type of documentation that you'll initially refer to most often. After all, this is what being a "black box" troubleshooter is all about: starting high level and then moving to the details. Functional maps are used as a sort of "org chart" of your network, and, appropriately, they indicate how data travels and what choke points exist. By looking at this map, you will be able to determine which devices depend on other devices in order to work. Details are not as important; again, flow is what you're looking for. You'll want to be able to determine, without being confused by unnecessary details, why department A can't talk to the server, but department B can.

Is there more than one type of logical map? Are there hybrid types of maps?

You can bet that in most organizations, there will be. For instance, perhaps you have a map of wire closets in a large building (see Figure 3.1). This might be a good thing to refer to when you are receiving calls about a *total* outage from certain departments; it is both a functional map *and* a physical map!

FIGURE 3.1

A functional map of physical closets.

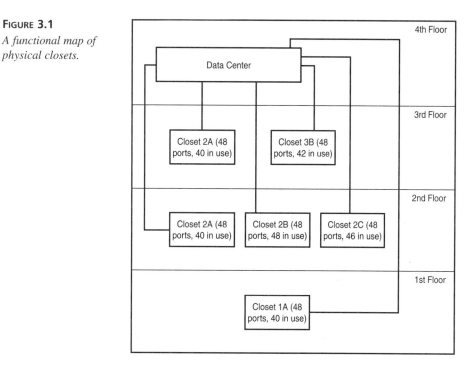

3

You might also have a map (shown in Figure 3.2) of the various VLANs (Virtual LANs) that exist in the building, which is separate and distinct from the physical map. Because VLANs aren't a physical construct, they are considered *logical* entities.

I touched on VLANs in Hour 1, "Understanding Networking: The Telephone Analogy," but don't worry if you don't understand what VLANs are at this point. You'll get more information on VLANs in Hour 10, "Ethernet and Switching."

FIGURE **3.2**

*A functional map of
logical entities: VLAN
layout.*

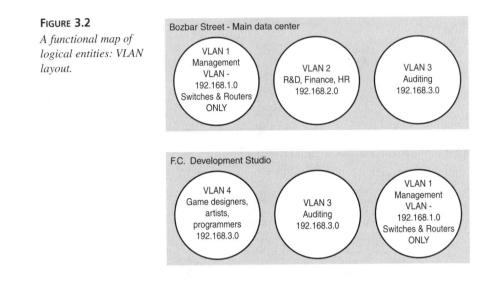

Obviously, not every PC or printer needs to be on a functional chart, but every device
that somebody else relies on (such as a mail gateway or a router) for data flow does.
You'll need to make a per-case decision whether to include individual devices on this
type of chart, based on whether these act as a group or are standalones. In the case of
Figure 3.1, the documenter decided to combine all the switches in a closet into one
object and represent them with one symbol because, for this map, showing all the
switches would clutter what is a very simple "major flow" map. The person who drew
the map decided that several facts were important:

- How many ports were available in the closet
- How many ports were in use in the closet
- How the closet switches connected back to the data center

If you have a network that's complex or larger than one site, it's time to grab another
piece of paper. (It's not worth it to try to cram everything into one map—that just makes
your map hard to read.) Typically, an organization with multiple sites needs both a big-
picture view, as well as separate site maps. In your big-picture view, each site will be
represented by a symbol that refers to a separate map and indicates how that site links to
other maps. See Figure 3.3 for a sample map of a multi-campus network map. (Certain
software, like WhatsUp Gold, enables you to create a map that has other maps contained
within it.)

FIGURE 3.3

A more complex functional site map, showing the entire enterprise.

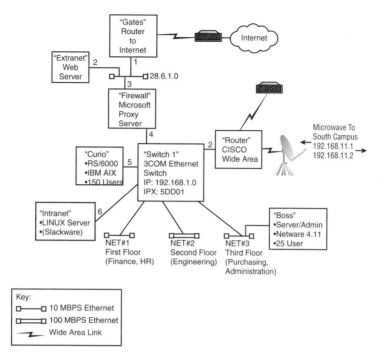

Physical Versus Logical Maps

Physical maps, of course, refer to the physical world—that is, how things really are. Logical maps refer to virtual constructions: how physical devices interact to create a virtual entity. The two are often related. For example, every modern operating system has the concept of "virtual memory," that is, a total amount of memory that programs can allocate. Although virtual memory is a logical construct, it is made up of two physical constructs managed by software: RAM memory and disk space. The *OS (operating system)* software manages the two physical constructs so that all a program has to do is ask for memory. The OS's memory manager will "swap" out the RAM to disk as it runs out of RAM. The point I'm trying to make is that every virtual construction has a physical representation.

Physical maps can be incredibly detailed, so you'll want to chew them off in bite-sized chunks. Some sites (usually those with fewer than 50 network runs) can get away with just one physical map. Most sites usually need a physical map for each floor of the building. This is usually a good breakdown for most sites because it shows each and every wire running along with each and every PC, printer, switch, and hub; this can get rather large. Accordingly, for simpler sites, it's really terrific to be able to lay your hands on the architectural floor plan of your building and add the network wiring and wire closet layout to it. If you can't get the actual floor plan, you can draw an approximation when you are labeling either wire runs or wall box locations (see Figure 3.4).

FIGURE 3.4

A floor plan labeled with major landmarks and with wall box locations.

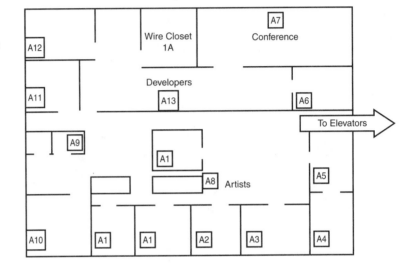

 The world of VLANs can make what used to be a straightforward documentation process somewhat more complex. VLAN assignments of a given switch can change quite often as users move. You will definitely want some sort of method for knowing which physical ports are assigned to which VLAN. (If you're using a Cisco switch, typing **show vlan** will quickly print out your VLAN assignments.)

Most folks keep some sort of physical documentation worksheet; if you have VLANs, this is one place where your logical and physical worlds collide. See Table 3.2 for sample headings for this worksheet.

TABLE 3.2   Physical Documentation Worksheet Sample

		Frobozz Corporation Closet Documentation Worksheet			
Switch #	Port #	Wall Box #	Tel#	VLAN	Description
1	1	A1	x7501	2	Jon
1	2	A7	x7750	2	Scott

TABLE 3.2   continued

		Frobozz Corporation Closet Documentation Worksheet			
Switch #	*Port #*	*Wall Box #*	*Tel#*	*VLAN*	*Description*
1	3	A5	x7505	2	George
1	4	A2	x7703	2	Matt
1	5	A3	x7708	2	Waldo
1	6	A4	x7710	3	Hakka
1	7	A8	x7506	2	Leppitsch
1	8	A11	x7700	2	Gabe
1	9	A10	x7801	2	Shelly
1	10	A9	x7508	2	Vlad
1	11	A5	x7702	2	Olivier

Should this worksheet be hand-written or typed into your computer? It depends on the size of your organization. You might discover that a pencil and paper works as well as an Excel spreadsheet for a small organization. However, the principle is the same whether you are using NetViz (`http://www.netviz.com`) or Visio (`http://www.Microsoft.com`) for 10,000 users or a #2 pencil for 20 users.

No matter what type of network you have, a physical documentation worksheet can act as a quick reference sheet for all data about that particular physical network. Need different headings? By all means, use them. Some folks used to record the physical (MAC) addresses of their computers on these worksheets.

In general, when in doubt, you'll want to get as detailed as you can. (I've never seen someone crying after a network outage because the maps were too detailed.)

Tips for Mapping

Here are some tips that will help you manage your mapping:

- **Update your maps.** Things change, and your maps need to show that. Make this part of your SOP (Standard Operating Procedure) with your consultant, network provider, or PC guy—particularly if you add or change things on your own.
- **Date your maps!** Because things do tend to change, you'll end up with multiple maps of the same general area. If you have a date on each map, it's easy to figure out which map is current.

- **Use symbols instead of color.** Using color in your maps can make them easier to understand, but you might find it harder to share your maps with associates and vendors who are trying to help you. (Although color copiers are pretty pervasive now, color maps are hard to read via fax, for example.) An alternative to color is the use of differently shaped symbols for items that need to stand out.

- **Use simple software (or a pencil).** Software for mapping or flowcharting can help you a great deal, but don't make the mistake of laying out your network map at the same time that you're learning the new software package. Draw your network map out by hand if you're unfamiliar with the software—this will make the layout go faster. Software is great because minor changes are easy to update. (Besides, having an "autoflow" feature for line drawing can really make your life easier!) However, complex software just isn't necessary—any simple drawing program will do. In other words, you don't need to make a career out of network mapping when you've got troubleshooting to do.

  Some of the possibilities include

  - SmartDraw (www.smartdraw.com). Good flowcharting capability and great symbol library (clipart).
  - Visio (www.microsoft.com). The Microsoft Word of network diagramming.
  - NetViz (www.netviz.com). This is a drawing utility, but it also has the ability to interface with and draw information from various databases.

- **Keep it simple!** Other people will have to read your document, and you want them to actually understand it. Accordingly, try to stay with straight, clean lines and avoid flow chart spaghetti (crossed lines). If you have more detail than you can really fit into one page, add another page.

Device and Cable Labeling

A map does you no good, of course, if you can't find a device that's shown on the map. Don't laugh—I've seen plenty of shops in which nobody knows where the router is. (Naturally, you'll want to include the physical locations on your maps.)

But if the router isn't labeled, it's hard to know which router it is. How can you reboot the router if you don't know which one it is? A good troubleshooter makes it a point to label each device clearly and concisely before trouble strikes; a lack of labeling can really increase your downtime by a remarkable margin.

If you ever visit the *USS North Carolina* or a similar World War II battleship, you'll marvel at all the hoses and pipes that run throughout the ship—particularly in the machine rooms. Take a look at the meticulous way all these pipes are labeled; believe me, they didn't do this for fun. They needed to know which pipes were air, steam, fresh water, brine, gas, or oil—a delay in a repair could literally sink the ship.

If you weren't fortunate enough to have had the U.S. Navy meticulously label your network (and your installer hasn't done it either), you'll need to start *today* with "as you go" labeling. Each time you find out what a device is or where a cable is going, slap a label on it. Don't assume that you'll remember—you might have a great memory, but during a crisis, that memory might be on vacation. (Also, remember that you want to go on vacation yourself one day and let someone else troubleshoot all this stuff for you.)

Go out and buy a label maker. They only cost about $30 and are really useful. They pump out quick, clear, and neat-looking labels. Also, you can print a label twice, cut once, and have a two-sided cable label, as shown in Figure 3.5. I've used models by Brother and Casio with good results.

3

FIGURE 3.5

Use a label maker to make two-sided cable labels.

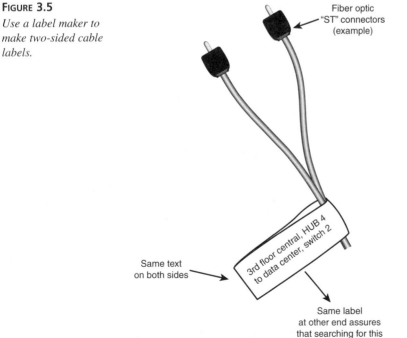

Fiber optic "ST" connectors (example)

3rd floor central, HUB 4 to data center, switch 2

Same text on both sides

Same label at other end assures that searching for this cable is easy!

Tips for Labeling

You'd think labeling is a fairly simple and straightforward project, but here are a few practical pointers that you might not have considered:

- **Test labels for adhesion before you buy.** There's nothing worse than making 250 labels, only to see them all flutter to the ground after a month. As with anything else in networking, a simple pilot test can save you a big headache later.

- **Paper or plastic?** Cable labels should be plastic rather than paper, to avoid their ripping as cables get handled.

- **Can you read it?** Any cable label should be put a good distance from the end (anywhere from 12 to 18 inches, if you have the room). This way, you can read the label once there are 50 or so other cables plugged into the same switch or concentrator.

- **Keep them current.** You really need to keep up with your labels when items change or are moved. Troubleshooting can take much, much longer if you think you know which cable is correct but find out later that it's not.

Let's say you have a router that connects your earthbound headquarters with your company's moon base. If the router's name is LOONIE, a good device label would be

```
LOONIE: Router for moon base, Lockheed Satellite transmitter
```

I've seen folks slap a label with an IP address on such a router; however, this is optional if you have good functional documentation clearly stating that LOONIE has two IP addresses (say, 167.195.160.1 on the earth side and 167.195.161.1 on the moon side). Still, as my grandmother would say, "It couldn't hurt." LOONIE's label including IP addresses could look like this:

```
LOONIE
167.195.160.1 (EARTH Interface)
167.195.161.1 (MOON Interface)
```

LOONIE has two connections in the back (one to your local area network and one to the satellite transmitter); you should label each connection with the device name and its endpoint. For example, the cable going to the satellite transmitter could be labeled:

```
LOONIE -> Satellite Transmitter
```

Then, the other label might be

```
LOONIE -> Data Closet #1, Hub #3
```

Why label the cable that's directly connected to LOONIE as "LOONIE"? Well, suppose that you have to disconnect the cable. It would be nice to know where to put it back.

Perhaps even more importantly, suppose that someone else disconnects the cable and you (or anyone else) has to put it back. Those labels can be very important.

I like to label each end of a cable with both devices that will be connected with the cable so that I don't have to think about which end to put in the cable. I've been at sites where some poor, confused soul has labeled each end with the source rather than the destination, so all you know is that the LOONIE router has a cable that goes to, uh, LOONIE. Oops! It's best to look at cable labeling from both sides. (After all, you bought a $30 label maker, and making labels is easy.) It really does save aggravation.

Detail/Description Documentation

The difference between a well-documented site and a professionally documented site is in the details. Detail documentation—although the least practiced documentation type—can augment the other types of documentation very nicely.

Detail documentation in the form of a formal write-up of how a system was configured, along with site-specific standards or frequently used troubleshooting practices, can make it easier for others to retrace your footsteps. This type of documentation, which includes how-to's and cheat sheets, contributes greatly to your ability to actually take a vacation.

The Art of Logging

You're the captain, so keep a log. It's hard to find a block of time to sit down and write a formal description of previous troubleshooting techniques, but if you keep a logbook near each crucial device (such as main servers, firewalls, routers, and so on), you can document as you go. Make it part of your SOP to write down anything done to a server, switch, or router (and at what date and time this operation was performed)—you'll save yourself a bunch of time when it comes to retracing your steps. Logbooks are also great for providing backup documentation with a vendor. For example, an entry such as "The new server has crashed each week at 10:00 on Monday night" might lead a vendor to realize that the hard-drive cleanup program scheduled to run on the server at 9:50 on Monday nights might be causing a problem.

Do paper logbooks get lost? Oh, heck, yes—particularly by "nobody."

For those of you who are part of a large IT staff, it might be a good idea to use some sort of centralized change tracking system. I'd be willing to bet that your help desk system has some sort of change management function built into it. If not, this is a really simple kind of intranet application to build. I've seen quite a few custom-written Web log programs. (One hint: Web programmers like cookies and become quite receptive to suggestion after a sugar glow.)

Dealing with Undocumented Networks

Is it possible to reverse engineer an undocumented network? Sure, but this requires a good bit of knowledge. What's more, it's really a waste of time if the network is being installed or changed while the documentation is taking place. The sad part is that most networks aren't very well documented; most professional troubleshooters readily agree with this. It's no wonder that many networks have so much downtime: avoid it by having good documentation practices.

If you run into someone else's network nightmare, see Hour 24, "Reverse Engineering, Discovery Tools, and Other Black Magic."

Is this a hint that you should insist on good documentation when you contract out for someone to build a network for you? Yes! Any professional worth her salt will probably be labeling like crazy anyway, but just in case you run into someone who thinks that an undocumented network equals job security, you need to get tough. Insist on labels on all cables and ask for maps. If you have to pay more, either pay a reasonable amount, which should be nominal (plus you'll save time and money in the long run), or find a different vendor. A lot of vendors are out there, and, ultimately, you're the person who either suffers or benefits from the documentation of the network and cable plan.

Summary

You can be the best network troubleshooter in the world, but without documentation, you're out to sea in a leaking boat. Documentation can mean the difference between ten minutes of downtime compared to two hours or so; therefore, a little work up front can really pay off in the long run.

Each type of documentation is important in its own way—for example, labels on cables, maps of the network cable runs, and functional diagrams of server placement are all valuable assets. Also, keeping a logbook can keep history from repeating itself. In other words, it gives you a point of reference when the network goes down.

In Hour 4, you'll learn how many network problems are the result of human-initiated change—and what to do about it.

Q&A

Q I label cables by number because each cable function can change and it's time-consuming to replace the cable labels. Is this adequate?

A Not in my experience. Folks don't always keep track of what numbers are being used, and a number doesn't describe what's at the other end, thus requiring a separate table to translate the numeric cable number to the physical device (which you'll have to update when you change devices, anyway). Do yourself a favor and just put the description on the cable.

Q What should I document on my maps? What shouldn't I document on my maps?

A Completeness is the key here. After you get some experience doing this and practice the techniques in future hours, you'll probably look at your initial maps and say, "I didn't need to write that down." However, you'll only know this after you get some experience under your belt. For now, write it all down; you can edit later.

Q This all seems overwhelming. Where do I start?

A Start simple and you'll be fine. You can start by writing down everything that you know about your network—your server name, where it's plugged in, what hub your computer is plugged into, and so on. Then, you can write down the categories of documentation, along with to-do's for each category.

Workshop

Workshop time! Here's a brief quiz to help you make the most out of this hour's lesson as well as activities for you to try on your own.

Quiz

1. True or false: Logical documentation shows wire runs and cable boxes.

2. Physical documentation should include which of the following?

   a. Electrical outlets

   b. A small area of very specific equipment and cables

   c. An overall picture of the network

   d. Server-to-server information exchange

3. When labeling the router end of a cable, you should include what?

    a. The router name and the port on the hub

    b. The router name

    c. The port on the hub

    d. Either A or C

4. SOAP stands for what?

    a. Some Other Person

    b. Standard Occupational Parameters

    c. Standard Operating Procedure

    d. Some Operational Processing

Answers to Quiz Questions

1. False

2. B

3. D

4. C

Activities

1. Go to http://www.smartdraw.com and download the evaluation version of SmartDraw. Draw some of the diagrams from this hour. See how easy it is?

2. Pick a *non-computer* system, one with which you're pretty familiar, and document it. Some suggestions: the "org chart" of your company; the color belt progressions of your favorite martial art; or the telephone or home audio setup at your house.

HOUR 4

The Delta Method: Identifying Network Change

The changes are small
"It ought to work," he says, yet:
The network is down.

—*The Mighty Quizro,* The Law of Unintended Consequences

It can seem like gremlins are lurking in every server, wire center, and particularly in every Windows PC. Usually, however, what we attribute to gremlins is actually the result of a change. Frequently, this means that a user has changed something and subsequently has forgotten (or denied) making the change.

We all do this; we're our own worst enemies. For example, say you install a new application on your computer, decide you don't like it, forget to delete it, and then have trouble accessing your company's intranet the next day.

If you're lucky, you won't forget you installed a new app, and you might uninstall it to find that, voilá, you can now access your company intranet. Typical application conflict, right? Easy.

But what happens if you have a really great weekend in between and forget? You might "spin your wheels" for hours while trying to figure out what's wrong. No shame in it; I've been there, too!

For as many times as we might think that there's a ghost in the machine sometimes, there isn't. For all their potential complexity, computers and networks, once set up, are rather predictable devices, and tend to function exactly the same, all the time—until something changes. One of the most essential pieces of knowledge in troubleshooting, then, is finding that change, or as the math geeks might say, "finding the delta (Δ)."

Several common vectors of system change that you will want to consider are as follows:

- Person initiated (yourself; your peers; vendors such as ISPs, VARs, consultants, and perhaps even a malicious outsider)
- Equipment failure (a marginal component, perhaps, causing an intermittent or strange problem)
- Resource allocation failure (your database running out of a resource, such as system inter-process communication structures and perhaps giving you and your users a *false error* rather than giving the proper error message about the resource failure)

The Fat Finger Factor

Let's look at person-initiated change first, starting with my favorite person to blame: me. Many times, when you might make a change to a router or server in order to offer a new service or to fix a problem, you introduce new and wonderful problems, simply because to err is human. If the error that you introduce does not take effect immediately, the change that you initiate seems to work, and will be the last thing you think of if a problem surfaces later. (This is a really, really good reason to keep a log of changes; rather than having to remember or ask others what network attribute has changed, you can simply look it up.)

For example, one time, I was fixing the startup file for a NetWare server to automatically make a certain volume available upon the next bootup. I rebooted the server that night and tested the users of that server; all seemed well.

The next day, we found that Windows NT—but not Windows 95—users were complaining that their time was off by five hours. Related? Couldn't be! We thought, surely this has to be something that had globally affected our NT users' configurations; it couldn't possibly be the server, particularly because the users in the affected department did not log in to this server for file services.

Of course, it was the server I had touched. Although I *thought* that my change was benign, in fact, I had accidentally introduced an error into the startup file; this is what I call the *fat finger factor*—while editing any configuration file (no matter how benign your changes are), you might introduce a stray character or two that makes a key command or parameter unintelligible to the server.

In my case, the problem was that I had edited the NetWare startup file for something quite innocuous and hit a random key by accident at the top of the file. The first line of the file was responsible for setting the time zone. Instead of reading

```
SET TIME ZONE=EST5EDT
```

the line as accidentally edited to read

```
\SET TIME ZONE=EST5EDT
```

When I saved the file with my "benign" changes, all of a sudden the server had no idea what time zone it was in because it didn't understand the \SET command. The server in question was not the *file* server for the department, but it *was* the time server!

Novell-connected Windows NT synchronizes the time from the server differently from Windows 9x; it relies heavily on time zones. So, my fat finger threw every NT workstation on our network off by five hours. (We're in the Eastern time zone, which is five hours off from universal time.) Ouch!

The lesson is this: Always point the finger at yourself first. Always be thinking, "What have I done lately?" Then, be prepared to undo your changes. As I discussed in the last chapter, keeping good notes—particularly a formal logbook—is a really good idea. That way, you can compare the date when the problem started to the dates of changes entered in your logbook.

Of course, others in your organization might be equally at fault—particularly if you share responsibility for your network. A logbook helps here, too, but don't solely rely on the logs—it helps to talk to each other and discuss what you've been working on.

When starting to troubleshoot a problem, if there are others who work on your network, you should definitely query them about changes they've recently made.

It can be particularly troublesome when you, or someone else responsible for the network, does a "fat finger" on a device and doesn't immediately restart it. When the device does finally get restarted, the change is no longer recent and is therefore hard to point to as the culprit. When you consider this, it makes sense to think of any device that has been recently restarted as a suspect device.

Of course, problems after a restart won't always be as subtle as the previous problem: I knew a Unix consultant who restarted a server to ensure that the new application he had installed would start up after the operating system started, only to find that the entire server operating system failed to load upon reboot. After much hair-tearing ("Jonathan, I SO did not touch anything to do with the OS loading, man!"), fixing the problem, which was unrelated to the change he made, and later investigating, we found that a system programmer with way too many security rights had accidentally removed the files in the startup filesystem and replaced them with his own files. He had done this a *month* previously, so this was a time-delayed fat finger factor. The programmer wasn't even the one who got burned; the consultant and I were the ones who had to fix the system by booting from removable media and replacing the files from backup.

> In general, you should always restart a device after a change has been made to it: You want to *know* if your change does something bad so that you can undo it while it is fresh in your mind.
>
> What about the problem of being wrongly accused of making a bad change? I combat this problem in two ways: First, for devices that I am responsible for, putting them on an automated restart schedule (see Hour 18, "Managing Change: Consistency and Standards," for some tips on how to do this); second, if I am able to, I like to restart a device *before* I start performing change operations. This way, I know that I am about to change a device that isn't already seriously broken.
>
> Finally, Bill's 1st Law of Network Changes: Always, always, always make sure that *everything* is backed up *before* making changes!

Vendors and Change

Your vendors, whether consultancies, ISPs, ISVs, VARs, and so on, get repeat business based on how well you are treated, and so, if they're smart, they do have your best interests at heart. Still, vendors can be a major source of unintended consequences at the worst possible times.

Several factors will affect the types of changes—and the timing of changes—that vendors cause to your network. Although vendors do want to do a good job for you, they have several other warring desires at work. Remember, like people, there are good vendors and there are bad vendors. (Of course, this is also true of internal staff.)

The following are some factors that might affect the way a vendor performs on a job on your network. The really good ones don't let any of these factors stand in the way of performing well for you. Still, you should at least consider that vendors might

- Have a schedule to keep and other jobs to do.
- Have a bottom line that is affected by the hiring of top talent, and thus often will deploy less-than-top talent unless they feel that top talent is necessary.
- Have the sense that there is no short-term consequence for poor quality (doing a bad job might mean losing you as a customer, but there are a lot of customers out there); and providing high quality is an expensive proposition, requiring an investment in training, lab gear, and so on.
- Have a vested interest in selling you new software, services, and hardware.

For example, because your vendor has various projects scheduled, this can mean that someone might show up on your doorstep at a random time (not necessarily when it's convenient for you or your organization). When someone shows up randomly, perhaps the correct staffer at your location is not available to give this vendor proper information—which might cause this vendor to make mistakes; or, it might be that a critical, uninterruptible process is in process when the vendor staffer shows up—which might force the vendor to cut corners, like making changes but not restarting a service.

The bottom line is to give your vendor the benefit of the doubt, but keep a watchful eye for these things.

I know it sounds obvious, but you do have a right to insist that changes to your network—no matter how necessary for a given project—must be scheduled. You wouldn't let your plumber walk into your house at any old time and fiddle with your water heater, would you?

Project Panic

When projects are large, of course, the cost of undoing a bad change is also large. For large projects, you should always insist that a sensible rollout and rollback plan be built into the project; the gradual rollout lets changes be introduced slowly; the rollback plan is how to undo the changes in case of problems.

For example, I was called into a medical office where the character-based medical office system was being upgraded to a graphical, windows-based system. Not a lot of planning or testing had gone into the upgrade; basically, someone had thought to himself, "It loads and runs on my 50-user test database, so surely it will work with the 5,000-user database with hundreds of thousands of detail records." Apparently, there was a real problem with network-based record access in the graphical version, and when faced with database sizes several orders of magnitude larger than the test system, the system became *excruciatingly* slow. At first, the vendor would not confirm this; but when faced with a packet trace (see Hour 20, "In-Depth Application Troubleshooting," for more information on when a packet trace is appropriate) that proved it, the vendor backed down.

Because there had been no gradual rollout, *all* the many workstations had to be rolled back until the vendor could fix the problem. Clearly, this cost a significant amount of labor, and thus money.

Moral of the story: No matter who makes changes, you or your vendor, an incremental rollout of changes followed by real-life testing, with a rollback plan in the wings (in case testing does not point out the problems) is a sure recipe for success!

Incremental rollout means that after a limited deployment to key individuals (who are perhaps good testers or expert users of the system), you start giving the application or system to batches of users in increasing quantities as you proceed. That is, you do the rollout in small chunks that get bigger as the rollout becomes more successful. For example, you might give five people a new application. Later, you give the application to 10 more people; then 15, 20, and in your final increment, you might be rolling out 30 people a week (once you're sure that things are working fine). Using an incremental rollout ensures that if you have a problem early on, the least number of folks are affected.

When possible, *always* roll out changes or new systems incrementally.

It pays to negotiate *up front* with your vendor about a rollout/rollback plan for a major project. The cost for "making it work in a disciplined way and putting it back if it doesn't work" might be a different price than "throwing it in and then dealing with it later if it's a problem." If you're dealing with an expert and reputable vendor, he won't mind if you bring up these types of things during project negotiation.

Don't be a pushover, but don't be a pit bull either. Having a good relationship with your vendor is really important; your vendor can either be a cause of trouble or a troubleshooting partner—you want to shoot for the latter.

Remote, "Invisible" Change

Vendors responsible for ongoing maintenance of your network devices might tend to use remote access to accomplish some of these maintenance tasks, such as patching or enacting manufacturer-supplied security recommendations. As such, you will have little or no idea that these things are being done, short of catastrophic failure.

As I mentioned in Hour 3, you might want to investigate the possibility of an intranet application that allows various folks to key in their network changes. You could make this available to outside vendors as well.

Patching and tweaking, particularly security tweaking, are good things to do, and if your vendor is on the ball about this, this is awesome. The important thing is to make sure that you get a phone call prior to or just after the change, or you will not have complete information to go on when you are troubleshooting a problem.

Remember, ISPs and the telephone company don't need you to give them a remote access account to make changes that will affect your network. It is a fact that ISPs and telephone companies make changes on the weekend or over holidays when utilization is low, so it's smart to call your provider and politely ask about possible network or equipment changes if you come back from the weekend or a holiday, and things aren't working quite right.

Unfortunately, when you ask "What's changed?" the answer will likely be "Nothing" unless you have a *very* together provider. To make matters more aggravating, even after you verify that nothing has broken over the weekend at your end, the problem might mysteriously vanish around lunchtime.

But the problem might not vanish around lunchtime.

For problems that don't, you might have to convince your provider that nothing's wrong with your computer equipment (or figure out that there is something wrong and apologize for having doubted them).

You can set up an alternate path between the two networks in question. One way to do this is to create a VPN between the two networks; another way is to simply dial up from one network to another. There are several ways to skin this cat.

For example, on one fine Monday, my brother had remote access cease functioning at one site. After tearing around and verifying that his servers were okay, he was able to ascertain that, in fact, using a different path, he was able to get in to his remote access. Although he could have dialed in, he simply changed the parameters of his remote access server to use a different TCP port (see more about TCP ports in Hour 1, "Understanding

4

Networking: The Telephone Analogy"), and was able to work. He then found out that the provider in question had blocked the original remote access port.

When the line is totally down, obviously, you can't set up a VPN (but you still can do dialup). When you are totally down, you actually have some more options: As long as you can't communicate anyway, you can truck the equipment from site No.1 to site No.2, and see if they are functioning when connected directly. If this works, you have pretty compelling evidence for the telecomm provider that nothing has changed with your equipment and that something *has* changed between the two sites.

Here's one warning, though. Although there are instances when you *can* connect two devices together with no additional equipment or configuration (for instance, ISDN routers with RS-232 ports can be connected with a crossover RS-232 cable), there are many other instances when you *cannot* do this. (Using a crossover cable with two cable modems is *not* going to work because there isn't a server in the middle to automatically configure them.)

The Risk/Benefit Ratio

If this chapter has pointed out one thing to you, it's probably that any type of change can dink up your network. It's enough to make you run screaming away from *any* type of upgrade or project, much less the installation of new software. Software, though, tends to be so problematic that it's a good jumping-off point to talk about the *risk-benefit* ratio: the risk of change in relation to the benefit that the change will introduce.

The breakneck speed of Internet time means that software developers have unbearable pressure on them to be first to market. This usually translates into quick/nonexistent product testing, which means that the programs are released with at least a few bugs. (The practice of shipping software with problems so serious that it might not even perform its intended function used to be so common that software developers themselves coined a phrase for it: "shipping a brick.")

Experience also shows that for every new feature introduced, there are probably two new bugs in a product; when do you decide to risk the problems and upgrade?

And, at what point is it worth it to you make your network even more complex than it is by introducing a new application?

> If you don't see *any* bug fixes or service packs posted on a new product's support site, it probably means that the product is not mature. Wait a while to deploy.

Because you have better things to do with your day than report bugs to the software vendor, it's a good idea to *not* be the first one on your block to put a new application or operating system on your network. Unless you desperately need the new features of a new product, you should wait until six months have passed or the first service pack is released—or perhaps both—until you seriously contemplate rolling it out. (For example, many industry observers were pretty sure that nobody would roll out Windows 2000 before the advent of the first service pack.)

This is a clear example of the *risk/benefit ratio*—the amount of risk compared to the potential benefits. Unless there is a *very* clear benefit (the old product doesn't work well anyway, you're losing money by not having a working product, and the new product promises to clear up the old problems), taking the risk of green software isn't too appealing.

Again, the risk/benefit ratio applies to *any* kind of change, not just software. It's pretty easy to think about the benefits, but thinking about risk is harder. Some of the things to consider when thinking about risk are the following attributes of a proposed change:

- **Scope**: How far-reaching is the new system or the change to the system? For example, for end-user software, you'd consider increasing levels of risk to be *one* person; a *department*; and *organization-wide*. Minimizing scope is the primary reason for an incremental rollout.

- **Distribution**: Is this a centralized change (for example, one server), or is it a change that gets replicated to many servers? Although it is easier to roll back a change to a centralized system, it is less risky to modify a decentralized system; if one component of a decentralized system fails, other parts of the system still function.

- **Inspection**: How well inspected is the proposed system? A system becomes more perfect as it is widely studied, criticized, and improved. (The cryptography world, where *no* cipher is trusted until it has been pounded on for several years, is a good example.) Hidden systems tend to have more hidden flaws, and thus are riskier to use; well-used and inspected ones generally have fewer flaws and are less risky.

- **Reversibility**: How difficult is it to undo the change? Some system upgrades are easy to undo; these are the least risky; others are a one-way trip: Clearly, these are the riskiest. One way to reduce the risk of low reversibility is to enact the change in a lab; that is a "mini" reproduction of the large network that includes most aspects of the system before the change. This, obviously, is pretty expensive to do both in terms of time and money, but can be worth it when the scope of change is large.

4

- **Interactivity:** How much does the system interact with other network components? Upgrading a word processor would have a very low score here, and thus, low risk; upgrading a Windows 2000 domain controller or the firmware for an Ethernet switch would have a higher scores, and thus higher risk.

The interactivity of the change in question can be quite serious and hard to fathom: Even if you don't have problems during a rollout, a new application or device can produce secondary effects in another item that don't seem to be related to the new item. Accordingly, a good rule of thumb is to reverse recent changes (if feasible) during network or communications trouble. (Perhaps you can shut down that brand-new Cisco switch that you're test-driving or your pilot-test installation of Active Directory.) The trouble might not be related to the new device or program that you've installed, but if you shut it down, you've ruled it out as the source of the trouble.

If the trouble goes away, you can then kick the problem back to the vendor you bought the offending item from (or to the manufacturer). However, make sure that the problem is reproducible (that is, make sure that it happens repeatedly when you reintroduce the program or device back into the network) before going to your vendor, or you will likely not get taken seriously.

For example, where I work, a certain Nortel switch started crashing on a regular basis. Nortel support couldn't help us; they recommended patches, which we applied to no avail. We then realized that the most recent piece of gear to be put on the network was a new model Cisco switch. When we turned the Cisco switch off, we discovered that the Nortel switch would stay up all the time. When we told Nortel, they admitted that there was indeed an interoperability problem with Cisco's *CDP (Cisco Discovery Protocol)*; it did, in fact, kill certain Nortel gear. After we disabled CDP on the port shared with the Nortel gear, all was well.

Discovering change in a large-staff environment is no accident, although informal means, such as quick morning meetings, are good ways for everyone to be tuned in to what's happening on the network at large, documentation such as logs, work orders, and incident reports are also highly important.

Summary

Many network problems are the result of human-initiated change. Finding the change can involve inspecting documentation and communicating with co-workers and outside vendors. Even unintended changes because of the "fat finger factor" can seriously damage a network, so it's worth considering where you've been, no matter how unrelated it might seem. You'll also want to figure out where others have been; however, don't rely solely on logbooks. (Although to document is divine, people aren't perfect. They'll sometimes forget to write down what they've done.) Vendors, including VARs, ISPs, or the telephone company can be problematic because there is no direct profit motive in being good at communicating change before it happens.

Before deploying any new network toy, whether software or hardware, it's worth considering whether the risk is worth the potential benefit. Risk is always much higher with new products—you're better off waiting a couple of months before using what might be a pretty, green product. Limited rollouts can also limit your potential network risk. You should also always think about a rollback plan, just in case things don't go as expected with a new project. When considering levels of risk, it helps to think about the change's attributes in terms of scope, distribution, inspection, reversibility, and interactivity.

In Hour 5, we'll look at *dividing and conquering,* another powerful troubleshooting technique.

Q&A

Q I've just upgraded all of our workstations from Windows 98 to Windows 2000. Now, one of my Windows applications isn't working anymore, even though it used to run under Windows 98. What could be wrong?

A A couple of things are somewhat different between Windows 98 and Windows 2000. Consider the following potential changes: different filesystem, NTFS (NT File System) version 5, versus FAT (File Allocation Table) or FAT32 on Win98; totally different video drivers; different DOS subsystem. Here's the question: Is the new operating system the *only* thing that's different? If so (you haven't upgraded your hardware as well), the problem is likely OS related. Try rolling back one of the workstations and seeing if the app starts working again.

Q Someone in my organization keeps changing things but never admits to it, particularly when things break. What can I do?

A Unless you're this person's boss, you can't do much. However, this person's boss probably sees that he contributes chaos and fear to your organization. This isn't a technical problem, it's a social one, and is best handled as such.

Workshop

Workshop time! Here's a brief quiz to help you make the most out of this hour's lesson as well as activities for you to try on your own.

Quiz

1. An external tape backup unit comes back from repair. You plug it in and boot up your PC. Your PC hangs at the BIOS screen. What do you do?

   a. Call your local repair shop.

   b. Disconnect the tape drive.

   c. Call your brother-in-law who's "into" computers.

   d. Press Ctrl+Alt+Del.

2. You add non-system software (that is, software targeted to the end user, not a system utility or anything like that) to your NT server that requires a reboot. However, you don't remember the last time the server was rebooted. Upon rebooting, you get a message saying that a service failed to start. You uninstall the software and reboot again. You get the same message. What do you do?

   a. Call Microsoft.

   b. Ask around to see if anybody else has changed anything recently.

   c. Reinstall the software.

   d. Ask around to see if anybody else can install this software.

3. True or False: New products are typically "bug free."

4. True or False: Scheduled visits from your vendor (versus drop-in visits) save you time and aggravation.

5. Everybody has been experiencing network disconnects since yesterday. The only changes that have occurred include John installing new virus protection to his PC and Mary receiving a new PC. What's the correct first step in resolving this problem?

   a. Turn off both Mary's PC and John's PC.

   b. Turn off Mary's PC, but leave John's PC on.

   c. Turn off John's PC, but leave Mary's on.

   d. Fire John and Mary for endangering the common good.

Answers to Quiz Questions

1. B

2. B

3. False

4. True

5. A

Activities

1. Call a vendor with whom you have a good relationship. Talk about change management procedures in place at that organization, and see if you can garner some tips that are useful to you.

2. Some equipment vendors have white papers about change management in their environments. Fire up your browser and check out this one from Cisco Systems: `http://www.cisco.com/warp/public/126/chmgmt.shtml`.

HOUR 5

The Napoleon Method: Divide and Conquer

We must all hang together, or assuredly we shall all hang separately.

—Benjamin Franklin

Any system, when divided, is much more tractable than the whole. Napoleon knew this: One of his favorite tactics was to send the whole of his army against a fraction of the enemy army, and in this way, slowly wear down what was once a formidable force. Having divided the enemy into small, manageable pieces, Napoleon's conquest was assured.

Your troubleshooting battles can be similarly successful if you take a page from the book of "Le Petit Caporal." From a troubleshooting perspective, divide and conquer is the concept that the problem system or problem location can be found more easily by splitting the problem area into smaller, manageable pieces. Divide and conquer can sometimes locate the source of the problem for you pretty easily, end of story. Sometimes, however, it's just one more tool in your arsenal: a way to prod at a problem to reveal more of the problem's characteristics.

I like to think of divide and conquer as having two major components:

- Problem localization
- Binary search

Problem localization is the technique to use when you have no idea where to begin searching for the problem. It is a method of isolating the process or system that is experiencing the problem. Problem localization can be as much art as science; yet some of the ways to approach it are more scientific and are included later in this chapter.

Binary search is a more straightforward divide-and-conquer technique. It is used when you know where the problem is localized, but not *what part* of the system is at fault. It systematically splits a system into smaller and smaller parts and hones in on which component is at fault. When you are lucky, the binary search will identify the precise system or subsystem that is causing a problem. Binary search is a very powerful tool because systematically dividing and using the process of elimination can isolate the root cause in very few steps (see the section "The Numbers Game: Binary Search").

Nine times out of ten, only *one* root cause of a given problem is at work at any given time. Unless you've been struck by lightning recently, the odds of you having more than one problem simultaneously are very slim. (That's not to say that domino effects don't exist, though.)

Problem Localization

It is not always obvious where the cause of a problem lies in a complex system that might have many participants, and that's where *problem localization* comes in; that is, discovering the general area or specific group of systems causing the problem. This often simplifies the problem by cutting away extraneous systems or details.

This is pretty great because one thing that can make network troubleshooting difficult is the level of complexity on even the most modest of networks. That is, all network devices—possibly thousands—have the potential to interoperate. Being able to quickly localize a problem becomes extremely important because nobody wants to consider thousands of devices as a potential source of trouble; it is far better and quicker to only consider a few.

Sometimes, when multiple systems are at work in a given virtual or physical location, you can isolate the interacting systems in order to see how the overall system reacts. If the subsystem is still exhibiting abnormal behavior when you have isolated it, you have tracked the problem to that subsystem; if the abnormal behavior goes away, you know that the subsystem is perfectly fine and that there is some external force at work.

This is kind of an abstract way of talking about what is really a very practical method, so let's chat about an actual problem and how to localize it.

Let's say that "nothing has changed on the network," (you will start to chuckle every time you hear these words, I promise) yet you begin getting calls about a certain department's Telnet sessions getting disconnected in the middle of the day. Everyone swears up and down that nothing has changed. You know, naturally, that something has; you just don't know what it is yet. It's time to divide and conquer and to do some problem localization.

Because this problem seems to be happening on a regular basis, you schedule some downtime for testing after work. You know that the only systems necessary for the user to be able to boot up and then Telnet into the server are

- A DHCP server (for automatic configuration of TCP/IP)
- The Unix/Telnet host
- A sample workstation
- The switch in the department closet
- The "Layer 3" switch in the data center

Scads and scads of *other* network devices are on the network, any one of which might be doing something unknown and bad. To truly localize this problem to the preceding five devices, it's best to make sure that the problem still happens when the devices are isolated from the rest of the network.

Your testing involves removing all hosts other than the DHCP server and the Unix/Telnet host from the data center switch. (Perhaps there is another switch to move other hosts to; or perhaps the other servers on the switch can have an hour or so of downtime for this troubleshooting.) You power off all the department's workstations except for one. See Figure 5.1 for the resolution to the scenario.

Sure enough, you are able to see the problem re-occur. If it did not, you might power-on all 50 of the department's workstations at once (don't do it one at a time at this point because you want to treat "workstations" as one group) to ensure that the department doesn't have a malfunctioning workstation that is causing the problem. In this way, you have *verified* that the problem does in fact exist in the group of items listed previously.

5

You have *localized* the problem, and thus you have nailed down a finite number of items that could be the problem. (It's beyond the scope of this hour to discuss the final solution to this problem, which I actually dealt with a year or so ago; if you're interested in the solution, see Hour 19, "Intranet and Internet Troubleshooting: TCP/IP at Work.")

FIGURE 5.1

Simplification of the problem scenario means that there are a minimum number of devices to consider in the balance of the troubleshooting.

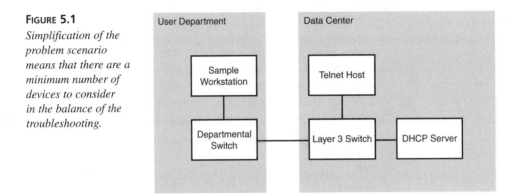

The Network Is Down!

A simpler type of problem localization becomes really important when someone runs into your office gibbering and screaming that the network is down. The very best thing you can do in this circumstance is to keep your cool and try to get some coherent information from a very upset person. After all, you're using divide and conquer; all will be well.

First of all, how do you know when the network is *down*? Is it really down—that is, nonfunctional—is it slow, or is an application acting funny? If it is truly non-functional, is it a physical network problem or a server or router problem? What part of the infrastructure is affected?

Sure, the person in your office has no idea. So let's get simpler.

You'll probably start by asking whether the problem is with one person (a *local* problem) or with a group of people (a *systemic* problem).

If you determine that it's just one person, you're done with your problem localization and can now proceed to local troubleshooting (which can require a combination of techniques, including divide and conquer). If it's more than one person, you need to gather more information. Is *everybody* down? Usually not.

Okay, so I actually *have* seen a situation in which everybody *was* down because of an electrician accidentally pushing the emergency off button of an equipment room's central UPS (uninterruptible power supply, or uninter-ruptible power source). Here's one problem that caused a "domino effect" of a whole bunch of other problems, including no phone service, no net-work services, and general chaos.

Notice how even though many systems were down, the *root cause* (or to use the doctor geek term, the problem etiology) rested with a single device.

It's worth a brief mention, in the spirit of proactive troubleshooting (preven-tion), that it is good to be very paranoid about putting all your eggs in one basket from the power standpoint. Sure, you might have servers with multi-ple, huge honkin' power supplies, but if the power *source* goes off, those multiple, huge honkin' power supplies are useless. Multiple power supplies on your servers, connected to multiple uninterruptible power sources, are now becoming common and are an excellent way to assure uptime. Most serious data centers now have multiple uninterruptible power sources; so the preceding scenario would be fairly unlikely nowadays.

Be prepared to actually have to do some digging on your own; although someone who reports a problem might give you a highly detailed and objective account of the situation, the greater likelihood is that you will have to take the report with a grain of salt and investigate on your own.

People will tell you that they can't log into the server, that their drive letters are gone, or even that all the PCs in their area have locked up. As I said, when you find out that more than one person is affected, you will want more info: Which department or location is the group in? In a large organization, you might want to call some different departments and see if they are working okay. Again, you are trying to localize the problem to a func-tional group.

After you determine which functional groups are not working properly, it's time to haul out those maps you so diligently drew after you mastered Hour 3, "Documentation: Your Essential Discovery Tool."

Take a look at where these folks are on your functional maps, and see what they have in common or where they connect through. When you do this, it will probably become painfully obvious where the problem likely is. If two departments are saying that they are down, it might be that the server they use is down—check your detail documentation. On the other hand, if you see from your functional map that all the groups which go through a particular router or switch are down, it's time to check that device.

5

If your users are getting a Web page login, but can't log in, and the Web server is on the other side of a router, you're clearly *not* going to check the router first because, apparently, it is passing traffic just fine. (Otherwise, the users wouldn't be getting the login box.) Your level of general server and network knowledge will guide you in this.

So, the essential questions for problem localization "triage" are

- What functional group has the problem?
- What functionality is impaired?

We'll talk more about problem determination in Hour 17, "Where Do You Start?"

The Numbers Game: Binary Search

The binary search technique is used when the problem location is known, but there are many subsystems to choose from. Remember, usually only one *root cause* exists at a time, and when the problem has already been localized, binary search is a quick way of finding that needle in a haystack.

For example, let's say that I'm thinking of a number from one to one million, and you want to guess what that number is. If you proceed sequentially and guess every number, you could potentially go through 999,999 numbers before getting it right. However, if you divide the maximum number in half, and I tell you "higher" or "lower," and you keep dividing that result in half, you will take *at most* only 20 guesses. Yup, just 20. That's quite an improvement. Don't believe me? Here's an example:

Me: Okay, I'm thinking of a number from 1 to 1,000,000.

You: 500,000?

Me: No, lower.

You: 250,000?

Me: No, higher.

You: (pausing to calculate 250,000 / 2 + 250,000): 375,000?

Me: No, lower.

You: (getting mad at me for picking a number between 250,000 and 375,000): Let's see, there are 125,000 numbers between 250,000 and 375,000, so the middle of that would be…312,500?

Me: No, lower.

You: (whipping out your calculator): 281,250?

Me: No, lower.

You: (getting good at this now): 265,625?

Me: (astonished): How'd you guess?

Naturally, this would probably go on for a couple of more guesses, but you get the idea. The range is initially 1-1,000,000—a huge range. Then it goes to 500,000, to 250,000, to 125,000, to 62,500, to 31,250, to 15,625, to 7,812, and so on. You can see that you lose zeros pretty fast in only seven guesses; by the time you guess another seven times, you're down to only about 60 possibilities. That should come as no surprise. You can see in Figure 5.2 how fast dividing an area in half cuts down your search.

Here's a bit of geeky party trivia: You can express the maximum number of guesses in a binary search by using the following mathematical formula:

$n = \log_2(x)$

Here, x is the maximum number in the sequence, and n is the maximum number of guesses. Log2 (1,000,000) = 19.93156857, which gives us a maximum of twenty guesses to find a number between one and a million. Smaller numbers are similarly friendly; Log2 (1,000) = 9.

FIGURE 5.2

In a binary search, the search area gets smaller and smaller as the number of guesses progresses.

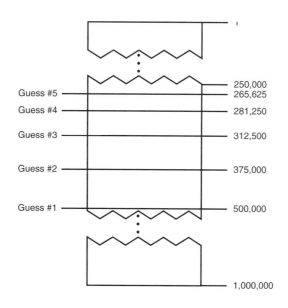

How does this numbers guessing game translate into the real world? Well, let's discuss an alternate resolution to the preceding "problem localization" example, where the Telnet session was getting disconnected. If you had discovered that the problem went away when you localized it to just one workstation and the required infrastructure, your next step would have been to turn on the departmental PCs. If you discovered then that the problem came back because of a rogue PC, you would *not* want to test each and every PC; instead, you would divide them into groups, and test again. Log2(50)=5.64, so you would potentially have a maximum of six guesses before you found the problem PC.

Hub Hoppin' With Binary Search

Hubs are exquisitely suited to troubleshooting via binary search. Why does a physical network segment go down? Usually, because these are shared networks, the hubs aren't terribly smart, and they do not detect and isolate a faulty workstation. All sorts of fancy new technologies are built into "smart hubs" (and most switches, for that matter) to detect this and stop it; therefore, this sort of problem isn't as common today.

Still, depending on the type of switch or hub you use and how brain-damaged a workstation is, it is still possible for a workstation to bring down a physical network—or even an entire VLAN. Why? Because even smart hubs aren't as smart as you are (nor are they as smart as manufacturers like to think they are). And, sometimes, being smart is not the default behavior; it needs to be turned on at the device.

For example, if a malicious user stuck a loopback plug in a wall jack that went to a switch, and Spanning-Tree (see Hour 10, "Ethernet and Switching") was not on, the entire VLAN would be taken down due to infinitely repeating traffic. So, stick binary search in your toolkit as a potential technique to use if you suspect evil in the world of physical networks or VLANs.

Segment Searching

The best way to handle a rogue workstation that is bringing a data link domain down is to use a properly configured switch, as previously noted. But let's say that either dumb hubs are in use and there is no money to upgrade; or you're new on the job, and the last person wasn't as diligent as I know you are. This is why it's still worth discussing some of the finer points of using binary search for data link problems.

You'll want to be sure that before you do a binary search for a rogue workstation— which does take time—that you refer to the physical documentation first and make sure that things are connected properly; then perform problem isolation on the hubs or switches themselves.

- Have you determined whether the functional group of hubs or switches, when disconnected from the main network at large, has a data link problem? If there is no problem when you are disconnected, *there is no local problem;* look upstream to the data center. Isolating the functional group by disconnecting the uplink (because the data link isn't working anyway, nobody will care) and then pinging from one workstation to another is a good approach for this. (See Hour 19, "Intranet and Internet Troubleshooting: TCP/IP at Work," for more on ping.)

- Have you determined which switch or hub is malfunctioning? If you have a large number of switches or hubs in the group, doing a binary search on the hubs or switches themselves might be appropriate. (Again, ping is a good tool here to affirm or deny basic connectivity.)

After you have determined that the hubs or switches are okay and that there is not an *upstream* problem in the data center, you can then move on to troubleshooting the individual ports of the switch or a hub. (Figure 5.3 shows visually how you'd divide this.) And, after you determine which hub or switch is causing the problem, you can isolate it from the rest of the network while you continue troubleshooting.

FIGURE 5.3

A group of four 8-port switches with 32 ports total requires no more than five guesses to determine which port is bad.

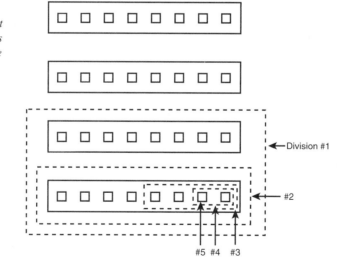

32 Ports – 5 Divisional Guesses

If the problem lies with the hub or switch that is connected back to the data center, simply connect a different hub or switch to the data center while you continue troubleshooting the problem hub; obviously, you want to make sure that most folks have as little downtime as possible.

Be sure that you have adequate labeling before you start isolating or moving hubs or switches; you certainly don't want to create additional problems by connecting the wrong cables to the wrong places when you put things back!

When you find the port that's causing the problem—and even when you first find the hub that has the problem port—make sure that you perform a *control* experiment on it. That is, put it back into the main network and make sure that it's still causing the problem.

Then, it's time to refer to your physical documentation to figure out which workstation on the network the port belongs to; you can then disconnect the workstation and visit to do local troubleshooting. In many cases, you'll find a mangled network cable, a bad network card, or even just a locked-up PC.

Again, most smart hubs and properly configured switches will automatically work around most port-based problems, so performing this process is somewhat primitive in this era of "automatic transmission" networking. If you have the means, a properly configured switch in your closet is the way to go.

Software Searching

Ah, I remember the good old days of my Apple II. You could load *one* program in at a time, and that was pretty much it. Things either worked, or there was something wrong with the program you loaded. The pervasive software conflict issues of today simply didn't exist.

Fortunately, in this day of modern PCs—fairly complex machines, running all sorts of programs simultaneously, with unintended consequences when the wrong programs get mixed together on the same machine—we have binary search on our side when things start dinking up.

Most seasoned tech support operators recommend that the first thing you do with a problem PC is to *boot vanilla*—that is, boot without all of your startup programs—and see whether the problem persists.

Guess what this technique boils down to? Binary search! Instead of dealing with a zillion little programs, you get rid of all the ones that aren't necessary to run the computer, and then see if you still have problems.

However, Windows is complex, and there are a bunch of ways that program code can get launched, going from the most commonly modified to the least:

- As a startup item from the Startup folder in the Start menu
- As a startup item from the login user's registry (`HKCU\`
  `\Software\Microsoft\Windows\CurrentVersion\Run`)
- As a startup item from the system registry
  (`HKLM\SOFTWARE\Microsoft\Windows\CurrentVersion\Run`)
- As an NT/2K service
- As a device driver
- As an old-style TSR (Terminate-and-stay resident) program (loaded from
  `c:\autoexec.bat`, on Windows 9x only)
- As an old-style startup item from the [windows] section of the
  `c:\windows\win.ini` file with the `load=` or `run=` items (No program designed for
  WinNT, ME, or 2K does this)

Other operating systems, such as Unix and NetWare, are far simpler in their startup
options:

- Unix users need only check out their `/etc/inittab`, and `/etc/rc.d` startup scripts.
  A good link on Unix startup is
  `http://www.infocom.cqu.edu.au/Units/aut99/85321/Resources/Print_`
  `Resources/Textbook/chap12/`.
- NetWare users should check `c:\nwserver\startup.ncf` and `SYS:\system\`
  `autoexec.ncf`.

5

> Windows startup is complicated! Here are some tips on how to boot vanilla
> on various Windows platforms:
>
> - Several packages enable/disable startup items on a temporary or per-
>   manent basis. These are called startup managers. Try a freeware tool
>   like Startup Control Panel: (`http://www.mlin.net/StartupCPL.shtml`).
> - Other startup automation utilities are listed on `http://www.govital.`
>   `net/~soz/lists/Startup_Tools.htm`.
> - Get smart on *all* the ways that startup occurs. A good reference page
>   on the Web is `http://www.tlsecurity.net/auto.html`.
> - Booting to safe mode is always a good step toward eliminating
>   unnecessary drivers, but unless you generate a boot log, you don't
>   know which. Start the computer in safe mode by pressing F8 right
>   after you turn on your computer. (If you choose to log the boot, the
>   log will be in `%SystemRoot%\ntbtlog.txt`.) You can choose Safe Mode
>   or Safe Mode with Network, depending on whether you can test
>   whatever it is without the network (not available on WinNT).

- If you are troubleshooting an NT-family server that has been around for a long time, you probably want to confirm that anything in the files AUTOEXEC.NT or CONFIG.NT are in fact necessary: These load 16-bit drivers, which you probably don't want or need in this day and age.

Again, when dealing with large quantities of software components, it's best to divide them in half, see if the problem remains, and try, try again. This technique vanquishes *many* local workstation problems.

Although most network workstation problems are caused by change, as we discussed in the last hour, those changes are not always immediately apparent.

Good examples of not-so-obvious changes include browser updates, browser plug-ins, and virus protection patterns. Therefore, when the change is not obvious, you want to stop banging your head against what appears to be a brick wall and get back to basics.

For example, let's say that everybody in your office starts having problems shutting down. They all get stuck at the "Please wait while your computer shuts down" screen. It seems, at first glance, that everybody is going to have to deal with it. Nobody has changed anything recently that they know of, and no one is capable—or willing—to wade through the guts of what's going on with some sort of software debugger.

It isn't a network problem? Well, the fact that it just started spontaneously on a bunch of networked computers seems very odd, so it gets dumped in your lap. Fortunately, you realize that even if social engineering does not reveal the source of the change, something *has* changed, and you can at least use divide and conquer's binary search method to figure out what it is.

You decide to use the Startup Control Panel program mentioned previously as a good way to start your search.

You start by disabling roughly half of the items, and all of a sudden, you can shut down again. You return half of the programs to the Startup folder and keep restarting until you find the source of the problem. It turns out to be your email notification program. However, you decide to start up with *just* the email notification problem, and you're able to shut down.

In this case, you've got a software interaction problem; it is pointed out by binary search. You put back in half of the programs that were in the startup file, and you manage to track the problem down to a situation in which you have both the virus protection program and the email notification program loaded. As you might have guessed, this troubleshooting session actually happened—the virus protection program, which automatically got updated from the Internet, had started to interfere with the email notification program. A quick search of the vendor's Web site found a patch for the email client (not the virus protection program), and an annoying problem was fixed.

Obviously, although binary search is incredibly useful in your daily troubleshooting efforts, it doesn't always work to ultimately solve your problems. In particular, it's tough to troubleshoot intermittent problems, as well as problems that don't involve a black-and-white (broken or not broken) scenario.

For example, the divide-and-conquer method might lead you to believe that a new application is causing your network slowdowns (and you might be right). However, it's not always feasible to get rid of a new application, and, furthermore, it might not be clear whether the trouble is *that* particular application or just that the network itself is at a saturation point in general. In this case, you might try a different application, but can you really switch a largely deployed application in a short period of time? You'll probably just end up checking the application to see if it's misconfigured and taking measurements to ensure that the application is behaving properly on your network.

Again, the bottom line with divide and conquer is this: Even when the divide and conquer method can't directly find your problem, using it sometimes reveals some aspects of a problem, and can at least point you in the right direction.

Summary

A problem that seems insurmountable can become easier to solve if you break it down into smaller parts. Problems tend to be split in two ways: by location or by component (whether it's software or hardware).

Although networks are complex and dependent systems in which one failing component can make it seem like everything has failed simultaneously, typically only one problem is causing a domino effect. The divide-and-conquer method allows you to find the problem component without knowing why it's causing a failure. When you don't know *where* a problem is, you can sometimes isolate components and see if the problem goes away: A process known as *problem localization*.

When you know where the general area or problem originates and have large numbers of components or locations involved, divide-and-conquer troubleshooting (also known as a *binary search*) can change your number of guesses from millions to dozens, thus saving you a lot of time.

5

Although the divide-and-conquer method isn't always the end-all and be-all of the troubleshooting process, it's still a powerful method that can usually pinpoint a culprit in many situations.

In the next hour, "The *Sesame Street* Method: Using What Works," we'll discuss comparing "broken" objects on the network with ones that are not broken, discovering the differences—and thus the problem.

Q&A

Q **If my router port is having problems, won't it seem like the whole network is down?**

A Well, sure—if you are on the wrong side of the router port, and if you have servers local to you. In this case, you can try to contact workstations on your physical segment—as discussed in this hour, ping is a good connectivity tool.

Q **Although I'm having *some* problems on my workstation, the divide-and-conquer method is problematic for me. I can't get rid of everything in my Startup folder; otherwise, I won't be able to work. Any other suggestions?**

A Each situation is obviously different. The divide-and-conquer method might not be your best strategy here. Instead, you might need to ask, "Which of these things is not like the other?" For more information on this troubleshooting strategy, see the next hour.

Workshop

Workshop time! Here's a brief quiz to help you make the most out of this hour's lesson as well as activities for you to try on your own.

Quiz

1. The divide-and-conquer troubleshooting strategy enables you to do what?

    a. Mathematically calculate a problem resolution.

    b. Solve any problem in the world by performing a binary search.

    c. Locate a problem by splitting the problem area in half (or removing half of the components involved).

    d. Divide the problem-solving labor among several people.

2. You're thinking of a number from 1 to 500. If I am using binary search to guess the number, what might my second guess be?

    a. 25

    b. 250

    c. 300

    d. 125

3. What's the first thing you should determine when hearing of a network problem?

    a. Determine whether the problem exists for one user or for multiple users.

    b. Check the router.

    c. Check the documentation.

    d. Determine whether the server has crashed.

4. You track a network problem down to the switch that leads to the rest of the network at large. To maximize uptime for everyone, what do you do next?

    a. Start port-level binary search proceedings.

    b. Build a router.

    c. Start to check the switch documentation.

    d. Bring the rest of the group up to the network at large while you troubleshoot the problem switch.

5. True or False: If you want to check startup items on a Windows PC, all these items are located in `HKLM\SOFTWARE\Microsoft\Windows\CurrentVersion\Run`.

Answers to Quiz Questions

1. C

2. D

3. A

4. D

5. False; although this is one possibility, there are many possible locations for startup items.

Activities

1. Teach a child in your life the "pick a number" game, using binary search. Use a relatively low range, like 1-100. Before you play, ask the child how many guesses it will take. Prove that you can guess the number this way in, at most, seven guesses.

2. Download and install one of the startup managers mentioned in the tip in this hour's "Software Searching" section. How many startup items are listed on your workstation?

HOUR 6

The *Sesame Street* Method: Using What Works

I'll never forget when I ran into the doctor's office as a rookie parent, sure that my baby's skull had somehow gotten broken. Panicked, I showed the doctor how a certain area of the baby's head had an odd-looking depression. The doctor laughed because he had seen this reaction about a million times from other rookie parents. He showed me a symmetrical mark on the other side of the baby's skull, saying, "It would be highly unusual for a skull to get broken symmetrically, don't you think?" He then went on to explain how this depression was a normal feature of a newborn's skull.

The doctor could have taken many time-consuming and expensive actions, including ordering x-rays and so on; but because he not only had experience with newborns, but also a grip on the concept of comparative anatomy, all he had to do was compare the two sides of the baby's skull, write me up a bill for an office visit, and send me on my merry (and embarrassed) way.

You can avoid expensive and troublesome testing in the network troubleshooting world as well by using comparative anatomy on network devices. I call it the *Sesame Street* method because of the famous "One of these things is not like the others" song and game from the *Sesame Street* television series. The *Sesame Street* method *can* truly be more of a game than it is hard work. The principle involved is as follows: Given a group of two or more items on a network, all that's required to troubleshoot the one item not functioning correctly is to perform a comparison to an item that is functioning correctly.

Typically, the way in which items are different is also the reason for an item malfunction. For example, let's say your children are twins and one of them—the one who eats Super Sugar Bombs instead of Wheaties for breakfast—is hyperactive. Assuming that the twins have identical activities, are in the same environment for their classes, wear the same types of clothes, and are physically identical except for their diets, it makes sense to try to align what they eat in order to *rule out* diet as a possible cause of hyperactivity.

The same principle applies to a misbehaving network appliance: If you find an identical item that is working, changing the problem item's configuration to be just like the one that is working can oftentimes fix the problem.

Servers, Routers, and Switches

You can apply this principle to just about any object on your network, but it has limited use when troubleshooting devices such as routers and servers. Routers and servers are hardly ever really identical, although they might be similar in function. Sometimes, the similarity of function is enough to compare, but you need deeper knowledge to be able to compare servers that are "mostly the same." It's a lot harder than troubleshooting devices that are "twins."

But just as humans have similarities, so too do servers and routers. That is, every human has 23 pairs of chromosomes; humans who do not have 23 pairs have serious problems. The same goes for servers and routers: They have "device integrity" characteristics. For example, a router that keeps crashing while others are doing just fine might show a different revision of its operating software (or *firmware*). Hardware routers and switches don't run Windows or DOS; instead, they run a "stock car" operating system (like Cisco's IOS), which is really pretty simple software (unlike Windows with its zillions of DLLs). The upside of this is that usually you only need to check one revision number; a difference in revision numbers might point out the difference between a working router and a problematic router.

Also, functional groups of appliance-like devices (whether they are switches, routers, or even things like print server or network-attached storage devices) tend to have similar configurations that are different in small ways (like an IP address). If you compare these configuration files, sometimes differences jump out at you.

Servers that run more complex operating systems, such as Windows NT, Unix, or Netware are going to be harder to compare: There are a *lot* more variables. (Thinking about comparing the thousands and thousands of entries in a Windows registry makes me want to scream.) Still, you might compare the more granular items, such as the patch level and perhaps the date stamps on system DLLs, of a problematic Windows NT server to a known "good" server. SRVINFO.EXE from the NT/2K Server Resource Kits can be of some help in this arena.

NetWare servers have the Config Reader (see Hour 14, "Netware/NDS Troubleshooting"), which does a wonderful job of automating the task of comparing the dozens of crucial NLMs (NetWare loadable modules) and patches that live on a given server. If you are a Novell premium support customer, OnSite Pro is available as well (also covered in Hour 14).

User Objects

Because servers are all configured somewhat differently, it's most useful to apply the *Sesame Street* principle to user-oriented objects that live on your network. By convention, user objects (user logins, profiles, associated security rights, and the user's workstation itself) are typically configured at least somewhat the same—if for no other reason than your vendor or internal systems administrator found it easier to roll them out this way.

In its simplest form, finding out what's different is pretty easy: You know that the group of users has been working reasonably well for a while. Let's say that one user reports that she can't use a particular application; because others are working using *their* workstations and *their* logins, the first step is to figure out whether her problem resides in *her* workstation or *her* user login. You can rule out workstation problems by having her log in to a different workstation. If the user is unable to run the application at another workstation, you immediately know that the problem is with her login, not her workstation. You can further prove this by having someone else log in to the user's workstation, proving that the application on this workstation does indeed work. You next must ask yourself how this user login might be different from the other user logins.

6

You need to compare apples to apples—in other words, if you try to run an application on a workstation that the application hasn't been installed on, you'll encounter problems. Also, some applications write user-specific files to a workstation, *not* to the network. Beware of these applications. You'll want to perform a controlled experiment for each type of application—before you have problems—to see whether a user who can work with the application on one PC can also work with it on another PC. If so, you know that the application can "float" from workstation to workstation.

When only a few users in a workgroup report a problem, you should first review what has recently changed (see Hour 4, "The Delta Method: Identifying Network Change"). If you come up with nothing (or even worse, if the change was mandatory and not undoable), it's time to start thinking about how those few users are different from the rest of the pack.

Remember, *ruling out* is essential to black box troubleshooting. If you can start thinking about what a problem *isn't*, you're one step closer to figuring out what the problem *is*.

You must rule out differences as a source of trouble when using the *Sesame Street* method, specifically when you find multiple properties that are different between objects. For example, if two workstations have different video cards, network cards, and different amounts of RAM, you might give them both the same amount of RAM to rule out the problem as a RAM problem. Then you can move on to giving them the same network card, and so on.

Keep It Simple

You're probably starting to see that a key component of successful troubleshooting is keeping things simple—and if they are not simple, changing the setup so that they *are* simple.

Keeping it simple is exactly what you do when you start with the highest level object to begin determining which thing is not like the others (see Figure 6.1). In the previous example, why even start investigating the workstation configuration before you can rule it out? Also, why start messing with the PC's video card or network card when you *know* there's nothing wrong with the PC?

FIGURE 6.1

Look at high-level objects first.

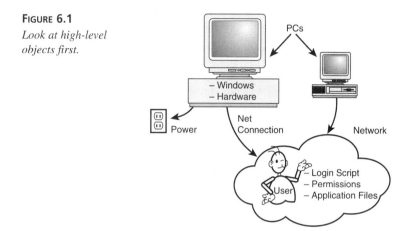

It's useful to think of these items as being in high-level containers that have lower-level containers within them. Until you rule out (or rule in) an upper-level container, it's silly to even look at its subcontainers.

You can think of a typical network setup as

- A box of workstations, which contains motherboards, memory, hard drives, and so on

- A box of networks, which contains wiring, hubs, and so on

- A box of users, which contains user IDs, login scripts, and various security attributes

Thinking of these high-level components in boxes allows you to concentrate on the task at hand without getting distracted, and it will make you a better troubleshooter. If you discover that the network is the problem, you won't get distracted by workstation subcomponents, for example. In other words, after you figure out that the network is the problem, you should only concentrate on the network subcomponents.

Identifying *which* of these boxes to start with really depends on the type of call you get. See Hour 17, "Where Do I Start?" for some tips on what type of information. The good news is that there are only three "big boxes" to deal with, and ruling these high-level objects in or out is fairly easy, even if you don't have a clear trouble report to go by.

To Shotgun or Not to Shotgun?

When you've identified, in general, where the problem lies, the fastest way deal with it is to use the *shotgun* effect—that is, to simply force a problematic network object to be identical to one that's working.

This means that you should point your troubleshooting shotgun in the general direction of the target. Have you ever seen a shotgun in use? It's pretty hard to miss your target when shooting with a shotgun because the shot scatters widely. Anything in front of the muzzle tends to get holes in it.

Shotgunning a particular object means that you replace all the components of that object in the same indiscriminate way—without spending time analyzing which component is the troublemaker.

Shotgunning a config is frequently done with appliance-like objects such as switches and routers. For example, because it is possible to use TFTP to update a Cisco router, it's a simple matter to download the config of a known good device, changing the config file so that it reflects the IP addresses of the questionable device. Then, you transfer the new config file via TFTP to the questionable device. If the device still doesn't work with a "known good" configuration file, you know to investigate elsewhere instead of investigating each port individually. (This is done on PCs with drive duplication.)

Where PCs are concerned, drive duplication (sometimes called *imaging* or *ghosting*) can be a big help here because it's fairly easy to "shotgun" a known good hard drive setup to a hard drive setup that's having configuration difficulties (see Hour 17, "Where Do You Start?" for more information). By doing so, you are verifying that the following components of the workstation return to a known good state:

- Operating system files, drivers, and configuration (such as the Windows Registry)
- Updates such as hotfixes and patches
- System-specific application files and configuration info

Remaking the user's home directory is another good method of shotgunning a problem after you've identified the general target. For example, because UNIX programs are dependent on multiple configuration files in a user's home directory, I sometimes rename a user's home directory, make a new home directory for that user, and then copy a known good user's home directory contents into it (see Figure 6.2).

You will also want to consider, in a Windows environment (particularly with Terminal Server, where all users are using the same server), replacing a user's profile with a known good profile. The profiles are located in

- Windows 9x and NT: `C:\windows\profiles\%username%`
- Windows 2K and above: `C:\documents and settings\%username%`

FIGURE 6.2

Shotgunning a user's home directory.

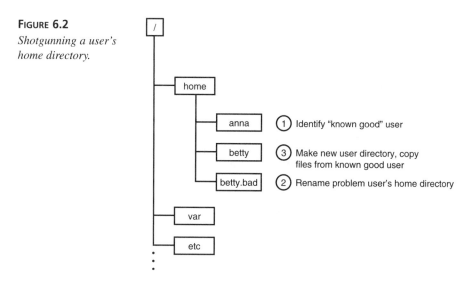

For those times when you can't use either the profile or home directory shotgun technique (for example, when crucial information would be overwritten), you'll want to consider and rule out the following components, listed from the highest level (to the left) to the lowest level (to the right):

```
- Workstation
    - BIOS / Manufacturer
    - Hard drive
        - Operating system configuration (startup files, Registry)
        - Operating system components (DLLs)
        - Local applications (versus network)
        - Virus? Or not!
    - Network card
        - Cable
    - Video card
    - RAM
    - Power
        - UPS
        - Surge suppression
- User login on server
    - Login script
    - Permissions
    - Application configuration files (user-oriented access list?)
    - User files (home directory)
    - Application itself (versus on hard drive)
- Port on the switch or hub
```

Most folks don't realize just how much trouble bad AC power can cause. Although it was true that a bad power source could cause serious problems some years ago, as processors and other workstation components become faster and faster, it becomes even more true.

It is really worth trying to rule out the power source of a PC that, for example, is locking up as it gets into the network. You can do this by plugging the PC in to a different wall outlet or adding a power conditioner. A *power conditioner* is a special filtering device that acts to get rid of the jitters and brownouts that can plague AC power (particularly in rural areas).

Finally, you know those little space heaters that lots of people use in buildings where perhaps the heating system isn't exactly up to snuff? Warning sign! These suckers pull a huge amount of current, and can brown out your sensitive PCs and network gear pretty quickly. Unplug the space heater, and see how things start to work just fine.

However, beware of chasing the low-level components. For example, operating system components can be an adventure in and of themselves; you can literally spend days doing comparisons of these lowest level objects. This might be worth it sometimes, but for most small areas of trouble, keep in mind that information you don't need is information you don't want. As I discussed in the introduction to this book, this is referred to as *information hiding*. Keep the fuel pump image from the introduction of this book firmly in mind when you're about to dive into more internals than you really care to deal with. Do you really need to learn all the icky details of what various Windows DLL files do if you can simply copy somebody's known good Windows configuration to solve the problem?

On the other hand, if an email program is complaining that it can't load MAPI32.DLL, it's certainly worth looking at the MAPI32.DLL file on the hard drive. Sometimes the file is damaged (it might show a size of 0, for example). Also, you might compare it to a known good MAPI32.DLL and realize that it's much smaller than it should be. In this case, copying one file from a known good workstation is faster than reloading and reconfiguring the entire workstation. It's a bit of a balancing act—you just need to look at the given situation, see what information you have, figure out how much time it would take to change something out, and take what seems like the quickest and most effective action.

This is actually the hardest part of the method: figuring out what to compare and getting a handle on the items that are proving the problem.

For example, if many (but not all) users are reporting a problem, particularly an intermittent problem, it can seem overwhelming at first. With intermittent problems, it can be hard to say where to start and where to look. (See "Problem Localization" in Hour 5, "The Napoleon Method: Divide and Conquer," when you're unsure.)

If problem localization doesn't work, you'll save your sanity if you start logging the calls and writing down in a tabular format what the problems are, when they happened, under what circumstances they occurred, and the configuration of the workstations and users involved. Such a chart might look like the one shown in Table 6.1.

TABLE 6.1 Sample Log Sheet

Date Time	Department	User	Problem	Type of PC
8/11 2:00	Finance	Jack	Illegal operation error—WordPerfect	Clone/Pentium-IV
8/11 2:20	Finance	Leona	Fatal exception 06 (during system boot). Seemed OK afterward.	Dell/PII
8/11 3:00	Finance	Tracy	Illegal operation error—WordPerfect	Clone/Pentium-IV
8/12 9:00	Finance	Tracy	Illegal operation error—WordPerfect	Clone/Pentium-IV
8/12 10:45	Finance	Jack	Illegal operation error—WordPerfect	Clone/Pentium-IV
8/12 1:00	Finance	Jill	Locked up. Had to reboot when reading email.	Clone/Pentium-IV
8/13 11:00	Finance	Jack	Illegal operation error—WordPerfect	Clone/Pentium-IV
8/13 12:45	Finance	Bill	Illegal operation error—WordPerfect	Clone/Pentium-IV

6

By looking at this detailed log, it becomes apparent that illegal operation errors are what you're getting the most of. (If you had more incidents listed in the log, it would become even more apparent. The other items are not repetitive and amount to "bumps in the road," not hard errors.) So now you know that "some of these things are not like the others." The ones that are alike are your persistent errors that you're trying to get rid of. Why isn't Bill calling as much as Tracy or Jack? A quick phone call reveals that he was out of town on the 11th and 12th, so he's not as much of a wildcard as the log implies.

Let's look at a concrete example. I was once involved in upgrading a department to a new version of Windows, which included upgrading to a new version of WordPerfect. The word from management was that this was a strategic change, making the possibility of rollback very small; it was up to us to make it work. Although the sample machines I had pilot tested worked just fine, we started to have problems a day or so after the upgrade. Certain (not all) users began to report illegal operation errors. I was absolutely sure that all users were configured the same—identical login scripts, file permissions, and home directory configuration—but, unfortunately, because we were using clone hardware, I wasn't as sure about the workstations.

I logged the incidents over several days and discovered that some users *never* reported the error. This indicated that the problem was not a moving target and that it was staying in the same places. This is important to establish; some errors do not pop up in the same places all the time—that is, they move from workstation to workstation. This typically indicates a systemic problem rather than a problem with the individual workstations.

Next, I saw that only the clone PCs were having a problem with the illegal operation error—none of the name-brand PC users had reported it. Finally, I saw that not all the users who had clones were reporting errors—only certain of the clones. This led us to believe that there were component problems with certain clones.

Obviously, one group of these things was not like the other. To rule out a user problem, I switched the PC of a user who didn't have the problem with the PC of a user who did have the problem. (This didn't endear me to either user, but it did tell me that the problem was definitely workstation related.)

I took inventory of the workstations that were acting up because I wanted to see what those workstations had in common. I made a new chart of the lower-level components (see Table 6.2). I left out the Windows OS and its components because I had taken pains during the rollout to make sure that all the workstations were identical in this regard. I also didn't scan for viruses because I rolled out a scanner along with the Windows installation.

TABLE 6.2   A Sample Chart of Lower-Level Components

Workstation	Mfr/Bios	Video Card	Hard drive	RAM	Hub/port
Jack	AMI	Brand-X	Quantum	16MB	8/2
Tracy	Phoenix	Brand-X	Connor	16MB	9/3
Bill	AMI	Brand-X	Seagate	24MB	8/1

After looking at the new chart, it became apparent to me that although the PCs all had components *du jour* and had been built with whatever pieces and parts the vendors had lying around, they all, oddly enough, had the same video card.

Just because it was reasonably easy, I swapped out one of the problem workstation's video card with a different video card. As I continued to log problems, it became clear that the workstation with the new video card was no longer having a problem. I switched another workstation's video card, and the problem went away there as well. Although I tried to update the video drivers on the remaining problem workstations, this did not make the problem go away. The final solution was to replace all the problem workstations' video cards.

Obviously, getting a lot of workstations whose components tend to change on a regular basis isn't a good foundation for being able to easily troubleshoot workstation problems. Because fewer differences equals less time trying to figure out which of these things is not like the others, it makes good sense to practice proactive troubleshooting by attempting to keep all components—software, hardware, and otherwise—to a standard, particularly within the same department or workgroup. See Hour 18 for real-life information from the trenches on how to homogenize your heterogeneous network.

> A *heterogeneous* network is one in which the components are all different; it's more difficult to be a *Sesame Street* troubleshooter on a network like this. On the other hand, the components used in a *homogenous* network are pretty much all the same. This is a *Sesame Street* troubleshooter's dream.
>
> Are there really totally homogenous networks in which everything is always identical? Probably not. Like most things in life, the truth lies somewhere in the middle. However, in this case, the key is to keep as many things the same as possible; for example, buying PCs from one vendor if possible.

Summary

6

If you have something that is broken, comparing it to something that works can be a quick way to establish what *exactly* is broken. Although it's difficult to compare the configuration of seminally different servers, comparing their overall revision levels and file versions can help to rule out a difference problem. In the case of hardware appliances such as routers, switches, print servers, and network attached storage, you will want to consider firmware levels as well as the configuration file.

Comparative anatomy works particularly well when you're considering other objects on your network, such as user setups and workstation configurations. Sometimes, if you've troubleshot the problem down to a particular configuration, you can replace it wholesale (or *shotgun* it) with a known good configuration. This allows you to avoid dealing with complex issues that you might care nothing about.

For complex problems with multiple complainants, you should keep a troubleshooting log that contains the specifics of how users' workstations and configurations are different. This can help to establish a pattern of how the complainants' configurations are the same.

The next hour, Hour 7, shows how SOAP notes, a technique borrowed from the medical world, can help you perform structured analysis on a tough problem.

Q&A

Q How can I tell whether a problem workstation is similar enough to a known good workstation to compare apples to apples?

A You need to have a good sense of when a workstation was installed, who installed it, and so on. Your site's detail documentation will come in handy for determining this. Even documentation in the way of receipts can determine whether a workstation was purchased (and therefore configured) at the same time as another. If you work for a large organization, your purchasing department most likely has asset tags on the PCs. Also, the date of purchase can probably be found somewhere in a database.

Q How do I shotgun a known good user setup?

A A user setup consists of the user object, the profile, and perhaps the home directory. Take these one at a time: create a new user; copy a known good user's profile; and/or copy a known good home directory. (Don't forget to back up the old profile or home directory just in case!)

Q Do all switches or routers have a downloadable configuration file that I can manipulate at my PC?

A No. One of the things you will want to consider if you have the opportunity to purchase new network appliances is whether they have the ability to upload and download the configuration. Also, you will want to find out whether that configuration is at all configurable when it is not on the device. (Some configuration files are binary—not text—and thus aren't editable when on your PC.)

Workshop

Workshop time! Here's a brief quiz to help you make the most out of this hour's lesson as well as activities for you to try on your own.

Quiz

1. True or False: A hardware router that's having problems should have all its DLL versions compared to a similar router that's not having problems.

2. A Windows user profile for Windows 2000 is located in

   a. `C:\Documents and Files\%login%`

   b. `C:\Documents and Settings\%username%`

   c. `%SYSTEMROOT%\Profiles\%login%`

   d. `%SYSTEMROOT%\Profiles\%username%`

3. What is *not* part of the high-level workstation "box"?

   a. The hard drive

   b. RAM

   c. The video card

   d. The login script

4. True or False: You need to be a Windows programmer to investigate an error message about a *bad* DLL.

5. When you log problems on a given network switch and different people report the same problem each day, the problem is most likely related to what?

   a. The workstation

   b. The user object

   c. Both A and B

   d. The switch

Answers to Quiz Questions

1. False. Hardware routers don't have DLLs; they typically just have one version number for their internal software.

2. B

3. D

4. False. You can compare the DLL's file size and date stamp to a known good DLL on a different workstation.

5. D

6

Activities

1. Identify two hardware on your network that should have the same configuration except for unique properties such as IP address. Check up on this (for example, for two Cisco routers, do a line-by-line comparison; for two hardware print servers, print their configuration sheets).

2. If you have ruled a problem into a user's Windows Profile, how might you identify which particular file is causing the problem? (Hint: Start to think about file comparison or registry tools.)

HOUR 7

The SOAP Method: Structured Analysis

The road to wisdom?
Well it's plain
and simple to express:
Err
and err
and err again
but less
and less
and less.

—Piet Hein

I hope you've liked all the note taking involved in the last hour because the method of troubleshooting in this hour involves a great deal more of it.

Treating a complex problem usually involves a lot of note taking because you have to fill in the gaps where your understanding of the problem is incomplete. Up until now, you've treated problems the way you treat a multiple-choice test—with change analysis, divisive reasoning, and matching. Now, we're talking about a fill-in-the-blank test, and it gets a little bit harder; this is the hour in which you have to wade through the subjective, match it up with the objective, analyze your data, and plan on what to do next. In other words, this is the technique you want to refer to for tough problems. You can think of it as writing a journal much in the same way that adolescents do: time-consuming, but ultimately a good way to sort out some serious knots and figure out even the toughest of problems.

Doctor Network

First, here's a little bit about SOAP notes. I first encountered SOAP notes while I was deciding *not* to be a doctor like my father. Although I had absolutely no interest in sticking needles into people or cutting them open, hanging around my father in his office taught me a lot about troubleshooting and diagnostics in general.

In a sense, medicine is *much* harder than computing—there are hardly any standards, the designer never released the data sheets (much less the full documentation), and the device you're trying to troubleshoot can sue you if you make a mistake. The medical profession has come up with all sorts of diagnostic methodologies—we as network troubleshooters can learn a great deal from the medical profession.

One of those diagnostic techniques is the SOAP method of note taking. On their patients' charts, some doctors write down (on separate lines) the letters *S*, *O*, *A*, and *P*, standing for *Subjective*, *Objective*, *Analysis*, and *Plan*, respectively. Therefore, if I went to see the doctor about my stomach, he might write

S: Patient reports stomach pain; ate hot chicken wings last night; extra work lately.

O: Palpation reveals tenderness in upper right quadrant.

A: Suspect acute gastritis.

P: Treat with antacid × 5 days, bland diet, follow up in 5 days to assess condition.

The subjective is what I say to the doctor, the objective is what the doctor sees, the analysis is what he deduces from his additional questions and reasoning, and the plan is what he will do to try to treat the problem, plus the next step. Doctors are used to not being able to get a black-and-white answer; however, if they have a plan, they are going in the right direction.

Going in the right direction is what the SOAP method is all about. Not every problem you run into as a troubleshooter is going to be solvable within that day or week— particularly problems that are not show-stoppers (emergency room visits). In particular, problems that come and go (intermittent problems) are usually long-term and complex troubleshooting jobs. To be able to start to get a handle on a complex problem, you have to segregate the problem into its component parts—that is, the subjective report and the objective facts. It's particularly important to be able to separate the subjective out—someone might be reporting something that has *some* bearing on the problem but perhaps is not pointing directly at the problem. Consider someone who's reporting chest pains—is this person reporting a heart attack or a muscle problem? The report of pain in the chest is a subjective feeling—the active investigation that reveals a heart attack or muscle pain is the objective finding. The subjective is useful but can only be borne out by investigation.

Just the Facts

When considering the facts in an intermittent or complex network issue (also known in the industry lingo as "troubleshooting a weird problem"), you need to categorize a basic list of objective items that can help point toward a solution:

- Duration of problem (all the time or intermittent?)
- Start of problem (date and time)
- Place (on the network; physical location)
- Number of users involved
- Configuration of workstation (like or unlike others?)
- Number and types of applications involved (running simultaneously with?)
- User name(s) involved; security group(s) belonged to
- Measurements
- Behavior of similar applications

Even though you might have a lot of objective data, you might not have the right objective data to analyze in order to come to the right conclusion. Therefore, your *plan* item on your first couple of tries on a tough problem will probably be to gather more data. Don't give up; the more data you have, the better guess you can make.

SOAP in the Real World

Let's take a case in which a user says she can't run a particular Web applet that she needs for her job. In particular, we'll take a case in which the problem seems to be intermittent—again, those tend to be among the toughest problems. Figure 7.1 shows a logical map of the site; her PC lives at point A on the map.

You visit the user's PC and can run the applet just fine. She frowns at you and says, "Well, it doesn't work for me." She tries right after you, and it works, but she reports the problem again the next day. You decide to use SOAP on this one:

S: Web applet does not run when user tries it.

O: Web applet runs *when I try it.*

A: Perhaps the time of day has something to do with it?

P: Come back during the time she usually tries the applet.

FIGURE 7.1

Troubleshooting a time-related problem.

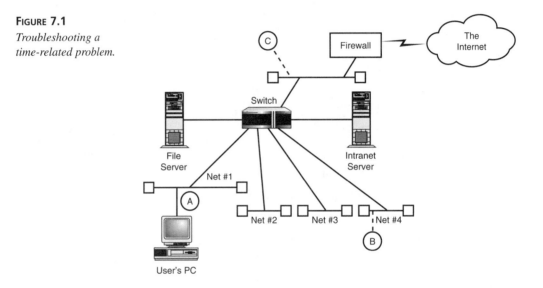

Your analysis of the problem is a good one, and your plan to gather new information works. You visit her when she usually tries her Web applet, and, sure enough, it won't work for you. What's going on? This time through, you're the one supplying the subjective data; it's your guess:

S: I bet that the time of day has something to do with the applet not working.

O: Web applet does not run at 8:00 a.m.

A: Could it be related to another network activity on that segment happening at the same time?

P: Try using a different network segment (point B on the map).

An okay plan, but it doesn't work out, as shown from your notes:

S: Network activity might be different on her segment at 8:00 a.m.

O: Web applet still fails on a different segment.

A: My head hurts. What else could be different at this time of day?

P: Investigate what goes on at 8:00 a.m. on the network as a whole.

She still has problems at 8:00 a.m. on a different network segment. That's fine. You've now ruled out her network segment, and that's very important to do. You've made a deduction, and it's wrong. Don't sweat it.

Is It a Virus, Doc?

After getting a cup of coffee, you briefly think about the possibility of one of those viruses that "go off" at 8:00 a.m. on a certain day, but you dismiss it—you have pretty good virus protection. What's more, you used a different workstation that you're sure is virus free when you tested the different segment. That's a good guess because things like this have happened—even viruses that don't *do* anything until a certain day at a certain time in the morning can interfere with system operations every day while it checks to see if it's the *right* day to ruin you.

So, it's back to the drawing board.

Getting a Consultation

This is the crucial part because you're frustrated, and you think you can't possibly solve this problem. It's tempting to give up. Guess what? Pros feel that way, too. The difference, however, is that the successful troubleshooter takes a break and looks at the facts again. Then, much like a doctor, the troubleshooter might "get a consultation" and go right back at it.

Do you have to get a consultation from a pro? Not necessarily. You get a consultation because you're too close to the problem, and you already have preconceptions as to what's going on. Let's say that you ask somebody—anybody—what goes on at 8:00 a.m. every day. The answer is going to be "everybody turns their PCs on" or "everybody gets in to work" or some variation on this. That turns on a lightbulb for you—because everybody is turning their PCs on and logging in at 8:00, might this be the computer equivalent of rush hour on the network?

7

The answer, of course, is yes, there is a network rush hour. How do you verify this? Well, it's sort of tough. There are two ways:

- Actual measurement (relatively difficult unless you've already read Hour 23, "Network Management Tools")
- Changing the situation (moving the workstation to a place where traffic will be quieter)

Even though you've already moved the workstation to a different segment, you hadn't considered that the segment you were moving to might also be problematic. You can think of this as the equivalent of moving from the Long Island Expressway to the Grand Central Parkway—it doesn't do you a lot of good at rush hour. (You've been treating the situation as though there was construction or an accident on one but not the other.) Now, your SOAP looks like this:

S: The problem might be network congestion.

O: The problem occurs at the same time on different major network segments.

A: Login congestion is likely on major segments, but not as likely on a segment with fewer users.

P: Check maps and try the applet on a "low traffic" network segment (perhaps nearer to the Internet segment and away from segments with server login traffic on them).

You deploy your plan: You temporarily set up a workstation at point C on the map. When you try the applet at 8:00, it works. You have now pointed the finger squarely at network congestion. The next question is, whose problem is this? In other words, is this something that the applet vendor is responsible for, or is this your problem for having a network that's too busy?

Your response to this problem might vary. On one hand, it might be practical to move this person to a less busy segment. However, this might not work because you can see from your physical maps that the network segments near PCs tend to have a lot of PCs on them and are smack in the middle of the servers. In other words, physical constraints might prevent you from putting this person on a segment without other PCs because the only hubs near her probably are being used for other users. Note here that if you were using switches that supported VLANs instead of hubs, you *could* switch her effective segment (the virtual data link domain) without physically moving her workstation— that's what VLANs are for. But in this case, we're dealing with hubs, so no such luck. Worse, we discover that all low-population segments are either in your data center or in another building, outside of her physical reach. (The smart aleck might ask, "Why not ask this person to stop doing her work process at 8:00 in the morning?" Not a great solution—the network is supposed to work, darn it!)

At this point, if you really needed to have this person's workstation stay where it was on the busy segment, you have to start application troubleshooting. Why is it that this person doesn't have any other problems, say, with local applications? As you'll see in Hour 19, "Intranet and Internet Troubleshooting: TCP/IP at Work," comparing a local application to an Internet application isn't a good idea; using Internet applications is like taking an international flight versus hopping in your car to go to the store. A lot of things can happen between here and Paris. You write down your SOAP again:

S: Applet is not working; other applications are.

O: The applet is the only Internet application in the mix.

A: Internet applications are not local applications.

P: Try a different Internet application during peak hours.

You've now done five SOAP lists. Long and tedious, isn't it? Yet, as you can see, SOAP is a powerful process for refining what you know, as well as a way to take guesses and turn them into fact and a way to keep you moving forward.

You try a different Internet application at 8:00 the next morning, and it works like a champ. Even though it doesn't do exactly the same thing, at least you're now comparing apples to apples—that is, a firewall-dependent, wide-area application to another firewall-dependent, wide-area application. You try yet another Internet application, just to make sure, and it, too, works just dandy. Here's your latest SOAP:

S: The application itself seems to be at fault.

O: Only have tried two other Internet applications.

A: Measurement of congestion and delay might help but would still lead to vendor.

P: Contact supplier of the applet and relate all notes that led to this conclusion.

Fortunately, this is not a free applet, and the supplier is eager to make it work for you. The supplier talks you through taking a network trace, and you email it off to him. He responds that you have quite a lot of traffic, but not an unreasonable amount. Because you've gathered a lot of notes and have sent them to him, he has a good idea of what's going on and understands that it's probably his problem. Because he wants you as a customer, before too long, you've got a patched program emailed to your desk, which you install to your user's PC—problem solved.

In a situation such as this, you want to make sure that you document the problem—either informally (via email to your colleagues) or formally (say, as an addendum to the product documentation in your library). You might write something like this:

10/20/98, JF: Applet has problems running on a busy network, use Patch 1.2, located on the 'Barbarian' server's 'FIXES' share.

Sound crazy? A software supplier fixing something you reported? Not really. Our shop has reported many bugs to suppliers over the years using this procedure with great success. When you follow careful SOAP note-taking procedures, you're likely to convince your technical support people that you have a *bona fide* problem that needs to be addressed. However, it's even more likely that you'll come up with the answer yourself—which is really the objective.

Summary

Computer networks have been around less than a century—as network troubleshooters, we should learn troubleshooting techniques from any source we can. The medical profession uses SOAP notes, which can be highly effective in pursuing complex problems. Because you don't necessarily have all the facts when you start chasing a problem, using the SOAP format for note taking encourages you to analyze your data objectively, collect more facts, and form a plan. This method enables you to take small objective steps in your road to problem resolution.

In the next hour, we'll dive into getting outside help for your network problems, without spending a lot, using the Simple Simon Method.

Q&A

Q A user says that her workstation hasn't changed, but I've traced the problem down to her workstation. What could it be?

A Remember that what a user *says* is always subjective. You need to take a look for yourself to see what the facts are. Also, talk to other people in her office. Look at her workstation yourself. Odds are that something has changed. This is change analysis, to be sure; however, SOAP reminds you that any user reports are subjective—you need to corroborate the facts yourself.

Q I've reported bugs to manufacturers before, with no success. Granted, there are manufacturers who listen, but how do you tell which ones will?

A Assuming that you reported the problem in great detail, my sense is that the smaller software vendors are really the ones who tend to respond to their individual users' problems. The larger software vendors, without naming names, tend to send you a form email that says something like "This will be fixed in the next release" or "Software is operating as designed." Believe it or not, even shareware vendors tend to be really, really responsive to you—particularly after you've registered a large number of licenses with them. They appreciate the business, and it shows.

Workshop

Oh, boy! Workshop time! Here's a brief quiz to help you make the most out of this hour's lesson, as well as activities for you to try on your own.

Quiz

1. *Subjective* means what?

    a. The way someone sees an issue

    b. The cold hard facts

    c. The world according to Garp

    d. The truth of the matter

2. True or False: SOAP notes always lead to a conclusion the first time.

3. A piece of subjective data should be _____.

    a. ignored

    b. collated

    c. divided

    d. investigated

4. Which of the following is not an example of a piece of objective data?

    a. How a user perceives a problem

    b. A measurement

    c. The number of users involved

    d. The timing of a problem

7

5. Analysis is usually the process of thinking about what?

    a. The cold, hard light of reason

    b. Reasonable subjective data

    c. Objective data only

    d. Subjective data plus objective data

6. True or False: Gathering more data is a common plan.

Answers to Quiz Questions

1. A
2. False
3. D
4. A
5. D
6. True

Activities

1. The next time you're reading the news, surfing slashdot.com, or even listening to your children complain, think very carefully about what portion of what you are taking in is *subjective* versus *objective*. You will be amazed at how much of the mainstream news media wraps subjectivity around very few objective facts.

2. See if you can find references to SOAP on medically-oriented Web sites.

HOUR 8

The Simple Simon Method: Consultations and Support

Nothing clears up a case so much as stating it to another person.

—Sherlock Holmes

Robert Heinlein's *Have Space Suit, Will Travel* tells a story about two frogs who jump into a milk bucket and can't get out. One frog sees how hopeless the situation is, quits paddling around, and drowns. The other is too stupid to quit and keeps paddling. Pretty soon, he's got an island of butter in the middle of the cream, where he floats until the milkmaid comes and throws him out.

Persistence can be one of the hallmarks of an unstoppable frog or a really good network troubleshooter! Even when you think you're beaten, that "one more try" can solve the thorniest of problems. Sometimes, that one last try can be admitting that perhaps you need a hand from someone else.

As discussed in Hour 7, "The SOAP Method: Structured Analysis," it's important to "get a consultation" when things seem hopeless. It's easy, fast, and doesn't cost much. What's more, with someone else's perspective in the picture, you can sometimes collect observations or facts that you've missed. Even better, when you explain the problem to someone else, you might be forced into diagramming the flow of the problem, reemphasizing important points, showing what you *know* to be irrelevant, and so on—which usually leads to you getting a better grasp on the problem yourself.

A multitude of ways exist to tap someone else's brains, and even to apply someone else's fixes, many of them not even requiring you to leave your office. Read on.

Tech Support Databases

Wouldn't it be great to quickly and easily get a consultation from an expert? Better yet, wouldn't it be great to get a consultation from an expert for free? You can!

As you might already know, most good software and hardware vendors allow you to search through thousands and thousands of pieces of detailed documentation from their own technical support personnel. In effect, you end up scanning the knowledge of some of the smartest technical support gurus in the world for that particular product. Searching a knowledge base or technical information database can be one of the best ways to avoid reinventing the wheel or rediscovering a solution, particularly with interaction problems (in which one piece of software or hardware affects another).

Knowing how to find the right tech support database and knowing good search strategies will save you tremendous amounts of time.

Folks who are new to networking frequently ask: "Why do vendors do this for free, and can we count on them doing it in the future?"

Well, to run a good technical support shop, managers need good databases that include the problem and resolution of every technical support call, no matter how trivial or tremendous it might be. This allows *them* to avoid reinventing the wheel; it also allows them to save tremendous amounts of time on the front line (and, therefore, tremendous amounts of money).

Having good support—paid or unpaid—keeps customers coming back; and having a free self-help knowledge base is a value-add that generates a tremendous amount of goodwill. The availability of these free knowledge bases also allows vendors to spend less on live operators because many customers, even paying customers, can simply help themselves just as well as they could with a first-tier tech support operator.

Web Search Strategies: Finding the Needle in the Haystack

8

Here's a fact of life: when searching a manufacturer's technical support database, you can do as good a job as the first-level support operator you'll get when you place a tech support call. (Actually, I'm being kind to first-tier tech support operators. The fact is that you will probably do a *better* job.)

The key lies in knowing *what* to search for, *where* to search for it, and *how* to formulate your queries. Even with all the excellent search engines on the Internet, a certain black box approach is necessary when looking for answers to network problems.

> Are you new to the knowledge base search game? Make sure that you don't perform a search from a company's home page because those searches typically search the entire company site, including nontechnical information such as press releases. Although there is usually a link to Support from the main company home page, large technology companies usually have a special Web address (a technical support home page) dedicated to support that offers tech-only searches. Just as a company's home page is usually found at *www.company.com*, most tech companies' support pages are typically found at *support.company.com* or *www.company.com/support*.

Searching, Searching...

Although it seems you would get the best search results by entering as many words as possible, bad search engines don't deal with this well and you'll end up with "search clutter." For example, let's say that a user reports trouble with his McAfee virus protection, telling you that he's getting the following error: "McAfee Internal Error 2735. StopAvSyncManager."

You have no idea what this means, so it's tempting to simply search on the entire string. But if you did, some sites might list hits on the word *McAfee,* on the word *Error*, and on the word *Internal*—all of which will match an insane number of documents. Worse, depending on the search engine that you use, the engine might decide that multiple instances of "McAfee" or "Internal" or "Error" in a document are more worthy of showing you than a document with a single instance of the word "StopAvSyncManager." In this case, you'd get many listings of the former cluttering up your display before the search engine decided to show you the latter.

You're best off, in this case, to try a search on "2735," or perhaps "StopAvSyncManager," which one would hope are fairly unique terms.

Good news, though. Although you should be wary of bad search engines, they are a dying breed. *Most* sites (but sadly, not all) offer sophisticated search engines, and picking and choosing search terms isn't quite as important (they'll "know" that common words shouldn't be given quite as much weight as less common ones.) Even better, sophisticated sites should allow you to clearly specify what exactly you want, as in

```
Internal Error StopAvSyncManager +2735
```

or

```
"Internal Error" AND "2735"
```

The first looks for the word "internal" or "error" or "StopAvSyncManager," and mandates that all hits must have "2735" in them. The second search phrase mandates that all hits must have the literal phrase "internal error" and also must have "2735."

If you're not sure how the site you're searching works, check around for an "advanced search" or help button, which usually spells out the way that you should key in more specific searches

Practical Searching

To get a better idea of how to formulate *your* search strategy, let's look at how my team and I used a black box approach to search for the answer to a Windows NT issue. (The principles for formulating a search strategy are the same whether you're using NT, XP, ME, 2K, 9x, UNIX, NetWare, or even Macintosh.)

Several years ago, we planned to roll out Windows NT in our offices. Naturally, we did a pilot test and after everything seemed okay, we went into limited production. Halfway through the first part of our rollout, a user complained that she was having problems when using DOS EDIT and other DOS utilities. Apparently, she was being asked to insert a disk into drive A whenever she ran a DOS program, regardless of whether a floppy disk was actually involved. This was really odd. We asked ourselves, "Which of these things is not like the other?" and ran to another user's machine. We tried the same thing using another user's machine and login, and got the same results.

We discovered that every single machine we rolled out was having the same problem. Obviously, we stopped the rollout. But we had an odd problem—why was a fresh new machine acting this way? As a matter of fact, each machine we had was acting this way. Was it a hardware error? A software error? If so, which software? Was this a network-related problem at all?

There was a lot that perhaps could go wrong here, so now was a good time to spend a few minutes searching. Fortunately, we had something to search for—in the form of a very rude error message: `NTVDM: No disk. Please insert a disk into drive A:`

8

The most obvious place to search, Microsoft's site, revealed nothing of tremendous interest when we did a search for this specific error message, except that we were told to check the PATH variable for references to drive A. No such luck; the PATH didn't include references to the floppy.

In order to figure out where to search for our answers, it was time to reach into our black box troubleshooting toolkit, simplify the system into high-level objects, and then determine what vendors were involved:

- Windows NT setup
- Intel virus protection
- WordPerfect Suite 8
- GroupWise email and scheduling software

At first glance that seemed pretty complete, but on further reflection we realized that, in fact, we were missing at least two more pieces of the puzzle. We were thinking about application software, but of course there were more pieces than are on the preceding list. So, we took it from the top and wrote down what was done, action-wise, to create this new machine. The possible sources of the problem omitted from the previous list appear in bold:

1. Unpacked **Dell PC** from box.
2. Setup was automatically run. NT and **Microsoft's Service Pack 3** were installed.
3. Installed **Novell Client32** (necessary for connection to NetWare server).
4. Configured **3Com Ethernet** network card.
5. Installed Intel Virus Protection, Corel WordPerfect Suite 8, Novell GroupWise.

Enumerating the steps we took to create the workstation led us to come up with a better vendor list to search. Our final list contained the following vendors:

- Dell
- Microsoft
- Novell
- 3Com
- Intel
- Corel

Rather than build a new PC from the ground up, and keep testing for the error after adding each component—which might take anywhere from an hour to two hours (if all went well!)—we figured it would be faster to do a quick search on the pertinent vendor sites. So, we searched for the error message at the following Web sites:

- `http://support.dell.com`
- `http://support.microsoft.com`
- `http://support.novell.com`
- `http://support.3com.com`
- `http://support.corel.com`

We began by entering NTVDM by itself because this was a fairly unique term. (Again, when searching, you don't want to get hits on common words such as *disk*.) After getting a bazillion hits, we proceeded to search for the entire quoted error message. (Remember that unless you specify a "weight" to a word—which is not an option on some vendor sites—each word counts the same; therefore, entering **NTVDM no disk** might match documents with multiple instances of *no* and/or *disk* more than it would match a document that has one mention of NTVDM; entering **"NTVDM: No disk"** as a quoted entity will match the entire phrase, and therefore *only* match documents that match this error message.)

Quoting phrases can *seriously* limit you; don't assume that just because the literal phrase doesn't exist that *no* pertinent document is out there. Documents that discuss a given situation might not give the exact, quoted error text, yet still might be useful. Use quoting with care.

Dell, at the time, had nothing about NTVDM. Microsoft had zillions of information documents, and NTVDM, by itself, pulled up close to 100 documents. We decided to come back here if nothing else panned out. On the third try, eureka! As shown in Figure 8.1, a search on NTVDM on Novell's site pulled up only nine documents, a very manageable number. A quick glance revealed a technical document that precisely described our problem. In this case, we learned that the Novell Client32, in conjunction with a bug in Windows NT Service Pack 3, has caused the problem. The documentation also detailed a fix, which was to copy NTDOS.SYS from the original Windows NT CD-ROM to the C:\WINNT\SYSTEM directory.

When troubleshooting a potential multivendor problem, don't spend too much time on each site at first—one vendor might have an obvious solution that jumps out at you, whereas the other vendors might have so many possibilities that you will end up sifting through hundreds of documents.

FIGURE 8.1

Searching several sites rather than spending a lot of time on one can generate small yields and make the solution obvious.

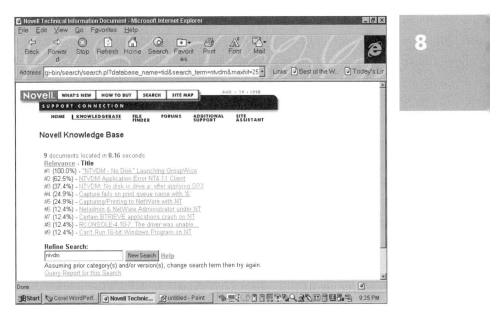

Five minutes after firing up the Web browser, we had solved the problem. Whoa! Talk about standing on the shoulders of giants. We might have spent hours playing divide-and-conquer on this problem if it weren't for the incredible power of tech support search.

Other Web-based Help

There are a huge number of Internet-based support forums that are both product and technology related, and they can also lend as much of a helping hand as a vendor site.

Generally, these sites fall into one of several categories:

- Paid expert sites. Much like eBay, individuals have something to sell; in this case, their expertise. Your mileage might vary quite widely. Exp.com (http://www.exp. com), one of the first paid expert sites, is one example.

- Free expert sites. Usually, an established provider of technical expertise, such as a consultancy or a technology magazine, providing free advice as a service to customers and the community/potential customers. Network Computing Magazine (http://www.networkcomputing.com/forum/askexp) is a good example of a site that does this: The site gets its editors and partner consultants to answer real-life reader problems, and then keeps those in a public information base.

- Usenet. Usenet has really fallen into disrepair over the last couple of years, because of high spammer activity among other issues. Still, it can be useful. If your provider doesn't offer an nntp (news) feed for you, you can always try Google's Web-based Usenet interface at `http://groups.google.com`.

- Mailing lists and digests. You'll have to do some searching to find these in the first place. Because there can be a good deal more editorial control with these, the content can be far superior to Usenet. The downside is that there doesn't seem to be a central place that will search all of them. The Atlanta Linux Enthusiasts (ALE) mailing list is an example support list that doesn't have a vendor affiliation; look for it at `http://www.ale.org`.

- Web boards. Web-based forums that are run by interested consultants or hobbyists. For a good example of what these look like, check out one Web-board's support site: `http://www.phpbb.com/phpBB`.

Searching these resources can be just as fruitful as going to the manufacturer's site. Not all manufacturers promote these groups on their corporate home pages because they don't have editorial say on what is posted and the public isn't always kind to them. Nonetheless, the preceding list can be a source of real-world information—stuff you won't get from the manufacturer. (Although depending on the source, you might have to wade through piles of useless expletives before you hit useful information.)

I'm not always impressed by the individual search engines that power various mailing list archives; it's certainly better to try to use them when they are good because a targeted search is generally best. But if a given forum's search engine is lousy, the good news is that unlike *vendor* tech support databases, public forums are indexed by and searchable using generic Internet search engines like Google.

Don't forget to search manufacturers' support sites before you hit the Web at large. Searching the whole darn Web can be pretty scattershot and time-consuming; remember, it's best to use a targeted search where possible before doing a global one.

Love to use Google? May I suggest the +site search flag? For example, if you wanted to search Network Computing for all articles written about Socks proxies, you might search Google for "socks +site:networkcomputing. com". Also, rather than performing a generic Web page search, go to groups.google.com when searching Usenet.

If the information that you're looking for doesn't seem like it's been posted, don't be shy about posting your problem to public forums. There are plenty of friendly and smart people out there who are willing to help. You will want to exercise courtesy and follow etiquette when asking for help. Specifically,

- Use a specific, yet brief, subject line. "Help" is a terrible subject and sure to cause readers to gnash their teeth and hit the Delete key. "Group Policies on Win2K failing" is a better subject line because it provides a concise description of the environment and problem.

- Make sure that you are posting to an appropriate forum, and don't cross-post. Although it's tempting to post your installation problem to a "general" forum in the belief that the "general" forum has more readers, if an "installation" forum is available, use it.

- Provide organized and concise information about the source of the problem, along with what you have ruled out or ruled in.

- Make sure that you have read the appropriate manual or FAQ (Frequently Asked Questions document) *before* asking a question. Many FAQs can be found at `ftp://rtfm.mit.edu`.

- "Lurk" on the forum for a while to get a sense of what might be unwritten rules of the forum; that is, read the forum for a while before writing to it.

The experts that answer questions publicly usually do so free; and, presuming that they are really good at what they do, they are usually busy people and don't have time to wade through a wandering message that is full of complaint and conjecture. To get the most effective response, stick to the facts, explain your methods and what you have already ruled out—and why. Keep it as short as possible too, but not so brief that you are not being complete. See "Being Taken Seriously" later in this hour for some ideas on what to include in your help request.

Pay to Play

All free support entails very little obligation on the part of the vendor. Despite this, your results can be pretty good if you take ownership of the problem and follow up aggressively. Nonetheless, there are times when you need more than you can get free, particularly if troubleshooting is a major part of your job.

Ultimately, only you can decide what level of convenience and response time you need. Your contract cost will be based on the complexity of your environment, response time, and whether your equipment or software is still under warranty. Here are some options that you might want to consider for your support organization:

- Technical support software subscriptions—Usually covers only what's available from the vendor: maintenance releases, upgrades, special knowledge base CDs, and so on.

- Specific training for software or hardware—Available either from the vendor or from a third party, these can range from in-person classes to computer-based training and simulation.

- Per-incident telephone support —Available from the vendor or a qualified third party, this is a pretty flexible way to get support when you need it on a limited basis. If you need help on a lot of support incidents, this is less cost effective than an annual or monthly agreement; but if you have only a few, this is more cost effective.

- Annual or monthly telephone support—"The whole enchilada," available from a qualified third party or the vendor. Typically is an "all-you-can-eat" type of agreement, where there is no limit placed on the number of support incidents you can generate. Obviously, this is usually the most expensive option.

A CD-ROM technical support knowledge base can be a very good investment.

Some Web-based knowledge bases, such as Microsoft's, are so busy that it can be aggravating waiting for each page to download. Instead, you can buy a subscription to Microsoft's TechNet for a couple of hundred dollars. Whether you love or hate Microsoft, you've got to love TechNet. As with most CD-ROM knowledge bases, you get what you pay for—much more sophisticated features, which result in speedier access. For example, you can refine your search results by product type and you can bookmark. TechNet has every single technical information document available on the Web site, but it runs about 10 times faster (see Figure 8.2).

FIGURE 8.2

A Microsoft TechNet session.

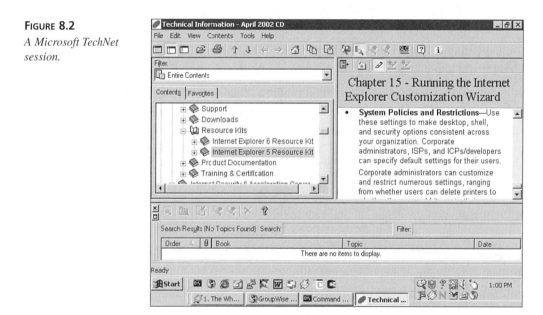

> **Talkin' TechNet**
>
> Because I deal quite a bit with problems with Microsoft products, I tend to hit TechNet rather heavily. However, it's sort of embarrassing because TechNet makes you look like a hero when all the heroism you've shown is a couple of mouse clicks in the right place. For example, a couple of technicians came to ask me for advice on a fatal exception error that had been going on for a while. Instead of running upstairs to look at the workstation in question, I keyed the exact error message into TechNet, which brought up a couple of hits—one of which seemed applicable. We ran upstairs to apply the TechNet suggestion, and the user was fixed in 10 minutes.
>
> TechNet's not only for searches, either. You can also browse by topic, including Microsoft whitepapers and resource kits, making it an excellent source of learning and study.

Investing in a CD-ROM technical support knowledge base is cost effective, even if you only avoid one or two visits from your $150-an-hour consultant.

Obviously, if a problem isn't solvable in a reasonable time frame, you'll have to go to the outside for help: Time (particularly downtime) equals money, and a couple of hours of consulting time can be money well spent in comparison to lost man-hours when something critical is down. If you end up having to pay for help from the outside, take heart— your work has not been wasted. Doing your troubleshooting homework can and will save your company hundreds or even thousands of dollars because you've decreased the up-front work of the consultant.

Being Taken Seriously

If you've read the manual, checked the databases, and you're still stumped, it's time to call the vendor. Whether you pay as you go for what seems to be a hopeless problem or have a support contract, a couple of strategies exist that will help maximize your encounter with a professional technical support person.

Primary in your efforts will be how well you've documented the problem during your troubleshooting efforts. If you've used SOAP notes during the problem, you probably already have exactly what a tech support person is wanting:

- Type of hardware involved
- Type of network involved (maps)
- Application(s) involved
- Time relationship (ongoing, time of day)
- Reproducibility

If you cannot reproduce a problem, neither can the folks at the other end of the phone. However, if you can reproduce the problem on a different workstation or a server, you're that much closer to convincing technical support that your problem is a legitimate problem and not just a product of your network environment.

People who call tech support before they gather this crucial information typically receive the brush-off. (The irony is that once you've done the requisite research and documentation, the culprit is usually apparent, thus canceling your need to call technical support in the first place.) One brush-off technique is the finger-pointing game. Because you, a non-expert, can't prove that a problem is unrelated to a different vendor, it can be difficult to refute technical support's claim that the problems lies with the other guy.

You can combat this by insisting on documented proof that you can submit to the maligned vendor—the vendor doing the maligning can tell you how to collect this proof—or by administering a test on your own. As you'll see in Hour 21, "Protocol Analyzers," you don't have to be a network expert to be able to submit network traces to technical support. Network traces are basically blow-by-blow accounts of what's happening on the wire, and they can be very useful to the network analyst on the other end of the line.

You can also combat finger-pointing by trying the same type of operation "manually," without the influence of the item being pointed at. In other words, if a program complains that it cannot write a file to a server, but you think it should be able to, try writing the same kind of file by yourself under the same login and session circumstances (don't reboot or log out). Therefore, if the setup program says this,

```
Can't copy "FOO.EXE " from D:\setup\foo to G:\myapp - Retry?
```

You might want to get to a DOS prompt and try typing the following:

```
C:\> COPY D:\setup\foo\FOO.EXE G:\myapp
```

Alternatively, you can use Windows Explorer to copy FOO.EXE from d:\setup\foo to g:\myapp.

Finger-Pointing Fun

I once had a bizarre problem with a server—certain applications simply would *not* install. The common thread was that the install program involved complained that it could not write certain files to a certain directory. The application vendors said, "It installs fine on thousands of other servers just like yours!" The server vendor's response was that these programs must be doing something odd while they're installing. "No," I protested, "more than one program is doing this—it must be the server!" The problem was set aside, until one of my technicians had the idea of performing a manual file copy of the files involved. In other words, one of the applications I was trying to install failed while it was copying the file KBSTUFF.SYS, so I simply typed

```
f:\> copy d:\setup\kbstuff.sys f:
```

and sure enough, I got an error—even though I could copy differently named files to that directory (and even though I had file permissions to write to the directory). I called the server vendor's technician back, who said, "I've *gotta* see this!"

The technician requested that I capture the network traffic in between the workstation and the server (the network equivalent of a wiretap). Sure enough, one day after submitting traces to the server vendor, we were told that, yes, the server was replying wrongly to the workstation. The vendor asked, "Do you have virus protection on the server? Software licensing software?" I did, and after removing the virus protection package, I no longer had problems installing any of the applications. Apparently, some sort of interaction problem existed with the various applications I had installed on the server—not the least of which were the vendor's bug-fix patches! The virus protection package was reasonably old, so it hadn't been tested with the latest patches—an upgrade to the virus protection package was in order, but at least I had tracked down the problem.

A given vendor might supply wonderful tech support in addition to a killer Web site. I've been fortunate to deal with some of these vendors—unfortunately, though, they're sort of rare. If you find one, buy its product as much as you can and offer up prayers that it sticks around forever. Seriously, good tech support technicians *can* be major help, so you certainly don't want to rule out calling them.

Summary

Sometimes, the best way to solve a problem is to find out if anybody else has had the problem. Internet search engines, Internet forums, mailing lists, and CD-ROM knowledge bases are excellent ways to extend your troubleshooting efforts. Technical support should be saved as a last resort; if you approach tech support with a documented reproducible problem, you're much more likely to be treated with respect. Brush-offs, such as finger-pointing, can be combated with good notes and a reproduction of the problem without the component that the vendor is pointing its finger at. Working knowledge of diagnostic gear, such as network analyzers, can really help to gather data that ends the finger-pointing game as well.

Q&A

Q Why don't you list every technical support site that you know of here?

A This stuff changes every six months; the techniques that you've learned so far will not. (You know, "go to lunch, fall behind.") You'll need to learn how to find particular sites in addition to how to search them once you get there. Just follow the aforementioned guidelines to find a manufacturer's Web site, and you should be okay. There are not many technical support sites outside of the ones provided by manufacturers, but just for fun, you can search for them using Dogpile, Google, and so forth—for example, type in `"Linux free support"`, making sure you enter the quotation marks, because each word on its own would result in a huge match.

Q I can't reproduce an intermittent problem. I understand that it's tough to get vendor support until the problem is reproducible, but try explaining that to my boss. Help! What can I do?

A You need to go back to the divide-and-conquer technique, take SOAP notes, and compare the problem area to other working areas. If other workstations or application installations are working fine, it might be time to burn down the barn and build it again. Other than that, disciplined note taking and follow up are your best friends when dealing with an intermittent problem. I feel your pain. Believe me. However, you will prevail if you keep at it. If the problem is important enough, feel free to go ahead and ask your vendor; tech support might be able to give you clues as to what you might have missed in your ruling-out process.

Workshop

Workshop time! Here's a brief quiz to help you make the most out of this hour's lesson as well as some activities for you to try on your own.

Quiz

1. Which of the following is it best to search a support site with?

    a. As many keywords as possible

    b. One unique keyword

    c. A quoted phrase or error message

    d. Both B and C

2. A support CD-ROM you want costs $300. Your boss asks you to justify buying it by telling him how many hours of consultant work you can avoid. At $150 per hour (which is the going rate for your consultant), you calculate that you would

8

only have to avoid _____ hours of calling the consultant to justify the cost of the CD-ROM.

    a. 2

    b. 9

    c. 5

    d. 15

3. True or False: Usenet discussion groups are always correct about technical issues.

4. To search the support database of the Frobozz Fabulous FiberSwitch Corporation, where might you start?

    a. `http://www.frobozz.com/frotz`

    b. `http://www.support.frobozz.com`

    c. `http://support.frobozz.com`

    d. `http://frobozz.com/www/support`

Answers to Quiz Questions

1. D

2. A

3. False

4. C

Activities

1. Identify the most crucial system on your network. Is there a topic mailing list that you can subscribe to? A Web-based forum? Go check it out.

2. Create a chart of all critical systems in your organization; what kind of support you have (paid, per-incident, and so forth), and what the contact numbers and contract numbers are. Keep this by the phone in case of trouble.

PART III

The Care and Feeding of Network Equipment

Hour

HOUR 9

Overcoming Hardware Phobia

We only truly learn by destroying.

—Usenet post, `comp.sys.unix` (circa 1980)

Network geeks don't live in a vacuum; we all have to learn how to deal with the things our networks live on. Whether it's a bad circuit board or a corrupt spot on a hard drive, network functions are picky, picky, picky; they stop working when underlying pieces and parts (collectively called the *infrastructure*) stop working. Networkers have been fixing (and accidentally breaking) hardware for years. (People might *think* all we do is stare at blinking lights all over our network command center and stroke our chins thoughtfully, but sadly, no; we've actually got to roll up our sleeves and actually work on pieces of the system more often than you would think.)

When a problem has been troubleshot down to a hardware component, further hardware troubleshooting is often necessary. Today, I'll cover what to do and what not to do with hardware, and you'll learn the basics of the following topics:

- PCs
- Circuit boards and other pluggable electronics
- Cables
- Monitoring system resources

 Because many servers are nothing more than pumped up PCs with faster and better hard drives, CPUs, and so on, many of these hardware techniques apply to servers as well: everything from Intel-based servers to Sun SPARC servers.

Typical Workstation Troubleshooting

A user's PC is often the culprit of a network problem. Although a PC is essentially just an assemblage of pluggable circuit boards and chips and can be troubleshot from that angle, you should also consider its low-level *software* configuration when troubleshooting. The PC's lowest level software is its *BIOS (Basic Input/Output System)*, which is responsible for making all the boards and chips talk to each other in a civil manner.

The BIOS

You can get into a PC's BIOS by pressing the proper setup key right after you power on the PC. Each BIOS manufacturer uses a different keystroke: Del, F1, or the F2 keys are all popular choices; you will usually see a message right after power on that indicates which one you should use.

The BIOS setup screen can range from fairly complex to reasonably simple. Typically, a name-brand PC's BIOS is simpler than a generic clone's because the name-brand manufacturers don't care much about motherboard expansions and options. Clone manufacturers, by comparison, want to allow for as many permutations of hardware as possible, so their BIOSes tend to be more complex. At any rate, a typical BIOS screen is text based, with no Windows-style controls.

A BIOS setup screen can be compared with other *known good* PCs from the same manufacturer in order to verify that the settings are correct. If you don't have another PC of the same type, you can always reset to the defaults. This can often correct a problem with your PC that some "nut loose behind the keyboard" might have caused.

For example, certain memory settings are configurable at the BIOS screen, as are certain Plug-and-Play settings. If one of these is changed to an incorrect value, your system might start malfunctioning in the most interesting of ways. In particular, certain non–Plug-and-Play network cards, for example, have limited *IRQ (Interrupt Request)* numbers they can use; if the BIOS reserves these IRQs for Plug-and-Play devices, your network card will either not work at all or will behave erratically.

> Be sure to write down your BIOS settings before you reset to the defaults because you might need some of those settings later. Typically, resetting your BIOS to its defaults won't hurt anything, but you never can tell.
>
> Some PCs have the option to print BIOS settings to a local printer—if yours does, go for it. Printing out your settings beats the heck out of writing everything down.

Name Brand Versus Generic PCs

The components within most PCs are reasonably consistent:

- The case typically has a built-in power supply that provides proper voltage and current for reliable operation.
- All PCs have a motherboard with a hardware *bus*: The bus is a common interface that allows all motherboard and daughterboard components to inter-communicate.
- The motherboard also houses memory, a CPU, a chipset, and expansion slots for daughterboards.
- All motherboards have a BIOS that, in addition to performing functions that facilitate component communication, performs a *Power-On-Self-Test (POST)*, and then *boots* the operating system from hard disk or other media.

> If your PC starts beeping when you turn it on and you don't get a video signal, it's easy to panic. Relax; one of two things is likely causing the problem: either your "Bank 0" (or first bank) motherboard RAM or the video card. (See "Plug and Pray" later today for instructions on reseating memory and cards as a first step.)

The differentiating factor between PCs tends to relate to the physical layout of components. My experience has shown that cheap clones, as opposed to name-brand machines, can be poorly designed, which can become a factor in situations requiring you to troubleshoot. This can be true both from the digital perspective as well as the physical perspective.

Suppose, for example, that the PC you're troubleshooting sports a poorly placed mother-board jumper block that comes into contact with an expansion card. (A *jumper* is a mov-able and removable mechanism that electrically ties two pins together on the motherboard; a *jumper block* is a group of these pins, usually controlling some kind of configuration of the motherboard.) All of a sudden, a jumper set that wasn't connected becomes connected through the metal on the expansion card bracket, and chaos ensues.

Clone PCs are often not compatibility tested the way name-brand machines are, which can add to the fun. The bottom line is this: Spending a few extra dollars for a name brand can help you avoid problems. What *name brand* means, I leave up to you. To me, it means "non–fly-by-night."

Of course, buying a brand name doesn't always mean that things work 100 percent of the time; any hardware you use might still add to network trou-bleshooting fun! But in a networked environment with large numbers of PCs, it's important to be able to have some sort of accountability when things don't work as promised—which you don't often get when buying from the here-today-gone-tomorrow clone market.

Plug and Pray

Each PC also has pluggable components in the form of expansion cards (modems, net-work cards, video cards, and so on). There are also pluggable microchips that usually have two rows of 8 to 16 pins that fit into a similarly sized socket. Each of these types of components is susceptible to physical movement or "chip creep" due to the metal expansion and contraction that happens during heating and cooling. What's more, con-tacts that aren't made of gold are also susceptible to oxidation, much the same way iron rusts, and of course, oxide does not conduct electricity as well as metal.

Any pluggable component (even a cable) is susceptible to these two problems. Fortunately, two simple solutions exist. Many times, pressing down on chips or boards can make an intermittent problem go away. If that fails to fix the problem, try to reseat the component by pulling it out and putting it back in. Chips don't usually need reseat-ing; typically, pushing down on them does the trick.

If you choose to reseat a chip, be very careful when pulling it out. Otherwise, you can ruin it by bending the small pins. Also, be careful not to allow the pins to fold underneath the chip. You'll want to make certain that each pin aligns correctly with its socket hole.

This problem isn't as bad with modern CPUs because their *ZIF (zero insertion force)* design does not require you to exert any force on the chip. Zero insertion force, like it sounds, means that there's no resistance when you first drop the chip in—the socket isn't "engaged" yet. Only *after* you put the chip in do you engage the socket, normally using a lever. You want to make sure to *raise* the lever next to the CPU before you start yanking on the chip—this will disengage the socket and release the tension on the CPU pins.

Therefore, if your PC seems totally dead, you can probably reseat your CPU without worrying too much about hurting anything.

9

I realize this is common sense, but it's worth saying anyhow: You can cause serious damage to electronic components if you work on them while they're turned on. Make sure that any device you're about to work on is powered down.

Electronic components are extremely sensitive to even the smallest amount of static electricity. You must *ground* yourself before touching any components. By touching a metallic ground, you discharge any static electricity that might have built up on your body while walking around. Most computers have a three-prong outlet that includes a ground. If you leave your computer plugged in (but turned *off*) while working on it, you can ground yourself by touching its internal metal chassis.

The interface cards that connect to your motherboard aren't as fragile as single chips. You can pull them out and push them back in; this sometimes fixes an intermittent connection or knocks dirt away from the pins.

Dirty Deeds

Cleaning a component or PC can also help clear up odd hardware problems. Dust and dirt can seriously impede the performance or reliability of a component. If you're not lucky enough to have a climate-controlled data center, dust is likely to be one of your enemies.

Some people get good results from using a vacuum cleaner to remove excess dust and dirt from the inside of their machines' cases. However, an overly powerful vacuum cleaner can suck up loosely connected jumpers, so be careful. Also a vacuum can create static electricity, which can ruin your whole day.

Although buying canned air is more expensive than using an existing vacuum cleaner, using canned air can give better results because it's portable and you can aim it with pretty good accuracy. Although you can actually fix problems this way, bear in mind that you don't get rid of the dirt—you merely relocate it. Just make sure to aim properly so that the dirt is forced *outside* of your equipment.

Some people who work with electronics like to use electronic cleaner spray on just about any dusty component. In fact, it works amazingly well, but I use it as a last resort. I don't like to use this kind of cleaner as a first step on network or computer components—maybe I'm squeamish, but apart from the fact that this stuff tears a hole in the ozone the size of Kentucky, it seems like overkill to me to spray a volatile compound all over your gear. Most times, the aforementioned methods work just fine.

> You can use a soft pencil eraser on the contacts of your interface cards to clean dirt or oxidation off of them.

Finally, don't overlook any manufacturer-recommended cleaning regimen that a particular piece of equipment might need. I'm embarrassed to admit that one time, I completely disassembled an Exabyte 8mm tape drive to discover why it wasn't working properly, only to realize that all it needed was cleaning with the cleaning cartridge!

Swap Session

You would be amazed at what can be fixed via a simple hardware swap. As a perfect example of black box troubleshooting, most hardware repair is accomplished by swapping circuit boards and other distinct and separate components. Even pros don't engage in component-level repair anymore; the days of a field technician soldering a new capacitor or microchip on to a broken circuit board have been gone for some time now. To save time, people in the field repair business simply swap out a suspect component for a new, presumably working component.

> It always bothered me that people never repaired these types of things—until I looked at the costs involved. At anywhere from $85–$200 an hour for labor, it's insanely expensive to repair cheap ($10–$50) electronic gear rather than replace it. Why spend $100 to fix your $25 Ethernet card? You can buy four for the price of fixing one! This probably doesn't make Greenpeace happy, but it sure makes sense economically.

Swapping components is something you can do yourself. Suppose that, for example, you've troubleshot a network application's problem to a particular workstation, and you've ruled out the user login and network files.

You've tried to run the Microsoft Exchange client for a user on her workstation, but got a fatal exception error. You logged her in to a couple of other workstations, which worked fine every time.

So you know that it's a workstation problem, but you don't pass the buck—you're interested in finding out *what* the workstation problem is.

This problem is a good candidate for swapping components. Sometimes it can be obvious what to swap first—for example, if someone's Microsoft Word is repainting the screen badly on one workstation, but not another, you would probably swap the video card first. In this example, it's hard to say what might be causing the fatal exception; fatal exceptions are caused by bad operating system components, local applications, faulty hard drives, bad video cards or drivers, and so on.

While noting whether the problem remains, you swap the following items:

- The hard drive with a known good hard drive from a similar PC (This is important to rule out a software problem with the OS, and is less drastic than re-imaging the user's hard drive for diagnostic purposes.)
- The video card
- RAM DIMMs
- The network card

When you swap the memory, the fatal exception error goes away. Furthermore, when you install this memory into a known good PC, that PC starts exhibiting the same lockup problem when you run the network application. It doesn't matter *how* the memory is broken—that is, whether it has bad circuitry on it somewhere or is simply somewhat incompatible with this brand of PC/motherboard. It only matters that it *is* broken. (Thank goodness you *swapped* hard drives here: Wouldn't you be embarrassed if you re-imaged the user's hard drive, only to later find out the problem lay with the memory?)

There are two kinds of common memory nowadays:

- SIMMs (single inline memory modules)
- DIMMs (dual inline memory modules)

SIMMs

SIMMs are getting less and less common, mostly appearing in laser printers and other appliances, and not PCs. A DIMM has contacts on both sides and is therefore more dense pin-wise (168 pins) and data-wise. Although a SIMM has contacts on each side of it, each side leads to the same place on the board. This means that there are actually 60 contacts on a 30-pin SIMM, and 144 contacts on a 72-pin SIMM. SIMMs are also typically slower than DIMMs.

To remove a SIMM from a motherboard, pull outward on the metal clips holding it. This makes it pop from its 90-degree angle from the motherboard to a 45-degree angle. You're then able to remove the SIMM. To insert a different SIMM, reverse the process: Put it in at a 45-degree angle, get it nestled in, and push it to a 90-degree angle. You should feel a click when the metal tabs engage the SIMM's holes. (If it's not easy to do, turn it around; you might have it backward.)

DIMMs

A DIMM is even easier because you don't have to fool with any of that 45-degree angle stuff. Instead, simultaneously push down (toward the motherboard) the plastic levers on each side of the DIMM. The DIMM pops up, and you can remove it. To insert a DIMM, simply line it up correctly—it has a different number of pins on each side of its bottom notch—and push it in hard. The plastic levers engage by themselves.

Depending on which type of memory the machine has, you might have to replace it in pairs or fours—whatever your motherboard documentation refers to as a *bank of memory*. The best practice is to swap the entire bank of memory with another known good bank—that way, you don't have to worry about whether you need to keep pairs of memory together, even though some computers consider a *bank* to be one SIMM or DIMM.

When swapping memory member, look at the edge connectors: they're not all gold plated. Some memory bars have zinc (silver in color) contacts, and should not be put into a gold-plated socket. You also should not put memory with gold plated contacts into a zinc-plated socket.

Why? When you mix metal types, you are creating a mini-battery that results in bizarre problems and possible memory failure.

Some might laugh at how strange this sounds, but it's fact, not folklore. Companies like Intel (www.intel.com/support/motherboards/desktop/genmbfaq.htm) and OnTrack (www.ontrack.com/hardwareinfo/memory.asp) verify this.

You'll frequently find that network application problems are related to component problems; taking half an hour to swap components can save you blank looks from a repair technician. In other words, an intermittent problem on your network might not occur when an outside technician runs diagnostics on what you have determined to be a problem PC. If you can localize the problem, you'll probably save time and aggravation in the long run.

The Cable Is the Network

UTP (unshielded twisted pair) is the most common cable used in networks today. Some less-common, but worth-knowing-about cable include

- **STP (shielded twisted pair)**—Used for Token-Ring (very obsolete) and older wide-area applications.
- **Fiber (fiber-optic cabling)**—Completely immune to electromagnetic interference, high distance limitation, has the highest theoretical (and practical, as of this writing) data rate possible. Tough to work with because it requires special (and reasonably expensive) equipment.

For our purposes here, we will assume that UTP is in use in your network, which is subcategorized as CAT-3 and CAT-5, and is used for 10Mb (megabit) and 100Mb Ethernet, respectively. The newer CAT-5e (pronounced Cat-Five-E) supports gigabit data rates as well.

> The categories of wiring are simply an industry-standard way of referring to the manufacturing specifications for the cable: the thickness (gauge) of the wire, the number of twists per foot, and the electronic resistance of the wire.

No matter what type of cable is in use, the important thing to remember is that all cables are fallible. For example, one of the most common (and smartest) things to do when a user is having network connectivity problems (no link light on the network card, perhaps) is to simply swap the cable with a known good cable. It's pretty easy to swap a cable, regardless of the cable type you're working with. Running diagnostics on the network card might take a *lot* longer than swapping the cable, so swapping is definitely what you want to do here. If the cable proves to be the culprit, you can simply toss it in the trash and buy another.

> Although Radio Shack (and even Home Depot) sells the gear to crimp your own cables, unless you make really, really good cables, and have a cable tester to verify them with, you're better off buying your cables ready made. At $8–$20 for various flavors and lengths of cables, it's definitely worth it. Good cables make a good network.

When troubleshooting UTP wire runs, you'll want to verify that the UTP is nowhere near motors or fluorescent lights because *EMI (electromagnetic interference)* can create very odd problems on your network. Because UTP is so easy to work with, a lot of people (trying to save a buck) run their own cable. (It's actually easy to slice the housing off of a cable, insert it, and crimp down on it.) However, many times, folks run cable without realizing that EMI even exists. Save yourself trouble by verifying that your UTP runs are nowhere near it.

Using Cable Testers

It's easy to test patch cables (that is, cables that go from your wall box to your PC) simply by swapping them. But what about the cable in the wall?

If you have ruled the wall cable in as a potential source of trouble, you might well want to replace the wall cable. But because it's expensive to get someone in to pull a cable back into the wall, there might be times when you'll want to verify that a cable is in fact broken (that is, the problem you're experiencing is because of a cable problem rather than stemming from some other source, such as EMI or a bad component).

For many purposes, checking wires for *continuity* (whether wires are conducting electricity end-to-end) and *pin configuration* (whether the wires are connected to the right places) will tell you what you want to know.

If you're a do-it-yourselfer, you might want to check out `http://www.hobbyelectronics.net/links/measuring.html#cable` for some nifty projects. But assuming that you simply want to plunk down some dough and start testing cables for continuity and correct pinouts, here are some to check out. Street prices for these brand-name devices are about $65–$90 as of this writing; but generic equivalents are even cheaper.

- Belkin's Multi-Network Cable Tester (Part #F4F315-T)
- Paladin Tools LAN ProNavigator (Part #1543-1)
- Microtest Micromapper Cable Tester (Part #8200-40)

These inexpensive testers are pretty cool in that they have a remote loopback device (see "Loopback" later today) that you can plug in at the far end of a wire run. This means that you don't have to even try to be in two places at once—whew!

Still, these testers only test the basics: continuity and pinout (if these basics aren't correct, you won't even get a link light on your Ethernet card, much less connect to the network). They do *not* test for CAT-5 compliance of your cable plant. Being out-of-spec on CAT-5 can cause less obvious problems, such as performance problems, or high error rates, and application failure.

Here's the bad news: Testing for Category 5 compliance is pretty expensive. Even the cheapest CAT-5 scope runs you about the price of a PC. Obviously, if you are responsible for a small network, it would be hard to justify the purchase of this tool.

Here's the good news: Unless you're a cable installer, you shouldn't usually have to test a wire for CAT-5 compliance. First of all, if you've used a reputable installer, it was tested after it was terminated. But even if CAT-5 problems pop up after installation, you can use logic and deductive reasoning to reveal this.

As I said before, if you suspect weirdness with jumper cables, you can simply swap them with known good jumper cables; this applies to suspected CAT-5 problems too. So, you can also apply the known good principle to in-wall cable runs.

That is, it's enough to simply swap an affected workstation to a different wall outlet to see if the problem goes away. Let's say that a user has been getting disconnected from her application on a regular basis (or perhaps her network performance is really terrible), and you've already ruled out her workstation and user configuration as a source of the problem.

A good next step would be to connect her workstation to another user's wall box—and thus a different internal wire run. If the problem goes away, it is extremely likely that the wire run is the problem. (Don't forget to rule out the port on the switch/hub!) You will likely find out (as I have) that there is some sort of EMI near the wire run. For example, I've seen a case in which building maintenance upgraded the air conditioning system, installed a new compressor just a bit too near a CAT-5 run, and created enough EMI to mess it up. This, coupled with testing patch cables, should help you troubleshoot the problem.

Loopback

Any type of cable issue can be easier to solve when you use loopback. The cable testers that I mentioned previously use a remote unit to test for continuity and cable pin-out; this remote unit connects transmit wires to receive wires and allows the unit to connect in a loop back to itself, effectively talking to itself. If it can do so reliably, the cable plant is okay in both directions.

Loopback is a powerful diagnostic technique that can pinpoint which part of your hardware is broken. When you're in a situation where you cannot swap a network card (suppose that you only have one high-speed network card in your server), you'll probably want to run the diagnostics program that comes with the network card. To ensure that both transmit and receive are working properly, the diagnostic program transmits a known piece of data and makes sure that it receives the data properly—to do this, the program needs you to hook up a loopback plug.

Figure 9.1 shows how to wire an Ethernet loopback plug, which you'd then insert into a device under test. Should you put loopback plugs into *production* devices? Heck, no—in particular, an Ethernet hub with a loopback plug in it creates an infinite amount of traffic and floods the hub. Just use them with devices that aren't in production, and you'll be fine. Need a different type of loopback? Check out `www.alliedtelesyn.co.nz/documentation/rel772/html/hw25.htm`.

FIGURE 9.1

A loopback plug for any networking technology connects the receive pins to the transmit pins; shown here is an Ethernet loopback plug.

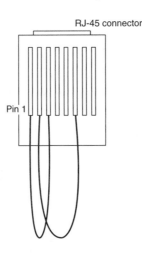

If your network card seems okay when you connect the loopback plug to it, you can rule out cable problems by moving the loopback plug farther up the line. For example, you can connect the workstation's cable that normally plugs into the wall in between the network card and the loopback plug. You might need a gender-changer to do this (which looks very much like a telephone coupler for an RJ-45 plug). You plug the loopback into the coupler, the coupler to the network cable, and the network cable into the network card, and then run the diagnostic test again.

If that seems okay, you can connect the loopback plug to the end of the cable that normally plugs into the hub and then test again. This rules out the entire cable run as a source of transmission or reception problems.

Out of Gas on the Information Superhighway

Running out of system resources is enough to make any operating system sing the blues—and stop you from operating properly. Knowing how to rule out (or rule in) a resource problem gets you closer to a solution. *Any* operating system requires hardware resources; the most common ones that you'll run out of include

- CPU cycles
- Physical RAM
- Hard drive space
- Fixed operating system data structures

Ideally, any program that you use will raise a red flag and alert you when resources become low, but two real-world issues that sometimes prevent this.

First, some programmers don't code well; that is, they don't make sure that the operating system said, "Yes, you may have some," before assuming that a resource allocation was successful. If they do not do correct error checking, you will *not* get a program error when resource problems happen. Instead, you will simply see strange problems, some of which might not even be obvious until later.

For example, one calendar program that I have dealt with didn't check properly for resource availability, and blithely told the user, "Sure, I wrote your calendar to disk." Of course, it didn't. The user got there the next day, and her calendar updates weren't there.

Second, it does take resources to discover problems: If an acute lack of resources, because of a program bug, and so on manifests itself, the lack might be so profound as to make reporting the problem impossible. (A locked-up PC can't exactly tell you much.)

Both of these issues mean that you cannot always rely on a resource problem to be obvious.

Out of Space = In Deep Water

Although it's generally obvious when you run out of disk space, it's a good idea to periodically check how much free space you have left. Remember, every modern operating system allocates "swap" space dynamically; therefore, if you're really low on disk space, swapping might become problematic and could lead to application and potential operating system problems.

> You can think of swap space as an overflow area for your computer's RAM—when you run a lot of programs that don't necessarily fit into the RAM area, an overflow area is used. (This is a special file on your hard drive called the *swap area*.) When an overflow is about to occur, the operating system copies the least-used RAM to your hard drive. If there's no overflow area...well, you get the point.
>
> Because swapping slows down your machine, you might want to consider simplifying the desktop, which will save a good deal of RAM. Most users can stand to lose a little desktop weight, particularly complex wallpapers, screensavers, and Microsoft's Active Desktop. If you like your desktop the way it is, go for it and buy more physical RAM—you'll be amazed at how fast your machine can go with enough RAM.

Windows

Because there are more Windows versions than you can shake a stick at, you might think that it would be horrendously complex to learn all the ways to monitor resources on all the platforms. Take heart, however. In this book, in the spirit of black boxing, I classify Windows into two major families, the Windows 9x family and the Windows NT family, and discuss them together unless there's a major difference between versions. The Windows 9x family includes Windows 95, Windows 98, Windows 98SE, and Windows ME. The Windows NT family includes Windows NT 4, Windows 2000, and Windows XP.

Each version of Windows comes with a different resource meter; but my favorite way to check that Windows has enough physical resources is to install a freeware resource meter called "CoolBeans Resource Meter" (see http://www.coolbeans.ws), which shows CPU, RAM, and swap for all versions of Windows.

> The Windows 9x family, like other early operating systems, has fixed operating system data structures; for example, there are a fixed number of GDI (Graphics Device Interface) data structures, and on a loaded system, they'll run out before things like RAM and hard drive do. You can check these fixed data structures using the Win9x System Resource Meter because many weird Windows 9x problems arise from a lack of these system data structures.
>
> For example, I've seen folks complain that they couldn't print, only to find out that because they were multitasking, they were running out of these resources; the solution was, "Don't multitask quite so much," (as adding memory wouldn't help), or "Use the Windows NT family" (which doesn't have this limitation).

On whichever Windows you use, CoolBeans Resource Meter will start off as a small, unobtrusive meter graphic, expanding to show a full dialog box, as shown in Figure 9.2, on demand.

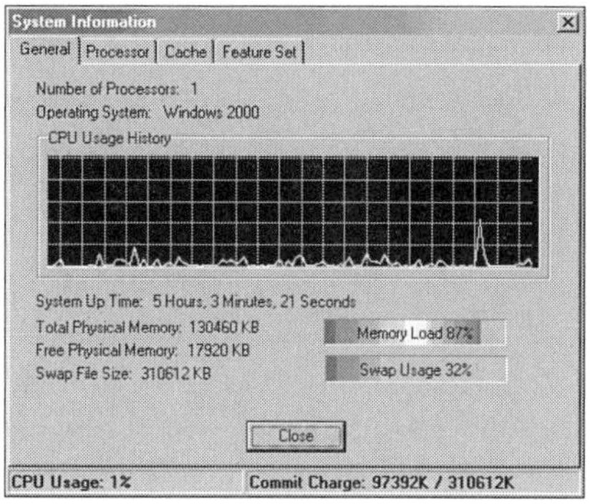

FIGURE 9.2

CoolBeans Resource Meter's "full" display mode.

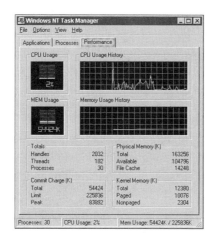

If you don't want to download/install a third-party tool, naturally, you can rely on the Windows 9x family's Resource Meter (add it from the Add/Remove Windows components panel, under System Tools), or you can use the Windows NT family's built-in performance monitor (available from Administrative Tools).

The Task Manager

The Windows NT family's Task Manager has a real-time performance monitor built into it; just press Ctrl+Alt+Del, and select Performance (see Figure 9.3).

FIGURE 9.3

The NT Task Manager's Performance Monitor is a good way to get a quick and succinct status of an NT-family workstation.

ScanDisk and CHKDSK

The hard drive is probably the most fragile resource of your system because it is still a component with moving parts. It's a good idea, after you rule in a workstation, to run its disk checker on the hard drive to rule out errors there. Sure, most versions of Windows now run automatically when an abnormal shutdown occurs; but how many users do you know of (like me) who manually skip it?

This can mean that days and weeks of disk problems due to power blips and user resets can go unnoticed. These errors, along with wear and tear on the drive, can accumulate and cause truly strange problems.

It's a really, really good idea to run the workstation's disk checker on a regular basis—say, every week. Most weeks you can probably get away with the a standard check, but every so often (every month or so), you'll probably want to run a thorough check, just to be safe.

The Windows NT family uses CHKDSK, which is a disk checking program that can be run from the command line. If you want to use the GUI, you can right-click on a drive, and then choose Properties, Tools, Check Now. The Windows 9x family uses ScanDisk from the Programs, Accessories, System Tools menu.

For both families, you can also check disks by right-clicking your hard drive in Explorer and then selecting Properties from the shortcut menu that appears. You'll see a dialog box with a Tools tab, similar to the one shown in Figure 9.4. On this tab, you can see when you last checked the drive. You can also start a new check from here as well.

FIGURE 9.4

A ScanDisk a day (or week, as the case may be) keeps the trouble away!

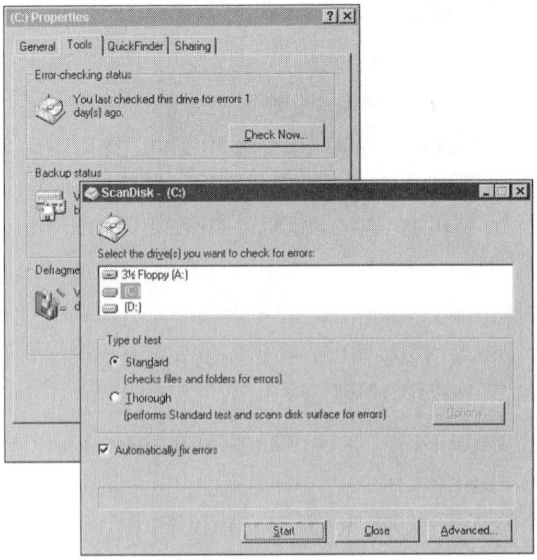

Doesn't Do Windows

Not a Windows user? Fret not. Unix and NetWare were resource checking when Windows was just a glimmer in Bill Gates's eye. Although the methods differ—and aren't as graphical, unless you're using X Windows or NetWare 5—the basic idea remains the same: Check your resources when you're having problems and compare these results to what your resources look like when you're *not* having problems.

Unix

Let's say that you're a Linux user, and you want to check your available memory and swap. You can simply type this:

INPUT

```
moria:/$ free
```

OUTPUT

```
          total     used      free      shared    buffers
Mem:      7220      6948      272       2524      3356
Swap:     16416     2396      14020
```

Most Unix users can check real-time resource use through the vmstat command, like so:

INPUT

```
$ vmstat 1
```

OUTPUT

```
procs   memory            page          faults      cpu
--- .  ----- ----.  -- -------------  -------- ----- ----
r  b    avm  fre re   pi po fr   sr cy in    sy  cs  us sy id wa
0  0   13376 233 0    0  0  2    6  0  144   807 81  4  5  84 7
0  0   13376 233 0    0  0  0    0  0  129   757 89  2  8  89 2
0  0   13376 233 0    0  0  0    0  0  143   768 85  2  7  91 0
0  0   13376 233 0    0  0  0    0  0  140   567 124 5  1  94 0
0  0   13376 233 0    0  0  0    0  0  147   387 39  1  3  96 0
```

This output looks like Greek, but it's not too terrible when you know the translation. Here are the salient points you should look for:

avm	Active virtual pages (amount of swap plus physical memory)
pi	Page in activity per second (how much overflow goes to swap)
po	Page out activity per second (how much overflow drains out)
fre	The free memory list
us	CPU utilization by users
sy	CPU utilization by system processes
id	CPU idle time
wa	CPU time spent waiting for disk activity

If you want a report, you should check out the `sar` command; using it shows you a report similar to this:

```
smp smp 4.0 2 PENTIUM    01/15/2002
00:00:00    %usr    %sys    %wio    %idle
07:00:00    0       0       3       97
08:00:00    0       1       4       95
08:10:00    1       2       9       87
08:20:00    2       4       11      83
08:30:00    3       5       57      35
08:40:00    2       5       23      69
08:45:00    3       6       61      30
```

Notice how the situation starts to get really ugly at 8:20 (when everyone's had their coffee and is now tearing into things). At 8:30, the system is only 35 percent idle, as opposed to 97 percent idle at 7:00. As you can see, the `sar` command can help you with long-term monitoring. Both `sar` and `vmstat` have manual pages that you can access online by typing this:

```
man <sar or vmstat>
```

NetWare

If you're a NetWare user, unfortunately, you have no long-term resource monitoring solution built in, although add-on solutions are available. You can, however, use the NetWare monitor screen to check out various resources. Simply type

```
load monitor
```

at your console prompt, and you'll see the processor utilization on the front page. Go to the Processor, Memory, or Resource Utilization sub-menus for more details.

Probably the most important thing to keep track of is the number of cache buffers, which you can track from the Resource menu. If the number of cache buffers falls below 40 percent or so, you'll probably experience problems.

Summary

Knowing how to troubleshoot basic hardware problems can save you a lot of time. PCs as a whole are reasonably simple machines, consisting of pluggable electronic components, some of which can be reseated. Poorly designed cases or motherboards can cause problems, so you can avoid problems by avoiding these.

Keeping clean is just as important as your mother told you; all hardware components react badly to dirt. Use a vacuum or canned air on visibly dusty components; use a pencil eraser on board contacts that seem to have dirt or oxidation on them.

Swapping components is an integral part of troubleshooting, and that goes double for hardware troubleshooting. As with the fuel pump on your car, you don't need to know how it works, just that your problem goes away after you swap it.

Unshielded twisted pair cable (UTP) is the most common network cable type. Inexpensive cable testers are available that will check for pin faults and cable breaks. A cable's Category-5 rating is highly affected by external *electromagnetic interference (EMI)*; although testing for CAT-5 compliance requires a very expensive meter, you can use substitution to rule in or rule out a cable run.

If your workstation is running out of gas, it can hardly be expected to drive down the street, much less to the onramp of your personal information superhighway. Knowing how to check your system's resources is really useful, no matter which operating system you run.

Q&A

Q Shouldn't I leave this hardware stuff to a hardware tech? I might break it!

A If this was stuff that cost thousands to millions per component, I might agree with you. But let's face it: If you destroy a floppy disk drive or a video card, you're out $50–$100, and believe me, you'll never make that particular mistake again. Consider it the cost of learning. Be careful with static electricity, powering off before you work, and putting components back in the same orientation, and you should be just fine.

Workshop

Workshop time! Here's a brief quiz to help you make the most out of this hour's lesson, as well as activities for you to try on your own.

Quiz

1. How do you get into most PC BIOS setup screens?

    a. Spacebar

    b. Compose-Compose-Execute

    c. F5, Ctrl+Alt+Del, or Enter

    d. F1, F2, or Del

2. True or False: Power should always be on when you're working on a hardware device.

3. You can ground yourself by touching which of the following?

   a. The plastic of the PC case

   b. The screw of your wall outlet

   c. The chassis of your PC (while plugged in)

   d. The dirt in your plants

4. True or False: Marginal or incompatible memory can cause network-related problems.

5. To verify a cable's integrity, a cable tester tests both the pinout as well as the _____.

   a. Compatibility

   b. Continuity

   c. Craftsmanship

   d. Culling

Answers to Quiz Questions

1. D

2. False

3. C. Surprisingly, the screw on your wall outlet is *not* always grounded.

4. True

5. B

Activities

1. Find the network diagnostics program for your network interface card. (You can usually find these at www.companyname.com, in the support or downloads section.) Fire it up. Can you run it in Windows, or do you have to boot up in DOS? What happens when you run it without a loopback plug?

2. While monitoring system resources, try to run out of physical memory on your workstation. (Run a lot of things like WinAmp, Word, Excel, Solitaire, and so forth at the same time—trust me, you'll run out of physical memory at some point.) Is there a noticeable difference once you start to "swap" to hard drive?

HOUR 10

Ethernet and Switching

The great thing about standards is that there are so many to choose from.
—Andrew S. Tanenbaum

Ethernet is the dominant wired LAN technology on the planet, the battle-scarred victor of more than a decade of LAN wars. This is great news because you *really* don't have to learn more than one LAN technology to be an effective troubleshooter. Other technologies such as ArcNet, PhoneNet, AppleTalk, and Token-Ring, if they're not already gone, are quickly melting off of the landscape.

In some sense, technology wars are neither here nor there for us as troubleshooters. We want to understand enough about the technology to be able to troubleshoot it: Extraneous details like political and marketing wars aren't really too interesting. However, as champions of sustainable and serviceable networks, it is worth noting that using a technology that is available, widely used, and well understood is always a plus for network uptime. All of those descriptions fit Ethernet to a T.

The 1998 edition of this book had an entire hour devoted to Token-Ring, which was widely available and supported by third-party vendors at the time.

This is no longer the case, and as a matter of fact, one can make the case that using an old and obsolete technology like Token-Ring can contribute to maintenance problems on your network. (Where are you going to get parts? modern drivers? bug fixes?) Accordingly, in this edition of the book, we've dropped all Token-Ring coverage. (If you're interested in dropping *your* Token-Ring, check out `http://www.networkcomputing.com/1208/1208ws1.html` for an article on how to do so relatively painlessly.)

Ethernet Evolution

One of Ethernet's success secrets is that it is able to change with the times. As an implementer and troubleshooter, what this means to you is that you need to understand where Ethernet came from before you can truly understand and work with today's Ethernet.

For example, when you purchase Ethernet gear today, you most commonly buy a switch, not an Ethernet hub. But even though the Ethernet on the switch behaves differently than old-school Ethernet, the same old-school rules apply when examining the connection between the switch and the PC. (For instance, you still cannot exceed Ethernet's *cable budget* of 100 meters, data payloads still have the same limits, and so forth.) So, before starting out on a discussion of switching, let's chat about the basic rules that apply to Ethernet. The following discussion is based on *shared* Ethernet; we'll discuss the way switches work in the "Switching" section later in this hour.

Shared Ethernet Characteristics

First of all, what does a *shared* network mean? And *how* does a shared Ethernet share?

A network that uses shared media is also called a *broadcast* network because all traffic is universally receivable by all nodes on that network bus. The bus (also called the *segment*) is the collection of everything that ties these nodes together (typically hubs). This is opposed to a point-to-point network like your PC's dialup connection, where only your PC and the dialup server see the traffic.

Media Access Control

Obviously, some sort of sharing method is necessary on a broadcast network. The way that any shared network, including Ethernet, implements media sharing rules is called its *MAC*—Media Access Control. Media Access Control basically means, "How is access to the shared media arbitrated?" Ethernet's MAC is pretty simple; it only *sounds* horrendously complex. The acronym for Ethernet's MAC is CSMA/CD, which stands for Carrier Sense Multiple Access Carrier Detect.

What the heck does *that* mean? In a nutshell, "Listen before you talk, and if someone interrupts you, wait a second before trying to talk again." That is, just as you can listen even as you start talking at the same time another person starts talking, Ethernet network cards listen as they start to transmit to the shared line. The carrier in CSMA/CD, like the "dueling banshees" you hear when your modem connects to another, is a predefined signal that information can ride on top of.

Collisions

On a given segment, if one network card transmits while another network card is also transmitting, the signal becomes garbled—the bus can only hold *one* signal at a time. This generates a network error called a *collision*. When a collision occurs, both network cards wait a random infinitesimal amount of time, and try again. Eventually, as shown in Figure 10.1, they do succeed, on a low-population segment. Because each workstation transmits in small, discrete data units called *frames* (discussed in the "Ethernet Frames" section later in this hour), it's possible (believe it or not) for a workstation to get a word in edgewise in between another workstation's transmissions. This has always seemed like black magic to me, but it works. (In fact, Ethernet uses a random back-off to determine when to try transmission again. That's no lie!)

FIGURE 10.1
Collisions!

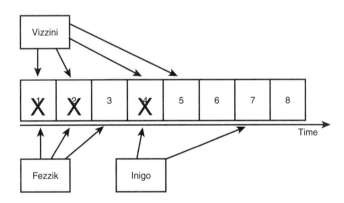

At moment 1 in Figure 10.1, Vizzini and Fezzik simultaneously try to transmit and thus collide. They randomly retry, but it happens to be at the same moment (2). They retry again, and Fezzik gets in at moment 3, followed by Vizzini at moment 4. Poor Vizzini collides with Inigo at moment 4. Vizzini retries at moment 5, nobody does anything at moment 6, and Inigo finally gets the final word in moment 7.

On a small network, collision detection works pretty well. But just as informal meeting rules start to break down when you get more than 10 or 15 people in a conference room, Ethernet, too, turns into a babble fairly quickly when a particular segment is scaled to more than a couple dozen workstations.

The entirety of one shared Ethernet bus, called a *segment* or *bus*, is also referred to as the *collision domain* because collisions can only occur on a shared segment. Makes sense, right?

> If you are unfortunate enough to have to troubleshoot a large shared network, here are a couple of tips: First, large shared networks are *always* problematic and are a bad idea to keep around nowadays; perhaps they were necessary years ago, but switches make them obsolete. Switches are really cheap and it might be worth replacing the hub with a switch, which will reduce or eliminate your collision domain. (How much is your labor worth? Is it better for you to spend a lot of time troubleshooting or to upgrade your equipment?) Second, if you absolutely must keep the shared network, bear in mind that you need special hardware to detect collisions (and in fact many hubs come with a collision indicator); software won't do it. However, a universally high error rate (as shown on a workstation's Ethernet card diagnostics) usually indicates a lot of collisions.

Wiring

The bad news is there are a bunch of ways to configure old-school Ethernet cabling. The good news is you should *never* have to deal with any of these ways. Coax or thick Ethernet cabling is obsolete, hard to work with, and it's included here simply to state that if you want a reliable network, you need to *get rid of it!*

> It will save you time and money in the long run to replace any of the following network types. They are obsolete and can be replaced fairly cheaply.
>
> | Name | Connector Type | Problems |
> | --- | --- | --- |
> | Thinnet | BNC (Coaxial) 10Base-2 | Bus cabling means that one disconnected workstation or cable break takes down the entire segment. It's trouble prone in general and harder to work with than modern 10Base-T. |
> | Thicknet | BNC (Coaxial) 10Base-5 | Bus cabling. It's expensive, trouble prone, and hard to find parts for. |
> | AUI | DB-15 | Expensive and hard to find parts for. |
>
> All these bad old network types came before the advent of modern UTP technologies (10Base-T, 100Base-T, 1000Base-T).

The *Base* in Base-T refers to the fact that Ethernet is a baseband—rather than broadband—technology. This is just a geeky term that refers to its method of signal encoding. The *T* simply stands for twisted pair.

Modern Ethernet uses one of two cable types:

Cable Type	Connector	Max Cable Length
UTP	RJ-45	100 meters
Fiber-optic	SC or ST	Varies depending on equipment

Generally, UTP (unshielded twisted pair) is what you'll see hooking workstations together; fiber is normally used to connect buildings together or to connect wiring closets to a data center.

UTP

Just as you thought, "Whew! I don't have to worry about all of those old types of cables," along comes UTP with *its* various flavors! Sorry.

There are four distinct categories of UTP: Cat-3, Cat-5, Cat-5e, and Cat-6. Using the wrong category cable causes slow performance and high error rates, even though you might still get a link. Here is a table of supported Ethernet speeds on each category of cabling.

Category	10Mb	100Mb	1Gb
Cat-3	yes	no	no
Cat-5	yes	yes	*
Cat-5e	yes	yes	yes
Cat-6	yes	yes	yes

* = Not guaranteed, but possible depending on cable manufacturer. Not a good idea, probably.

All speeds of Ethernet running over UTP use the same type of connector: RJ-45. This is both a blessing and a curse: RJ-45 is really easy to work with, but it's *really* easy to mix up your cables.

Don't try running a category of Ethernet on wiring that's not certified for the appropriate category. You can use a *higher* category safely (for example, you can run 10Mbps on Cat-5), but not a lower one.

If you use a lower one, all sorts of intermittent network errors can occur, which can domino into your applications. What's more, because you're getting a signal and are talking to the network, you might not realize that the problem is because of wiring until you've run around looking at everything else.

A cable plant fails wire category certification in at least five ways, so you should ask the installer to "certify" the cable plant as part of the installation process. This means that he or she will install using plugs, jacks, cabling, and techniques that are category compliant and will actually put a meter on the end-to-end product to ensure that theory has become practice.

Some folks prefer to use certified cable installers—that is, professional network cable installers with a networking industry affiliation (for example, BICSI-certified)—rather than an electrician, who might be more comfortable with A/C power cabling rather than network cables.

Wire Pairs

10Mbps and 100Mbps Ethernet use only two pairs of wires: Specifically, they use pins 1, 2, 3, and 6. The other two pairs should remain *unused* for 10Mbps and 100Mbps runs.

Gigabit Ethernet uses all four wire pairs to transmit.

If you are working with a Cat-3 or Cat-5 cable plant, beware of amateur cable installation. Someone might have decided to use the two remaining pairs for either another Ethernet jack or a telephone jack. This will drive you nuts with intermittent problems until you realize what's going on. Take a look inside the jack; it's pretty easy to spot. You should see *nothing* connected to the two remaining pairs. You have to disconnect those pairs on that cable and run another 4-pair cable for the phone or the other Ethernet jack.

With a 10Mbps or 100Mbps cable jack, it's perfectly okay, if one pair is damaged, to replace it with one of the unused pairs. Just make sure that the appropriate pins on the Ethernet jack are paired up: 1 must be paired with 2, and 3 must be paired with 6.

Only NIC-to-hub cables should be straight through—that is, pin to pin. (Pin 1 goes to pin 1, pin 3 goes to pin 3, and so on.) Cables that are used to connect hubs together should be crossover. If you have a cable tester (see Hour 9, " Overcoming Hardware Phobia," for more detail), you might want to experiment to find out which pin on one side of the cable goes to which pin on the other side.

UTP cables are entirely too easy to "home make," and I have seen problems stemming from this. As such, it's worth mentioning that all UTP cables require proper pairing. For 10Mbps and 100Mbps Ethernet, pins 1 and 2 need to be from the same pair, and pins 3 and 6 need to be from the same pair (see Figure 10.2). Although the intuitive way to make a cable might be to put pins 1 and 2 together, and then 3 and 4, 5 and 6, and 7 and 8, this is *not* correct. 10Mb Ethernet will run on this, but you might encounter strange problems under 100Mb. If you see a cable that looks like it was crimped the wrong way, you might want to exchange the cable with a known good one. Using premade cables usually avoids problems like this!

10

FIGURE **10.2**

Correct 10Mbps and 100Mbps Ethernet wire and pin configuration.

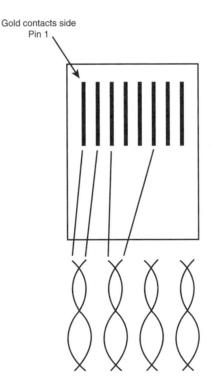

Gold contacts side
Pin 1

Crossover Cables

Straight-through cables are what you use to connect a workstation to a switch. But there are many cases when, for troubleshooting purposes, you'll want to connect a workstation to a workstation, a switch to switch, or a hub to a switch. In these cases, you'll need a crossover cable or a crossover coupler. The crossover simply crosses the pairs so that the cable is no longer straight through: Transmit is swapped with receive, and receive is swapped with transmit. (For those of you familiar with serial cables, a crossover is just like a null modem cable.)

When might you use a crossover in a troubleshooting situation? Let's say that you have exactly *one* switch in your office, and nobody seems to be getting a link light. You have already taken a laptop (or lugged a desktop) to the switch and plugged it in with a known good cable, and the problem remains. To verify that the Ethernet cards on your workstations are okay, you might plug two workstations together using a crossover cable. Voilá! You see a link light, so you know that the two workstations are okay. It's a pretty good bet that the switch is *not* okay. You can even ping between the workstations to make sure that you're passing data. (In fact, you can even play multiplayer games this way. Cool!) Just make sure that you have valid IP addresses on the same network. See Hour 19, "Internet and Intranet Troubleshooting: TCP/IP at Work," for more info on TCP/IP addressing.

Traditional shared Ethernet is really, really easy to *cascade*; that is, you can extend the bus by simply adding a crossover cable and an additional hub. Similarly, you can hook switches together using a crossover.

Using a shared 10Mbps network? Although it's easy to add a hub or two via cascade/crossover, you don't want to go crazy with this. Be careful about how large your Ethernet bus gets—if you add too many hubs, you're going to run into trouble. Make sure that you follow the 3-4-5 rule (see "The 3-4-5 Rule" sidebar). If you're using a shared 100Mbps network, be aware that at speeds above 10Mbps, there is a propagation delay issue that really rules out using more than one repeater and severely limits cascading. (Avoid this. Use a switch; they're so darn cheap nowadays.)

> ### The 3-4-5 Rule
>
> The Ethernet 3-4-5 rule applies *only* to 10Mbps Ethernet and states
>
> - You may have *three* populated subsegments (applies to coaxial only, so forget this one).
> - You may have *four* repeaters or concentrators.
> - You may have *five* subsegments in a series—that is, one connecting to the next, as with Christmas tree lights.
>
> Because the 3 rule applies only to coaxial networks, let's concentrate on 4 and 5. A *repeater* is a device that regenerates whatever signal is on the wire in order to overcome a wire length limitation (100 meters with UTP). In a nutshell, when you echo a signal down the line, it takes time; too many echoes result in a critical loss of timing.
>
> The 5 rule means that you shouldn't cascade more than five hubs in a row. (A stackable hub with a proprietary link between hubs counts as only one hub.)

10

Finally, it might sound obvious, but it bears saying that you can't plug a 10Mbps card into a 100Mbps hub. You can plug a 10Mbps card into a 10/100 switch, but *not* into a regular old hub.

Ethernet Frames

It's worth briefly looking at the frame structure of Ethernet. Why? Here are a couple of reasons:

- Ethernet's maximum frame size is 1,514 bytes.
- Ethernet has several ways of encapsulating protocol data (TCP/IP, IPX/SPX, LAT, and so forth).

Ethernet's maximum frame size includes six bytes for the MAC address of the source NIC, six bytes for the MAC address of the destination, a two-byte value indicating what kind of frame this is, and a "payload" portion that holds your data, such as a TCP/IP packet (this can be a maximum of 1,500 bytes). There are considerations and troubleshooting consequences for this maximum TCP/IP packet size (called the MTU or maximum transmission unit) of 1,500, but we'll cover those in Hour 19.

Some people (even those who design network analyzers) refer to a maximum Ethernet frame size of 1,518 bytes. This number just includes a four-byte error-detection field at the end of each frame. Another 20 bytes of overhead can be found at the beginning of the frame. (But this is only of interest to Ethernet switch designers.)

The minimum size of an Ethernet frame is 60 bytes. Any Ethernet frame less than this is considered a *runt*, also called a *short* or *fragment*, and is a totally abnormal condition on a switch; these can be caused by collisions on a shared network, so if you see a lot of these, you might want to consider dividing up your users among switches.

Finally, there are several ways that your computer can put together an Ethernet frame (called *encapsulation)*. Unless the two devices that you are hooking together agree on the encapsulation scheme, your devices aren't going to talk to each other—at least in any way that counts.

Some might say, "Well, there's only *one* modern way to lay out an Ethernet frame," and they'd be right. But just the other day, an associate of mine, a smart cookie and well-known IT professional, entered a plea for help on a mailing list that I'm on. He said, "I can't make my brand new RS/6000 talk to my network," and those of us on the list recommended that he try many things; but nothing worked until he realized that his RS/6000 had been configured to encapsulate TCP/IP in the older 802.3 fashion, rather than Ethernet_II. (Figure 10.3 shows the difference.) What's the lesson? Make sure that your encapsulations agree. If there's no choice, you're probably using Ethernet_II. (You can always switch until things seem to work.)

FIGURE 10.3

Two different Ethernet frame types, or encapsulations.

Ethernet Framing for Ethernet_II

Ethernet Datalink Preamble	Destination MAC Address	Source MAC Address	Data Payload	Data Payload	Frame Check Sequence

Ethernet Framing for Ethernet 802.3

Ethernet Datalink Preamble	Destination MAC Address	Source MAC Address	Length of rest of frame, w/o FCS	Illegal SAP of "FFFF"	Data Payload	Frame Check Sequence

You'll note that the frame has a field for the Source and Destination address. As I discussed in Hour 1, "Understanding Networking: The Telephone Analogy," this MAC address is how a broadcast network keeps track of who's sending what to whom. Each Ethernet card has a unique MAC address: a 48-bit number, expressed in hexadecimal, usually with the digits separated with a colon or dash. So, 00080A051E52 would be written as 00-08-0A-05-1E-52. Each card "knows" that it should listen to a transmission if the transmission has the card's MAC address in the "destination" field of a given frame. Similarly, the network software then knows how to respond to a given transmission: It simply examines the "source" field and knows which address to respond to in its reply.

Switching

So, all we know so far about switching is that it isn't shared. In fact, we're told that each port on a switch has "dedicated bandwidth." But those are marketing buzzwords. Let's delve a bit deeper, starting with the progenitor of the switch: the bridge.

Bridges: Old School Versus New School

In the old days, you'd split your collision domain with a bridge when you had too many Ethernet stations on one segment. What does a bridge do? Well, it splits your collision domain (groan). Seriously, a bridge connects two different network segments, and it does so in a way that not all traffic is shared.

Here's how it works. Take a look at Figure 10.4 and follow along with me. There are two network interfaces on an old-school bridge; call them A and B. Similarly, whereas there are many workstations on each side of the bridge, we'll concentrate on workstation #1, on side A of the bridge, and workstation #2, on side B of the bridge. The bridge listens to all transmissions, learns the MAC addresses of every station, and associates those addresses with that side of the bridge. If a transmission is destined for its own side of the bridge, the bridge does nothing. If the transmission is destined for the other side of the bridge, the bridge picks it up and transmits it appropriately.

If a station is quiet (not bloody likely because most workstations are chatty as heck, but *possible*), the bridge will broadcast to both sides to elicit a response—and then listens for the response and associates that workstation with the appropriate side of the bridge. In our example, station #2 is unknown, so the bridge broadcasts on both sides. But for the return trip, it already knows which side #1 is associated with, so it simply picks up the response transmission from #2 and transmits it on side A of the bridge.

FIGURE 10.4

How a bridge works.

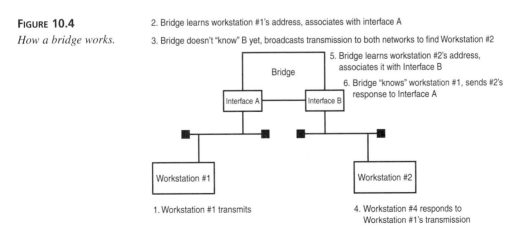

2. Bridge learns workstation #1's address, associates with interface A

3. Bridge doesn't "know" B yet, broadcasts transmission to both networks to find Workstation #2

5. Bridge learns workstation #2's address, associates it with Interface B

6. Bridge "knows" workstation #1, sends #2's response to Interface A

Bridge

Interface A   Interface B

Workstation #1   Workstation #2

1. Workstation #1 transmits

4. Workstation #4 responds to Workstation #1's transmission

10

That's it. So instead of having 50 workstations in a collision domain, you'd have 25 workstations in each collision domain. That was the function of a bridge. Here's the good news. If you understand how bridges work, you now know the most complicated part of the theory and operation of switches. A switch is simply a multiport bridge.

Spanning Tree

It's entirely possible to connect several bridges in such a way that they form a circle. (A goes to B goes to C goes to A.) If left unchecked, traffic would keep getting forwarded in a loop and start to occupy all bandwidth available. Furthermore, because a switch is in fact a multiport bridge, if some malicious user (or malfunction) looped back a switch port, the same phenomenon would happen: infinitely looping traffic. I've seen this happen: It takes down the entire data link domain.

To keep this from happening, bridge designers created a protocol called *spanning tree*. In a nutshell, a magic frame (called a Bridge Protocol Data Unit, or BPDU) is created by one bridge every once in a while, with the signature of the bridge that created it. The switch that created the frame should theoretically never see that uniquely identified frame ever again. If that bridge does see its own magic frame coming back to itself, it shuts down the port that the frame came in on. It's easy.

Symptoms of infinite-loop syndrome include mysterious "Ethernet down time" even though ports have link lights, combined with high utilization. Naturally, bridges or switches are in the picture. Enabling spanning tree on your equipment in this scenario couldn't hurt, and it might help!

> Cisco equipment allows for two types of spanning tree per port. Cisco recommends that you use the `spanning-tree` command for ports that are connected to other switches, but that you use the `portfast` qualifier for ports that are connected to workstations. The `portfast` qualifier, as its name implies, allows the port to come up a bit quicker. If you don't use `portfast`, some things like DHCP or Novell's Client32 may timeout while spanning tree is being negotiated. See your Cisco documentation for details on how to use the `spanning-tree` and `portfast` commands.

Cut-Through Versus Store-and-Forward

There are two ways that a switch can propagate traffic: cut-through or store-and-forward. *Store-and-forward*, like it sounds, first stores the frame in a temporary location, and only after it is stored in a buffer (memory location), checked for errors, and determined to be error free, is it then forwarded to the appropriate interface. As you might imagine, this is the way to go if you want to maximize trouble-free operation. Unfortunately, this also introduces a bit of delay, or latency.

Cut-through, on the other hand, starts to forward the frame as soon as it sees the *destination* on the frame. Because it forwards the frame on-the-fly, there's no chance for catching errors such as a checksum error or a runt (a frame which is too short, also known as a *short*). Naturally, this is faster—but riskier—so when you suspect many Ethernet errors, you will not want to use cut-through switching. Check your switch documentation to see how to change your switch from cut-through to store-and-forward.

VLANs

Just because switches reduce the amount of traffic seen by all stations doesn't mean that some broadcast traffic isn't necessary. There are times when a station *needs* to broadcast something to all stations; for example, when a station has an IP address on the local subnet, but doesn't have the MAC address, it broadcasts the IP address in a special TCP/IP packet (contained in a broadcast Ethernet frame) called an ARP (address resolution protocol) request.

However, in large switched networks, large groups of stations in the same broadcast domain create large amounts of broadcast traffic. Even in a switched network, where you don't have to worry about collisions, network designers have found it best to keep the number of stations in a broadcast domain low (less than 200 or so). All sorts of broadcasts exist, ranging from print servers that feel the necessity to announce themselves every 30 seconds, to bad NICs that generate "noise." Trust me on this: you *want* to keep your broadcast domain low as a proactive troubleshooting step.

The way you partition your LAN's broadcast domains—whether on the same switch or a different switch—is called a VLAN, meaning Virtual LAN. Typically there is *one* TCP/IP subnet associated with a VLAN.

VLANs are also flexible. In the old days, your entire hub or switch *had* to be associated with *one* subnet. With VLANs, you can pick and choose which ports on a switch are associated with a given subnet. This means that you needn't change someone's network number just because you move them to a different switch. This makes moving servers or workstations pretty easy.

To sum up, folks use VLANs to

- Keep the broadcast domain low
- Easily reconfigure the network

10

VLANs are incredibly useful, but things can get *really* confusing—unless your documentation is great. For example, say that switch #1 in the data center has VLAN #1 on ports 1–10 and VLAN #2 on ports 11–12. Your laptop is numbered with the TCP/IP network for VLAN #1; if you plug it into port 11 or 12, you will not be able to browse, connect to a fileserver, or even ping, even though you will see a link light. Again, documentation is the key to avoiding confusion or going on a wild goose chase for a problem that doesn't exist.

Duplex and Auto-Negotiation

A fully switched connection is actually a point-to-point connection between the end-station and the switch port. There aren't *any* other participants until *after* the switch works its magic and forwards frames. Because a switch can offer a point-to-point connection, it is possible for that switch port to offer a *full duplex* connection, that is, the capability for both ends to receive and transmit at the same time. Full duplex connections do not have collisions because no MAC arbitration is necessary.

> Full duplex is pretty cool, but not as cool as manufacturers would have you believe: 100Mbps upstream + 100Mbps downstream does not equal 200Mbps worth of download capacity; it equals 100Mbps of upload and 100Mbps of download. The line capacity stays the same.

Just like some people, some applications and server processes can't deal with talking at the same time that they listen. I have seen situations, particularly with low-end network cards and drivers, where putting the card into full duplex creates strange anomalies that only went away once we put the card back into half duplex.

Also, many switches ship with their ports set to auto-sense, theoretically allowing workstations to connect at whatever speed and duplex is best for them. In practice, this doesn't always work.

Because of the potential anomalies, auto-sensing, whether on a computer or a switch, is generally not a good idea.

Ideally, auto-sensing allows everything to work properly. But time and time again, I see problems caused by differing vendors' equipment that has differing ideas of what exactly entails auto-sensing. This is true particularly when both ends are set to auto-sense. For example, when I boot Win2000 on my laptop, my 100Mbps Xircom Ethernet card will not give me good performance on my home LAN (which happens to have a NetGear switch) unless I disable auto-sensing.

Much documentation is available out on the Net and on vendor sites that suggests auto-sensing itself is not bad. Although I would agree with this, I would go further and say that although auto-sensing itself might not be bad, the *implementation* of auto-sensing as it stands in the industry right now is not exactly a reliable technology, particularly when multiple vendors are involved. It's one of the first things that I suspect when someone reports a switched Ethernet performance problem.

Summary

Ethernet is a really simple physical networking technology. However, like all networks, it has hard-and-fast rules for its design and implementation. Although Ethernet has used many different types of physical cabling in the past, the simplest and most reliable cabling today is UTP or fiber-optic. Older cabling should be replaced.

10

Knowing how shared networks work is a good thing, but in the name of good uptime, you should use switches. Hubs are pretty much drop-in replaceable by switches; this reduces the collision domain and eliminates hassles like the 3-4-5 rule. The 3-4-5 rule only applies to 10Mbps Ethernet.

Bridges work by monitoring Ethernet bus traffic and forwarding it if the destination station is not on the originating side of the bridge. Switches are basically multiport bridges. Spanning tree is a bridge and switch technology that can help avoid bad LAN days, and some vendors have a "spanning tree lite" (for example, Cisco's PortFast) that is suitable for workstation ports. Finally, if you have a switch that defaults to auto-sense, you probably want to configure it directly in order to avoid problems down the line.

Q&A

Q Should I use a switch port for every PC?

A Yes, if humanly possible. Shared Ethernet is dead.

Q Are there errors other than collisions?

A Collisions cause other errors, such as CRC errors and runts (shorts). But on the whole, most errors are collision related.

Q Hard-setting my switch will force me to reconfigure it if things change. Isn't there an easier way?

A Sure. Use the same brand of Ethernet cards as switches. You'll be okay. Probably.

Workshop

Workshop time! Here's a brief quiz to help you make the most out of this hour's lesson as well as activities for you to try on your own.

Quiz

1. During normal error-free transmission, there can only be _____ signal(s) on any given Ethernet segment.

    a. 5

    b. 10

    c. 2

    d. 1

2. What is a collision?

    a. When two network cards try to transmit simultaneously

    b. When two network cards develop bad microchips

    c. When a user accesses the wrong database

    d. When a user transmits incorrect data

3. True or False: Errors are a normal part of Ethernet operation.

4. True or False: Thinnet, Thicknet, and AUI are the most desirable types of Ethernet you can buy.

5. True or False: The 3-4-5 rule applies to 100Mb Ethernet.

6. A bridge or a switch can reduce the _____ domain of a data link segment.

    a. Crucial

    b. Collision

    c. Runt

    d. Jabber

7. An Ethernet port that is looped back to itself (without the spanning tree protocol present) can cause the network to

    a. Go down

    b. Have intermittent problems

    c. Slow down for certain protocols

    d. Work better

8. True or False: when auto-sensing is in use, turning it OFF is one of the first troubleshooting steps you should take.

Answers to Quiz Questions

1. D

2. A

3. True

4. False

5. False; it just applies to 10Mbps Ethernet.

6. B

7. A

8. True

Activities

1. Create a mini-network with a hub or a switch; that is, composed of two machines plus a hub or a switch. If the switch has spanning-tree on, turn it off. Connect your two PCs to the hub or switch. Make sure that you can ping between the two PCs. Now, take a crossover cable and connect two of the ports together. What happens? Can you ping? Are other network operations affected?

2. Do the same thing with a switch with spanning-tree enabled. What happens?

HOUR 11

Wireless Networking

You can have peace, or you can have freedom. Don't ever count on having both at once.

—Robert A. Heinlein

Wireless networking untethers you from earthly constraints, and makes cable snags, broken connectors, and Cat-V specification problems all things of the past. Of course, this freedom is just a trade-off: Although wireless *is* wonderful (and in fact, much of this book was written using an 802.11b wireless network), you can say hello to a host of new problems to troubleshoot. Lucky you!

At this writing, *wireless* refers to two specific technologies: wireless Ethernet and Bluetooth. WLAN (Wireless LAN) Ethernet, specifically 802.11a and 802.11b, is intended for applications like sitting out on the patio and browsing the Web with your laptop. Wireless Ethernet (802.11b) is also used heavily in distribution and warehouse environments for automated data capture with respect to one and 2D barcodes. Bluetooth's lower-power personal area network (PAN) range is designed more for applications like wireless headsets, wireless PDA synchronization, and other devices that are in your personal space.

Wireless Ethernet has caught on in a big way. I mean, jeepers, you can toss wireless Ethernet gear in your shopping cart while you're picking up photocopy supplies. Clearly, 802.11 (a and b) is here to stay.

Access Points

Basically, 802.11 *access points* are bridges that plug in to your wired infrastructure and allow wireless terminals and PCs to access that infrastructure. The wireless LAN (WLAN)—that is, the radio spectra in the area that the WLAN operates in—is a shared medium, and does *not* have dedicated bandwidth the way a switch does.

In fact, a wireless access point, for all intents and purposes, can be considered to have many of the properties of an Ethernet hub. It scales about as well because its MAC (Media Access Control) method is similar to Ethernet's: Although wireless access points theoretically support thousands of nodes, in real life, only about 20 or so per access point are practical. (For what it's worth, 802.11b's MAC is called CSMA/CA, *Carrier Sense Multiple Avoidance/Collision Avoidance*—as opposed to Ethernet's *Collision Detect*. CA does a little bit better than CD, but for our purposes, all we care about is "How many can I use before it gets ugly?"—and that answer is about 20. However, this also depends on the types of application in use as well as the throughput requirements for each wireless user.)

Wireless Ethernet Characteristics

To understand how wireless can fail in different ways from wired Ethernet, let's first enumerate how wireless is different. The following table lists some characteristics of wireless technologies, all of which are important in wireless problem determination. Don't worry if you don't understand all the terminology—we'll get to that in a moment.

Attribute	802.11b	802.11a	Bluetooth
RF Band	2.4 Gigahertz	5 Gigahertz	2.4 Gigahertz
Modulation	DSSS	OFDM	FH/GFSK
MAC	CSMA/CA	CSMA/CA	Master/Slave TDD
Security model	WEP	WEP	PIN/Shared Key
Max data rate	11Mbps	54Mbps	750Kbps
Typical range	300 feet	300 feet	30 feet

The typical range listed in the table is a maximum. Data rate goes down when signal quality degrades because of obstructions or interference (see Figure 11.1). Here are a couple of notes:

- Different equipment tends to have different maximum range because of transmitter power.

- Wired network technologies have a fixed speed. For example, Ethernet is 10Mbps or 100Mbps. Wireless technologies have an "ideal data rate," which adjusts downward when it needs to based on the quality of signal. Higher signal quality means that the equipment is able to achieve higher data rates.

Figure 11.1

Signal strength goes down (as does the data rate) as distance increases. Lighter areas indicate weaker signals.

100 meters (328.08 feet)

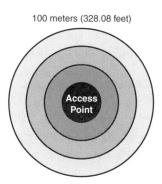

Access Point

11

Radio Frequency Characteristics

To begin with, wireless is all about RF (Radio Frequency) transmission. As you can see from previous table, 802.11b and Bluetooth, this means broadcasting in the 2.4-gigahertz band, whereas 802.11a broadcasts in the 5-gigahertz band.

Freaked out by all of this frequency and band stuff? Don't sweat it. Wireless works just like any other radio—you just can't listen to it in your car. A frequency that indicates a radio channel really indicates a point on the radio spectrum; the channel actually includes a "band," that is, the distance (see Figure 11.2) between two frequency points. For example, if your favorite station is 105.3FM, you're really listening to the FM band going from 105.2 to 105.4MHz, with 105.3MHz being the center point.

The first thing you might guess is that Bluetooth and 802.11b have some interoperability problems. And, you'd be right. In fact, the less-powerful transmitters in Bluetooth gear will be overwhelmed by the more-powerful transmitters in 802.11b gear. According to a really nerdy paper released by the Ericsson corporation, Bluetooth operations don't get seriously disturbed by 802.11 as long as you are within 6 feet of a Bluetooth access point; however, when you're 30 feet away, the probability of data errors increases significantly, to about 1 out of 10.

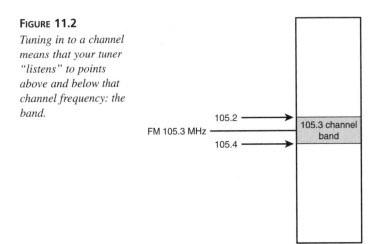

FIGURE **11.2**

Tuning in to a channel means that your tuner "listens" to points above and below that channel frequency: the band.

In general, though, it probably goes without saying that unless you're begging for trouble, you don't want to deploy radio transmitters that use the same frequency range unless you enjoy pain. The 2.4-gigahertz band is pretty crowded: not only is it used by Bluetooth and 802.11b Ethernet, but also certain wireless telephones use it. To top it all off, certain microwave ovens generate 2.4G interference!

In a nutshell, when you are not getting the signal strength you expect, or perhaps aren't negotiating the speed that you expect, check your location for interference.

How can you check for interference without expensive equipment? Well, you can't. But the good news is that you *can* rule out interference simply by turning off possible sources of interference and seeing if the problems persist. Got a wireless phone? Turn it off! Got a microwave? Make sure it's off while you're testing! (If it turns out to be the problem, have your local appliance repair store check the door seal.) Your neighbor has a wireless phone? Turn it...okay, maybe you can't turn your neighbor's phone off. But you might be able to relocate your access point to the other side of the house, out of range of your neighbor's phone.

The same technique, of course, applies to *you* when your spouse/neighbor/children accuse your wireless gear of interfering with *their* toys or appliances. Turn yours off and see if the problems persist.

Now let's talk about modulation, or the way that information gets encoded into a radio wave. Does it matter to us as troubleshooters what kind of modulation is used? It does only in the sense that we want to match up equipment when vendors of two different wireless technologies use different modulation. That is, 802.11 supports both FH

(Frequency Hopping) and DSSS (Direct Sequence Spread Spectrum)—make sure that you buy matching equipment. The more common wireless Ethernet standard in use is 802.11b, and it supports DSSS only.

More obvious stats that you'll want to have in hand when checking for trouble on a wireless network are the range (uh, yeah!) and the data rate. I've been approached by someone very dear to my heart, saying, "How come the wireless LAN is so slow? Is there something wrong with it?" Well, no. Not to reveal the identity of this person or anything, but the WLAN in my home runs 802.11b, which has a max data speed of 11Mbps—and, when in my kitchen, with quite a bit of masonry and beams between the laptop and the access point, usually runs at 2Mbps. It's not at all surprising that stuff runs slower than our 100Mbps wired Ethernet LAN, being that it's running several orders of magnitude slower.

Identity and Security

Finally, wireless Ethernet, unlike regular Ethernet, has two extra attributes: network identity and encryption. The identity attribute affects data link connectivity—you can think of it as the VLAN identifier of wireless—whereas the encryption attribute affects the ability to unscramble and understand the data payload. If any one of these is misconfigured, you're not going to be able to talk on the WLAN.

An access point, when first configured, is given an ESSID: its Extended Service Set Identifier. (This is also referred to as SID, SSID, or merely Network name by different vendors.) The ESSID, again, is kind of like a VLAN identifier—it's not a security identifier. As such, your ESSID must be the same on two 802.11 devices for them to establish data-link communications. You won't get a link light on your wireless card if the ESSID is incorrect.

On the other hand, you do get a link light if data encryption, Wired Equivalent Privacy (WEP), has been enabled on your access point, even if your workstation doesn't produce the correct WEP key. If your access point and your wireless NIC don't agree on the WEP key, you won't be talking, even though your wireless link light is on. You'll "see" the data, but won't be able to understand it without the key.

Usually, there's some sort of utility such as Linksys (shown in Figure 11.3) that can let you know if all is well.

> You can use utilities like this to do simple site planning. How would you, ideally, plan out a wireless telephone base location? Sure, you'd walk around while talking to a friend—making sure that no critical locations were full of static. Similarly, you can walk around with your laptop and check out the signal strength location in various locations.

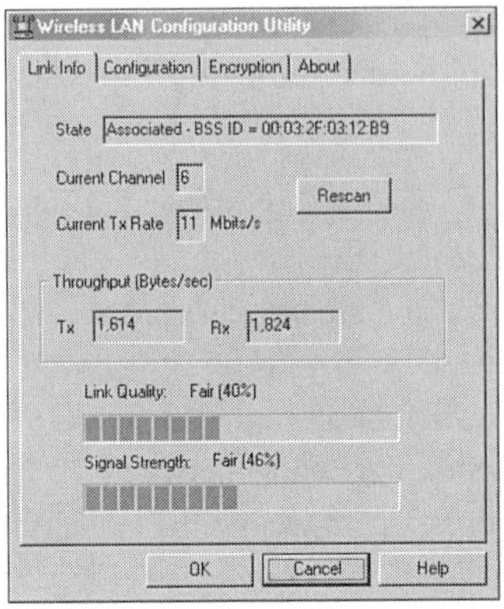

FIGURE **11.3**

Linksys utility, showing current throughput, signal strength, and data rate. WEP status is on the Encryption tab.

Premature Blamestorming

It's easy, with all the things that can go wrong, to prematurely blame wireless for a given network problem. But from the size of this book, it's pretty apparent that there are a lot more things that can go wrong. So before blamestorming wireless, make sure that the problem does *not* exist when you are using wired networking.

For example, say that you're getting kicked out of your client/server application every once in a while. You might suspect that there was some sort of wireless interference going on—and without being able to shut down every other device in the place, it would be hard to rule them out. Instead of following this difficult path, you might simply want to swap your wireless interface with a wired interface. Don't *have* a wired interface? (Don't laugh, I've seen devices, particularly handhelds, that don't even offer wired interfaces.) Well, if you can use the same application from another device (say, a laptop), *first* see if the problem persists on that other device when using a wireless connection.

If the problem does not persist, you might be looking at a problem with the original device. If the problem does persist, check to see if it persists with a wired connection. You might indeed find out that the problem only exists within the wireless network. But you might find that the problem exists whether or not you use wireless technologies. As with other technologies, it's important to do this problem determination before you decide that wireless is your problem—you don't want to waste your time chasing a problem that is not wireless related.

Finally, if you do find out that the problem is wireless related, and you cannot seem to track it down to range or interference, you might want to check out another vendor's wireless gear, particularly if you have low-cost wireless gear. Unfortunately, I've seen problems with low-end gear where TCP connections are mysteriously reset (for example,

SSH or Telnet) in the middle of a session. Those problems have gone away when I've switched cards and used higher-end gear. Although this won't affect many applications (like Web browsing or certain games), it's something to be aware of.

Summary

You can think of a wireless access point as a hub that just happens to use radio frequency (RF) transmissions as its "wires." There are several different types of wireless technologies: 802.11 Ethernet is used for LAN replacement, and Bluetooth is used for short-distance inter-device communication.

802.11 can reliably scale to about 20 or so stations per access point. Both 802.11b and Bluetooth use the same frequency range: the 2.4GHz band, and so there can be interoperability problems, but these usually aren't terrible if you are willing to put up with shorter distances between nodes. 2.4-gigahertz is pretty crowded, what with certain wireless telephones and even microwave ovens emitting RF in this band. You might have to change channels or stop using other devices if you have problems with wireless in the 2.4GHz band. As usual, "rule out" is your friend here.

It's important not to blame wireless prematurely for a given network problem. See if the problem persists if you use a wired network.

Q&A

Q If I can't buy all my wireless Ethernet gear from the same vendor, how do I make sure that it will interoperate?

A It's probably a good idea to buy 802.11b gear labeled "WiFi." WiFi is a vendor consortium that sets certain tolerances which ensure that different brands of gear will play well together.

Q The card I bought at Best Buy is WiFi, but for some reason, it won't talk to my access point at work. What gives?

A It's likely you have a Linksys NIC—these, although hugely popular, WiFi branded, and inexpensive, don't guarantee that WEP will interoperate with non-Linksys gear. Sorry, man. Check Linksys' Web site. Maybe by now there's an update.

Workshop

Workshop time! Here's a brief quiz to help you make the most out of this hour's lesson as well as activities for you to try on your own.

Quiz

1. A wireless access point is most like

   a. An AP

   b. A switch

   c. A hub

   d. A router

2. Bluetooth networks, in specific, are meant for

   a. WLAN

   b. PAN

   c. MAN

   d. DCAN

3. The two technologies that use the 2.4GHz band are

   a. 802.11a, 802.11b

   b. 802.11b, Bluetooth

   c. Bluetooth, 802.11a

   d. None of the above

4. When two technologies use the same frequency range, there is a very real possibility of

   a. Interference

   b. Jabber

   c. Strengthening of signal

   d. Chipping

5. WEP is used for

   a. VLAN equivalent

   b. Encryption of data

   c. Wireless Enhancement Protocol

   d. All of the above

6. SID is used for

   a. VLAN equivalent

   b. Encryption of data

   c. Wireless Enhancement Protocol

   d. All of the above

7. If a new application exhibits strange behavior on a wireless-connected network, it's a good idea to

   a. Change applications

   b. Boost the signal

   c. Change the WEP key

   d. Try the application on a wired network

8. If you prove that a problem is caused by the wireless network, it might be a good idea to

   a. Stop using wireless for those PCs

   b. Try a different manufacturer's wireless gear

   c. Reboot

   d. Use a different Network Name

Answers to Quiz Questions

1. C
2. B
3. B
4. A
5. B
6. A
7. D
8. B

11

Activities

1. Open up your Web browser and check out `http://www.fcc.gov/mmb/asd/bickel/oddno.html`. It's an interesting discussion of why FM frequencies in the U.S.A. end in odd numbers.

2. Grab a geeky friend, child, or other warm breathing body, and see if you can locate two wireless telephones that operate in the same frequency range. (900MHz is common, as is 2.4GHz.) Set them up in a location that has two phone lines, and call each other. See if you can create interference. (You might have to change channels.) How bad is it?

HOUR 12

Windows Networking Basics

There is more to life than increasing its speed.

—Mahatma Ghandi

Whoa! Stop the world, I want to get off. In less than a decade, Microsoft has blown through what seems like a million versions of its Windows operating system. Although this gives end users much-improved functionality (just the ability to avoid rebooting more than once daily makes many of us sing hosannas), it also makes system administrators and budget officers tear their hair out over the technology and cost implications of this upgrade treadmill.

Less-than-infinite budgets at many organizations means that it's likely that you'll run into many, many versions of Windows; but take heart, underneath the slick exterior of even the latest Fisher-Price look of Windows XP, the guts can be simplified, understood, and conquered. That's the purpose of this hour.

You'll want to know the basics of using Windows networking before cruising through this hour; this hour dives into the theory behind Windows networking, and gives you enough practical knowledge that you'll definitely be able to solve most Windows problems that come your way. (Don't worry, when I say basics, I really do mean basics. If you already know how to map a drive in Windows, share files, and so on, you're in good shape. If not, don't fret; just check out `http://support.microsoft.com/support/kb/articles/q152/5/62.asp`. I promise, we'll still be here when you get back.)

So, given that the Windows family tree has grown up sort of wildly, how do we simplify it? Well, for starters, let's subdivide that tree into two sub-families, the Windows 9x family and the Windows NT family. As you might guess, the Windows 9x family will be going bye-bye at some point; but there is still plenty of it out there, and we might as well know how to deal with it. Here's how the current operating systems divvy up:

- **Windows 9x Family**—Windows 95, Windows 98, Windows 98SE, Windows ME
- **Windows NT Family**—Windows NT 4.0, Windows 2000 Pro, Windows 2000 Server, Windows 2000 Advanced Server, Windows XP Home Edition, Windows XP Professional

Okay, good deal. We can deal with two branches of a family tree, right? Here's how we'll tackle the material itself. We'll start by chatting about how Windows networking works, laying some foundations for troubleshooting Windows networking, and transitioning naturally into networking tools. Finally, a troubleshooter requires resource monitoring and process trace tools for *all* operating systems, and Windows is no exception. Accordingly, we'll finish up with a discussion of these tools, with a nod to tools that allow you to rescue your Windows machine if you find you're unable to boot or login.

File and Print Foundations

Although Windows allows you to connect with everything but the kitchen sink (and I hear that Microsoft is working on this), we'll focus only on the networking tools Microsoft has invented and provides. If you've got a good handle on the theory behind Windows networking, you'll be better able to troubleshoot it when it's not working. (It's always nice to know what you're looking for with the flashlight.) Not surprisingly, there are actually several components to a successful Windows network (I'll define these further as we go along):

- Naming services (WINS/NetBIOS, DNS)
- Authentication services (NT Domain, Active Directory Domain, or Workgroup Sharing)
- File and print services (SMB)

As you might expect, running a peer-to-peer Windows 95 network is a lot simpler than setting up a Windows 2000 network over a wide area connection; however, the building blocks are very similar. If you use Microsoft file and print networking, your computer is either part of a workgroup or a domain. Either way, though, you are likely using TCP/IP as your protocol, and as such, rely on infrastructure services such as DHCP and DNS. (For more on DHCP and DNS proper, see Hour 19, "Internet and Intranet Troubleshooting: TCP/IP at Work.")

Name Resolution and Server Location

Name resolution is an important building block for Microsoft Networking, as with any network service. After our discussion in Hour 1, "Understanding Networking: The Telephone Analogy," you're probably comfortable with the fact that any network name needs to be resolved to a network address—that is, when you point your browser to www.jotto.com, the name gets resolved via *DNS (Domain Name Service)* to the network address 205.134.224.21.

The great news is that the latest versions of Microsoft networking do just this: they use DNS as their primary means of name resolution and server location. The bad news is that there are a couple of backward-compatible issues that you will need to understand to effectively troubleshoot. Furthermore, even if you are an old hand at DNS, you'll need to learn a bit more about how Microsoft does it. All the methods of Microsoft name resolution and server location (which in aggregate are called the Windows Locator Service) can be summarized as

- NetBIOS standalone (broadcast or static name files)
- NetBIOS point-to-point and flat (non-hierarchical) name server (WINS)
- Hierarchical name server (DNS)

12

Let's start by discussing how standalone NetBIOS works, both from name resolution and server lookup ("browse") standpoints, and then we'll be equipped to understand both WINS and DNS.

NetBIOS: Standalone

First of all, what *is* NetBIOS?

NetBIOS (Network Basic Input/Output System) provides name and session services to the file-sharing and print-sharing programs between two computers. You're using NetBIOS when you share files between two Windows 9x family computers.

NetBIOS handles name services for Microsoft file and print services. It also serves to carry messages pertaining to the creation of workgroups on the network and makes sure that no duplicate workstation names exist within the workgroup or domain.

When a duplicate workstation name does exist, NetBIOS tells you about it in a hurry. For example, when a technician duplicates a known-good hard drive (see Hour 18, "Managing Change: Establishing Consistency and Standards") to a known-bad hard drive and then reboots both stations, he or she immediately sees the following Windows error, which is in fact a NetBIOS error:

```
Microsoft Networking:

The following error occurred while loading protocol number 0.

Error 38: The computer name you specified is already in use on the
network. To specify a different name, double-click the Network icon in
Control Panel.
```

NetBIOS has queried the network to see if the name exists, and, in fact, it does. Of course, the tech simply goes to the Control Panel, clicks the Identification tab, and changes the PC name to fix this problem.

The question becomes: How does NetBIOS know that the name is in use? Well, when there's a name server in use, NetBIOS simply queries the name server for its own name before announcing itself.

What do you do when you don't have a name server? There are two methods you could use: broadcast and static host tables.

Broadcasting means that each NetBIOS station communicates with the subnet's TCP/IP broadcast address for the purposes of finding out "who else is out here," and announcing itself. It's pretty simple, and works similarly to NetBEUI (a nonroutable protocol that transports NetBIOS), except that it's using TCP/IP. (We'll discuss the good points and bad points of NetBEUI in a little while.)

What about static host tables? First of all, what *is* a static host table? By definition, a static host table is a file or database that is *local* to a workstation; it does not look changes up from the network the way that DNS does.

Here's one example of a static host table. As you probably already know, a Windows PC's TCP/IP stack can use a HOSTS table on its hard drive to resolve hostnames to IP addresses. The HOSTS table is used for normal TCP/IP networking (as in Telnet sessions to a host system as well as pings). A HOSTS file looks like this:

```
192.168.10.5 elmo
```

```
192.168.10.5 grover
```

This means that `192.168.10.5` is the numeric address for `elmo`, and `192.168.10.6` is the numeric address for `grover`.

Each Windows PC can also use an `LMHOSTS` file—a different kind of static host table—which is formatted much the same as a `HOSTS` file but used for NetBIOS name resolution. Why? Well, a `HOSTS` file only specifies a name-to-address mapping; it does not indicate what service is offered by which host.

Contrast this to `LMHOSTS`, where one can actually specify, "Hey, if you're looking for the main server to logon to, here it is!" For example,

```
192.168.10.5 elmo
```

```
192.168.10.5 grover #DOM:feldmonster
```

specifies that `grover` is not only IP address `192.168.10.5`, but is also the main server for the domain `feldmonster`. See the difference? Again, the `HOSTS` file only specifies name resolution; the `LMHOSTS` file specifies where services are located; for this reason, the entry is known as a *mapping* rather than just a resolution.

> Historical/trivia note: The LM stands for LAN Manager, which is what Windows networking evolved from.

Both the `LMHOSTS` and `HOSTS` files live in the `C:\WINDOWS` directory in the Windows 9x family; the Windows NT families locate these files in the `%SYSTEMROOT%\etc\drivers` directory (`%SYSTEMROOT%` on XP defaults to `Windows\System32`; NT and 2000's default is `WinNT\System32`.)

`LMHOSTS.SAM` is a sample file you can look at to see the file format and so on. I **strongly recommend** that you *not* use `LMHOSTS` files (or `HOSTS` files) as a normal practice unless you have the smallest network in the world; the tedium of updating many of these files makes you wish you were running after really tough network problems instead.

Although you should consider static host mappings (and static host tables in general) to be a day-to-day no-no, you should know about them for two *troubleshooting* reasons. First, if there's a name resolution problem with a workstation, you might want to see if somebody has been monkeying around with `LMHOSTS` at a given client computer. Second, you can play with an `LMHOSTS` file to rule in or rule out name resolution in a given problem. (For example, say that you get a `no domain controller could be located` error for the `feldmonster` domain. If you manually insert the correct IP address in the `LMHOSTS` file—and it works—you definitely have a problem with service location between this workstation and the server.)

Whether or not you're using static mappings, it is highly useful to be able to find out what a particular Windows station *thinks* that current mappings are. That's where the `nbtstat` tool comes in. The rub here is that you need to know how to translate hexadecimal values into actual usable service information. For example, here's the output from a machine on my home network, using the `nbtstat -n` command (I have modified the table to include the actual meanings of the hexadecimal numbers):

```
Name                 Type      Status      Meaning
-----------------------------------------------------
MONSTER      <20>   UNIQUE    Registered   File & Print Server
MONSTER      <00>   UNIQUE    Registered   Computer name
FELDMONSTER  <00>   GROUP     Registered   Workgroup name
FELDMONSTER  <1E>   GROUP     Registered   Backup browser
```

This might be a little early to discuss this because I haven't covered some of the concepts in the definitions, but it's important to know that `nbtstat` is usable no matter whether you're using a name server or running standalone with a static host table. One concept that hasn't been covered yet is browsing; but worry not, we'll get to that in the next section.

Ordinarily, the meaning of the hex numbers doesn't appear; but you can get a listing of all NetBIOS hexadecimal numbers from `http://msdn.microsoft.com/archive/ default.asp?url=/archive/en-us/dnarwnet/html/msdn_browse1.asp`. You can also retrieve the NetBIOS name table from a given IP address, say, `10.1.2.3`, by using the `nbtstat -a 10.1.2.3`. If you were to do this to an NT 4.0 domain controller, normally, it would look like this (but without my addition of a Meaning column):

```
Name                 Type      Status      Meaning
-----------------------------------------------------
SHREK          <00>   UNIQUE    Registered   Workstation services
FELDMONSTER    <00>   GROUP     Registered   Legacy  "Lan manager" type domain
SHREK          <20>   UNIQUE    Registered   File & Print Server
FELDMONSTER    <1B>   UNIQUE    Registered   Primary Domain Controller
FELDMONSTER    <1E>   GROUP     Registered   Master Browser, Domain-type
SHREK          <03>   UNIQUE    Registered   Messenger service
INet~Services  <1C>   GROUP     Registered   Internet group name
IS~SHREK.......<00>   UNIQUE    Registered
FELDMONSTER    <1D>   UNIQUE    Registered
..__MSBROWSE__.<01>   GROUP     Registered   Alias of MasterBrowser for subnet
SHREK          <01>   UNIQUE    Registered   Real name:MasterBrowser of subnet
```

What about Windows 2000 servers? Well, here you would be more interested in DNS, which we'll discuss in a little while.

NetBEUI

NetBEUI is for networks that don't have TCP/IP; typically small networks or workgroups without the need for Internet access. If you have TCP/IP, skip this unless you like history lessons. Or, if you see NetBEUI in your network configuration *and* you have TCP/IP, read on to see why you should get rid of NetBEUI.

NetBEUI is a *nonroutable* protocol that transports NetBIOS. Again, it is only used when TCP/IP is not available. It is simply the way the NetBIOS messages are packaged and delivered to the wire. The plus used to be that you didn't need to have a TCP/IP stack loaded on your PC to be able to do useful networking functions. The downside was that because NetBEUI is very simple, it relies on network broadcasts to get a lot of information across: There aren't any network addresses, so everything is addressed to everyone.

A broadcast (when a network node sends information to *all* other network nodes on a segment) obviously causes a lot of network traffic. NetBEUI does this so it doesn't have to keep track of all the nodes on the network—if a station doesn't differentiate whom to talk to, there doesn't have to be a facility on the network to keep track of who's currently available on the network.

There are two consequences: First, a name server isn't necessary with NetBEUI (good if you don't have a name server); and second, NetBEUI traffic *cannot* traverse a router (bad if you have a router and you want your people to be able to share files across it).

Considering that nowadays it's pretty easy to bring up a name server, why does NetBEUI even exist? Well, if you had less than 30 stations, no server, and no Internet connection, NetBEUI was pretty attractive: There was no need to allocate TCP/IP addresses (therefore requiring tracking of static IP numbers or a DHCP server) and no need for a name server. A lot of people used it for this reason. But if NetBEUI is in use on a network *nowadays*, it is just there because of inertia: most folks now have a server and the associated TCP/IP infrastructure required for TCP/IP operation.

Accordingly, you really shouldn't be using NetBEUI. Broadcasts are the pits; in large enough quantities, they will lead to broadcast storms (that is, one workstation broadcasts, leading other workstations to broadcast). On a large scale, this creates unnecessary network traffic that can wreak havoc on your network. Get rid of it if you can. (Naturally, the same argument goes for TCP/IP workstations without name servers, by the way, because they must broadcast.)

12

Browsing

The Windows networking literature refers to *browsing* as the process of listing all available Windows networking resources, as opposed to when you know a server name and you simply ask for a connection.

When you're using a peer-to-peer network (no server involved), one computer gets arbitrarily designated as browse master; others are designated as backup browsers. Any client computer can get information about network resources, whether the resources are servers, workgroups, NT domains, and so on. For example, when you click your Network Neighborhood icon, the computer list you see is obtained from the browse master of your workgroup or domain. As you can see, browsing is pretty important—if you can't see the resource, you can't use the resource.

The *browse master* of a workgroup or domain is the machine that's responsible for keeping a list of participating workstations. If the browse master leaves the workgroup, another browser from the backup browser list must take over. If a backup browser erroneously believes that it is in charge, problems spring up. Staying current on service packs usually prevents this type of misbehavior.

The browse master of a domain is always the *primary domain controller (PDC)*. If it's not, you've got a problem. The Browser Monitor on the NT and Win2K resource kits (BROWMON.EXE) can help you check on browser status on a subnet.

Workgroup browsing problems might simply be a typo because no joining is involved when the workstation is set up. It's really easy for the person doing the setup to walk away without verifying browse-ability. I once saw a case in which a user absolutely could not browse others in her workgroup. After checking the network card and cable and finding nothing wrong, we were on the verge of reinstalling Windows—we had tracked the problem down to something about the OS. Before doing this, we checked the Control Panel one last time; this time, we noticed that the workgroup name had a space in front of it. Argh! We removed the space, and suddenly we could see everybody else.

I've also seen a case in which a workgroup was mistyped using a zero rather than the letter O.

Although an NT domain can exist across subnets (that is, via a router), workgroups cannot. Instead, the workgroup exists twice on the two different segments—each one with its own browse master and browse list. This means that the browse master on network A has no idea what the browse list is for network B. Computers on segment A will not be able to see those on segment B in their network neighborhood, and vice versa.

WINS: The "Flat" NetBIOS Name Server

Windows Internet Naming Service or *WINS*, was invented to make routable Windows Networking possible. As you'll recall, using TCP/IP in its simplest form (without a name server) means that NetBIOS must use broadcasts or static name tables, both of which are horrible for reasons already outlined.

WINS is the answer to how machines can resolve names without broadcasting and without static name tables. When a client machine is configured to use WINS, instead of broadcasting to register itself and check for duplicate names, it contacts the WINS server. The WINS server keeps track of Windows workgroups, domains, and machine names on a TCP/IP network.

When a machine contacts the WINS server directly to register itself and look up other hostnames and services (such as domain controllers), this is called *point-to-point* name resolution; machines that resolve names this way are called *p-nodes*. Broadcast machines, as you might expect, are called *b-nodes*; machines configured to do both (hybrid) are called *h-nodes*.

WINS servers are available for Windows NT, UNIX (as part of the Samba package), and Windows 2000. There is no WINS server for workgroups.

WINS has several limitations:

- It is flat, rather than hierarchical. In a large organization, this means that it's pretty easy to accidentally duplicate machine names.
- Although WINS does have replication options (the capability for two or more servers to share data), in practice, this is fairly annoying to administer because there is no master relationship: each server is peer-to-peer, and equally able to mess up the database.
- In a busy and large WINS system, database corruption happens, not infrequently.

Here's some advice about WINS:

- If you're using Windows 2000, use DNS instead of WINS.
- Use NBTSTAT (built-in) and WINSCHK (available from the Windows resource kits) as good rule in/rule out tools when you suspect problems with WINS servers and/or their databases. Bear in mind that you always want to get multiple perspectives from these tools; that is, point them at several different machines to see "which one of these things is not like the others."
- Make sure that your DHCP servers distribute the correct WINS servers to clients! Sounds simple, but in practice, people do forget this.

12

- Don't be shy about deleting the WINS database if you even suspect corruption—remember, the database is *dynamic* (built by client machines as they connect), so what harm can you really do? It's probably a good idea to do this when things are quiet, though; you'll need to stop the WINS service, delete the database files (typically located in %SystemRoot%\System32\WINS), and then restart WINS. Make sure that your server machines *explicitly* contact the WINS servers shortly afterward so they can re-register themselves, and be available for clients.

- Use few (if any) static mappings. They're annoying to keep up with; you should only use them if a server (for instance, a hardware CDROM server) doesn't support WINS.

- Keep it simple! Don't use more WINS servers than you need.

- Be consistent! Unless there is a compelling reason not to, make them all replication partners. The last thing you want is an inconsistent database, where server #1 says that a workstation is a certain IP address, and server #2 doesn't know that the workstation exists. A good rule of thumb is, "what you do to one, do to the other." For example, if you delete the WINS database on one machine, make sure to delete it on the other—or the corrupted info will flow back.

Finally, you should know that WINS is "history": it's not something that Microsoft has future plans for. If you must support Windows NT servers and workstations, you need it. But if you don't have to support these, by all means, do not use it; use DNS instead.

DNS: Hierarchical Naming and Service Location

As we'll discuss in Hour 19, DNS is capable of serving up more than just name-to-ip-address translations. DNS can host many types of database records (standard ones include NS, or name server records, and MX, or mail exchanger records), and Microsoft's latest iteration of its networking protocol takes advantage of this by ditching the old NetBIOS and hosting both naming services and service locations in the DNS.

Nothing clears the air like a good example, so let's take a look at what grover, the Primary Domain Controller for an Active Directory domain, would look like if DNS was being used as the resolution mechanism for Windows networking (as is the default behavior for a Windows 2000 network). Using the standard DNS tool, nslookup, to find the primary domain controller, you might type: **nslookup _ldap._tcp.dc._msdcs. feldmonster.com**, producing this output:

```
Server:  grover.feldmonster.com
Address:  10.1.62.2
```

```
_ldap._tcp.dc._msdcs.feldmonster.com      SRV service location:
        priority     = 0
        weight       = 100
        port         = 389
        svr hostname = rover.feldmonster.com
grover.feldmonster.com internet address = 10.1.62.2
```

Don't worry too much about the convoluted format of the DNS record; the important thing to understand is that certain types of services have certain types of lookups.

> I highly recommend that you read one particular Microsoft tech note; it covers how to integrate a Windows 2000 domain's name resolution into an existing DNS system. I don't recommend actually *doing* this—to avoid problems, it's really best to use 100% Microsoft DNS—but it is interesting and instructive to see how traditional DNS and Microsoft DNS mesh. Here's the URL: `http://www.microsoft.com/windows2000/techinfo/reskit/` `deploymentscenarios/scenarios/dns04_integ_adnspace_with_` `nameoverlap.asp`.

Again, understand that DNS is used as a name resolution and service location mechanism only. DNS does not perform username and password authentication: *That* is done by the domain controller, not the DNS servers.

File and Print Services and Authentication

12

We're going to talk about file and print services *before* we talk about authentication, merely to acknowledge that it exists. We won't get heavily into it because it's pretty simple, and typical problems don't actually have much to do with the file and print services themselves. Problems getting to files and printers are usually related to protocol problems, name service problems, WINS problems, DNS problems, and authentication problems.

As Figure 12.1 shows, once service location and name resolution is finished, authentication is done, Windows file-sharing and print-sharing happens through a mechanism called *server message block*, or *SMB*. SMB exists in all versions of Windows, with some modifications that have to do with authentication, which we'll get to in a moment, and service location/name resolution, which has already been discussed. The SMB service (the "server" service in the Windows NT family) is what makes it possible to offer access to a Windows computer's files and printers. The SMB client program (the "workstation" service in the Windows NT family) on a client PC makes it possible to use SMB-offered files and printers on a server.

FIGURE 12.1

After a client makes a Windows Networking request, there is a very definite order of operations.

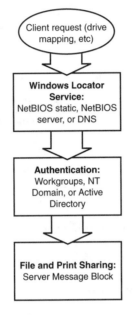

Authentication: Domains, Trees, and Forests, Oh My

Three types of authentication are performed on Windows networks:

- Workgroup (password per-share)
- NT Domain (username and password)
- Active Directory (username and password)

There's nothing remarkable about workgroup sharing. If one share doesn't work, a good strategy is to create another and see if it works. If it does, you might have to re-create the share that isn't working.

NT domains and Active Directory are a little trickier, but they share a lot of common features. A notable one is that they implement the concept of "secure workstations;" that is, workstations that are explicitly allowed to join the domain by an administrator. In a world where physical access to a machine allows a user to decrypt passwords, there's a lot of debate about just how secure this is, but for our purposes, we just need to know a couple of things.

In particular, because part of the concept behind a secure NT workstation is the idea that you cannot access a given workstation until you've identified yourself, we as troubleshooters roll our eyes and think to ourselves, "Great, so I can't try to fix it if it's having trouble authenticating. That's just grand."

Don't sweat it if you can't get logged in; see "Non-Bootable OS Recovery Methods," later in this hour.

NT Trust

Because NT domains are not hierarchical—that is, they are flat, rather than tree-structured—there needs to be some way for a user on one NT domain to use the resources of another NT domain. The mechanism that allows users of one domain to use resources of another is called *trust*. Trust relationships can be a one- or two-way relationship.

Say that your boss gives you access to the file cabinet with everybody's salaries. He has placed trust in you that you won't blab everybody's salaries all over town. Similarly, you trust your boss to pay you on Friday. This is a two-way trust relationship. On the other hand, your small children must trust you to put food on the table. You do not trust the older child at the tender age of 6 years old to stay with his 2-year-old brother; his idea of fun would be to feed his dinner to the dog and to feed the dog food to his brother. This, of course, is a one-way trust relationship.

You make NT domain trust decisions in a similar fashion. If you need for folks in domain A to be able to access resources in domain B, but not vice versa, you establish a trust relationship between domains B and A. You would say that B *trusts* A.

If one person in one of your NT domains (domain B) cannot access a resource (a share or a printer) in another one of your NT domains (domain A), you probably want to check the trust relationship. Make sure that the domain providing the resource is *trusting*, and that the domain needing the resource is *trusted*.

If you are administering NT, you use USRMGR.EXE to generate *explicit* trusts (that is, trusts that you tell Windows about). Be aware that *implicit* trusts also exist: For example, your Windows NT Workstation implicitly trusts the Domain Controller once it joins the domain.

Here's one interesting note about how name resolution and service location can affect trust relationships and thus authentication: I was called in to troubleshoot a trust relationship that had apparently been set up correctly; but even though it had, the system administrator got the following message when he attempted to administer the remote domain:

```
There are no logon servers available to service the logon request
```

The key was in the fact that these were wide-area linked domains, and the two WINS servers were not replicating properly; once they were, the problem went away.

12

Active Directory: Hierarchical and Scalable Domains

I find that a lot of folks tend to be uncertain about exactly what Active Directory Services (AD) does, and if you're uncertain about its exact function, it's kind of hard to rule it in or out as a problem.

So, you already know that although AD *needs* DNS as a name resolution and service location mechanism, you know that DNS is a separate entity from the AD—it in fact runs as a separate service on your server. Like any directory service, AD offers authentication services for more than one server in a hierarchical and distributed manner: That is, more than one server is capable of serving the database; and even within the AD namespace, sub-containers are used so that not all network objects are in the same place. Basically, AD is what you get when you hook up a bunch of NT-like domains to a DNS-like hierarchy.

A *domain*, like in the NT world, is a database that contains fields like usernames, passwords, and groups. In the AD world, these fields are called *object classes*; the sum of all these fields are called the *schema* of the directory. Unlike NT, the schema is not fixed; programs can add object classes to the database. The *global catalog server* is, among other things, responsible for the schema, which makes it the proper server to turn your gaze upon should you get schema errors.

A *tree* is a collection of domains—the first of which is known as the *root domain*. The tree is known by the same DNS name as the root domain; other domains in the tree have child names, as shown in Figure 12.2. Domains in the same tree have a trust relationship, which works similarly to the NT 4 trusts I just discussed.

FIGURE 12.2

The hierarchical relationship between a forest, a tree, a domain, and a child domain.

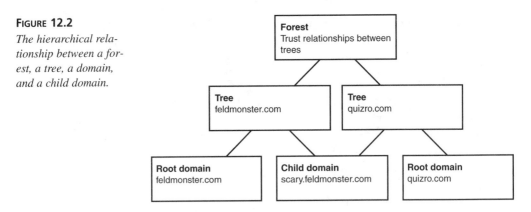

Forest
Trust relationships between trees

Tree
feldmonster.com

Tree
quizro.com

Root domain
feldmonster.com

Child domain
scary.feldmonster.com

Root domain
quizro.com

For organizations that want to keep administration separate, separate trees are used; but, trust relationships are still allowed. A group of trees that have trust relationships between them are known as a *forest*.

In reality, many smaller organizations using AD use perhaps one or two servers, so they use one root domain living in one tree—with no forest.

Microsoft does a pretty good job of offering a knowledgebase about common problems at `support.microsoft.com`—but keep in mind, many AD problems are either resource related, infrastructure related, or, ultimately, design related. Whether you are trouble-shooting someone else's AD gone wild, or deploying a new system, following Microsoft's design guidelines is not only a good idea, it will likely save you many hours of trouble. One good design document is located at `http://www.microsoft.com/technet/prodtechnol/ad/windows2000/plan/w2kdomar.asp`.

Because AD not only supports, but integrates the *LDAP (Lightweight Directory Access Protocol)* into AD operations, many folks are starting to hook third-party devices to AD's LDAP, such as firewall appliances and other devices that require authentication. Pretty cool, but, alas, my experience shows that you will definitely want a troubleshooting tool to do this—that is, the ability to tell a vendor, "Well, I'm able to use the LDAP with another tool, but your device is acting funny." Shazam! LDAP browsers come to your rescue. Plenty of LDAP browsers are out there, but my favorite is the Java-based LDAP Browser/Editor from the University of Chicago's Jarek Gawor. Check it out at `www.iit.edu/~gawojar/ldap`.

It's worth noting that AD does not allow an "anonymous bind" (where bind means "con-nect," in this context) to LDAP; you *must* specify a username and password. Most of the time, the mapping of your Active Directory name space is pretty easy; Figure 12.3 shows an LDAP browser attaching to the `feldmonster.com` domain, using the administrator login.

12

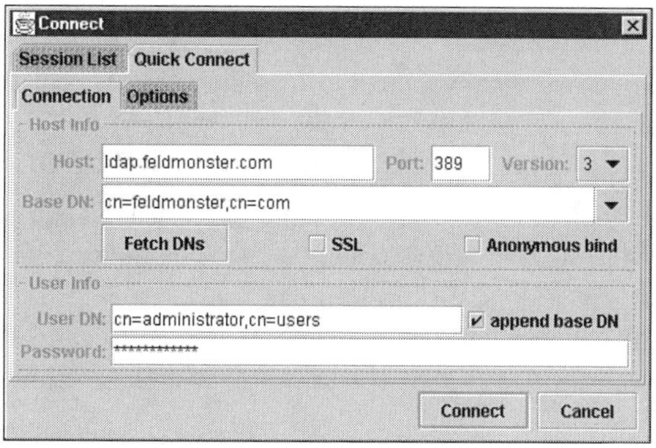

FIGURE 12.3

An LDAP browser attaching to the feldmonster.com *domain using the administrator login.*

Tools: Command and Conquer

Cool! We're done with the theory behind Windows networking; now, armed with your knowledge, you know enough to make effective use of the tools that I introduce in this section. I'll start with network-layer diagnostics, and then move on to resources and process tracing tools.

`ipconfig` and `winipcfg`

Your basic IP configuration can be shown using `ipconfig` (Windows NT family) or `winipcfg` (Windows 9x family).

Both of these commands enable you to manually release or renew your DHCP lease, or to display basic TCP/IP information, whether or not your station has been configured for DHCP.

If you're using Windows 9x, you should actually use `winipcfg /all` because this shows all configuration, not just the IP address and netmask. Here are some other useful command switches for the Windows NT family:

- `ipconfig /all`—Shows all configuration info, not just IP address and netmask. (See Figure 12.4.)
- `ipconfig /release`—Releases DHCP addresses for all adapters (specify an adapter name to avoid all of them).
- `ipconfig /renew`—Renews DHCP addresses for all adapters (specify an adapter name to avoid all of them).
- `ipconfig /flushdns`—Windows 2000 and above only, flushes the local DNS cache. This is extremely useful if you have made a DNS change and need it to propagate to this workstation. (If you don't do this, the change won't show up on your workstation for a while.)
- `ipconfig /displaydns`—Windows 2000 and above only, shows the DNS cache. Useful to see if "what you get" is what the server is actually distributing.

Insanely Useful Basic TCP/IP Diagnostic Commands

If the problem is more thorny than a configuration issue, it can be useful to know the perspective of the problem workstation; that is, what the workstation can see, what it cannot see, and the state of various informational commands as run from that workstation. You can use various informational commands, as listed in Table 12.1, to see the workstation's perspective on the network (these commands apply for both Windows 9x and NT families).

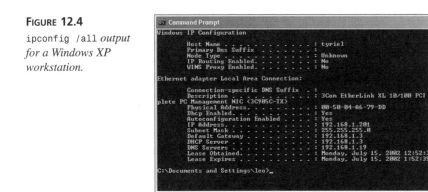

FIGURE 12.4

ipconfig /all *output for a Windows XP workstation.*

TABLE 12.1   Useful Basic TCP/IP Diagnostic Commands

Command	Description
arp -a	Displays the MAC-to-IP address translation table.
netstat -rn	Shows TCP/IP routing table (numerically).
netstat -an	Shows all TCP/IP sockets in use (numerically) for all clients and servers.
ping *hostname* or *address*	Checks basic IP connectivity with *hostname* or *address*.
tracert *hostname* or *address*	Traces the route that a packet takes from the current workstation to *hostname* or *address*. Shows each router that the packet goes through on its way to *hostname* or *address*.

All these commands are more or less lifted from UNIX; rather than redundantly discuss them here redundantly, let me point you to Hour 13, "UNIX and Linux Troubleshooting," for examples of their use in basic TCP/IP troubleshooting. Note that many more command switches exist than are listed here. Remember that the /? usually shows what other switches are available for a given command—play around a bit, and you'll discover some more useful things for your environment.

More Useful Network Diagnostic Commands

Of course, maybe you've already checked basic TCP/IP, and you're pretty certain that the problem doesn't lie here. If the finger is pointing at Windows itself, check out the diagnostic tools in Table 12.2. Some of them (the ones marked with a *) are from the Windows Resource Kit—which I *highly* recommend that you get, if you're doing a lot of Windows troubleshooting. The Resource Kit is not only a source of tools, it is an excellent source of additional Windows knowledge; just don't expect to get through it in 24 hours.

12

TABLE 12.2 More Useful Network Diagnostic Commands

Command	Description
netsh	Interactive command-line utility that allows you to list and change network-layer configuration. (Two hints: First, type **int ip** when you first enter the program; these options are the most useful day-to-day. Second, typing **?** at any time shows available options.)
net session	Shows all Windows networking sessions (shares and so forth) active on this machine.
net share	Lists all Windows shares that are available on this machine.
* service.vbs /L /S monster	Shows status of all Windows services on the "monster" server.
* service.vbs	
* netset /display	Shows a list of network components (that is, network protocols and basic services) that are associated with network interfaces.
* srvinfo //server	Connects to a remote or local server and shows uptime, protocols, network cards, service packs, hotfixes, drive space available, and so on.

Windows Throughput, Resources, and Rescue

Here's where the rubber meets the road: The part in which, if you don't have the necessary resources, or if some bit of configuration fluff gets dinked up, all of the preceding fancy file and printer sharing simply seizes up and stops working.

The first bit of good news is that you can say what you want about Microsoft, but it built some killer statistic-gathering mechanisms into *all* Microsoft Networking server and client programs. This, coupled with System Monitor, enable you as Joe User to see how you're doing in terms of performance at any given time. This means that you can quickly and easily profile a particular server or network segment. This is something that used to take a network expert and a $10,000 piece of equipment to do, but, whoa, you can do this on pretty much any Windows workstation. (Did I mention that I like this feature?)

Throughput Thruway

In all seriousness, the powerful statistics-gathering abilities of Windows really allow you to do some powerful troubleshooting cheaply. Let's look at a two quick examples.

Scenario 1: Suppose we have an application that's running very slowly for a given person. Other folks are running the application just fine, but our confidence level is pretty low concerning how alike each workstation is. We discover that the user can log in to someone else's workstation and work just fine.

Somebody suggests that we nuke the user's hard drive and make it just like a setup that works. This is greeted with stony silence by the user, who happens to be a big shot in the company. Apparently, this is not the path that we will take. At least, not if we want to continue our employment.

The user says that his machine runs like molasses, and he seems right from what we can tell of other people's workstations. What's going on? Is it the client or the server? Is this subjective slowness, or is there an objective way of measuring this?

We could break out the network analyzer to measure the network throughput by attaching it to the network segment and analyzing packets between the client and server. However, because network throughput is easy to measure with the Windows 9x family's System Monitor, we install this to the user's workstation and add the Microsoft Network client's Bytes Read/Second statistic to our chart. Figure 12.5 shows a monitor session; it reveals that the Microsoft file and print session is running reasonably fast on this user's 10Mbps network: 625KB–991KB per second. You can't expect much faster than that on a 10Mbps Ethernet network. But would an upgrade to 100Mbps help? Well, it's an older workstation, and you can tell that it is working hard keeping up (look at the CPU utilization and free memory). Both drop when this file transfer is happening. In this example, we would see normal output like this when running the application on a different server.

We keep the System Monitor minimized and run the problem application. Yes, indeed, it's slow. We're seeing wide-area speeds on a LAN connection. Right away we know that there's truly a speed problem on the network; it has nothing to do with his workstation.

Or does it? We have a different server that runs another department's stuff, so in the spirit of ruling in or ruling out the problem, we decide to do the same measurements on a different server using the same application. In this case, the measurements are more in line with what we're seeing on other workstations on the LAN. It seems that this particular server and this person's workstation are not happy with each other. The five minutes we spent with the System Monitor accomplished a couple of important things:

- This person is not imagining things; we have objective data to prove it.
- We've discovered that the workstation can connect to a different server without the slowdown problem; we now have a workaround while we further diagnose the problem server or workstation.

12

FIGURE **12.5**

A Windows 9x monitor session.

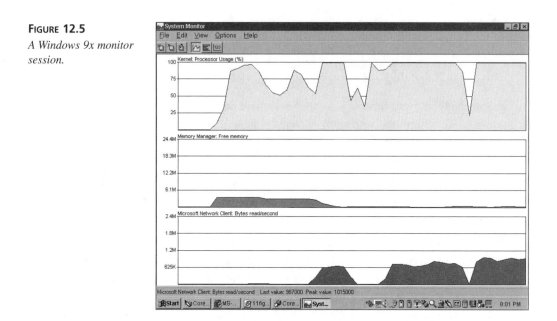

But life isn't always simple. It turns out that the original server is *not* a Microsoft server, it's a UNIX server running Samba—the UNIX/Linux SMB server. Is this the same type of server as the test server we just used? Well, no. So, we do the tests again, this time to a different UNIX server running the same version of Samba. Ah hah! It turns out that this user's workstation seems to have problems talking to this version of Samba. (Others in the department are not having a problem.)

The solution to this problem consisted of (very carefully) reinstalling the Microsoft file and print client to the workstation and repatching the workstation, consistent with other workstations in the department. (Yes, indeed, because we were dealing with a VIP, a backup of his hard drive was done—just in case more problems got caused through this process.) After the application of the client and the service pack, we tested again with the System Monitor. The problem was gone, and the VIP was happy.

Scenario 2: Many, but not all users in a department were complaining about slow application performance. These happened to be users of Windows 2000, so I used the Windows 2000 Control Panel applet (Administrative Tools, Performance) to take some measurements. The first statistic I added was "Redirector—Bytes Received per second," followed by "Redirector—Bytes Transmitted per second." (The *redirector* refers to the client portion of SMB that redirects server resources to look like local resources, such as drive letters.)

Unlike the first scenario, this network was 100Mbps to the desktop, with a very, very fast server at the other end. There was no reason at all for many people to be complaining, so I thought I'd take a look from my office.

The server itself was connected to a SAN, had huge amounts of memory, and so forth, so I became concerned that any file transfers from that server would be limited by *my* hard drive. So, I mapped my "O" drive to the server, identified a very large file to use as a test file, and then dropped to a command prompt and typed:

```
COPY O:BIGFILE NUL:
```

The NUL: parameter allows you to say, "Don't actually copy the file to my hard drive, just throw it in the bit-bucket," enabling you to avoid your hard drive as a limiting factor.

Because BIGFILE was huge (it was a SQL server database backup, and was about 10GB), I had plenty of time to switch over to the Performance applet and view how fast, on average, the file was transferring to my workstation. As Figure 12.6 shows, it was averaging around 6.1 megabytes per second, which was not bad.

FIGURE **12.6**

Reasonable performance on a 100Mbps network.

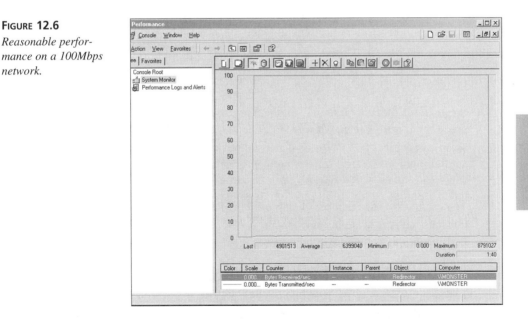

12

I went down to the wire closet used by the folks who were having problems, using the same laptop that I had used in my office, hooked it into the Ethernet port of one of the problem workstations, and ran my tests again.

Whoa! As Figure 12.7 shows, there was quite a difference. We went down from 6.1MB per second to about a third of a megabyte per second. Also, see how the indicator is jerking up and down? There's no steady stream as you might expect.

FIGURE 12.7

Poor performance, given a nominally fast server on a 100Mbps network.

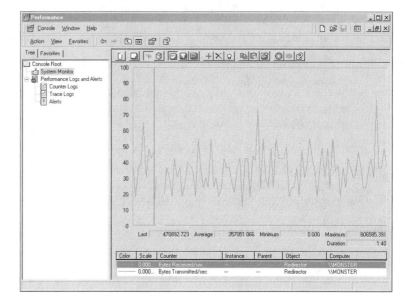

So what was the deal? It turned out that the closet switch hadn't been properly configured for our environment—it was left as default; that is, autosense, instead of explicitly set to half duplex, 100 Mbps. As discussed in Hour 10, "Ethernet and Switching," autosensing can cause all sorts of problems, including this type of throughput problem. But, thanks to the Performance applet, it got tracked down pretty quickly.

You can track a huge number of stats with the Performance applet—tracking redirector transmission speeds are just the beginning. You'll definitely want to get familiar with the Performance applet before trouble strikes.

Process, File, and Registry Tracking

Although you can use the Performance applet to track things like processor utilization, it won't tell you *which* process is using *what proportion* of processor resources. Fear not, though, the Windows NT family does in fact keep track of such things, just like a real operating system.

The simplest way to check out per-process utilization is to bring up the Windows Task Manager (Ctrl+Shift+Esc is a shortcut key for this) and to sort the columns by CPU time—this is the amount of total CPU time used by a process since it started. On a healthy computer, the System Idle Process should be the *highest* number. (One other interesting thing to do is to sort by Mem Usage, letting you know which processes are hogging memory.)

Of course, there are other, more buff ways to track processes. SysInternals (`www. sysinternals.com`) provides one freeware program called Process Explorer, which, put simply, rocks the house. Process Explorer (`ProcExp.Exe`) not only shows various resources used by processes, but it also sports a tree view, showing which processes started which others. It also identifies which files a given process has open, as shown in Figure 12.8. If you've ever been frustrated by `file in use` errors, kiss them goodbye once you download Process Explorer. Sweet!

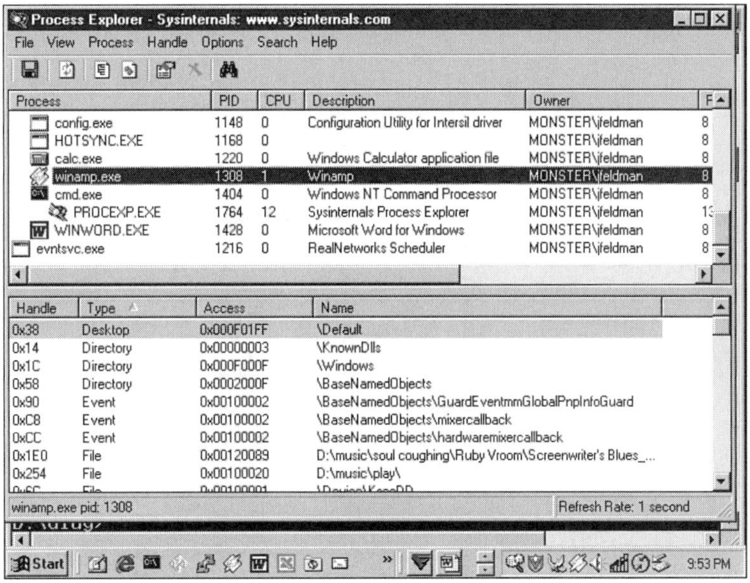

FIGURE 12.8

Process Explorer shows a tree view of the process table, as well as additional process info, notably files open.

Similarly, if you've ever asked, "Which actual process owns that socket pair that I'm seeing in the `netstat -r` output?" check out TCPView. It identifies all currently used socket pairs (UDP and TCP) and maps them to processes. This can be hugely useful; I once saw a bug in a program that kept infinitely opening sockets, and basically created a denial of service (DOS) because it was opening them so fast that other programs couldn't open sockets. It's pretty good to be able to track this sort of thing and kill the offending process rather than reboot and pray.

SysInternals also provides two other tools that no self-respecting system administrator should be without: `FileMon` and `RegMon`. Both utilities work on the Windows 9x and the Windows NT families.

`FileMon`, as it sounds, tracks all file access on a Windows system. Depending on your troubleshooting scenario, this can be a huge help. I can't even count the number of times I've been hit with some weird application error, "can't access file," and I had no idea what file, what error, or what the deal was. By reproducing the error in a small time frame on an otherwise idle system, `FileMon` quickly identified which file this was. Why not use `ProcExp`? Well, `ProcExp` only shows files that are currently open by processes, not open *attempts*.

`FileMon` actually shows failed attempts as well, which is awesome if you are a troubleshooter. (You might not *know* which application file you need to restore from backup, and this tells you.) Figure 12.9 shows `FileMon` tracking a Notepad session that is attempting to load a nonexistent file called `Ouch.txt`. As you can see, `FileMon` fingers both the nature of the error as well as the name of the missing file.

`RegMon` looks and works similarly to `FileMon`, but it deals with the registry instead of the Windows file system. Both tools are extremely powerful for dealing with corruption or security issues.

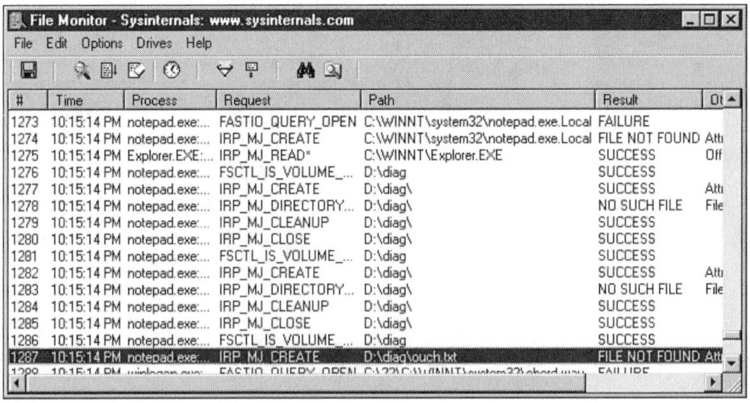

FIGURE **12.9**

`FileMon` *and* `RegMon` *show current activity on the file system and registry, respectively.*

Nonbootable OS Recovery Methods

There are two ways in which you might not be able to access your Windows NT family machine: First, you might not be able to logon; second, you might not be able to boot into the OS at all.

In the good old days, you might boot an operating system diskette, fix the problem on the hard drive, and then reboot the hard drive. Well, there are a couple of problems with that nowadays. First, the Windows NT family doesn't offer a bootable OS diskette. Second, booting to a different operating system (such as DOS) presents a problem: The NTFS (NT File System) isn't readable by DOS, so restoring files that way is a bit of a problem. Besides, you can't exactly make registry tweaks here.

Microsoft has a couple of recovery methods that it recommends. First is the "Last Known Good" boot prompt. This has its uses, but I can tell you from experience that this does not always work. "Last Known Good" means, "restore the registry to the last known good point," where "last known good point" means "after Windows goes graphical." If Windows goes graphical, and *then* you have your problem, you're sort of out of luck.

For example, one time I ran the viewer application for a certain type of remote control package, and it randomly decided to modify my Windows 2000 workstation and install remote control. When I rebooted, I couldn't log in because it was complaining that it couldn't find a certain DLL. Well, sure, I hadn't installed the remote control piece. I tried using "Last Known Good" to no avail. How about the Emergency Recovery Diskette (ERD)? Well, I hadn't updated my workstation's ERD recently, so that was out.

There were a few methods I could have tried, in order, from most annoying and complex to least. First, I could have installed another copy of Windows 2000 in a different directory on the hard drive, and then manually copied the required file to the dead installation. Second, I could have moved my hard drive to another Windows 2000 workstation, and fixed it there. Third, I could have shared my hard drive from another Windows machine, and copied the remote control DLL to the proper place.

Clearly, the third option was, in this case, most preferable. But the first and second would have worked if my workstation was so dinked up that I could not share the drive from another machine. This happens with servers more often than we'd like to think.

If you find yourself doing a lot of recovery work, I'd like to recommend that you invest in some more utilities, produced by the same folks that write the SysInternals ones. They are

- NTFSDOS Professional—Allows you to read and write files from an NTFS hard drive after booting from a DOS diskette.
- Remote Recover—Allows you to read and write from a dead server over the LAN, by providing a LAN boot diskette for the server.

Summary

Windows networking has many similar attributes between versions of Windows. In particular, Windows can be split into two distinct families: Win9x and WinNT based. The various versions of Windows Networking also have many similar attributes: The naming and service location has traditionally been accomplished via NetBIOS, and still is done so on many currently available versions of Windows, but DNS will eventually supplant this. NBTSTAT is the tool of choice for diagnosing NetBIOS issues; nslookup is the tool of choice for dealing with DNS. As with most other networking functions, configuring for broadcasts is a bad idea for all but the very smallest networks.

The process of locating a server via explicit name is different from searching for available servers; the latter process is called browsing. Service location for NetBIOS via a router is accomplishable via WINS, a simple database that registers computers, and allows computers to look others up. WINS has several limitations that seem to be addressed by the future DNS model; great if you're using Win2K and above. Static name resolution using host tables should be reserved for troubleshooting purposes—and you should check for static resolution if name server changes don't seem to propagate.

Three types of authentication are performed on Windows networks: workgroup, NT Domain, and Active Directory. It's worth knowing how Active Directory is structured so that you can identify where potential problems might lie. No matter whether you're deploying AD or coming in after the servers have been switched on, it's a good idea to get familiar with Microsoft's AD design guidelines. One additional wrinkle to AD is that third-party devices can use Active Directory's LDAP capabilities to authenticate, even without a Windows client on board; getting an LDAP browser for troubleshooting purposes is a good idea.

Windows has a plethora of TCP/IP commands at your disposal, with even more Windows-specific commands distributed with the Windows Resource Kits. These have *a lot* of built-in commands and programs for diagnosing and configuring the network; it's worth spending some time investigating them now so that you can use them when problems arise.

The statistic-gathering capability of Windows is immensely valuable to troubleshooters. Throughput is one key element to a well-functioning Windows Network. By using the System Monitor or Performance tool, you can rule in or rule out problems with a workstation, a server, or even infrastructure such as an Ethernet switch.

Real operating systems allow you to keep track of processes, files "handles" and other resources. The Windows NT family is really good at this. With third-party tools, notably those from SysInternals, you can track open files, processes, process correlation to TCP and UDP socket pairs, file access attempts, and even registry activity.

Finally, although the Microsoft-recommended recovery methods work in some cases, sometimes (like when you forget to update your ERD as your system configuration changes) they don't. Apart from third-party tools, booting from an alternative Windows install on your hard drive, moving your hard drive to another PC, or connecting to it via the network (assuming that it gets far enough in the boot sequence to offer file and print services) are all ways that you can attempt to fix your Windows machine if it doesn't boot up right.

Q&A

Q I'm using TCP/IP and networking just fine without WINS. Come again? Why do I need this?

A You're likely in a nonrouted environment or your configuration has been set in stone in the LMHOSTS text files on your hard drive. Hey, if it's working for you, great! Just be aware that if you start to add workstations or add a router (which includes using some types of VPN), you will have to make some decisions.

Q Any other recommendations for counters to track in the Performance applet?

A Sure. Apart from the obvious Processor and Memory counters, the Server set of counters are pretty useful, too, for Bytes Received and Bytes Transmitted. The `PhysicalDisk` set is also useful; `% Idle Time` is a good one to track if you're trying to see how hard users are hitting your server drives.

Q I'd like to learn some more about Windows Services. Any good resource for me?

A You bet! Check out `www.microsoft.com/windows2000/techinfo/howitworks/management/w2kservices.asp`.

12

Workshop

It's workshop time again. Let's do it.

Quiz

1. True or False: NetBIOS is best used with no name servers.

2. NetBIOS is

    a. A protocol for name resolution and file service

    b. A service for file services and service location

    c. A protocol for name resolution and service location

    d. None of the above

3. True or False: WINS is the only naming service available to Windows users.

4. NetBIOS can be transported via _____ and _____.

    a. UDP, TCP

    b. TCP/IP, NetBEUI

    c. TCP/IP, DNS

    d. WINS, DNS

5. The third-party authentication supported by Active Directory is

    a. LDAP

    b. NetBIOS

    c. DNS

    d. WINS

6. True or False: You must use a network analyzer to measure throughput of SMB.

7. True or False: It is possible to access a Windows 2000 Server's hard drive, even when you cannot boot to it.

Answers to Quiz Questions

1. False

2. C

3. False

4. B. NetBIOS can be *transported* via TCP/IP or NetBEUI. Remember, DNS is an alternative to NetBIOS. WINS is a NetBIOS name server.

5. A

6. False

7. True

Activities

1. Use some of the troubleshooting tools outlined in this chapter on your functioning network. A good one to play with is NBTSTAT. Compare its output to the outputs listed in this hour. Are the types consistent with what you would expect? Try `srvinfo` on several of your servers. Are they patched to the same levels? Do they have as much free space as you would like?

2. The time to experiment with recovery tools is now, not when an emergency arises. Plan a fire drill, and either write out what you would do, or actually *do* what you think you might have to do if your server became inaccessible (this is probably preferable) to another, non-production server.

12

HOUR **13**

UNIX and Linux Troubleshooting

Every society honors its live conformists and its dead troublemakers.

—Mignon McLaughlin

When I wrote this chapter for the first edition of this book, back in the stone age of 1998, UNIX varieties were many, and no one UNIX variety seemed to be dominant. Well, that's changed. Linux is perhaps the most successful UNIX ever, with even nongeeks installing it in their homes and offices. The bad news is that Linux, like UNIX before it, also has many flavors. But the good news is, a lot of network innovations have come out of the UNIX melting pot, and we can expect that trend to continue—the Internet itself probably owes its existence to UNIX-based network inventions. Of course, TCP/IP itself grew up on UNIX computers; therefore, many TCP/IP concepts and commands from UNIX are extremely applicable to other operating systems, notably Microsoft's family of Windows operating systems. (Microsoft reportedly lifted the TCP/IP stack source code from FreeBSD, a UNIX variant, to use in Windows 2000.)

Even if you have no UNIX or Linux in your environment, my advice to folks who are newer to networking is to get yourself an older PC—perhaps even a couple—and load one of the free UNIX flavors, such as Linux or FreeBSD. It is amazing what you can learn while you're dabbling with UNIX, and there are no expensive licenses to buy.

This hour does not attempt to teach UNIX to the completely uninitiated, and in fact mostly speaks about UNIX in general rather than the specific varieties such as Linux, FreeBSD, or SunOS. If you're a complete beginner at UNIX, you might want to check out either http://www.ee.surrey.ac.uk/Teaching/Unix/ (a general UNIX tutorial) or http://www.ctssn.com/ (a Linux and UNIX tutorial).

> The various flavors of UNIX handle certain specifics differently, for instance, the way that you refer to your Ethernet card. But overall, the general paradigm is always the same, and many basic commands are the same.

UNIX Functionality Overview

Let's take a 20,000-foot view of how most UNIX servers are configured. Yes, they have the capability to act as file and print "share" servers, just the way Windows servers do, and you can connect your Windows drive letters or printers to a UNIX box. But just as Windows NT has client/server apps (such as SQL Server) in addition to file and print services, so too does UNIX.

File and Print Services

If your UNIX box is running Samba, a freely available software package, your Windows PC can connect just as if your UNIX host was another Windows PC.

However, bear in mind that from a troubleshooting standpoint, Samba on UNIX is *not* the same thing as "native" file and print services on an NT server; when performing "one of these things is not like the other," comparing a UNIX host that supports SMB to windows doesn't work. See Hour 12, "Windows Networking Basics," for more details.

If you don't have Samba on the UNIX end, you are likely using *NFS (Network File Services)* on the UNIX server, and are using a third-party *NFS client* for Windows to be able to map drive letters and use printers. Windows NT, 2K, and XP include Print Services for UNIX, which, like it sounds, only supports printing. (It's available from the Add/Remove Windows Components applet in the Control Panel.)

If you are using third-party software, it's important to understand that the client software is perhaps the first thing to rule out as a problem because it is not native to Windows. (Can other workstations perform the same operation without trouble? What is the version of the client on the troubled workstation?)

If you are using UNIX file and print services, here are some important network ports to know about:

- tcp/515—printer (also called LPD, for Line Printing Daemon)
- udp and tcp/2049—Network File System
- udp and tcp/111—Port Mapper

We'll discuss which server programs use these ports in a little while.

Client/Server

I'll get into client/server a bit more in Hour 20, "In-depth Application Troubleshooting." For now, it's enough to know that client/server is basically a fancy way of saying, "If I ask somebody for the price of a widget, he gives me an answer." (This is unlike file and print, where you would get the entire catalog.) Think of client/server as being question/answer oriented. For example, domain name services (DNSs) are a great example of client/server. When you pull up www.jotto.com, you don't ask your name server for a list of everyone in the .com zone; instead, you ask it for the IP address of www.jotto.com. It responds with 205.134.224.21. It's a very simple transaction. The client asks the questions, and the server provides the answers. If configured to do so, any machine can act as either the client or the server: Basically, it's a matter of running the right software.

Software that runs without user intervention is called a *daemon* (the equivalent in the Microsoft world is a *service*); we'll discuss daemons in a little while.

Configuring UNIX

As with any computer, you network a UNIX computer by sticking a network card into its motherboard, plugging it into a hub, turning the computer on, configuring it, and away you go. That's not so hard, huh? The trick with UNIX is that the only standards that exist are TCP/IP-based standards. There are no UNIX standards for NetBEUI and IPX/SPX; however, these are available through third parties as vendor add-ons (and are beyond the scope of this book).

UNIX servers tend to house mission-critical databases as well as service users via client/server applications. In the past, this has largely been via Telnet, which is a way of

13

running a character-based terminal session on a UNIX computer over the network. (Think of this as "thin client" without graphics.)

Lately, Telnet has been replaced by one of two things: Windows front ends or Web-based front ends. Both of these typically communicate to the host computer via TCP/IP, and because TCP/IP is the dominant network protocol on the planet, this is rarely a problem.

UNIX's chief problem with most people is that it is very command-line based. That is, instead of using pretty graphical user interfaces, administrators usually type in commands for configuration and troubleshooting purposes. If you're a Windows user, think of this as having to use the Command Prompt screen for most administration purposes; instead of using Explorer's Tools, Map Network Drive to map a drive to \\server\ share, you instead type **net use \\server\share**.

The good news, if you're intimidated by a command-line interface (CLI) , is that certain UNIX distributions include graphical front ends for these commands. Many of these graphical front ends are just as user-friendly as their Microsoft Windows counterparts; Red Hat Linux does a good job at this, for example.

The bad news is, just as Windows users are discovering, if you really want to know what's going on (and be able to exert a fine degree of control), the use of the command line is almost unavoidable. It is also almost unchanged between flavors of UNIX. Accordingly, I'm going to talk about command-line network configuration and troubleshooting. Don't let that deter you—think of it as an excuse to brush up on your typing. What's more, once you learn this stuff, much of it works under every flavor of Windows: 95, 98, ME, NT, 2000, and XP—it's just hidden behind the scenes.

We truly do learn by destroying, and I certainly don't expect you to want to experiment with your production UNIX system. That, as they say in *Ghostbusters*, would be *bad*.

Instead, install UNIX on a test system, and do your "learn and destroy" on that system. You'll know when it's safe to work on your production system. (I'm not saying that it's ever truly safe. Even experienced sysadmins make mistakes; but as with everything else in computing, as long as you have good backups, there's not much you can do that's irreversible.)

If you have a UNIX distribution that can be Intel based, such as Linux, FreeBSD, or even Solaris, you're in luck. Creating a test system is as easy as downloading a CD image of the operating system in question, burning the CD, and installing it to a spare PC.

But certain UNIX distributions, such as IBM's AIX or Hewlett-Packard's HP/UX, simply don't exist on Intel platforms (that is, PCs). And, if you're using Sun Microsystem's Solaris, even though Solaris is available for Intel platforms, the OS works somewhat differently. Never fear. Check out ebay.com or other auction sites. You can pick up an old, obsolete UNIX machine for a couple of hundred bucks—and the operating system works the same as it does on your bazillion-dollar production system. I *highly* recommend this. There is nothing like hands-on experience, and I find that when you're familiar with how to install the OS, this reduces the fear factor that can sometimes lead you to make mistakes. The installation of what seems to be a complex operating system will actually be pretty easy, and this will build your confidence.

Some used systems will come with installation media; some won't. Make sure that you ask; the cost of buying a new license for the OS can be high, so you are much better off if it comes with the used machine.

Daemons, at Your Service

First, here's a word about the UNIX way of keeping track of what programs are running.

A production UNIX server typically has a couple hundred programs running at once—particularly because each client that connects to the server usually causes a separate program to fire off (called *forking*) to serve the client. UNIX uses an internal process table that lists process numbers, the name of the processes, and other information.

Again, programs that are not interactive, yet are responsible for services are called daemons. All UNIX services, whether Telnet, HTTP, or FTP, run as daemons.

When looking at a process listing, you can usually figure out which process is a daemon: It has the letter d at the end of its name. When talking about a daemon, you usually pronounce the d at the end, as in *name-dee* for named.

13

Manually Restarting a Daemon

Suppose that a particular service is not running on a given UNIX server; say, for example, that the Web server doesn't seem to be responding. Rather than trying to reboot the server (other services would be interrupted by doing this), you might first investigate whether the Web server process is running and then start it if it's not or stop it and restart it if it is. You usually need to be running as the super user (root) to stop or start processes.

You can cause a great deal of damage when running as the root user; you should use the su (super user) command to temporarily gain root privileges, run your commands, and then exit, rather than logging in as root. Again, you can contribute greatly to your confidence (and competence) level if you install a play system on a PC—either Linux or another flavor.

Because the root prompt (#) is typically different from the normal prompt ($), I show it in the text to indicate commands that I would run as the root user.

Depending on the type of UNIX you're running, you would type one of the following commands to look at the process table:

ps -ef

ps -ax

What's up with the -ef and the -ax? Well, these are flags that indicate to the ps (process status) program that you want to view everything in the process table. They're just different on different systems. So, right away, you need a way to figure out which flag you need to use. Buck up! Most, if not all, UNIX systems have all the manual pages right on the system. The man (check manual pages) command can give you details on most any command you want. For example, to get specific details on what those -ef and -ax flags with the ps command mean, as well as to find out what other flags are available and how to interpret the output you would type this:

man ps

One of the best ways for you to learn UNIX is to use the man pages; to learn how to use the man command, you can type this:

man man

The ps command stands for *process status*. On a busy system, your screen will zoom by with zillions of processes. Fortunately, you can make the display pause, or, even better, search the table for what you're looking for. Suppose you're looking for the Web server, the HTTP (Hypertext Transfer Protocol) daemon, or httpd. You could type this:

ps -ax | grep httpd

You might get nothing back—it probably means that `httpd` has died, and you need to restart it. However, if it's not dead (just merely lost its mind), you might get this:

```
52  ?  S     0:01 /usr/sbin/httpd
```

The first number is the *process ID* (or *PID*). This is the number you refer to when you want to do something to this process. For example, the commands for killing and restarting this process might look something like the following, if you didn't have startup and stop scripts to use. (We'll discuss start and stop scripts in the "Start and Stop Scripts" section.):

```
$ ps -ax | grep httpd
  52  ?  S     0:01 /usr/sbin/httpd
$ su
Password:
# kill 52
# ps -ax | grep httpd
# /usr/sbin/httpd
# exit
$ ps -ef | grep httpd
  871  ?  S     0:01 /usr/sbin/httpd
```

You'll notice here that I don't need to use `su` until I actually kill the process and restart it. Then I immediately exit the su session so that I keep my super user time (and thus risk) at a minimum. I also like to recheck the process table before and after I've restarted the daemon just to make sure it's *not* out there after I kill it or to make sure that it *is* there after I restart it.

inetd: The Daemon Daemon

Should all daemons be there when you check for them? Actually, no. Back in the days when memory was a more valuable resource than it is nowadays, the concept of a receptionist daemon was invented so that daemons not in use weren't loaded into memory. This receptionist is called `inetd` (Internet daemon) and is responsible for listening for connections, telling the caller to hold on, and then waking up the right daemon and transferring the call. Daemons that are invoked this way include `telnetd` (Telnet daemon) and `ftpd` (FTP daemon), among others. You can see which daemons are invoked by `inetd` by viewing the contents of `inetd.conf`, which look something like this:

```
# If you make changes to this file, either reboot your machine or send
# the inetd a HUP signal:
# Do a "ps x" as root and look up the pid of inetd. Then do a
# "kill -HUP <pid of inetd>".
# The inetd will re-read this file whenever it gets that signal.
# Echo, discard, daytime, and chargen are used primarily for testing.
```

13

```
# Format is:
# <service_name> <sock_type> <proto> <flags> <user> <server_path> <args>
echo     stream tcp   nowait  root    internal
echo     dgram  udp   wait    root    internal
discard  stream tcp   nowait  root    internal
discard  dgram  udp   wait    root    internal
daytime  stream tcp   nowait  root    internal
daytime  dgram  udp   wait    root    internal
chargen  stream tcp   nowait  root    internal
chargen  dgram  udp   wait    root    internal
ftp      stream tcp   nowait  root    /usr/sbin/tcpd  /usr/sbin/wu.ftpd -a
telnet   stream tcp   nowait  root    /usr/sbin/tcpd  /usr/sbin/in.telnetd
```

You can start and stop inetd by using the kill commands outlined earlier. This tends to be a bigger deal than just killing one daemon because inetd acts as a receptionist for many services; it's best to use kill -HUP PID to make inetd reread its configuration first.

> Some distributions (Red Hat Linux in particular) have started to use xinetd instead of inetd. See the man page on xinetd for details; xinetd is configured somewhat differently, but the main idea is the same.

Start and Stop Scripts

Usually, systems that use SVR4 (pronounced ess vee are four, short for System V, Release 4) standards, such as UNIXWare or Red Hat Linux, will have these types of startup and stop scripts. These systems usually also allow you to use restart in place of stop or start.

> It's probably worth mentioning a shortcut that Red Hat Linux has, the service command, which basically invokes the startup or shutdown script for the given service, so typing
>
> # **service smb restart**
>
> is the equivalent of typing
>
> # **/etc/init.d/smb restart**
>
> This is a keystroke saver, if you like. Just be aware that it doesn't work with other UNIXs.

If your system is based more on the University of Berkeley revision of UNIX (*BSD*, or *Berkley Standard Distribution*), as is the case with AIX or Slackware Linux, everything will have a command that starts the daemon up somewhere in a file called /etc/rc. *something*, and a similar command that stops the daemon in another rc file, but you won't have fine control over starts and stops. These rc files usually have a *bunch* of daemons bundled together in one script. Bummer!

Common Services and the Daemons That Love Them

Following are some common services, listing the daemons that make them run, as well as some daemon-handling tips.

BIND (named)

Certain really important daemons run on their own, namely the DNS naming daemon (named), also sometimes known as in.named. You can stop and restart these in the same way as with httpd, earlier, without worrying about what other services might be affected.

The named process is part of a package called BIND (Berkeley Internet Name Daemon), which has several major revisions that are still in use. I still see version 4 out there, even though there's no support for it. (Some vendors have integrated it into their OS offering and haven't bothered updating it.) Version 4 is configured *very* differently from versions 8 and 9. Here's a quick reference of the major versions and some ways that they are dealt with differently.

Version	Config File	Control Method	Config Syntax
4	/etc/named.boot	kill	Free form
8 & 9	/etc/named.conf	rndc	C-language style

DNS is a complex beast, and is a hugely important piece of your infrastructure. We'll delve deeper in Hour 19, "Internet and Intranet Troubleshooting: TCP/IP at Work."

For the moment, though, from an OS perspective, here are some simple BIND trouble-shooting tips. If named is running but doesn't give out the right information even after a restart, you might want to check to make certain the named configuration files are okay. (You can always restore from a known good backup.) Check the main configuration file (see the preceding table) to find out where its database files live, and then check that those are okay, too.

13

You'll notice that the configuration syntax for BIND 8 and 9 is C-language style. What this means to you is that it's really, really easy to leave off a semicolon at the end of a statement—meaning that it's really easy to fat finger a BIND 8 or 9 file. Check your semicolons!

Again, see the man page for more information than you ever wanted to know about named.

NFS (`biod`, `mountd`, `nfsd`) and RPC Lookup (`portmapper`)

Not every service runs on a single daemon. NFS (Network File System, the file and print service for UNIX), for example, does not. It runs different daemons for different tasks—`biod`, `nfsd`, `mountd`—and relies on the RPC lookup service, which is provided by another daemon called `portmapper`. If you're lucky enough to use a system that has per-service startup scripts, you might be able to restart NFS by typing the following:

```
# cd /etc/init.d
# ./nfs stop
# ./nfs start
```

But note that the RPC `lookup` service, and its daemon, `portmapper`, is actually a *different* service than NFS. You might have to restart *it* as well.

You already know that certain programs use specific port numbers (HTTP uses TCP/80, for instance). But *RPC (Remote Procedure Call)* programs don't have fixed port numbers. These programs use *symbolic* service names; the ports can be different on every server machine. How do these programs figure out which UDP or TCP port their server lives on? Easy—they just ask the RPC lookup service, implemented in UNIX as the `portmapper`. Think of it as per-service name lookup.

Don't forget to check configuration files if you're troubleshooting file sharing!

You can check out who's allowed to use a given NFS (the equivalent of a share under Windows NT) by looking at the `/etc/exports` file. If you add or change access in this file, you'll need to run the `exportfs -a` command.

NFS hostnames in the `exports` file should also be listed in the `/etc/hosts` file or in your DNS zone (for example, `company.com`), or some NFS implementations won't allow them to connect.

Samba (`smbd`, `nmbd`)

When using Samba (SMB, or Windows compatible) file sharing, check the `/etc/samba/smb.conf` file for possible problems.

I frequently see new Samba users run into encryption problems. Basically, UNIX encryption isn't compatible with Windows encryption, so you have a couple of choices as to how to approach this. Your choices, in order of most preferable to least preferable, are either to have your Samba server join the NT domain, to maintain a separate Windows-style user database on the Samba server, or to turn off encryption altogether on both the Windows workstations and the Samba server. For more information on Samba encryption problems, see `http://de.samba.org/samba/ftp/docs/textdocs/WinNT.txt`.

You might also want to see the Samba documentation at `http://www.samba.org/samba/docs`. "Troubleshooting Techniques" from *Sams Teach Yourself Samba in 24 Hours* is available at `http://www.samba.org/samba/ftp/docs/Samba24Hc13.pdf`. Cool!

Error Checking

There are definitely times to quickly restart something and check *why* later, but sometimes, restarting services doesn't work quite as well as you might like. For example, say that the `httpd` is running out of memory and crashing badly. Restarting it doesn't do *anything* about the memory problem! You'll restart it, and be back where you started.

In such situations, you definitely want to check the logs.

Log Files

The logs typically reside in `/var/log` and subdirectories, but some flavors of UNIX have the logs in `/usr/adm`. Naturally, you want to check the most specific log and move on to the most general. For example, if I were having trouble with the `httpd`, I would check the `httpd` logs. Some distributions keep these in `/var/www/log`, but you might find them in `/var/log/httpd`.

At any rate, I would first check the date stamp on the log. If it's date stamped as of three days ago, forget it. You want today's log. Sometimes, when daemons have problems, they become unable to log. Next, I'd do a `tail` command on the log, which shows the last few lines of a file. For example, to see the last 100 lines, I'd type

```
# tail -100 /var/log/httpd/error.log
```

13

If there were no obvious problems (like, uh, "httpd can't allocate memory!"), I'd move on to the system logs. Those are typically kept in /var/log/messages, and /var/log/syslog. (Don't be alarmed if one or the other is missing on your system; it just means that the implementer decided to use one versus the other.)

System Logging: syslogd

The system logging service is known as syslog for short, and has a daemon associated with it, syslogd. syslogd listens for other daemon's messages and dutifully writes them out to disk. This is both a blessing and a curse: If your daemons are configured to write their messages to syslog, you only have one place to look. But then you also have to wade through syslog and look for messages that pertain to the daemon in question. You can do this pretty easily, though. For example, if I were looking for messages pertaining to the socks daemon, I might type

```
# tail -200 /var/log/syslog | grep sock
```

Be aware that syslog only records events that it has been told to record. Check out the man page for syslogd as well as the configuration file, /etc/syslog.conf.

Ports, Sockets, and Netstat, Oh My

When you've restarted a daemon, checked the log files, and nothing seems to be working, you'll need finer diagnostics. A good place to start is by checking the ports and socket pairs on your UNIX server.

Enter **netstat -a**. This command is to network sockets what ps is to processes. You'll remember from Hour 1, "Understanding Networking: The Telephone Analogy," that a listening socket means that a service is listening at a certain extension (*port*) for calls.

The netstat command can list each socket that's being used for a current connection or being listened to for a connection. It tells you whether things are backlogged, where they are backlogged from, and which socket is in use on both sides of the call. netstat -an allows you to look at the numeric values only, which is valuable when you want to keep name services out of the picture. Let's look at a specific example.

Suppose that someone calls and tells you he can't get into FROTZ. FROTZ is the Financial Remuneration with Overwhelming Trillions of Zeros system. This system is very important to your place of employment, Frobozzco, so you're alarmed when *anyone* can't get in. The user at the other end of the line is incoherent with rage and will not answer any of your questions.

You know by this person's name that he's in the Finance department. You can't get an answer to the basic question "Are other people having problems?" Therefore, you decide to find out for yourself. You quickly check the network map and see that Finance lives on the subnet `200.1.1.0`. In order to determine for yourself whether anybody else is having problems, you log into the FROTZ UNIX host and type the following:

```
netstat -a | grep 200.1.1
```

You're rewarded with this:

```
Proto send-q recv-q Local Address        Foreign Address    (State)
tcp   0      0      frotz.frob.com.telnet 200.1.1.10.1673   ESTABLISHED
tcp   0      0      frotz.frob.com.telnet 200.1.1.25.1975   ESTABLISHED
tcp   0      0      frotz.frob.com.telnet 200.1.1.27.1772   ESTABLISHED
tcp   0      0      frotz.frob.com.telnet 200.1.1.29.1968   ESTABLISHED
tcp   0      0      frotz.frob.com.telnet 200.1.1.33.1492   ESTABLISHED
tcp   0      0      frotz.frob.com.telnet 200.1.1.34.1444   ESTABLISHED
tcp   0      0      frotz.frob.com.telnet 200.1.1.35.2855   ESTABLISHED
```

I've included the column headings for clarity; you wouldn't actually get them when searching for an address. It becomes apparent very quickly that people from the `200.1.1` network *are* in, and they're working just fine: The ESTABLISHED socket status is what tells you this.

You now know that people from `200.1.1.0` are logged into the system, and you suspect that the user's problem is workstation related.

> The who command shows all users who have explicitly logged in, and many folks might use it to figure out who is logged in from what IP address. This would be fine to do if you were dealing with an interactive login service like Telnet, Rlogin, SSH, or an X Window session; that is, a session that runs a UNIX shell (the equivalent to a DOS command prompt).
>
> But, if you are dealing with a service that doesn't allow or require an explicit login, you'll still want to know how many sessions there are, and where they're coming from.
>
> That's where netstat comes in: It shows you *any* service, not just ones that deal with interactive login.

13

proto is the network-layer protocol. In most cases, it's tcp or udp, TCP being the equivalent of a phone call (circuit oriented) and UDP being the equivalent of tossing notes back and forth to each other (connectionless). You can find more on UDP in Hour 19.

send-q and recv-q are representations of holding places for sending and receiving data in the host's memory. You can think of them just the way you do a print queue; they hold stuff while waiting for processing. Unlike a print queue, they usually are *empty* during normal operation. That is, these values are typically 0 for local area networks because local networks move pretty fast.

What if they're not 0? Well, a changing send queue can mean that the other end is processing data but is keeping up somehow. This is usually a normal state for a LAN print server; it really is a print queue, so it processes some data, and then catches up, gets some more data, and keeps going. If you see a nonchanging, nonzero send queue for one socket but not others, it usually means that something on the other end has stopped accepting data.

A nonzero receive queue can mean that something on the UNIX host itself is running out of resources, and it's temporarily unable to process the incoming data. In practice, this is relatively rare.

The local address is, of course, the server you're typing `netstat` on. In this case, because we're discussing the Telnet service, the full address with extension is `wefrotz.frobozz.com.telnet`. Had we used `netstat -an`, it would have shown something like `192.168.55.10.23` (Telnet being port 23).

The foreign address is the other address—the client machine. The port number of the foreign end of the socket doesn't matter as much here—just about any high-numbered port number that isn't already in use can be used on the client side.

> You can count the number of client/server sockets in use at any given time, say, for the SSH (secure shell—the secure equivalent of Telnet) server, simply by knowing that the SSH service runs on TCP/22. Because you know this, you can search the `netstat -an` listing for a `:22`, and then do a line count on the number of matches—which tells you how many connections there are:
>
> `netstat -an | grep :22 | wc -l`

> You can find out which services your UNIX machine is offering to the world by typing this:
>
> `netstat -a | grep LISTEN`
>
> The output shows you which services are listening for new connections. Because the service names are usually close to or exactly the same as the program names (HTTP service/httpd program), you can easily figure out which program is responsible for a given service.

See Hour 20 for more information on tracking application problems.

The Name Game: Name Service Problems

Without name services, very little works because most clients are configured with symbolic names (www.quizro.com) rather than numerics (192.168.1.1). From a client perspective, it's usually pretty easy to rule out name server problems: You simply try to use the service using the IP address rather than the symbolic name. But from a *server* perspective, it's a bit trickier.

> When name services fail on a *server,* it's important to realize that existing connections continue to work; it's only the new ones that will typically fail.

A UNIX host typically performs a name lookup to whatever its name resolution host is *after* the connection is established in order to get the symbolic identity of the caller. Therefore, if name services have a problem, this can cause a domino effect that causes problems for other services.

The Hidden DNS Problem

I see a lot of problems in the field that are DNS related, even though some of them don't seem to be at first. For example, after a name server dies on a given UNIX host, Telnet sessions to that host can take a *long* time to show a login prompt. That is, even though the connection is accepted, and the netstat -an output *shows* there's a connection, *something* prevents the login prompt from being issued.

That something is the DNS server. The Telnet server is configured to look up all connecting Telnet addresses after they connect; although the name server is dead, the Telnet service keeps trying before it issues a login prompt. Depending on the operating system and Telnet implementation, this can result in long delays.

> When the Telnet service itself (or the xinetd) is dead, your connection is dropped. (And, your workstation's netstat -an shows *no* connection to that server.) If the Telnet service is up and running on the host, you *will* see an ESTABLISHED connection in the netstat -an. You just won't see the usual login prompt from your Telnet client.
>
> The same tip can apply to the sshd (Secure Shell Daemon), depending on whether it is configured to do DNS lookups after a connect. If all you see is a blank screen and a cursor upon connecting, and you don't see a login

13

> prompt until anywhere from 30 seconds to a couple of minutes later, *check the server's DNS!* For other services without a login prompt that seem to be "hanging" upon connect, just check `netstat -an` to see whether you have an ESTABLISHED connection to the server.

nslookup

The tool for checking name services is called `nslookup`. As the name implies, it can contact a name server (hence the *ns* in `nslookup`) and look up information from it. If you know your UNIX host is running `named` and should be answering name queries from itself and others, you can type this:

`nslookup hostname hostname`

You should get a response. If you get an error message, the `named` that runs on *hostname* is likely down.

> You can use `nslookup` on any UNIX host, not just the one that you're logged into.

There's also an interactive mode that's most helpful for resolving complex DNS issues. I'll go into this feature in Hour 19.

Physical and Network Driver Problems

Sometimes a UNIX networking problem won't be in the higher-level services and programs—in other words, there will be times when it's not the people behind the telephone, but rather the telephone or phone system itself. In order to make this determination, you can use a couple of techniques and commands.

> Think your server's locked up? Well, when *nothing* seems to be working from the network (that is, you can't Telnet or SSH into the server), you might have to find the UNIX console (the actual keyboard and monitor that is connected to the server itself) and log in from there. If the console isn't responsive, the UNIX server has locked up. That's pretty unlikely, however, and usually recoverable in some sort of graceful manner. Powering down is usually a bad thing, and can cause file system damage—but if it's your only option, you've got to grin and bear it.

Before hitting the power button, do your homework and figure out what the NMI (nonmaskable interrupt) key sequence is. For Intel CPU-based UNIX, this is Ctrl+Alt+Delete. Some Sun SPARC stations use Stop+A; and Sequent machines use Ctrl+P. Some UNIX servers have a button named Soft Reset on the server itself. In any case, check out your documentation. Pressing Ctrl+Alt+Delete on Linux will reboot the server; pressing Stop+A on Sun will put you into the BIOS monitor, where you can initiate a restart if you need to. Again, see your documentation for more details.

Assuming that the console is working, it's time to roll up your sleeves and see why your UNIX server can't be seen from the network. Let's work from the inside out, assuming that, like Dr. Freud, all analysis begins with the self. The basic notion here is that you need a network card to get to anything. Let's check that first:

```
# ifconfig -a
lo          Link encap:Local Loopback
            inet addr:127.0.0.1  Bcast:127.255.255.255  Mask:255.0.0.0
            UP BROADCAST LOOPBACK RUNNING  MTU:2000  Metric:1
            RX packets:0 errors:0 dropped:0 overruns:0
            TX packets:37231 errors:0 dropped:0 overruns:0

eth0        Link encap:10Mbps Ethernet  HWaddr 00:00:C0:82:26:94
            inet addr:167.195.160.6  Bcast:167.195.160.255  Mask:255.255.255.0
            UP BROADCAST RUNNING MULTICAST  MTU:1500  Metric:1
            RX packets:816928 errors:0 dropped:0 overruns:0
            TX packets:654019 errors:0 dropped:0 overruns:0
            Interrupt:10 Base address:0x350 Memory:c8000-cc000
```

The key things to look for are the words up and running. If you don't see them, something has caused your network card to go down. Some network cards go down because of a bad port on a hub, so try switching the port. A reboot might be in order to rule out a bad network card or corrupt driver. You can also try netstat -i to check the error count, or run ethstat to see what types of errors you might be getting. This might point to a network or a driver problem. Remember, the driver is what "perceives" the network, so a high error count can mean that the driver is at fault just as much as it can mean that the physical network is at fault.

Don't *assume* that a high error count is indicative of a current problem. Most networks experience some sort of errors on a regular basis. If you have a 24×7 server that has been up for 30 days and is showing 1,500 errors, don't forget that this error count is for the last 720 hours. That's an error rate of about 2 errors per hour: It's no big deal.

13

You want to see if the error rate is *climbing*. It's the *rate* that matters, not the total error number. So, if you do a netstat -i and get 1,500 errors, and then do it twice again in the next minute, and get counts of 1,580 and 1,720 errors, you likely do have a problem. What does this buy you? Well, at least you know that there is a problem somewhere between the UNIX driver and the switch. Maybe it's not the driver; maybe it's not the switch, but it is *something* that is part of the chain of driver–card–cable–switch port. By seeing this type of error climb, you have *ruled in* this component chain.

The next thing you need to find out is whether your machine can talk to itself. Try pinging it:

```
$ ping 127.0.0.1
PING 127.0.0.1 (127.0.0.1): 56 data bytes
64 bytes from 127.0.0.1: icmp_seq=0 ttl=255 time=8.5 ms
64 bytes from 127.0.0.1: icmp_seq=1 ttl=255 time=6.8 ms
<CONTROL-C>
-127.0.0.1 ping statistics-
2 packets transmitted, 2 packets received, 0% packet loss
round-trip min/avg/max = 6.8/7.6/8.5 ms
```

Pay careful attention to that address: 127.0.0.1 is the *loopback address*, meaning that the TCP/IP driver hooks into itself to try to talk. (See Hour 17, "Where Do You Start?," for more on TCP/IP's loopback address.)

If you can't ping it, you have something really odd going on. Again, a reboot might be in order. This is a *software* loopback, so a problem here does not point to hardware.

 The loopback address is a way for you to get your UNIX system to talk to its own TCP/IP programs rather than using the network card to communicate. When you successfully communicate through the loopback, you rule out the TCP/IP program (stack) as the cause of your trouble.

Next, try pinging your own network card. If, for example, your server's TCP/IP number is 192.168.99.5, try this:

```
$ ping 192.168.99.5
```

The output from this should look similar to the output for the loopback ping.

If this works out okay, try pinging the router. If that doesn't work, make sure you can see other workstations on the segment. Can they see the router? The router might be down, leading people on all other segments to assume that the UNIX host is down.

If you are running the `routed` or `gated` daemons, a software malfunction or network error can affect your connectivity greatly because both of these daemons affect the UNIX kernel's *routing table*. (See Hour 15, "Home and Office Routers," for more details on routing tables. Hour 15 also discusses `netstat -r`, which shows you which route the UNIX host *thinks* packets should take through the network.)

If you suspect router problems, you'll want to be familiar with the `traceroute` command, also discussed in Hour 15. The `traceroute` command is a great way to find the routers that a packet needs to go through in order to get from point A to point B. Not all implementations of UNIX have it, though. Most do, but there are still one or two proprietary implementations of UNIX that do not. However, you can always get it from `ftp://ftp.ee.lbl.gov/traceroute.tar.Z`. You'll need to be reasonably comfortable with the UNIX command line to use this because it comes in source code form—it requires you to use the `tar` command to extract the source code and the `make` command to compile it.

Process Tracing

No discussion of UNIX problems would be complete without mentioning process tracing. In a nutshell, because (by nature) the operating system *is* notified about system requests that a process makes, one can use tools that will trace this process. This can be highly tedious work, but if you approach it smartly, it can be quite rewarding.

For example, I was once the system administrator for an obscure UNIX database system, which was written by some folks who weren't too concerned with security. They recommended that all files be "world readable and writable." Naturally, I wasn't too keen on that and, after debate, we generated a list of what permissions were appropriate for the users versus administrators.

Some weeks later, there was a significant problem with one report; it was bombing out with no clear error message. The programmers, in their test environment, had no problem whatsoever. But in my environment, we did have a problem. The programmers kept telling our users that it was "a UNIX problem," in classic blamestorming style. Well, sure!

I did a process trace on the program, generated a log, and voila—the process trace indicated a `permission denied` error on a file write system call. The programmers had

forgotten to handle that condition (because they really weren't too concerned with security in the first place), so their program bombed when it happened rather than giving a
reasonable error message about *which* file and *what* had happened. Thanks to the process
trace, I had that information in hand, and was able to work around the problem until it
got fixed.

The process trace tool that you use will depend on which UNIX you use. Here's what's
available; you can see the man page for particulars on each.

- truss—Older UNIXes, mainly SCO UNIXware
- trace—AIX
- strace—SVR4, Sun, Linux
- tusc—HP/UX

Don't know which one is available on *your* system? Try doing a man on each until you
hit pay dirt.

Generic process trace tools can generate a truckload of output, so don't use them lightly,
and try to capture discrete events rather than an entire session. For example, if the problem happens after the user presses Enter at the report screen, don't capture the entire
process up to the Enter—instead, start tracing right *before* the user presses Enter, and
stop tracing as soon as the problem occurs.

One nongeneric trace tool is the lsof (List Open Files) tool, which generates very simple
and highly searchable output. It is a tool that indicates which process owns which open
files *and* network sockets. That is, although netstat can show you *which* sockets are
open, it cannot tell you which processes *own* those open sockets. Stick that one in your
tool belt. It will be useful one day; trust me on this.

An example that comes to mind is when one system administrator was trying out some
new print software on a production system. All of a sudden, after a reboot, nobody could
print to that host. The sys admin on duty had no idea what was going on until he saw that
the standard printer daemon was not running, yet the printer socket was open (tcp/515).
He did an lsof that correlated tcp/515 with the name of the running process, killed it,
ran the normal daemon, got back running, and dealt with the rest later.

Summary

UNIX hosts are typically reliable servers used to house databases, client/server applications, and Telnet/SSH sessions. They're also awesome for running Web services in
general.

UNIX services run through background programs called daemons. Some service problems can be solved by stopping and starting a daemon process. Others will require an examination of logs or configuration files to figure out what's wrong.

You'll often need to run commands as the root user. To get comfortable and become good at this, you'll probably want to set up a test system, where you're able to learn from your mistakes without affecting a crucial system.

You can keep track of the services and clients running on your system through the `netstat` command. A busy UNIX system can have hundreds or thousands of sockets open at any given time; you can track down the socket you're looking for by using `netstat` in conjunction with the `grep` command. If you need to, you can track down the process corresponding to the socket by using the `lsof` command.

Ping is your best friend (as usual with TCP/IP troubleshooting) in determining whether a problem lies with the UNIX server, the network, or the router.

Process tracing can be tedious, but rewarding when you have nowhere else to turn.

If *NDS (Novell Directory Services)* or Novell eDirectory is in use at your organization, you won't want to skip the next hour, "NDS and NetWare Troubleshooting." See ya there!

Q&A

Q I can't get to a file on my G: drive (it's mapped to my UNIX server's /home file system), but the person next to me can. When I log in as her, I can get to the file. What's up with this?

A UNIX security and file permissions is a reasonably large topic, and I touch on it in Hour 18, "Managing Change: Establishing Consistency and Standards." To answer your question, though, it's likely that the file or directory belongs to a group that you do not belong to. Look at the group on the file using `ls  -la` and add yourself to that group.

Q We've recently gotten a new Internet service provider, and all of our IP numbers have changed. Now, everytime I boot my UNIX system, I get "NFS Server Belboz not responding." What's going on?

A It's likely that the Belboz system is only listed in the `/etc/hosts` file of the UNIX system. View the file, and you'll likely see that the TCP/IP number is wrong; change it to the new number.

13

Q   **Can I use `syslogd` remotely?**

A   Well, sure! Glad you asked. In fact, you can centralize all of your UNIX error reporting through one `syslogd` on one host. Make sure that this is a bulletproof host, though, unless you feel like losing your error reports. Also, there are many network appliances (CD servers, print servers, firewalls, and so on) that can generate output to `syslog`—which is cool because these appliances only have a certain amount of physical memory, and no hard drives, so the days of losing error reports because of power failure or firmware freak out are over!

Workshop

Wah-hoo! It's Workshop time! Here's a brief quiz to help you make the most out of this hour's lesson.

Quiz

1. True or false: Root access is needed to use all networking commands in UNIX.

2. What does NFS stand for?

     a. Network File Server

     b. Nothing Falls Slowly

     c. Network Failure System

     d. Network File System

3. True or false: `named` does *not* use `inetd` as a receptionist server; `named` runs on its own, all the time, and is not invoked each time a user asks for it.

4. True or false: Linux is the only available free or low-cost UNIX flavor.

5. A daemon is a process that

     a. Interacts with the end user

     b. Runs in hell

     c. Runs in the background without user intervention

     d. Interacts with other processes in the foreground

6. It's most desirable to _____ when you encounter a problem with a UNIX service.

     a. Start and stop a process

     b. Reboot

     c. Call the police

     d. Ping

Answers to Quiz Questions

1. False
2. D
3. True
4. False
5. C
6. A

Activities

1. If you've never used UNIX or Linux before, grab a Linux distribution (www. redhat.com or www.suse.com are good choices) and install it to a spare computer.

2. Check out the `strace` command on your new Linux box. To keep things simple, let's follow the error you would get if a file was unavailable to an application. Type

   ```
   strace -f -o /tmp/strace.log cat blahblah
   ```

   where `blahblah` is a nonexistent file. You should get an error message on the screen saying `no such file or directory`. Now look at the output of `/tmp/strace.log`. Scroll to the end and see how the system call returns with an error.

13

HOUR **14**

NDS and NetWare Troubleshooting

> Life consists not in holding good cards but in playing those you
> hold well.
>
> —Josh Billings

Novell, at one point, had everything a networking company could ask for:
market share, good product, and a receptive audience. It literally owned the
entire networking map and was considered the only game in town for serious file and print networking. Obviously, it lost a major battle with
Microsoft some years ago, and Windows 2000 now owns this market.

So why is Novell still in business? And why am I devoting an hour to NDS
and Netware? Well, Novell's NDS is in use for millions of users all over the
world. It's one key reason why many large organizations are still running
Novell products; there's no really good multi-platform alternative. That is,
most importantly, NDS is available for UNIX platforms (whereas the
Microsoft equivalent, Active Directory, isn't). Of course, if you don't run
any Novell products, skip this hour. But if you use NDS on Linux, Solaris,

or Windows 2000, or whether you simply use NetWare as a file and print platform, stick around.

Still here? OK. Let's get started.

Networking with NDS

NDS has changed quite a bit over the last couple of years; its latest incarnation is called eDirectory. eDirectory can live on multiple flavors of UNIX (Linux and Solaris), as well as Windows 2000, although Novell still recommends its NetWare operating system as the best platform for it.

Great. So it can run on a lot of server platforms, making troubleshooting more complicated. How wonderful. But let's cut to the chase; while bearing in mind that the platform might always be an issue, let's first dive into what NDS does.

NDS Fundamentals

NDS is a network-available catalog that enables you to have all your server, user, login, security, and configuration information on a distributed, partitioned, hierarchical database. This makes for one-stop shopping when you're configuring the network.

Whoa! What's this distributed, partitioned, hierarchical stuff? This sounds like a marketing phrase. Well, it is, but it's also pretty cool. In a nutshell, NDS enables you to manage more users and servers with fewer people—which is pretty attractive to management. It also allows you to have greater fault tolerance for the information that you manage.

NDS is *hierarchical* because it has multiple levels on which information can be stored. This keeps each level uncluttered and makes things simple for you. Naturally, simplicity makes troubleshooting easier.

Old versions of DOS didn't let you create folders; all your files used to be just sort of plopped in one location on a disk. Can you imagine if you could only save your Office documents to one place? Doesn't that seem crazy? This probably gives you a sense of how important a hierarchy is to a network directory.

The downside to a hierarchical directory is that usernames now have multiple parts to them. They still have a name (referred to as the *common name*), but there's also an identifier for where this user fits in to the hierarchical *tree*.

For example, `Quizro.finance.ny.frob` refers to the user Quizro, who works in the Finance department of the New York office of Frobozz Magical Gadgets, Inc. You can think of this as an Internet address without the @ sign; it's just taken for granted that the first portion is the user's name.

The NDS is *distributed* because several copies of the database live on multiple servers, making it impossible to lose the entire database if one server suffers a hard drive crash. (All copies of a given database are called a *replica ring*.) For example, DHCP information can be stored in NDS—making it practically impossible to lose DHCP lease information when an individual server goes down.

Finally, the NDS is *partitioned* because different levels of the hierarchy can be treated separately. This means that the database can have several different segments, not all of which need to be updated all the time. Partitioning your NDS database allows you to cut down on network traffic; if you have 10,000 users, of which only 1,000 at a time are geographically close to each other, why would you want to exchange the entire 10,000 user database when you update it?

Even more importantly, partitioning lets you have a large, connected database without tying up your wide area traffic. Let's say that you run an importing company with offices in New York and Savannah. You have a leased line between these offices that connects the office networks together. Because you pay for the amount of time used or data sent, you're interested in using the line as little as possible. You're also interested in keeping the pipeline clear so that people who are trying to communicate between the offices do so as quickly as possible.

You would want to create a partition between the Savannah site and the New York site because this tells NDS that the Savannah and New York databases should be treated as separate *distribution* entities. Because they're not joined at the hip, the frequent replication traffic that occurs between the distributed NDS servers will not clog up the pipe between New York and Savannah.

If you are using NetWare or UNIX as your NDS platform, you configure it using a text-based console, similar to what you used to see under DOS. These servers aren't busy fiddling with graphics, windows, and the overhead that goes with those things. This lack of complexity and overhead makes for a reasonably easy-to-troubleshoot server that runs faster on less hardware.

Although the server runs in character mode, you'll use the Novell utilities for managing the NDS in a GUI environment; for example, the Java-based ConsoleOne tool runs on

14

UNIX as well as Windows. This tool gets used by the working network administrator to add, delete, and modify users, groups, security, and so on. Although this tool is windowed, it doesn't bog down the server because the windowing happens at your workstation.

> If you have a NetWare 4.*x* server (or lower, perhaps?), bear in mind that it is no longer supported by Novell. Upgrade to NetWare 5 or 6. It's not that painful, and there are a lot of reliability and network administration enhancements.

> The NetWare bindery (a per-server flat username and password directory) became obsolete with NetWare 4.*x* and higher, but NetWare servers still support a *bindery emulation mode*, which makes a NetWare 4.*x* server respond to NetWare 3.*x*–style bindery requests. If you don't need it, disable it by typing **set bindery context**=. This sounds good on paper, but beware: this might cause old style tools (for example, backups or older email servers such as GroupWise 5.2) to break.
>
> How can you tell if an application is configured to use a bindery-based username? Well, if it's just a plain username, such as wrockett, it's likely a bindery-based username. If it's a qualified username, such as wrockett.ranger.spaceforces.federation, it's definitely an NDS username.

Before we dive in to troubleshooting specifics for NDS, here's one final general note. Remember at all times that what a server says about the NDS is *that server's* perspective about the NDS. One common NDS error is a "-625" error. You'll always receive this when a server is unplugged from the network. But here's the thing: If you unplug the *Spiderman* server (or if its switch port or NIC fails), all servers on the network will report "-625" for the Spiderman server. If the Spiderman server is still on, it will report "-625" about all the other servers (see Figure 14.1). Who's right? Well, sure: It's the majority of the other servers. Spiderman's got the problem—he needs to get plugged back in, or whatever.

Got it? So, it's all about perspective. Keep that in mind, and you'll be okay. In general, do not take *any* action based on what *one* server says. NDS is a distributed beastie, and you need to treat it accordingly.

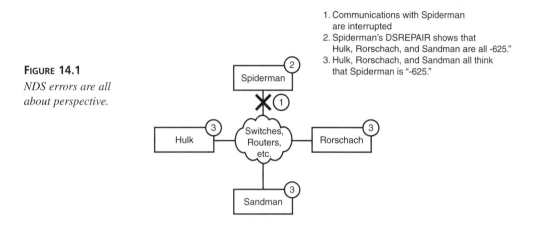

FIGURE 14.1

NDS errors are all about perspective.

1. Communications with Spiderman are interrupted
2. Spiderman's DSREPAIR shows that Hulk, Rorschach, and Sandman are all -625."
3. Hulk, Rorschach, and Sandman all think that Spiderman is "-625."

TCP/IP and NDS

TCP/IP is the preferred network protocol for NDS. As a matter of fact, the IPX/SPX network protocol is *only* supported on NetWare (can you say dinosaur), so, if you have a multiplatform environment, TCP/IP is where it's at.

Some quick TCP/IP notes are in order before we launch into repair techniques. The two most important IP services that NDS uses are *NCP (Novell Core Protocol)* and *SLP (Service Location Protocol)*. The SLP enables clients and servers to find each other, even on a routed network; the NCP is what allows them to perform transactions. (NCP is also used for file and print services.)

Some important points are as follows:

- NCP uses TCP/524.

- NDS SLP runs in one of two ways: point-to-point or multicast, unless you specify point-to-point SLP. By default, the multicast address for SLP is 224.0.1.35.

- If your servers aren't talking, you've ruled out physical problems (such as cable), and multicast is in use, check your router logs for potential explanations of the problem. (You might need to tweak up your log level; see Hour 15, "Home and Office Routers," for more information.)

- If static SLP is in use, make sure that you can access TCP/427 on the server in question. UDP/427 is also used, which is useful to know if you are doing a network trace, as we'll discuss in Hour 21, "Protocol Analyzers."

14

For more NDS troubleshooting information, search Novell's knowledge base. In particular, there is a good SLP troubleshooting document at `http://support.novell.com/cgi-bin/search/searchtid.cgi?/10060296.htm`.

Health Checks

Novell will tell you that regular NDS health checks are essential. Well, sure. But simply saying "health checks" is just like saying "eat right": it's pretty vague. So, here are the most important basic things to check on an ongoing basis. Use the DSREPAIR utility (`ndsrepair` on UNIX), and run it on the server that is Master of your [Root] partition.

- Time synchronization (should report + or - a couple of seconds on all servers)
- Report synchronization status (partition synchronization should show `all servers synchronized up to time`, where `time` should be within a few minutes of now.
- External references (should be zero)

If the time is not reported as synchronized, nothing will work properly. NDS needs time synchronization to work properly. On each member server of a partition, check to see whether TIMESYNC "thinks" that time is synchronized to the network. If it doesn't, the problem is likely with that server. Check to see whether other network services are functioning right; also, check TIMESYNC configuration. On NetWare, use MONITOR.NLM, Server Parameters, Time; on UNIX, use `ndsrepair -T`.

Novell has a pretty good whitepaper detailing various health checks you should run; check it out at
`http://developer.novell.com/research/appnotes/2001/may/03/a010503.pdf`.

Of course, even if you run regular health checks, there are times when the NDS—like every other database on the planet—gets messed up, because of communications problems, bad software, or other issues, and you'll have to repair it.

Some DSTRACE and DSREPAIR Tricks

DSREPAIR (`ndsrepair` under UNIX) is your friend. It will likely fix most of the problems that you run into. A user can't log in, and changing her password doesn't work? Use DSREPAIR. You can't install a new server into the tree? Use DSREPAIR. You get the idea.

Here's the thing, though. Don't run a full, unattended repair unless you must. It will do everything under the sun on that server, including scanning the entire file system on all volumes. If this isn't what you want, you are setting yourself up for a long and tedious wait for no purpose.

Instead, use Repair Local DS Database as an initial starting point. (Unless, of course, you have a more targeted purpose in mind.) Many times, this is pretty quick, and as soon as the *local* database is repaired satisfactorily, it is then propagated out to the other servers in the replica ring.

DSTRACE can also be your friend. It has about a bazillion options, but here are some pretty cool ones that I've found particularly useful over years of NDS troubleshooting. (For more than you ever wanted to know, see `developer.novell.com/ndk/doc/ndslib/dsov_enu/data/hujirj2n.html`.)

General Debugging

It's good to see what kinds of NDS error conditions exist on a given server; use the following DSTRACE options to start logging, based on which operating system you're using:

- `set dstrace=on` —Starts logging messages to the screen, but these messages will scroll off the screen. (NetWare)
- `set ttf=on`—Writes messages to the file `SYS:SYSTEM\DSTRACE.DGB`. (NetWare)
- `set ndstrace=on`—Turns on logging to the file `/var/nds/DSTRACE.LOG`. (UNIX)

Synchronization

Does the log show an object that refuses to synchronize or other sync error? A good way to force the server to sync with other servers is to use the following flags with DSTRACE:

- `set dstrace=+s` —Schedules the skulker, which means override the normal sync process and check all objects to make sure that they're current.
- `set dstrace=*u`—Resets the server communications status list. This forces the server's status to "up."
- `set dstrace=*h`—Forces the "heartbeat" process. It's much like the +s flag, except this exchanges time stamps between servers.

Schema

The schema of a directory is much like the field structure or data dictionary of a traditional database. If you're having schema issues or getting schema errors, you might want to try the following DSTRACE flags, in order:

- `set dstrace=+schema`—Starts showing schema messages in the trace.
- `set dstrace=*ssd`—Resets this server's schema target list, basically implying that this server will sync with all servers.
- `set dstrace=*ssa`—Tells the server to schedule a schema sync immediately.

14

Stuck Obituaries

An obituary refers to an old object reference from a different partition that won't go away. Obits normally stick around for a little while (less than an hour) when an object is deleted, and then go away. If there are communication problems, sometimes the obits won't go away. And if they don't go away, sometimes other NDS operations will fail or produce errors. Check `http://developer.novell.com/research/sections/ netmanage/dirprimer/2002/April/p020401.pdf` for more details than you ever wanted to have on stuck obituary problems. In the meantime, here are two useful DSTRACE flags:

- `set dstrace=+j`—Tells the server to start logging the janitor process, which deals with obits.
- `set dstrace=*f`—Schedules the flat cleaner process to start in five seconds on this server.

If your obits don't go away in a reasonable amount of time, you might need to call support. Or, one method that seems to have worked pretty well over the years is this: *Change* the master of the replica ring. Back in Figure 14.1, for example, if Spiderman *was* the master, and Sandman had a Read/Write copy of the replica, change the master to Sandman. (You can do this in DSREPAIR under advanced options.) Wait a while, and I'll bet that your stuck obits are gone.

The NetWare OS

Any Novell server is fundamentally a 32-bit program called SERVER.EXE that runs from a DOS prompt. (Yep, just like Windows 3.*x* runs from a DOS prompt.) This means that you still have an AUTOEXEC.BAT file on your C drive—it typically consists of one line: SERVER.EXE. This server program actually doesn't do much; for example, it can't network on its own or access hard drives. When you load the SERVER.EXE program, the server console screen opens. This screen, shown in Figure 14.2, is a text-based interpreter that can accept various commands.

NLMs and Java

In addition to accepting commands, the server program acts as a traffic cop for all the server resources, and it relies on loadable modules to provide specific services. In general, these modules are referred to as *NLMs*, short for *NetWare loadable modules*. NLMs provide everything from a statistic reporting program (MONITOR.NLM) to configuration programs (INSTALL.NLM); in addition, NLMs enable the server to speak certain protocols (TCPIP.NLM).

FIGURE **14.2**
TCP/IP-based RCONJ
or IPX/SPX-based
RCONSOLE (or
Remote Console)
allows you to remotely
control the server con-
sole from your desk.

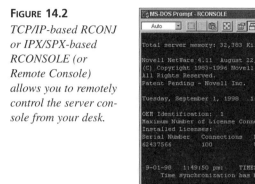

Special cases of NLMs include disk drivers (for example, IDE.HAM), and network card drivers (for example, NE2000.LAN). All these modules act in concert through SERVER.EXE to make your server talk to the network and respond appropriately to requests. Yikes! There are a lot of pieces and parts. A typical NetWare server has dozens of NLMs loaded at one time. When everything works, it's great.

Java has entered the picture with NetWare for certain non-system functions. The *JVM (Java Virtual Machine)*, which executes as JAVA.NLM, is in charge of all Java processes. You can show what processes are running by typing

`java -show`

You can kill a Java process by typing

`java -kill id`

where *id* is the process number listed by the java -show command.

NetWare Patches

One of the challenges presented to a NetWare troubleshooter is keeping track of all these NLMs and identifying any trouble presented by a malfunctioning NLM. This was really terrible in the past; you had to download many different files to fully "patch" your server. Nowadays, you can simply get the latest service pack from Novell (taking a cue from Microsoft, which has always offered one-stop shopping for fixes). Keep up with those service packs!

Just as Microsoft does for Windows NT, Novell considers certain problems serious enough to issue hot-fix patches (patches that are supplied to the user population before

14

the next service pack is issued). Although not all patches apply for all environments, you might find you need to patch the server in order to fix a certain problem.

> Any time you experience problems with your Novell server, check out the Novell Knowledge Base at http://support.novell.com. In addition to using it to search for your current problem, you can also use it to check out the minimum patch list. This can be a great first step in troubleshooting because you can easily verify that you have all the patches in the minimum patch list loaded on your server.

As a matter of fact, even if you have Novell's Premium Support, the first thing the support staff has you do is make sure that you've applied the latest and greatest patches. Many, many problems are patch related.

> Patches can fix, but patches can also destroy. You shouldn't get *too* paranoid, though, because the entire industry has come a long, long way toward making the patch process as safe as possible. For example, the patch process now keeps backups of your previous files. Nonetheless, for your own sanity, make sure that you have good, verified backups of your servers before applying any patches. (This applies to *all* patches, not just Novell patches.)

Third-Party NLMs

What about the NLMs that Novell doesn't provide? In other words, what about third-party NLMs? Examples of these include backup software, network card drivers, software metering programs, and server-level virus protection programs. If you're the type of person who doesn't go for nitpicky record keeping, keeping track of these revision levels will be a nightmare for you. This is particularly true if you have multiple servers in the mix and have multiple folks working on these servers; you never know if someone has updated one server but not the other.

Accordingly, when you're having problems with one server but not another, you must play the *Sesame Street* game and compare NLM levels. You can do this manually by typing **modules** at the server console prompt (see Figure 14.3).

If this seems like a lot of work to do manually, you're right! Go download (free) the CONFIG.NLM tool (along with the Config Reader) from Novell's site: http://support.novell.com/tools-files.html.

FIGURE 14.3

Getting a list of modules from a NetWare server.

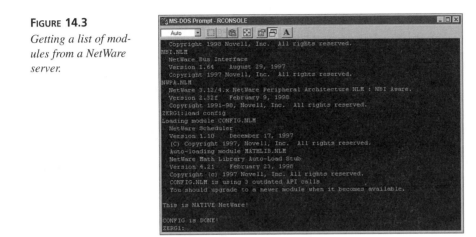

CONFIG.NLM reads the configuration of your server and writes a CONFIG.TXT report to your SYS:SYSTEM directory. The Windows-based Config Reader will read the output that CONFIG.NLM drops off in the system directory and process it to make it easy to read.

The Config Reader, shown in Figure 14.4, automatically downloads current information from the Novell Web site and then shows you an overview of your system, points out NLMs that are out of date, and automates the comparison of two given servers. This makes it much easier for you to see how one server differs from another.

FIGURE 14.4

The Windows-based Config Reader makes it easy to find out "which of these things are not like the other."

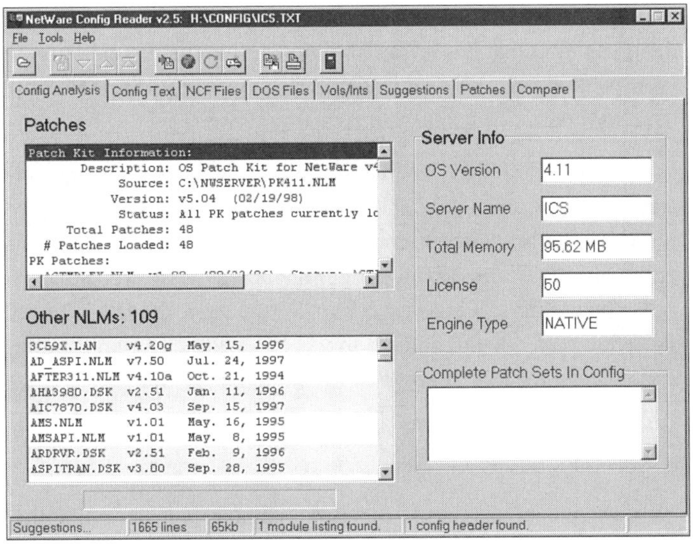

14

Premium support customers can download OnSite, a tool that makes comparisons of multiple servers *really* easy; there's no CONFIG.NLM required. OnSite also does a bunch of other stuff, so if you're a premium customer, go for it (see Figure 14.5).

FIGURE 14.5

OnSite Pro allows you to execute commands, compare server configurations, and monitor resources—all remotely.

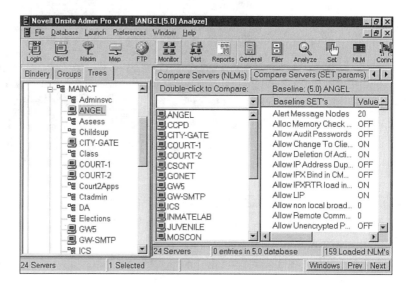

Your "Friend," the ABEND

If you've run Novell products for any length of time, you know how aggravating it can be to get an ABEND. An *ABEND*, short for *abnormal end*, is when the server can't handle a situation that has arisen and must terminate its operation because data might get corrupted otherwise. It's a difficult call—would you rather continue working and risk data corruption, or would you rather be down?

What causes an ABEND? In a nutshell, hardware problems and software problems cause ABENDs. It's understandable that a bad CPU or bad memory could take down the entire server—after all, without good memory or a working CPU, it's sort of hard to run programs. But why should one program (such as your Web server program, for example) cause the entire server to go down? Fortunately, the latest Novell server software has started to make distinctions as to what constitutes a major problem versus a minor one, and you can pick and choose between policies. (In MONITOR.NLM, use Server Parameters, Error Handling.)

Novell classifies applications in two different ways:

- Applications that use the same memory and so on that the server program uses (dangerous, but fast).

- Applications that use a special protected mode in which the amount of damage they can do to the server itself if they misbehave is minimized (slower, but safer). (Think of this as the rock climber who climbs bare-handed—and quickly—versus the rock climber using pitons, who is slower but safer.)

Novell calls the latter way "running a program in a different domain," but whatever it's called, it's a lot more reliable, and it's automatic in the latest releases. I don't know of anyone who will complain because the server runs two percent slower because of its increased reliability.

Monitoring System Resources with MONITOR.NLM

As much as I love the Microsoft System Monitor, I have room in my heart for Novell Monitor as well. Even though it's text based (it's not graphical at all), Novell Monitor is rather complete and can be a troubleshooter's best friend, particularly if you don't have Premium Support, and thus access to OnSite Pro (which does some of the same things, remotely and graphically). You simply type

```
LOAD MONITOR
```

at the console prompt, use the menus, and the world is at your fingertips.

Just about every resource on a Novell server is tracked by the Monitor, and this is a good thing. Here are some really good things the Monitor monitors:

- Server connections and session statistics
- File locks (who's using the file?)
- Hardware resources (CPU, memory)
- Processes (subprograms)

Out of Connections

Suppose a user reports that she can't get into the server. Once you've established that others are working with the server, you might try to get in yourself and discover you cannot. A quick check of the Monitor screen using the Connections option reveals how many connections are in use—you might see that you're out of server connections.

Each user who is logged in to the server uses one server license. If you run out of connections, you'll most likely have to purchase more licenses from Novell.

Using the User Connection List

When the server runs out of disk space, you can walk through Monitor's user connection list and see who has been using a lot of disk space lately; the results look something like those shown in Figure 14.6.

14

FIGURE 14.6

You can use Monitor to view connection information.

In this case, you can see that the evil user JFeldman has written 1,128KB (or 1.12MB) in the one minute he's been logged in. He might not be your culprit, though—1MB usually doesn't overflow a server volume. You should look through the other connections for something more like 5–10MB or more. Also notice the network address: JFeldman's logged in from network 1D, MAC address 00-00-f6-88-d9-4b, and port 404C.

After you find the offending user, you get a quick confession. For other ways of finding disk space wasters, see Hour 20, "In-Depth Application Troubleshooting."

File, File, Who's Got the File?

Sometimes, you might not be able to install software because a shared file is in use. Getting this message is really frustrating because all Windows will tell you is that you can't write to the file, not who is preventing you from writing to it.

You can find who's using the file by using the Monitor. Simply go to File Open, Lock Activity menu in the first Monitor menu and then select the file you're interested in. The Monitor will show you the connection numbers of the people who are using the file (see Figure 14.7). You can then navigate the connection list and find out the login names of those people; once you know who the people are, you can kindly ask them to get out of the program for the moment—or sever their connection (by typing **DEL**), if you can't get through to them.

FIGURE **14.7**

The Monitor can show you who currently has a file "locked."

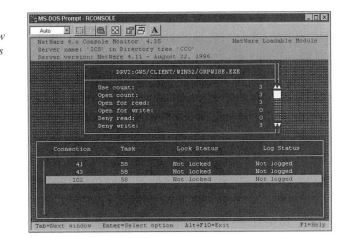

MONITOR.NLM Scenario: Monitor Man Is Here!

Monitor has saved my hide more than once. One time, the network administrator and I were completely stumped by what seemed to be a backup program problem. The backup program, which ran as an NLM, needed to log in to the NDS to do its work. Every week or so, the backup program would complain about being unable to log in, and we would reboot the server to enable the backup program to log in again.

The backup software people pointed the finger at Novell: "It's an NDS problem," they said. "There must be something wrong with your NDS; it's nothing to do with our software." Searches on the backup vendor's site as well as Novell's site revealed nothing; fortunately, when we called Novell, they concurred that it certainly sounded like an NDS issue. We pursued this for a while without getting anywhere.

Then, eureka! During one early-morning session of vain attempts to make the backup software behave before we rebooted, an early-rising user who had left his PC on the night before experienced workstation problems; when he tried to log back in, he couldn't. We checked the Monitor, and sure enough, we were running out of connections. Was this a coincidence? Could have been. The next time the backup problem occurred, we checked the number of connections on the server, and sure enough, we were running out each time.

Why hadn't we noticed this earlier? Normally, users were already logged in and working before the backup started acting up that evening. If the backup was acting up, it kept doing so until we got in at 7:00 in the morning, before most folks tried to log in. That meant it was rebooted before others could notice the lack of connections.

14

We licensed more connections, but even then we kept running out of connections. What was going on?

By looking at the Monitor's connection list, we discovered that all the extra connections were coming from the server itself. Remember from Figure 14.6 that a connection display shows the IPX address of the connection station. In this case, the extra connections were coming from the server's unique internal IPX number (see the later section "IPX/SPX"). This definitely pointed to an NLM.

> This situation would have been awful to troubleshoot without the Monitor. For example, it would have been very difficult to divide and conquer this problem because it was an intermittent problem and we needed all of our NLMs loaded during the workday. We could not arbitrarily run without given NLMs.

Because of the Monitor's close tracking of such things, we were able to find a resource called Service Connections and check each NLM's number of connections (see Figure 14.8). The one with the abnormally large value was our culprit. (How do you find the largest value? Sort the list by pressing F3 and choose Number in Use.) After we unloaded this module (which happened to be Novell supplied), all the extra connections went away, and the problem was solved.

FIGURE **14.8**

The module that was grabbing all of our licensed connections couldn't hide from the Monitor.

```
MS-DOS Prompt - RCONSOLE                                              _ □ ×
Auto        ▼  ▢   ▣  ▣ ☞▤ A
NetWare 4.x Console Monitor  4.35                    NetWare Loadable Module
Server name: 'ICS' in Directory tree 'CCO'
Server version: NetWare 4.11 - August 22, 1996
┌───────────────────────── Server Memory Statistics ─────────────────────────┐
│                                                                             │
│     Allocated memory pool (bytes):           22,745,088    23%              │
│     Cache buffers (bytes):                   50,610,176    51%              │
│     Cache movable memory (bytes):             6,365,184     6%              │
│     Cache non-movable memory (bytes):           565,248     1%              │
│     Code and data memory (bytes):            19,685,376    19%              │
│     Total server work memory (bytes):        99,971,072   100%              │
│                                                                             │
└─────────────────────────────────────────────────────────────────────────┘
┌───────────────────────── Resource Information ─────────────────────────────┐
│                                                                             │
│     Tag:        Service Connections                                         │
│     Module:     Unix->NetWare LPR Print SERVER                              │
│     Resource:   Service Connections                                         │
│     In use:     248                                                         │
│                                                                             │
└─────────────────────────────────────────────────────────────────────────┘
Esc=Previous list   Tab=Next window   Alt+F10=Exit                  F1=Help
```

We reported this to Novell. Although Novell already knew about the problem, the patch had not yet made it in to the mainstream. Once we did a search on the NLM's name, we found that there was a TID on this problem. Unfortunately, because we weren't really clear on what exactly was going on while we were searching, we didn't get a hit on this. The problem was quickly solved after we applied the patch. Three cheers for the Monitor!

Protocol Problems

If you're the one who installed your server, you're probably already familiar with the INETCFG NLM, which I call the Swiss Army Knife of Novell networking. This NLM, similar to the Windows Network Control Panel, loads network drivers and binds and configures protocols to them. You can use it to quickly glance at the way things are configured.

Alternatively, you can simply type **CONFIG** at the console prompt (*not* LOAD CONFIG; that's the configuration file generator). INETCFG tells you the way things *should* be, whereas CONFIG shows you the way things *are* (see Figure 14.9).

FIGURE **14.9**

The CONFIG output of a server that has one network card and one network protocol (IPX/SPX).

If CONFIG doesn't match up with INETCFG, you might have a problem. You can sometimes resolve this by telling the server to enact a networking "do over." Simply type the following:

```
REINITIALIZE SYSTEM
```

As scary as this command seems, all it does is reload network card drivers, if necessary, and bind protocols to those cards. It's really fast—so fast that I've run it on a test server, and my session didn't get dumped. However, I sure wouldn't try it on a live production server.

14

IPX/SPX

Although IPX/SPX is considered totally obsolete by many, it's still in use in a bunch of shops.

Each IPX/SPX segment needs a network number. This is not a big deal; you can select pretty much any hexadecimal number that is unique at your organization. The network number is a layer 3 concept; each VLAN must have a unique IPX net number. If it's not unique, you can run into problems, such as the inability for the servers and workstations to "see" each other.

NetWare is just full of unique prima donnas; there's another number, particular to each server, called the server's *internal IPX network number*. This number must also be unique, and it can be really useful in tracking down problems. (As you saw in the MON-ITOR.NLM scenario when I tracked down the extra connections to the server itself.) This number is hexadecimal; if it's the same as another server's number, it, too, can cause big problems (particularly if a server is acting as a router). In that case, duplicate internal IPX numbers will cause routing to stop working.

Even if your server has *no* IPX/SPX on it, Novell still generates a Unique Server ID, used in NDS communications.

If you don't know what a particular server's unique number is or what the network number is on the attached networks, just type **CONFIG**. I almost don't want to tell you about IPXCON.NLM, but I will: `IPXCON.NLM` is a diagnostic tool that can be quite helpful in diagnosing IPX/SPX problems. Just LOAD `IPXCON.NLM`—it comes with every NetWare server, and is menu driven and fairly easy to use. Although it is cool and can help you track down problems, you really should ditch IPX/SPX if you are having problems, and use TCP/IP instead. It is *much* better supported.

TCP/IP

You'll configure TCP/IP the way you do any protocol: from `INETCFG.NLM`. The basic configuration is just the way you'd configure a workstation. You do have, however, a couple more things to configure on a server, most notably the *services* that the server offers. To do this, use the UNICON utility. You can use UNICON to check the service configurations, as well as to start and stop the services if you suspect they've gone to la-la land. As you can see from Figure 14.10, UNICON will configure the following items:

- DNS (UDP and TCP/53)
- NIS (You probably won't need this unless you're a hard-core Solaris UNIX shop.)
- UNIX-style (LPD) print services (TCP/515)
- FTP (TCP/21)

FIGURE **14.10**

UNICON will config-ure UNIX-like services on your NetWare server.

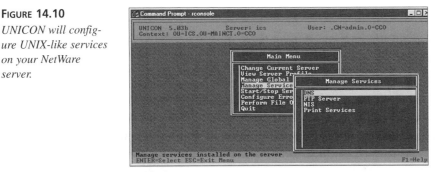

See the UNI in UNICON? Think it might be referring to UNIX? You're right! All these services, though ostensibly generic TCP/IP services, got their start in the UNIX world.

You can also check TCP/IP configuration files (or possibly restore the configurations from a backup tape) in the SYS:ETC directory.

In particular, the SYS:ETC/RESOLV.CFG is a really important configuration file—symbolic name lookup. (DNS won't work unless this is configured properly.)

The TCP/IP Console

When you load TCPCON, you can check more TCP/IP–related statistics and functions than you'd ever want to. TCPCON can handle many functions, as shown in Table 14.1.

TABLE 14.1 TCP/IP Functions Available from TCPCON

Function	TCPCON Navigation
Check TCP/IP statistics and error counts	Statistics menu
Check the routing table	IP routing table
Check current TCP or UDP socket table (just like netstat -a in UNIX or Windows)	Protocol Information, TCP *or* UDP, Connections
Check the MAC-to-TCP/IP address table (just like arp -a in UNIX or Windows)	Protocol Information, IP, IP Address Translations

Other lifesaving TCP/IP tools include these:

- **LOAD PING**   Standard ping (but you can ping multiple stations at a time)
- **LOAD IPTRACE**   Novell's answer to traceroute

14

Summary

Novell NDS is one compelling reason shops haven't totally abandoned Novell. NDS is a multiplatform directory services solution that millions of users still use. The two TCP/IP services that are essential to NDS are SLP (TCP and UDP/427) and NCP (TCP/524). IPX/SPX is obsolete and bad, but people still use it anyway. If you want the best possible NDS support, use TCP/IP.

NDS health checks should be regularly performed, but when trouble strikes, DSREPAIR and DSTRACE are both valuable tools to overcome NDS problems. Both have various options that help to address specific problems, such as sync problems, schema problems, or stuck obituaries, to name the most common.

NetWare servers run a DOS .EXE that bootstraps the operating system. The system is then run using various NLMs that operate as drivers as well as application programs. The modularity of the system means that one malfunctioning NLM can ruin your whole day, but fortunately, Java is also available as a console platform.

The Monitor can help you with tough troubleshooting jobs because it keeps track of every resource available to the server. In addition to keeping track of server connections, it keeps track of memory and CPU resources, as well as what each NLM process uses.

Both TCP/IP and IPX/SPX are configurable through INETCFG.NLM. TCP/IP applications can be configured through UNICON, and many statistics and internal tables can be viewed through the TCPCON. What's more, Novell includes standard tools such as PING and IPTRACE (traceroute) in its TCP/IP distribution.

Q&A

Q How is NDS (Novell Directory Services) related to DNS (Internet naming)?

A You might wish you hadn't asked that. If you are using a *federated* tree, NDS and DNS are *integrated*, that is, the DNS domain (like mycompany.com) is integrated with the NDS tree name (mycompany.com.dns). (See http://www.novell.com/ documentation/lg/dirxml10/index.html?taoenu/data/a6hhzgg.html for more info.)

But even if you have a non-federated tree (not explicitly integrated with DNS), DNS *can* be used to specify the addresses of servers that handle your NDS tree, even if you don't have SLP implemented. You do this by specifying your tree name in your DNS. For example, if you wanted "mytree" to be handled by two servers, you'd add two DNS records for "mytree.company.com" and make them hand out the IP addresses of two servers that had replicas of that tree. See `http://support.novell.com/cgi-bin/search/searchtid.cgi?/10014570.htm` for more details.

Ow! If this makes your head hurt, skip it. If you find out later that you need to know about this, come back. It'll still be here.

Q Why doesn't Novell just get rid of the concept of ABENDs?

A Every operating system, whether it's UNIX (kernel panics) or Windows (the Blue Screen of Death), has unrecoverable errors. It's just the nature of the beast. Nobody wants an operating system to keep running after the foundation has been undermined. The thought is it's much better to reboot than to have to restore all the lost data because of the server not showing the good judgment to stop playing with the data.

You should definitely upgrade to Java-based applications if you can; Java rarely causes an ABEND. However, things like drivers (TCPIP.NLM, IDE.HAM) will always be "metal-level" programs, and you can't avoid potential ABENDS—except by being *very* cautious about upgrades and patches.

Q My friend who runs a Novell server says that sometimes when he tries to unload an NLM, the console prompt never comes back. Isn't there any way to recover from this?

A I'm glad you asked. Indeed, there is a way. While standing at the console (this won't work remotely) press Ctrl+Alt+ESC. One of the options will read Spawn Alternate Console.

I will warn you that when the console starts to act funny, other nastiness is on the way. You should probably use the alternative console screen to reboot this server ASAP.

If you can't spawn an alternative console screen, you can press the keyboard sequence Ctrl+Alt+Esc at the console, and you'll probably see the following prompt:

```
Down server and exit to DOS?
```

That might be your only way out if things are really ugly.

Workshop

Workshop time! Here's a brief quiz to help you make the most out of this hour's lesson, and some activities for you to try on your own.

14

Quiz

1. What does *hierarchical* mean?

    a. Having hieroglyphic translation of ancient computer records

    b. Having multiple levels

    c. Having the ability to recover from errors

    d. Having multiple segments of a database

2. The preferred network protocol for NDS is

    a. TCP/IP

    b. IPX/SPX

    c. AppleTalk

    d. DNS

3. You can often repair the NDS by using _____ and _____.

    a. DSTRACE, NCP

    b. DSREPAIR, DSTRACE

    c. VREPAIR, NCP

    d. SLP, DSREPAIR

4. A distributed database can _____.

    a. Live on multiple servers

    b. Make a set of information more available

    c. Neither A nor B

    d. Both A and B

5. True or False: Partitioning of a large network database makes it more manageable.

6. The main NetWare server program is called what?

    a. `SERVER.COM`

    b. `SERVER.EXE`

    c. `SERVER.NLM`

    d. `SERVER.LAN`

7. When you experience trouble with your NetWare server, it's a good idea to check what?

    a. The hard disk

    b. The LAN card

    c. Patch levels

    d. Critical NLM BIOS

8. IPX/SPX servers each need a unique _____.

    a. Internal network number

    b. Internet network number

    c. Internet nucleus number

    d. Internal nucleus number

9. The TCP/IP protocol and basic services can be configured from

_____.

    a. TCPCON

    b. INETCFG

    c. UNICON and TCPCON

    d. INETCFG and UNICON

Answers to Quiz Questions

1. B

2. A

3. B

4. D

5. True

6. B

7. C

8. A

9. D

14

Activities

1. *Before* you need to, experiment with the various ways that you can repair the NDS. Use DSREPAIR and DSTRACE.

2. *Before* you need to, experiment with the various keyboard sequences on a NetWare server that is *not in production*! If you need to do these on a server that is in trouble, fine—but you should not do these just for fun on a server that is okay.

   Try Ctrl+Alt+Esc. Try Ctrl+Shift+Esc. And finally, try getting into the NetWare debugger by holding down *both* shift keys with the Shift+Shift+Alt+Esc key sequence. Definitely check out the following URL, which details one way of recovering from an ABEND by using the debugger to isolate the offending application: `http://support.novell.com/cgi-bin/search/searchtid.cgi?/1202963.htm`. This trick actually does work about half the time, in my experience.

HOUR **15**

Home and Office Routers

Every journey begins with a single step.

—Ralph Waldo Emerson

All routers are made to perform one basic task: to give network data a "single step" assist in its path from point A to point B. Everything else is window dressing. So, the good news is that, fundamentally, routers are simple. They *should* be simple to troubleshoot, right?

The bad news is that routers have a lot of options, different configuration methods, and bunches of theory behind them.

To make life easier on you, this hour aims to give you

- A sense of the difference between switches and routers
- Information about the troubleshooting difference between big beefy routers found in datacenters and their smaller cousins found in small offices and homes
- Some practical routing theory that will come in handy in a pinch
- Some practical tips about configuring routers

Routers Versus Switches

"Turn on the wayback machine, Sherman." Remember Hour 2, "The OSI Model of Networking: Understanding the Old School," where we discussed the difference between OSI layers? Sure; OSI layer 1 is physical, layer 2 is data link, layer 3 is network, and so on. The reason I bring this up is because the fundamental difference between a router and a switch is which OSI layer they operate on. (See Hour 10, "Ethernet and Switching," if you want a refresher on exactly what a switch does.)

That is, a switch is a *data link* device—it is specific to the type of interface device that is being used (for example, Ethernet or FDDI), and deals with MAC addresses and frames as the most complex form of addressing (00:02:50:50:82:a5). A router is a *network* device. It doesn't necessarily care about what type of interface cards are being used; it cares about things like TCP/IP addresses and packets (192.168.55.209).

The devil, as they say, is in the details.

By definition, *both* routers and switches are referred to as being *multihomed*—that is, they have more than one network interface connected to more than one datalink or network domain. You can think of this as routers and switches having more than one place they call home.

All modern servers—whether NT, UNIX, or NetWare—can be configured to be simple and cheap routers. Of course, they need to be multihomed in order to be connected to more than one network.

I have been known to swap out routers to rule out hardware router-related issues. If I suspect that a network problem might be router related, it's a lot cheaper to temporarily put in a PC with Linux on it *acting* as a router than it is to purchase a new $10,000 router just to rule out a router problem. See http://www.linuxrouter.org for an easy way to use a PC plus a boot disk as a router.

In reality, although routers and switches are spoken about in different breaths, many large switches have routers in them, and many routers have switches in them. Therefore, for practical considerations, it's worth realizing that your switch might be configured to perform routing functions, and that your router might be configured to perform switching functions.

In a simple world, they're different devices. For example, see Figure 15.1 for the practical difference between a router and a switch. (Note the different IP addresses of the networks connected to the router versus the networks connected to the switch.)

It's becoming common to see layer 3 switches. A *layer 3 switch* is a hybrid device: It is simply a switch that can also act as a router. Theses devices are usually extremely fast and costly.

It is not unusual to see two different management interfaces (CLI, Web page, and so on) for these devices: one for the router and one for the switch. The Cisco 6509 is a good example of a multi-interface layer 3 switch.

FIGURE 15.1

The basic difference between a router and a switch: All the networks connected to a switch have the same network numbers.

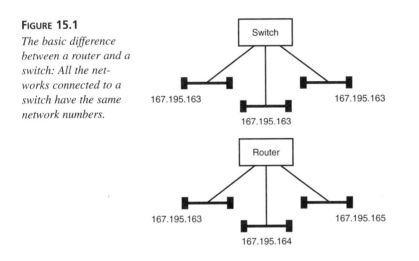

A switch is usually a wire-speed device that's able to spit out frames as fast as it sucks them in. You typically don't switch over a slow link because data link communication is very, very timing dependent. Thus, routers are the device of choice when dealing with wide area connections.

Router Types

Vehicles are also built for one purpose: to get from point A to point B. Still, there are many varieties, from backhoes to Porsches. This is also true of routers: There are many different types of routers, with many different varieties of options and control methods.

There are two main types of routers: SOHO (Small Office/Home) and enterprise. SOHO routers typically serve anywhere from 1 to 10 users, whereas enterprise routers can be responsible for the traffic of thousands of users.

Enterprise routers are built on the assumption that they will be dealing with a lot of traffic—so they typically devote a lot of processing power to dealing with their main task, forwarding network data to the next router.

A SOHO router, on the other hand, is usually the one and only network device on the premises, so it tends to have more "Swiss army knife" functionality built in, usually at the cost of large-scale manageability and (ouch) troubleshooting functionality, such as debug logging.

SOHO Routers

Consider these two SOHO routers: the Linksys BEF411 router, popular among cable modem and DSL customers, or the NexLand WaveBase, popular for branch office installations. Both include a router, a NAT firewall, and a DHCP server, as well as a four-port Ethernet switch. The WaveBase includes both a wireless access point as well as a VPN server; the Linksys, depending on which model you buy, can include a wireless access point or a VPN server.

Many SOHO routers also have a wide area access port for some sort of telephone network access, such as an ISDN or analog dialup.

The ones that don't have a port dedicated to a telco technology usually have the designation cable/DSL router or broadband router. The interesting thing here is that these *don't* have ports dedicated to DSL or cable. Instead, they have an Ethernet switch port dedicated to talking to your DSL modem or cable modem. (This way, they can be compatible with both cable and DSL because both types of modems typically support Ethernet as an uplink method.)

Because SOHO routers have so many components, troubleshooting them can be complex. Make it easier by identifying *which* of the components is failing, and then concentrate your efforts on component-level troubleshooting. Again, components to consider include

- **DHCP server.** Are IP addresses being handed out to the workstations on the local network? Check the configuration to make sure that DHCP is on. Getting IP conflicts after a power failure? This is because SOHO routers don't have a hard drive to store DHCP assignments. Here's a quick fix: Reboot all workstations; this will make each one of them get a new IP address. (See Hour 19, "Internet and Intranet Troubleshooting: TCP/IP at Work," for more on DHCP troubleshooting.)

- **Wireless access point.** See Hour 11, "Wireless Networking," for troubleshooting tips.

15

- **VPN server.** If you are using PPTP, make sure that you have PPTP pass-thru enabled. (For PPTP, you can try to Telnet to port 1723 from the outside.) If you are using IPSec, make sure that IPSec pass-thru is enabled. If your VPN connection is working, but sometimes randomly "drops," check for firmware updates after ensuring that you have good IP connectivity between the VPN and your PC.

- **Wide area port.** Can you "ping" the address of the cable modem or DSL modem? If you can't, check the modem lights; you might have a physical problem. Unfortunately, sometimes you have to suck it up and call your provider, particularly if you've reset the device to no effect.

- **Built in Ethernet switch.** Can workstations reach each other? Caution: If the DHCP server isn't working, and your workstations don't "autoconfig," it's likely that the workstations cannot see each other—but this doesn't mean that the *switch* is broken. Try assigning a *static* IP address to two known good workstations; this will let you rule out the switch as a cause of problems.

- **Logging facility.** Although SOHO logging usually isn't as robust as an enterprise router's, sometimes this can come in useful. For example, if your router is running slowly and you believe that workstation A and B are the only clients, you can at least rule out high traffic as a cause by verifying the known traffic in the logs.

- **NAT firewall.** If the router is working, the NAT firewall is usually working—at least for outbound connections. You can usually bypass the whole unit by hooking your PC directly to the cable/DSL modem and renewing your DHCP lease. (If you have a static IP for your router, use it, but change it back when you're done.) If you can get outbound connections, you know the firewall is the problem. (See Hour 16, "Firewall and Proxy Server Basics," for more on firewalls and NAT.)

  If your problem is inbound (that is, you have a host that needs to be accessed from outside of the firewall) make sure that your firewall configuration is pointing to the correct host. Again, you can always hook this host directly to the modem to rule the router in/out.

Individuals can't really do much if the cable modem or DSL is busted on the ISP end; you've got to call it in, and then grit your teeth and wait for them to fix it. However, you *can* make sure that the problem doesn't lie with you. Naturally, resetting the device is a good first move, and you should also check out the blinky lights on the front, and see what your device manual says about those—but there's more:

- **DSL.** Because DSL runs over a standard analog telephone line, your first order of business is to ensure that your standard telephone service is working. (Do you have a dial tone? Is there noise on the line?) Have you recently added a jack? Have you recently purchased a telephone? A bad telephone can do bad things to a telephone

line. Try unplugging *all* telephone devices except the DSL modem and see if it
starts to work. (Remove any DSL filters as well, and see if your DSL modem
works on a bare line.)

- **Cable.** Have you recently added splitters on the coaxial cable in your home? Try
  taking them out and seeing if things start to work. If you have spliced your own
  ends onto the cable, hook to the cable company's instead. (If its ends are far away,
  you can use a long coax cable and a coax coupler, at least for testing purposes.)

Enterprise Routers

Enterprise routers have a different set of features than SOHO routers. In particular, they
have much better logging facilities. Many router problems become readily apparent when
you look at the log. (In other words, the log mentions if the router is running out of
memory or if packets are failing checksum.)

However, sometimes the errors aren't apparent, so you might want to turn on everything
logging, also known as *debug* level. (We'll discuss one caution about this in a moment.)

Error Logging

Let's say, for example, that you've troubleshot a problem down to a Cisco router, and
you're at the end of your rope trying to figure out *why* the router is malfunctioning. You
might want to start logging level 7 messages (debugging) to a 16K buffer, try whatever
operation is failing, and then show the log to the screen:

```
logging buffered 16384

logging trap 7

show logging
```

Log levels on Cisco routers go from 0 to 7, where 0 is the least amount of logging (emer-
gencies only, 3 logs errors only, and 7 logs *everything*). Try to use the least you need. For
more Cisco information, check out `http://websrv.cs.fsu.edu/reference/itl/labs/`
`debug/debug.htm`.

For other manufacturers, see your reference manual for appropriate logging commands.

Do not use more of a logging level than you need, and make sure to turn it
off or tweak it down to an "informational" or "error-only" when you're
done. Verbose logging—particularly debug level logging—is very hard on any
device, and performance will suffer if you leave it on. The busier the router,
the harder debugging is on it; a busy router can literally be taken down by
enabling full debugging. Try to schedule debugging for quiet times.

Many routers (even SOHO routers) support logging to a syslog server, that is, a server that keeps logs for more than one system. The advantage here is that you can log to hard disk rather than relying on a memory buffer (which gets erased in the event of a real system problem such as a crash). UNIX systems have one built-in, but you'll have to use a third-party add-on if you want to run syslog on Windows (for example, the one made by Kiwi Enterprises: `http://www.kiwisyslog.com/products.htm`).

DHCP Forwarding

Because an enterprise can have many VLANs, but not very many DHCP servers, it's very common to use an enterprise router to forward DHCP queries from a VLAN that has no DHCP server to a VLAN that does have one; this is known as *DHCP forwarding*. (In the Cisco world, IP Helper (also known as a DHCP Relay Agent) accomplishes this, using the command `ip helper-address` *`dhcpserveraddress`* in the interface configuration.)

DHCP forwarding is not an automatic function; it's configured statically. If someone changes the IP address of the DHCP server and does not also change the router, people on subnets without their own DHCP server will have problems. Figure 15.2 shows how DHCP forwarding works.

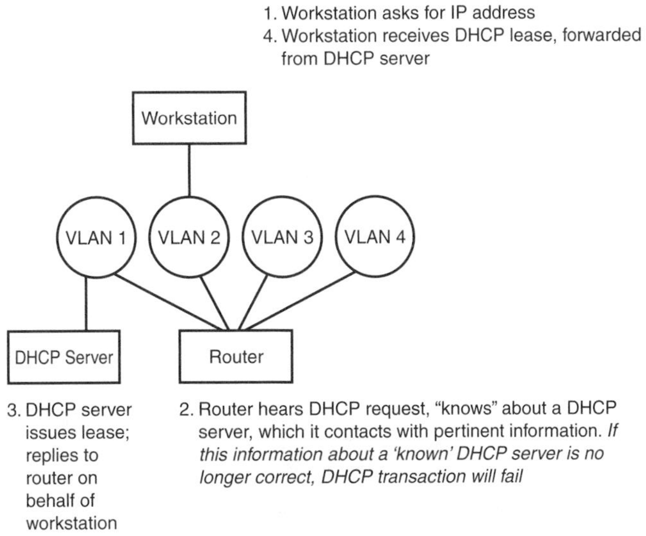
1. Workstation asks for IP address
4. Workstation receives DHCP lease, forwarded from DHCP server
Workstation
VLAN 1
VLAN 2
VLAN 3
VLAN 4
DHCP Server
Router
3. DHCP server issues lease; replies to router on behalf of workstation
2. Router hears DHCP request, "knows" about a DHCP server, which it contacts with pertinent information. If this information about a 'known' DHCP server is no longer correct, DHCP transaction will fail

FIGURE 15.2
How DHCP forwarding works, and how it can fail.

Router Theory

Each router listens on each one of its multiple interfaces for route (also called *forwarding*) requests.

When a router receives a packet destined for a different network segment, the router must decide to which of its network interfaces it will direct the packet. If the router is connected directly to the destination VLAN, it just plops it out of the interface that's connected to that VLAN; otherwise, it must hand it off to another router that either is attached to that VLAN or is closer to the directly connected router.

Routing Tables

Obviously, if the router has a direct connection to a particular segment, it knows how to route the packet there. But what if the router you hand the packet to isn't directly connected to the destination segment? How does the router know which path the packet should take?

Each router maintains an internal table of every network that it knows about. This is called a *routing table*. The routing table consists of a list of network numbers, which interface or router this network number is reachable through, and how costly this route is in terms of time or distance. A routing table for Router 1 in Figure 15.3 is shown in Table 15.1. (I'm intentionally not showing netmask values to keep things simple, but in real life you'd see them.)

FIGURE **15.3**

A sample routed network.

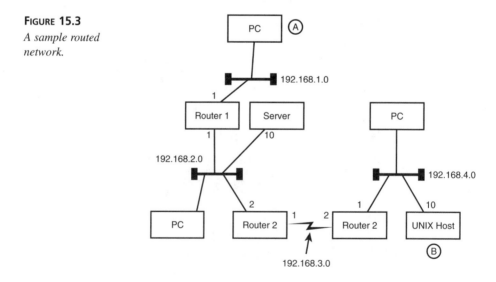

TABLE 15.1   Routing Table for Router 1

Network	Next Hop	Metric
192.168.1.0	192.168.1.1	0 (Direct)
192.168.2.0	192.168.2.1	0 (Direct)
192.168.3.0	192.168.2.2	1
192.168.4.0	192.168.2.2	2

Depending on your router, the words *next hop* in the router table might be replaced with words such as *destination* or *gateway address*. The word *metric* might be listed as *cost*. In this case, *metric* refers to how many hops away the network is from the router.

For example, look at the map in Figure 15.3; how many other routers must you go through to get from Router 1 to 192.168.1.0? The answer is none. You do not go through any other routers, so the hop count is 0. How many take you from Router 1 to 192.168.3.0? Right, one hop—through Router 2.

The format of this table differs depending on what type of router Router 1 is, but the content will be similar. Notice that a routing table can list only next hop destinations that are directly reachable by that router. In other words, a router only objectively knows about networks to which it's physically connected. All other networks are reachable by routers that are connected to a subnet to which this router is connected.

A Couple of Milliseconds in the Life of Joe Packet

Let's follow a concrete example by tracing a packet through the network shown in Figure 15.3. The PC at point A wants to telnet to the UNIX host at point B. Because we're talking about routing, we don't care about the specifics of the network conversation; we just want to trace how the call gets from point A to point B. Here are the steps:

1. The middleware that allows an application program to talk to your network card's driver is called a *stack*. Your PC's TCP/IP protocol middleware (stack) must open up a connection to the UNIX server at 192.168.4.10. The TCP/IP stack knows what its own IP address is (192.168.1.20) and also knows what its own netmask is (255.255.255.0), and therefore calculates the *network number* as 192.168.1.0. Clearly, 192.168.4.0 is a different network. Therefore, instead of establishing a conversation with the destination, the IP stack establishes a conversation with the router.

2. The IP stack on the workstation can only talk to stations on the same network, so it passes the first packet of the Telnet conversation to a router on the same network: the router at 192.168.1.1 (Router 1).

3. The router first looks up the destination network in its routing table. In this case, the destination is listed in Router 1's routing table as being reachable through the 192.168.2.1 router (Router 2).

> If the destination network is *not* in the routing table, the router drops the packet and sends back a special IP packet (ICMP, as opposed to TCP or UDP) saying that this destination is unreachable.

4. Router 1 starts a conversation up with Router 2, whose routing table is shown in Table 15.2.

TABLE 15.2   Routing Table for Router 2

Network	Next Hop	Metric
192.168.2.0	192.168.2.2	0 (Direct)
192.168.3.0	192.168.3.1	0 (Direct)
192.168.1.0	192.168.2.1	1
192.168.4.0	192.168.3.2	1

5. The packet still needs to get to point B from Router 2. Router 2 looks up the destination network (192.168.4) in its routing table and finds out that it does not have a direct connection to that network. Instead, the next hop is at 192.168.3.2 (Router 3), which is on the other side of the wide-area connection. Router 3's routing table is shown in Table 15.3.

TABLE 15.3   Routing Table for Router 3

Network	Next Hop	Metric
192.168.3.0	192.168.3.2	0 (Direct)
192.168.4.0	192.168.4.1	0 (Direct)
192.168.1.0	192.168.3.1	2
192.168.2.0	192.168.3.1	1

15

6. Finally! The destination, `192.168.4.10`, is on a directly connected network! All Router 3 needs to do is to establish an Ethernet-level connection with the UNIX host and hand off all the PC's packets that it receives from Router 2. The packets are flowing and the planets are starting to align—what could be better?

Of course, responses from the UNIX host destined for the PC at point A go from the UNIX host to Router 3, to Router 2, to Router 1, and then to the PC. This might seem confusing when you say it like that, but take a look at the map and refer to each routing table, keeping in mind that the destination is `192.168.1.0` this time, and you'll see that each lookup leads to the next correct router.

In real life, this can be somewhat more complicated. Instead of each routing table having four entries, it can have hundreds—or even thousands—of entries. However, the basic principles are unchanged; much of what you need to figure out from a troubleshooting standpoint is how to command your router to show you what its routing table looks like, so you can do a sanity check on it. For example, if Router 1's table showed that the next hop to `192.168.4.0` was `192.168.2.10` (the file and print server), you'd raise your eyebrows and start to investigate why Router 1 thought that the best way to `192.168.4` was through a server. (Going through a server isn't in itself terrible—if the server is a multihomed server that also acts as a router to the proper network. But in this case, it's a dead end.)

Checking Routes

Routing problems can be diagnosed from the router itself, but they can also be diagnosed via a network connected to a router. You can determine whether a router is up just by pinging it (be sure to ping it from a segment that it lives on because pinging it from a different segment involves different routers). Likewise, you can use the `traceroute`, `tracert`, and `iptrace` commands to see how a packet from the workstation is actually flowing through the network. Check the routing tables of multihomed servers with `netstat -r` to see what they think the routes are. After you do these things, you can compare the results with how things *should* flow according to your site documentation, and you're one step closer to resolving your problem.

Those Dynamic Routers

I heard you ask about four paragraphs ago, "How does the routing table get built?" I wasn't ignoring you; it's a good question. To begin to answer it, let's discuss basic route entry types.

Three types of routes can be established in a routing table:

- **Direct routes.** When you configure a router's interface for a certain network, it automatically adds this network in to its routing table.

- **Static routes.** A static route is one you type in yourself at the router console. This gets extremely tedious and isn't the greatest way to have a flexible and easily reconfigurable network.

- **Dynamic routes.** Dynamic routing entries are built via routing protocols. Like an application protocol, a routing protocol defines a specific method of communication of information—in this case, the automatic sharing of routes between routers. If not used carefully, though, routing protocols can cause problems.

> There's one special static route you'll want to know about called the *default* route. This is represented by the destination network 0.0.0.0 and is the route used when a packet has a destination that isn't covered by anything else in the routing table. In Ciscoland, this route is also called the route of last resort.

Routing protocols are based on the concept that each router "knows" which network it lives on and that it can communicate which networks it knows about to other routers. Looking at Figure 15.3 again, it makes sense that Router 1 could tell Router 2 about the 192.168.1 network and that Router 2 could tell Router 1 about the 192.168.3 network—along with the 192.168.4 network, after Router 3 told Router 2 about it. Whew! It's a good thing this happens more or less automatically because in a large network, writing this out could get really hairy. Again, here's how dynamic routes would work in this sample network:

Router 1	Tells Router 2 about 192.168.1
Router 2	Tells Router 1 about 192.168.3
	Tells Router 3 about 192.168.1
	Tells Router 1 about 192.168.4
Router 3	Tells Router 2 about 192.168.4

Route in Peace: LAN Routing Protocols

There are four common types of LAN routing protocols you should know about—more for configuration checking (making sure that routers are configured for the same routing protocols) than anything else. Clearly, as a network engineer, there are volumes of information that you'd want to assimilate about these protocols; but as a troubleshooter, you simply want to know the basics of how they work so that you can sensibly rule things in or out.

Three of the common types are TCP/IP based: RIP (Routing Information Protocol), RIP II, and OSPF (Open Shortest Path First). The fourth belongs to the IPX/SPX network protocol: Although IPX/SPX is essentially a dead protocol (because newer Novell products default to TCP/IP), enough of it is out there in shops that I hope you'll excuse me if I don't leave the poor folks who have to deal with IPX/SPX routing protocols out in the cold, and briefly talk about both RIP for IPX/SPX as well as NLSP (NetWare Link State Protocol).

RIP and RIP II

Both the TCP/IP RIP and the IPX/SPX RIP are *broadcast protocols*—that is, each RIP router announces its routing table to everybody on the network every so often. Both RIPs also calculate route cost based on number of hops rather than how fast a particular route might be (for cases in which multiple routers have a path to the same network). RIP can cause a lot of network traffic in complex networks because it talks too darn much. (TCP/IP RIP broadcasts to the network every 30 seconds.)

It's worth saying at this point that *route flapping* is when one router advertises the best route to a destination, and then is superseded by another router (or even the same router) that has another opinion. Route flapping is typically caused by bad router configuration.

First-generation layer 3 switches (which are really routers integrated within a switch, remember) were particularly bad about allowing configurations that led to route flapping. If you've got one of these, watch out!

If you're using TCP/IP, RIP II might well be offered as a routing protocol on your enterprise router. Among other things, it allows for authentication among routers, which is terrific because it will not allow a rogue router to mess up the network's routing tables. Any router that is allowed to participate in a RIP II network with MD5 authentication must have the correct key in order to offer routes. Obviously, if you're using authentication and you can't get a new router to join in the RIP II fun, you should check your key for typos.

All of these routing protocols are known as *distance vector protocols*, which means that they offer routing information about which interface leads to which destination, and how far it is. With this type of information, routers can't make decisions about link *quality*, so complex networks with many different speeds of links are not good candidates for these protocols.

OSPF and NLSP

OSPF (Open Shortest Path First for TCP/IP) and NLSP (NetWare Link State Protocol) for IPX/SPX are more advanced routing protocols than RIP. They take into account how fast a link might be and assign a cost accordingly (they're also known as a link state protocols). Each NLSP or OSPF router identifies itself to other routers on the same network and learns the routes that those other routers know.

The big difference between these routing protocols and the preceding ones is that they use point-to-point communication rather than broadcasts. If something changes, the routers communicate it to each other directly. Because they do a quick check on each other fairly often (usually every 10 seconds), a dead router is noticed and the routing tables are updated quickly. It's good stuff!

Router Rumble!

Routers that participate in routing protocols on your network can seriously damage your large-scale connectivity if they're misconfigured.

I once troubleshot a problem in which somebody plugged a router into network A that was configured to connect network A with network B. This was because the new router was intended to *replace* the router that currently served network B.

Unfortunately, the new router's second interface was configured as being on network B, and though it wasn't plugged into network B proper, it started to advertise via RIP that it knew the best route to network B. This caused confusion in the routing tables; some packets started to go to this router, only to discover that there was an entrance, but no exit! The legitimate router for network B was doing what it was supposed to do, but it was being usurped by the new router.

I found this out because I noticed that traceroutes from different locations were taking different paths. I then checked the documentation (praying that it was correct), and then checked each router's routing table to see whether reality jibed with the documentation. Naturally, it didn't, and the rogue router showed up in the other routers' tables. A few well-placed questions confirmed my suspicions.

This was, of course, a human error that could have been found by change analysis—if the guilty party had 'fessed up!

Here's the lesson: Don't plug a new router in to a production network until it's time; instead, test on a disconnected network. Test hubs are cheap enough—putting together a couple of test segments shouldn't cost more than $100.

Configuration Methods

15

Hardware routers are different from commodity PCs in one important way: They're *not* a dime a dozen. So, although it's easy to test out potential Windows or Linux changes on an easily built lab machine, it's not quite as easy to do on a hardware routing platform.

Familiarity goes a long way toward avoiding real-time mistakes. If you can get a hold of the device before it goes into production, so much the better. Being familiar with the commands, error-reporting facilities, and configuration procedure of a device makes you much more able to handle problems as they come up during production. Failing that, having another "lab" device that you can test on is really useful. After-market/used devices are comparatively cheap on auction sites such as eBay, and are well worth the investment.

One thing is reasonably consistent among most routers—they are all usually configurable via one of these:

- Telnet
- SSH (Secure Shell)
- Browser
- Serial connection (console)

The serial option is the most universal—it allows you to communicate with the device even if the network is down.

If your switch or router has a serial console, you can connect your PC's serial port to it using a null modem cable (available at most Radio Shack, Best Buy, and Office Max stores.). The connection at the device will either be DB-9 (male) or DB-25 (male); if the connection is something else, it's probably not a dumb terminal port. Cisco routers use a special RJ-45 (router) to DB9 (PC) cable, which you can get just about anywhere.

After you connect the cable, you can then use just about any modem program (ProComm, HyperTerminal, NetTerm, and so on) to connect to it. The most common settings for dumb terminal mode are as follows: 8 data bits, no parity, one stop bit, 9600bps. This is sometimes written as *9600-8-N-1*.

If you cannot access a router via Ethernet and are forced to update a router's firmware via serial port to solve a problem, set the serial port speed as high as you can (usually 115Kbps) or you'll grow old waiting for the firmware to transfer. Set the router's speed first; commit the change; and *then* set your PC speed. Naturally, after you finish, you either need to change back or document the change to avoid future problems.

Some SOHO routers don't allow for the backup of their configuration information. So, no, you can't hook up a tape drive to a router or switch, and most of them (although not all) won't let you download their configurations to a server that does have a tape drive on it.

> When using HyperTerm or another terminal emulation package, you can save capture text to a file for later analysis. If your router doesn't have a configuration file upload feature, displaying the configuration on your terminal program and then saving it can be a good way to back up this critical information.

Enterprise routers, naturally, are much better in this regard. Most allow you to write configuration files to a network location. You want to make sure that all router configurations are backed up so that you can both compare configurations ("The *Sesame Street* Method: Using What Works," Hour 6) and recover quickly in case of mishap.

Here's the bottom line: Make sure that you have all configuration information well documented. Regardless, switches and routers are particularly crucial places to keep good change logs.

Summary

You can think of routers and switches as being cousins. Routers switch packets at the network protocol (TCP/IP or IPX/SPX) level, whereas switches move frames at the data link (Ethernet or Token-Ring) level. Switches are usually wire-speed devices, whereas routers can handle delay (as is the case over a wide-area connection). Switches are typically used for one geographically separate area; routers are used to connect geographically disperse areas. A switch can be used as a hub replacement, allowing users to enjoy an unshared line to communicate to other devices on the network.

The documentation that comes with your switch or router should become bathroom reading material if you really want to be able to handle problems. Of course, the theory is really important, but router and switch theory by itself won't do you a lot of good; you'll also need to know specific informational and configuration commands for your devices.

Routers are much more complex than switches, and they communicate back and forth quite a lot via routing protocols. Switches, on the other hand, are pretty dumb, and they only talk to each other to avoid a duplicate path to a workstation. Both switches and routers, however, are more often than not hybrid devices that can route packets at a protocol level or switch packets at a data link level—all depending on how you configure them.

15

Q&A

Q **What's a layer 3 switch?**

A Layer 3 refers to layer 3 of the OSI model, discussed in Hour 2. Layer 3 is the network layer. A device that forwards traffic on layer 3 is a router. Manufacturers refer to routers as layer 3 switches when they are capable of operating at *wire speed*. *Layer 3 switch* is basically a marketing term for "fast router with built-in switch ports."

Q **I tried to connect to my router with a serial cable. I'm pretty sure that I'm using the right cable, but every time I use my communications program, all I see is a bunch of Ç characters. Why is my device speaking French to me? Does it think I'm cute or something?**

A Don't worry; your device isn't making a pass at you; it's not even speaking French! Any time you see garbage characters like these on a serial connection, it probably means that you're running with incorrect communication parameters. If you're using the correct default parameters, as specified by your documentation (probably 9600bps, 8 bits, no parity, and 1 stop bit—this is the most common configuration out there), somebody has probably improved the connection by ramping up the connection speed and hasn't told you about it. Try 19200bps, 38400bps, or 57600bps. If those don't work, you can always try changing the stop bits or parity—but realize that people usually don't monkey with these on the device end. This problem is typically the result of a speed issue.

Workshop

Workshop time! Here's a brief quiz to help you make the most out of this hour's lesson as well as some activities for you to try on your own.

Quiz

1. What's the principal difference between a router and a switch?

   a. Data link versus network protocol treatment

   b. Protocol versus network program treatment

   c. Data link versus MAC layer treatment

   d. Protocol versus data network treatment

2. True or False: It's a good idea to back up your router configuration if you can.

3. A routing table can be built by which of the following?

  a. Static routes

  b. Dynamic routes

  c. Neither A nor B

  d. Both A and B

4. A routing protocol is a way for routers to _____.

  a. Assume different bandwidth considerations via networking

  b. Advertise known networks

  c. Assume routing information internally

  d. Exchange network error information

5. Router 88 has a routing table that looks like this:

Network	Net Mask	Gateway Address	Cost
200.1.1.0	255.255.255.0	200.1.1.1	0 (Local)
200.1.2.0	255.255.255.0	200.1.2.1	0 (Local)
200.1.3.0	255.255.255.0	200.1.2.2	1
200.1.4.0	255.255.255.0	200.1.2.2	2

  Based on this routing table, how will Router 88 route a packet that's destined for 200.1.3.10?

  a. It will talk directly to the node at 200.1.3.10.

  b. It will talk directly to the router at 200.1.2.2.

  c. It will talk directly to the router at 200.1.2.1.

  d. It will drop the packet and generate an error.

6. How might you make Router 88 send packets that don't correspond to any of its routing entries along to Router 99?

  a. Add Router 99 to Router 88's routing protocol participation.

  b. Add Router 99 as a default route for Router 88.

  c. Add Router 88 to Router 99's routing protocol participation.

  d. Add Router 88 as a default route for Router 99.

7. SOHO routers can have each of the following options, EXCEPT for

   a. DHCP server

   b. VPN server

   c. File server

   d. Wireless access point

8. True or False: SOHO routers typically have diagnostic/debugging logging options.

9. When you decommission or move a DHCP server in your enterprise, you should remember to check to see if your routers have a _____ entry *before* you do the move.

   a. DHCP forwarder

   b. IP negotiator

   c. Poor connectivity layer

   d. Dynamic routing

10. When experiencing problems with cable or DSL, it's a good idea to consider whether the _____ is involved—has anything been done to it recently?

   a. Firewall

   b. Socket layer

   c. Routing protocol

   d. Wiring

Answers to Quiz Questions

1. A

2. True

3. D

4. B

5. B

6. B

7. C

8. False

9. A

10. D

Activities

1. Go to your workstation, pull up a command prompt (or shell window) and type "netstat -rn". What do you see? What is your network number? What is your default router? Do you have more than one? Do you see any unexpected addresses? What are they?

2. Grab three workstations; one of which will be used as a router. Set them up as shown in Figure 15.4.

FIGURE 15.4

Workstation #2 is the router for this activity.

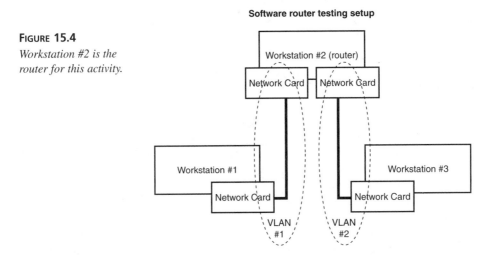

Install an additional network card to the "router" workstation. Download the latest images from the LRP (Linux Routing Project http://linuxrouter.org), and create a small routed network. Workstation #1 will be on VLAN #1, and will be connected using a crossover cable directly to the first interface card on Workstation #2 (the router). Then, use another crossover cable from Workstation #2's second interface card directly to Workstation #3. This will be VLAN #2. Think about what IP addresses you'll use (Hint: RFC 1918, Private Addressing) as well as whether you'll have to use DHCP (Hint: DHCP is not always necessary as long as you choose addresses well). Boot up Workstation #2 using the LRP boot disk, and see if you can ping the router, and whether you can ping the workstations. For extra credit, use netmasks *other* than 255.255.255.0 and see if you can get Workstation #1 to ping Workstation #3.

HOUR **16**

Firewall and Proxy Server Basics

Three can keep a secret if two are dead.

—Benjamin Franklin

This is a *scary* yet kind of fun hour. I hope you've brought your secret detective code ring and your security blanket. We're going to go seriously James Bond here; you can expect a couple of nifty devices, explosions, bad guys, good guys, and gunplay by the end of the hour. Okay, no. But we *are* going to talk about network security, and how firewalls and proxies fit into the security picture of most organizations.

For some reason, the public perception seems to be that a firewall or proxy server is the major security concern on any network. In reality, although a well-configured firewall or proxy server is really, really important, it's only one piece in a larger security model.

Although I won't get into these topics in tremendous detail here, network security relies on good password policies, server configuration, as well as the diligent application of security-related operating system and application patches, network auditing, and user dial-in policies (just to name a few things besides firewalls). Just as any responsible corporation has locks on its doors (the firewalls), it also probably distributes corporate ID tags, has receptionists to greet and keep the public from casually intruding on the work environment, has a burglar alarm, and has an accounting system to keep track of the disbursement of funds. Although not every corporation has security guards—much less security guards with guns—they do have locks on their doors and are basically secure.

> *Perfect* security on a network system means unplugging it from the network, disconnecting all dial-up ports, burning the Internet router, and using paper instead of the computer. (For some reason, this is not a popular security policy, and besides, all this does is move the security risk from networking to paperwork!)
>
> Failing this, all you can accomplish is best-effort security—and *keep good backups*. Firewalls are a good beginning to best-effort security. They keep your most obvious entry points locked down and act as a gateway from your inside network to the outside world.

Top-Secret Definitions

Let's lay out some definitions here. When most folks talk about firewalls, they usually mean packet-filtering routers. As you learned in Hour 1, "Understanding Networking: The Telephone Analogy," a *router* is the glue between two or more network segments. (We discussed routers in depth in Hour 15, "Home and Office Routers.") Therefore, a packet-filtering router refers to a router that has rules about *who* and *what* is allowed to be routed between its interfaces. Not so bad, huh?

What's a proxy server? First of all, it's *not* any kind of router. So what is it? Like any kind of server, a proxy server offers services. It's basically a multihomed server that accepts requests on a certain port and *forwards* these requests to a server on the other side.

Think of a proxy server as a big, bad security guard who will go into a bad network neighborhood for you, retrieve what you want, and return it to you—all without exposing you to harm. As in voting, the proxy server proxies you—that is, it acts as your agent to go do something and then reports back to you what the results are. Going back to our old friend the telephone analogy, bear in mind that a proxy server is not telephone equipment; it's merely an agent that has two different telephones connected to two different telephone systems. Some folks believe that proxies are more secure than packet-filtering firewalls, but there is some debate about this. Certainly, proxy servers do tend to have better logging features in general.

NAT firewalls are sort of a combination of packet-filtering firewalls and proxy—they act like a router, but they make network requests on your behalf. There is no application knowledge of what kind of monkey business is going on at the firewall end, and as such, this can lead to interesting problems.

Here's a request before we begin: Please don't take this hour as anything but "how to start to troubleshoot firewalls." This hour is about how to start to troubleshoot these devices when they bonk up. If you are setting up a firewall for the first time, I beg of you to avail yourself of the good security books and documentation out there before doing so. (Sams Publishing's *Maximum Security, 3rd Edition* is a pretty comprehensive survey of the subject; I'll list some more books at the end of this chapter during Q&A.)

That said, let's take a look at the theory, which will let you start to investigate a given situation and start to figure out what might be wrong.

TCP Versus UDP

Germane to the theory behind firewalling is the idea that connections can be limited based on the service being offered or sought. Because each TCP/IP service has a unique socket number that it listens to (remember from the telephone analogy that a *port* is the extension number that the service person for the company answers), it's reasonably easy for a router or proxy server to limit connections to these ports. Because limits are placed on the port numbers themselves, it follows that the service is also limited. This means that you can pick and choose among the services that might travel in or out of the firewall.

> Actually, services don't *have* to run on their default socket number; just as your boss can make you sit at a different telephone, a network administrator can change the socket number of a service. This is fairly unusual, but it does happen.
>
> For example, students sometimes run their own Web servers on different ports because the university has occupied the default Web port with the official Web server. So, to get to a student Web page that is running on port 8100, you might have to point your Web browser to www.college.edu:8100 instead of www.college.edu. The firewall upshot here is that if you run a service on a nonstandard port, people might not be able to traverse the firewall to get to you.

16

This is reasonably easy with *TCP (Transmission Control Protocol)* sockets. A TCP connection is a connection-oriented call—like a true phone call, where someone dials someone else and establishes a two-way link.

A *UDP (User Datagram Protocol)* conversation, on the other hand, is basically like when I throw you a crumpled-up piece of paper containing a message, and you throw one back at me. This is called a *connectionless* session. You can think of the difference between TCP and UDP as the difference between you and me using two tin cans and a string (TCP) to communicate versus you and me passing notes in class (UDP). Keep in mind that a note can be easily misdirected.

It's fairly trivial for TCP connections to be limited because the reply to the connection is basically within the same connection. It's a lot harder to do this with UDP sockets. A UDP connection throws out a packet and then waits for the reply. Because no connection exists, the firewall must be configured to accept random UDP packets, any of which might be a reply. Typically, a range of UDP ports has to be allowed in through the firewall, which implies a lot of trust.

Some administrators (depending on their site security policies) disallow UDP through the firewall—period. Others rely on *stateful* firewalls, which "remember" the originating packets that have passed through them and accept responses from the target appropriately.

Packet-Filtering Routers

A packet-filtering router usually depends on access rules—that is, rules you set up within the router software itself. A packet filter usually has a rule set that starts with least common and works its way up to most common. What's a rule set? Typically, a rule set looks something like a routing table but includes ports as well as addresses. Any packet that comes in is compared against rule 1, and then rule 2, all the way to the end. If at any time it matches up against a rule, processing stops. For example, for my 192.168.1.0 network, the rules might be as follows:

- Allow 192.168.1.0:any on interface 0 to connect to all:any.
- Deny all:any to connect to all:any.

This means that anybody within my 192.168.1.0 network (provided they come in on router interface 0) can connect to anything they darn well please. If condition 1 was not true, condition 2 would apply, which denies everything. This is probably the most common firewall configuration: Allow certain ports (or all ports) from the inside to go to the outside and disallow all other connections (for example, connections from the outside).

Some packet-filtering routers will have a filter on "which interface" the packet comes in on, in addition to what IP address the packet is from. This helps eliminate *packet spoofing*, where a packet *claims* to be from a certain network, but actually is not.

A complex rule set results in confusion and possible misconfiguration. If you're configuring a rule set, keep it simple.

You should know that certain applications (such as active FTP) will ask the *destination station* to initiate a connection back to the requesting workstation, even though it's a TCP application. It's sort of like, "Hey, Fred, find out when the movie is, and then call me back."

Under many firewall configurations, this is prohibited because it means that the firewall has to be configured so that a random workstation from the outside can initiate a connection to a random workstation on the inside. You might as well use a colander rather than a firewall!

You can usually get around this type of application problem by using a different mode of the application—for instance, passive FTP, where only the requesting workstation makes connections. Most browsers default to passive FTP (PASV), but not all standalone FTP clients (FTP Explorer, FTP Voyager, and so forth) do.

The availability of good logging facilities will largely depend on whether you're using an enterprise-class firewall. Here, troubleshooting is very similar to router troubleshooting, with ping, traceroute, and lists of the routing tables and rule sets being your best friends. As with routing problems, symptoms of packet-filtering firewall problems include the inability to reach a host on the other side; unlike a router, though, the symptom of a packet-filtering firewall problem might be the inability to reach a *service* on the other side. (For example, TCP/80 might be available, but TCP/23 might not.)

Stateful Inspection

Stateful inspection is a really neat technology. It allows inbound ports (TCP or UDP) on a *contextual* basis—that is, it reads your note to Jenny and then accepts a note back from Jenny only if it seems as though the contents of that note are relevant to what you sent. This can be very application specific. If the firewall doesn't "know" Jenny, it can't determine whether the note she sent back to you is real. Stateful firewalls typically come preconfigured with rules for common applications such as Telnet, email, FTP, and so on. If you're having problems using a custom application through a stateful firewall, it's best to check with the firewall vendor or the software manufacturer to see what your options are.

Alternatively, you might be able to enable a "poor man's" stateful inspection, that is, "allow the destination station to come back into the firewall as long as you've seen a source packet in the last two minutes." This certainly isn't as secure, but it might get you over the hump while waiting for vendor action.

Closed Versus Stealth Ports

If a client attempts to access an unavailable address/port through a firewall, older firewalls simply send back a *reset*, saying "Sorry, no such number." This response indicates that the port is closed. Newer firewalls "tease" the client, accepting the beginning of the session (SYNchronize), and simply never responding. This is called a *stealth* response; the end-station has a much harder time doing a malicious probe: It doesn't receive a definitive open/closed answer.

Although this is great for security, it's kind of annoying for certain applications. Let's look at an example.

One time, I was configuring the Exim *MTA (Mail Transport Agent)*, which is similar to sendmail; it's a daemon that deals with *SMTP (Simple Mail Transport Protocol)*. Everything seemed fine, until one day, I got a call from a client that could not send us mail. They claimed that they were timing out (taking too long to get an initial response). I verified this by using my home server to Telnet in to the Exim daemon, using telnet myeximserver.mydomain.com 25. Many TCP servers show a banner line upon connection, and SMTP servers are no exception. (FTP, HTTP, ICA, IMAP, POP, and SSH also do this.) Exim's SMTP banner shows something like

```
220 shrek ESMTP Exim 3.35 #1 Sun, 12 May 2002 16:23:54 -0400
```

However, when I tried this from outside of the firewall, it was 10–15 seconds before I would get the banner. No wonder this client was timing out.

It turned out that Exim was trying to run the ident protocol (a service that queries your host to find out your username) against any host that contacted it. The firewall did not have a rule to allow ident outbound, and it defaulted to stealth behavior, meaning that when Exim tried to run ident through the firewall, Exim would have to wait for the time-out before it knew that ident failed. Sure enough, when we allowed ident outbound, this fixed the problem.

NAT

Most modern firewalls have the option to perform *network address translation (NAT)*, which enables you to tell the outside world that you're a different address than you really are. Much like a proxy server (which we'll discuss in a moment), a NAT firewall modifies a workstation request to make it appear as if the NAT firewall is the one making the request (see Figure 16.1).

FIGURE 16.1

NAT modifies the packet as it gets forwarded through the router.

16

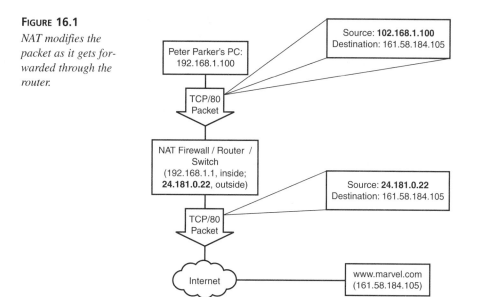

Like a proxy, this means that if you change Internet service providers, you don't have to change your IP numbers, which is nifty.

NAT can cause problems in certain applications, though, because it operates on OSI layer 3—the network layer—rather than on OSI layer 7, like proxy servers. Why is this important? Well, when an application is aware that monkey business is going on, it can compensate. But, when it's not aware that packets are being fiddled with on a lower level, problems arise.

For example, with certain client-server applications (for example, Citrix browsing), the application embeds the source or destination IP address in the application payload (not just in the packet). Obviously, if the IP address gets switched around by the router (layer 3), it's not going to address the IP address in the application payload (layer 7) and the application is going to fail. Although some NAT firewalls (Linux based in particular) deal with this, *each* application requires its own rule-set. Multiplayer games can be huge problems in this arena. (See Hour 22, "Network Troubleshooters Just Wanna Have Fun," for some tips.)

Proxy Servers

Let's dig a little deeper into the theory behind a proxy server. Think of the proxy server as a receptionist for a spy organization that has two sets of phones: the internal organization telephone (the "red phone") and the outside world's phone system. The outside phone system is not directly usable by any of the other agents in the spy agency; they must give a message to the receptionist, who then orders pizza, arranges for third-party hit men, and so on. The spy organization has it this way so that its circuits are not directly connected to the public telephone network—and a good thing, too! It doesn't mean that the receptionist is incorruptible, but at least he's within the organization, fairly trustworthy, very accountable for his actions, and, of course, easily monitored because he's the only point of communication between the organization and the outside world.

The important thing to remember is that there are two different types of phone calls because the receptionist hangs up one line (the red phone) and picks up the outside phone to relay the information on a different call. As such, there are two different routing domains (the two phone systems) involved. Although this sounds mysterious, it really isn't—all it means is that two sets of networks (the red phone and the outside world's phone system) are prevented from talking to each other because the router doesn't share a common network between the two networks (see Figure 16.2).

FIGURE 16.2

A typical proxy server setup.

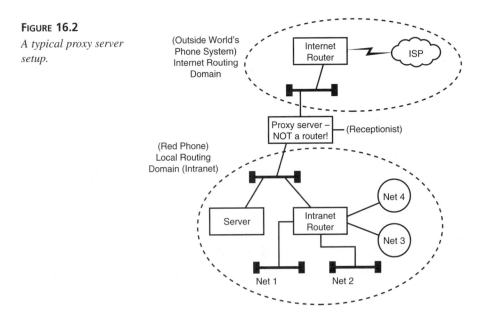

Are there still rules involved as to who may call in or out? Definitely. Similar to a packet-filtering firewall, proxy servers typically have a default policy of "deny everything but the following," and you define what *is* allowed. For example, let's say that the company executives all reside on network 4 in Figure 16.2. They have ruled that only they can have Internet access, so the only explicit rule that you would set would be this:

Allow all traffic from network 4 from the "inside" interface of the proxy server.

16

All other traffic, say from network 3, would be denied.

Proxy Type

Here are the two different types of proxy servers:

- **Application proxy**   An application proxy is a very, very specific proxy—it proxies only one type of application, such as FTP, HTTP, and so on. It does *not* proxy anything else—that is, an FTP proxy won't accept an HTTP connection. If you want to have more applications available through your proxy server, you must make sure that the proxy server is running the proxy services for those applications as well.

- **Circuit-level proxy**   A circuit-level proxy is a proxy that operates on the network level only. The most popular circuit-level proxy is called Socks (originally developed as a freeware package, but now available commercially from several vendors). This type of proxy understands protocol and socket number, but that's about it. Typically, circuit-level proxies are generic—they can act to handle any sort of port, as shown in Figure 16.3.

What's the difference? Well, for one, a circuit-level proxy is more flexible—it proxies *any* TCP/IP service. However, an application proxy has its merits, too. For example, a Web proxy (otherwise known as an *HTTP proxy*) caches Web pages and graphics it has already transferred and, as a result, serves them up much faster to your users. This is because an application proxy has inside knowledge about what's going on with the application. A circuit-level proxy doesn't know anything about the application—just something about the connection. In other words, a Web (HTTP) proxy "knows" that Web pages are being received from a server and will store them locally, as Figure 16.4 shows. The next time any user asks for those Web pages, the proxy serves them from the cache area, thus saving time. (Don't worry—if new pages are posted, the cache handles this, too.)

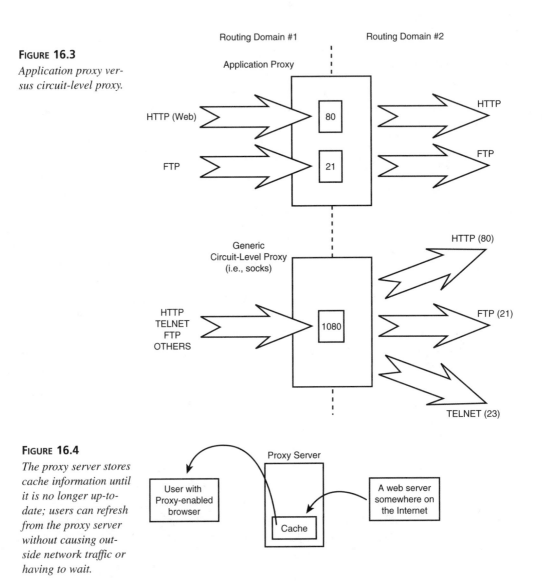

FIGURE **16.3**
Application proxy versus circuit-level proxy.

FIGURE **16.4**
The proxy server stores cache information until it is no longer up-to-date; users can refresh from the proxy server without causing outside network traffic or having to wait.

Just Add Software

Every proxy server has client software that needs to be installed on the workstation that will be using the proxy. This can be simple—every copy of Internet Explorer and Netscape Navigator or Communicator has support for the Socks circuit-level proxy, as well as built-in support for HTTP, FTP, and other proxy servers. Figure 16.5 shows the proxy settings for Internet Explorer.

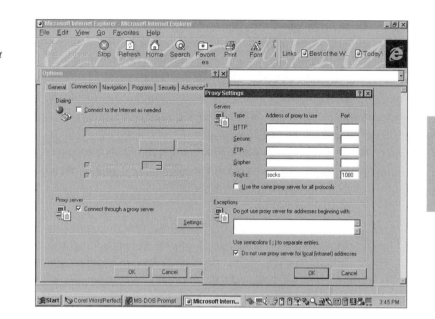

FIGURE 16.5

The Proxy Settings screen from Internet Explorer.

16

Configuring Your Proxy

The really important thing you should do when configuring the client software is to make sure that your proxy server is *not* used for local traffic. Most proxy servers do fine proxying the amount of traffic that can fit in the pipeline that goes from most sites to the Internet—T1 or 1.5Mbps traffic is a breeze for most servers to handle. However, when a proxy server finds itself forced to also deal with multiple people asking it to handle the local 10Mbps or 100Mbps traffic, things start…to…get…slow. You'll find yourself surrounded by angry villagers waving torches and axes, wanting to know why their Internet access is sluggish!

To configure Internet Explorer to avoid the proxy server for local traffic, just make sure that the Do Not Use Proxy Server for Local (Intranet) Addresses check box is checked (refer to Figure 16.4). Microsoft assumes that any address in your domain (http://server.mycompany.com) or a server name without a domain (http://server) is a local address. Clever. Netscape is a little more complicated to configure; if you want to do this, you'll need to offer the correct .pac file on your intranet. (This actually works for Internet Explorer as well. Check out http://www.microsoft.com/technet/treeview/default.asp?url=/technet/prodtechnol/ie/reskit/ie5/part5/ch21auto.asp for more details.)

Of course, even if you configure the software correctly, someone might "unconfigure" it later; it's best to prohibit this type of antisocial behavior at the server. Sure, someone who misconfigures his own workstation will experience malfunctions, but it's better to get one or two trouble calls than lots of pesky "The internet is slow" calls. Trust me on this. People who get slow stock quotes get really, really ugly.

> As far as slowness goes, if you see a lot of traffic through your generic proxy server, you might want to investigate specific application proxies. The fact that an application proxy caches frequently used pages can really cut down on your amount of traffic, provide users of those pages a boost in speed, and speed up everybody in general because those pages are not being loaded over and over again.

Proxy Trouble

You'll need to treat a proxy server as a server that just happens to be connected to two different networks. As such, you'll usually need to be able to log in to it in order to troubleshoot it.

> Presumably, your firewall will have some sort of secure login. Remember, though, what happens when you assume! Make sure that your login session is encrypted; if you don't know, ask your manufacturer. If the login is not encrypted (that is, if it uses Telnet instead of SSH), do not under any circumstances log in from the Internet—it's a trivial exercise for someone to eavesdrop on your login conversation, and all of a sudden, your secure firewall is not so secure anymore because someone from the outside can now log in to it.

When you log in, you can treat the proxy server just as you would a regular workstation. However, remember that it's a regular workstation with a double life: a life on your network and a life on the Internet. You'll do the normal troubleshooting procedures: traceroute, ping, and so on. Furthermore, you can see who's currently using your proxy server by typing **netstat -a** or **netstat -an** (depending on whether you want numeric output or not).

Pay attention to the LISTENING lines; they're the proxy services themselves. If one of them goes away, it's likely that the proxy program associated with it has died. For example, the Socks proxy service listens on socket 1080. If you don't see something resembling the following, you'll need to investigate whether the Socks program is still running (use netstat -a):

```
Active Connections
Proto  Local Address          Foreign Address  State
TCP    proxy.myhost.com:1080  0.0.0.0:*        LISTENING
```

In this case, the Socks program is definitely running. Whether it's acting nicely is another story. (For example, maybe the access rule for your network has been accidentally deleted: Although you can *connect* to the socket, it's *denying* you the right to use the proxy. You can only verify this by trying to use it from your network.) You can do a similar trick with other proxies if you know their socket numbers. HTTP is socket 80, FTP is socket 21, and Gopher is socket 70, for example.

DNS and Firewalls

What about name services? Don't you need to be able to speed dial all those servers on the Internet? Here's the scoop on DNS and firewalls.

Packet-filtering firewalls can be configured to let your DNS servers on the inside perform lookups from the outside (that is, to allow stateful TCP/53 or UDP/53). In this case, standard DNS troubleshooting rules apply. The DNS lookup looks something like this:

1. The client workstation asks the local DNS server to resolve www.jotto.com.
2. The DNS on the local server can't find jotto.com locally; it turns to the outside DNS server.
3. The outside DNS server returns the IP address to the local DNS server.
4. The local DNS server returns the IP address to the client workstation.
5. The client workstation attempts to connect; the packet-filtering firewall grabs the connection and allows it through.

You can determine whether DNS services are working simply by typing **ping *webname***. It's likely that the ping itself will fail—not all Internet servers allow outsiders to ping them, and your packet-filtering firewall might not be configured to let pings (ICMP ECHO) through. However, you should be able to resolve the address. For example, if DNS *is* working, a ping to an external host might look like this:

```
C:\WINDOWS>ping www.jotto.com
Pinging www.jotto.com [205.134.224.21] with 32 bytes of data:
Destination host unreachable.
Destination host unreachable.
Destination host unreachable.
Destination host unreachable.
```

The `Destination host unreachable` message might not be acceptable overall, but at least you know that name resolution is working. How do you know? Well, in the preceding output, `www.jotto.com` is followed by its IP address, `205.134.224.21`. If name resolution were not working, the ping session would look like this:

```
C:\WINDOWS>ping www.jotto.com
Bad IP address www.jotto.com.
.
```

This example doesn't resolve the IP address from the DNS name. The `Bad IP address www.jotto.com` message from Windows means that the name resolution has failed.

Some proxy servers allow you to avoid mixing your DNS servers with the outside world's DNS. This is called proxy DNS (sometimes called DNS forwarding), and it works as follows:

1. The proxy client software tries performing a local lookup on the name (`www.jotto.com`).
2. The proxy client software fails with the local lookup, assumes that the name is of a remote site, and asks the proxy server to resolve the name and then proxy the request.
3. The proxy server resolves the name from an outside DNS server.
4. The proxy server processes the request and hands the resulting Web page to the client.

Notice that at no time is the IP address passed back to the client. This means that you *cannot* perform the ping trick outlined earlier if you're using client proxy DNS rather than having your internal DNS servers talk to outside DNS servers. You'll always get the `Bad IP address host.outsidecompany.com` message.

> Not every proxy allows for proxy DNS. Socks version 5, for example, will proxy the DNS for you if you configure the client to do so, but Socks version 4 won't.

Summary

A packet-filtering router with stateful inspection is usually what's referred to as a firewall. These routers have rules as to what is and is not allowed into a network on a service-by-service basis. Older firewalls don't allow for NAT or stateful inspection. Small home or office firewalls typically don't have great logging or stateful features. NAT is famous for breaking certain applications because of embedded IP addresses in the application payload; certain video conferencing and games are good examples.

Proxy servers differ from packet-filtering firewalls in that they operate on OSI layer 7, not layer 3; they act as a workstation on the Internet, and they pass their results back to workstations inside your network. This makes for a bit more setup on the client end and has different troubleshooting characteristics than a plain router. (You need to establish that routing to the device is okay for both the inside and outside networks; and you need to verify that the proxy service running on the proxy server is alive and configured properly.) Because a proxy server, like a spy ring receptionist, has two separate "phone systems," you sometimes need to log in to the proxy server or be on the console in order to troubleshoot it.

DNS can be a thorny issue; you'll be well served figuring out what type of DNS resolution you have *before* you run into problems (so that you know how to verify DNS connectivity). Certain proxy servers will also proxy DNS resolution, making standard DNS troubleshooting tools unsuitable for troubleshooting Internet name resolution problems.

16

Q&A

Q **Our boss said to get a firewall, so we have one, and it seems reasonably good. Still, I'm concerned about the network internally because we have a lot of PCs with PC Anywhere that have arbitrary dial-in ports. Also, I'm hearing more and more about browser bugs that let the bad guys subvert my internal workstations, rendering my firewall useless!**

I don't have a lot of money to lock down our network, so I can't invest in expensive network-monitoring programs or audit systems. What can I do?

A Security people like to refer to most corporate networks as "crunchy on the outside, chewy on the inside," meaning that most folks simply do not invest the time in applying security patches for known security holes. If you're interested in how to improve your security without spending megabucks, check out http://www.cert.org, http://www.sans.org, and http://icat.nist.gov. Many vendor-related security vulnerabilities (and how to get fixes) are listed there. You should also make a concerted effort to learn as much as you can about network security policies. Good books on this topic include Cheswick & Bellovin's *Firewalls and Internet Security* and Garfinkel and Spafford's *Practical UNIX Security*.

But perhaps the best thing you can do is to keep current with your application and operating system patches. This includes browser patches. Case in point, the Klez worm would have been largely ineffective had folks patched their Internet Explorer and/or Outlook clients.

Q **My vendor says that its firewall isn't a packet-filtering router or a proxy server. What's up with that?**

A I love vendors. They're so funny sometimes. Here's the deal: Packet-filtering routers got a really, really bad rap a couple of years ago when someone figured out how to fake them out. They received a lot of bad press. Therefore, advanced firewalls aren't really considered to be packet-filtering routers anymore—even though they still route packets, they still deal with packets on a network level, and they still filter.

Basically, just make sure that someone other than your vendor has tested out the firewall in question and found it to be secure. For product comparisons, check out http://www.networkcomputing.com; but these reviews tend to be comparisons of market leaders. For a general stamp of approval, you can check out the ICSA at http://www.icsalabs.com.

Q **Can't my proxy server be compromised by all the bugs out there?**

A Anything's possible. Whether you have a proxy server or a firewall, stay in touch with your vendor and be sure to get security patches as they become available. In general, however, your proxy server should *not* be running other programs besides the proxy programs—unless you're a security expert and can warrant that these other programs won't put the server at risk.

Workshop

Workshop time! Here's a brief quiz to help you make the most out of this hour's lesson, and some activities for you to try on your own.

Quiz

1. What's the difference between a proxy server and a packet-filtering router?

    a. Proxy servers filter on the network level, whereas routers filter on the application level.

    b. Proxy servers filter on the application level, whereas routers filter on the network level.

    c. Routers are security risks with improper configurations.

    d. Proxy servers are security risks with improper configurations.

2. True or False: A proxy server is not considered "network glue." Instead, it's considered "just another server" (albeit a multihomed server).

3. A packet-filtering router and a proxy server are both _____.

    a. users of stateful inspection

    b. multihomed

    c. security loopholes

    d. socket rockets

4. TCP is _____, and UDP is _____.

    a. a pain to configure; wonderful

    b. problematic with government installations; okay with corporations

    c. easy; hard

    d. connection oriented; connectionless

5. A proxy server can be overburdened by which of the following?

    a. Users asking it to proxy local LAN connections

    b. Users asking it to link to infrastructure valence

    c. Too much T1 traffic

    d. Too much searching on a Web site

6. You can use normal DNS troubleshooting tools from within your network if which of the following statements is true?

    a. DNS is being routed through the local DNS servers

    b. DNS is being routed through the proxy server

    c. The router handles internal DNS requests

    d. The proxy server handles all DNS requests

7. NAT modifies the _____ address in the packet at the _____ layer.

    a. destination, source

    b. source, network

    c. network, source

    d. application, destination

16

Answers to Quiz Questions

1. B
2. True
3. B
4. D
5. A
6. A
7. B

Activities

1. Do some reading about why firewalls are *not* the only line of defense to be considered. A good place to start would be at www.incidents.org. What other lines of defense, both technological and policy-based, are available to network professionals? How might these systems fail?

2. Download the nmap tool from www.insecure.org. Among other things, nmap can quickly tell which ports are open on a given host. Run it against hosts that *you* own, not someone else's; doorknob-rattling (which is what this is) is frowned upon unless it's *your* doorknob. How quickly does nmap work on a host that is unprotected by a firewall? How quickly does it run when the same host is protected by a stealth firewall?

PART IV

In the Trenches

Hour

HOUR 17

Where Do You Start?

You are not obligated to finish the task; but neither are you free to neglect it.

—R. Tarfon, *Pirkei Avot* (Chapter 2, Mishna 21)

Networks are kind of like gardens: Without constant maintenance, and without proper planning, they quickly grow out of control. Coming into the middle of a network mess that your predecessor made (trust me, I feel your pain on this) can be quite daunting: You weren't the person who made the mess, and it's hard to know where to start to get your arms around it. If the network was built in an unnecessarily complex fashion, it can be difficult to see your way clear to solving even a simple problem!

But whether you're trying to tame a snarled-up network or tending to one that has been well-built from the start, the answer to "Where do I start?" is this: Every day, try to improve things just a little bit. As you improve the network, two things happen: You get fewer trouble calls, and the trouble calls that you get are easier to handle.

Okay, it's all very well to say "improve the network," but what exactly am I getting at here? Here's the scoop.

You start by continuously documenting (see Hour 3, "Documentation: Your Essential Discovery Tool"); you continue by establishing consistency and standards on your network (see Hour 18, "Managing Change: Establishing Consistency and Standards," for some good tips); and you'll finish by constantly monitoring your network for *potential* trouble—and getting paged or emailed about slowdowns or capacity problems *before* users have a problem (see Hour 23, "Network Management Tools," for more on this). Once you get a handle on these three critical proactive troubleshooting elements, you'll start to feel like the Maytag repair guy—you won't have nearly as much to do.

This is known as *proactive troubleshooting* in geek speak, and it's the best kind of troubleshooting: where you stop problems before they start. However, proactive troubleshooting is a little bit like peace, love, and understanding. (What's so funny?) It's all great and everything, and it's definitely worth shooting for (pardon the phrase); but understand that no matter how much you make things better, you still have to engage in *reactive* troubleshooting (firefighting) when things don't go as planned. Just as you'll continuously work on your proactive troubleshooting by documenting, observing your network, and planning, you'll also continuously be reactively troubleshooting. It's inevitable. The key here is to make the ratio of reactive to proactive troubleshooting very low.

Okay, so we've agreed: we'd all rather avoid problems before they start by learning what causes problems and by enacting policies and procedures to avoid them in the future. But even as we do this, new problems have a way of popping up. Proactive and reactive troubleshooting are simply the yin and the yang of the troubleshooting game. You'll never get done with either; all you can do is make each one less painful.

Accordingly, in this hour, we'll reexamine the basics of how to get started with reactive troubleshooting of networking problems, whether those problems are application related, network protocol related, or physical network related. This will enable you to then further hone in on what the problem might be, based on the theory and composition behind the component.

No book can provide you with a cool head during a network combat situation. However, as this stuff is demystified for you, and you start to form your own set of troubleshooting reaction habits, you'll start to see that whatever the spooky problem is, the source eventually rears its ugly head if you keep plugging away. At the point when this all becomes more familiar to you, and at the point where your proactive techniques are well established, your stress level during problem determination will definitely start to decrease.

Reaction Traction: Getting a Handle on a Problem

Unless you have a crystal ball or network management software (again, see Hour 23), your first inkling that something is wrong with your network will have nothing to do with your network and everything to do with your telephone. This is particularly true if your organization has multiple sites or multiple networks because you're not always going to personally suffer during a network outage; therefore, you won't know what's happening unless someone (or something) lets you know. For the moment, let's assume that you haven't invested in network management software and are relying on your telephone to explode at the speed of light when the network gets into trouble. (As my pop used to say, you need to learn how to use hand tools before you can really appreciate power tools.)

During any trouble call, you want to make sure that you understand two things about the problem: seriousness and scope. You'll want to understand early in the call both to what extent this problem or outage affects business (its seriousness), as well as how widespread the problem is (its scope).

Seriousness is typically communicated fairly early on in the call: "If I don't get this uploaded by the end of the day, I'm going to miss the bank's payroll deadline!" is pretty serious versus, "I can't seem to get to my retirement fund report on the Internet." So your first step as a multitasking troubleshooter is to make sure that you're working on problems in order of seriousness.

The problem's scope usually isn't communicated to you immediately, unless you're talking to a sophisticated user. But it's fairly easy to figure out: Simply ask the person at the other end of the phone whether other users have this same problem. It might take some doing to tickle this answer out of the caller (one popular answer is "I don't have *time* to go ask other people for you"); she is understandably upset, might have lost work, might have a deadline, and so on, and might not want to take the time to answer what seems to be trivial questions. You need to be polite but firm here. Emphasize that you can't provide help if you don't know whether other users are affected. If faced with an intractable user, of course, you can simply pick up the phone and query other, more friendly users yourself. The key is to gather as much information as possible about the problem before beginning your diagnosis.

If other users are experiencing the same problem, the problem is *systemic*—that is, it's a pretty safe bet that everybody's PC hasn't malfunctioned in exactly the same way at

17

exactly the same time, so the answer can be found in something that all the PCs have in common—their common network "glue." Here's a list of items PCs are commonly connected to (in the order of "more local" to "less local"):

- Hubs
- Switches
- Routers/Security devices
- Servers

If you're lucky, the first 90 seconds of the trouble call should tell you where the problem lies, which is pretty cool. When you know what *type* of problem it is, a solution or workaround pretty much takes care of itself.

To show you what I mean, let's say that everyone in the Finance department is down. It's "everyone," so you know it's a systemic problem; but everyone in HR is up. You check with your documentation, and see that HR is in a different closet than Finance. A quick check of the Finance closet reveals that the power has gone out, and switches without power don't do too well. One circuit breaker later, and everyone's back up.

As you can tell by the preceding example, systemic problems are often dealt with using the techniques we discussed in Hour 5, "The Napoleon Method: Divide and Conquer," in this case, divided and dealt with by considering physical location.

If you know the problem is local (PC related) rather than systemic, you can relax—at least you don't have a lot of people down. What's more, if you have built and maintained your network using the consistency techniques that we discuss in Hour 18, your likelihood of getting this person back up quickly is quite high.

Diving into Details

As we discussed in Hour 2, it can be quite useful to consider pertinent layers of the OSI model. When thinking of where to start on a network problem, go through the useful OSI layers again: physical, data link, network, and application. Rule out problems, in order, because each progressive layer depends on the one before it. If there's a physical problem, the data link isn't going to work; but if the network is working, it's a good guess that the data link is also okay.

To your users, *everything* is application oriented. That's the nature of the beast: If users can't get their apps, "the network is down." But not every situation is as clear-cut as "down" versus "not down." "I can't get to the Foo application" usually implies that something is down, but what about "The Foo application is not printing my report"?

Some network problems aren't directly related to the network protocol or physical network attributes. These problems are generally thought of as *application* problems, whether they're client/server programs or file and print–oriented programs. We'll do a lot of in-depth application troubleshooting in Hour 20, "In-depth Application Troubleshooting." Be sure to bring coffee and a hankering to tinker!

You still need to scope application problems because this allows you to rule in or rule out a component as a cause. Again, if one person can't print from the Foo application, you might suspect a workstation or user-related problem. But if nobody can print from the Foo application, you would start by looking at the server.

The way that you handle the call determines the quality of information that you get about the problem. And the quality of information that you get determines how fast you can troubleshoot the problem. As in military intelligence, more information is always a good thing. Don't accept "The such-and-such is down!" as a legitimate trouble call. Specifics are your friend.

Socializing a Solution: Basic Call-Handling Techniques

Accordingly, let's go over the basic call-handling techniques that are applicable when you're not presented with a clear picture of what's going on. Assuming that the user is having unspecified application problems, how do you probe for more information? Don't forget to apply the SOAP theory—getting as many objective facts as possible about any type of trouble can only help you. Ask the user as many factual questions as you can. Here are some examples:

- What happened?
- Can you make the problem happen again, even after a reboot?
- If you can't make it happen again, when did the problem happen?
- During what? With which applications loaded?
- What were you doing right before the problem?
- Was idle time involved?
- Has this happened before? How was it resolved?

17

Asking about previous instances of the current problem is really important. Sometimes the history behind the problem makes the problem come into focus for you. For example, someone might tell you that the problem happens repeatedly at the same time every week—a major clue. Sometimes, the user might go so far as to tell you how the problem was fixed last time. A doctor friend of mine says that history is nine-tenths of diagnosis; he's not too far off.

Asking about idle time might seem insane, but more than once, I've asked this question and come up with a solution. Remember, many things happen after you idle a workstation: screen savers kick in; client-server timeouts occur; and Trojans and viruses sometimes use idle time to work their evil. Problems that only occur during idle time can point to one of these three vectors as the source of the problem.

This whole process—particularly if you're not at the workstation involved—can be like groping in the dark. If you don't have a basis for your questioning, it's hard to know which questions to ask. Sometimes, you simply have to go see it for yourself (particularly when the problem being reported is a local problem). Before you do, however, you might want to try to reproduce the problem from *your* desk.

For example, to rule out operator error, you can have the user at the other end of the line reboot the problem workstation—soup to nuts. Have the user power down and ask her to describe to you what's happening at each stage of the boot process. When it's time to run the application, bring up the same application on your workstation, and have the user talk you through what she is doing to get the error; at the same time, you do the same thing on your end. This process can be tedious, and it takes a bit of practice, particularly if you're familiar with the application but the user is not (or vice versa).

Remote Control

A better option, particularly if it's problematic for you to get across town to a user's workstation, can be to invest in one of the many network remote control packages out there, such as one of the following:

- PCAnywhere
- RemotelyPossible
- Novell Z.E.N. Works Remote Control
- Microsoft SMS Remote Control
- WiredRed's E/Pop (instant messaging plus remote control)

These packages enable you to watch exactly what the person at the other end is doing, which is really, really helpful. Sometimes you can simply correct what the user is doing. If you can't, though, at least you'll realize whether she is reporting the problem correctly

 Of course, a network remote control program does you no good if a workstation is not talking to the network, so you might want to brush up on your over-the-phone troubleshooting skills anyway.

Web Desktop Sharing

If you find yourself doing a good bit of troubleshooting with really, really remote folks, who aren't on your campus network, or if driving or flying to these folks to install one of the remote-control packages is a hassle, consider using the desktop sharing features of a Web collaboration tool instead of traditional remote control. Some of these include

- WebEx.com
- Support.com
- PlaceWare.com
- GotoMyPC.com
- Microsoft NetMeeting
- eRoom

At this writing, some of these can be pricey; but they can be cheaper than troubleshooting via airplane. I am not impressed with the security model of GotoMyPC, but the others seem reasonably good. The .coms listed here are all subscription based, but if you are in the position to maintain a server on the Internet, you can run your own server for NetMeeting and eRoom.

Problem Determination Using TCP/IP

We've already established that more information is good information. So, when you get off the phone, if connectivity still isn't possible, and you have established that your physical gear is okay (power's on in the closets, and so forth), it's really useful to perform some basic TCP/IP troubleshooting steps to gather more data. I basically perform these measures as second nature; it's really useful to have objective data about what is reachable versus what is not. Here are some steps that I typically follow as an initial information-gathering process.

17

This discussion is going to be in the context of a Windows PC, but these steps can be taken on any workstation—you'll just use slightly different commands.

Step 1: Ping the Loopback Address

Ping, the basic IP reachability tool, tells you "up" or "not up." Interestingly, it's usable on your own PC as well as remote destinations.

Reachability always should start inside and work progressively out. ("If I can't hear myself, I can't expect anybody else to hear me either!")

First, you definitely need to identify your user's PC as well as the resource she is trying to get to on your network map. Because the user's workstation is off the network, there's no remote control for you. You'll have to make a personal appearance at the user's work-station, pull up a command prompt, and see if you can ping the loopback address (127.0.0.1), like this:

```
C:\>ping 127.0.0.1
```

Why ping the loopback address? Well, it allows the IP protocol program to talk to itself without involving any outside influence, such as the network card, as illustrated in Figure 17.1. This allows you to rule out the stack or the PC environment as the source of the trouble.

FIGURE 17.1

The TCP/IP stack of your computer can talk to itself, allowing you to rule out the PC environment as a source of trouble.

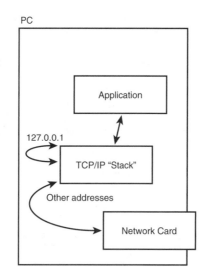

Step 2: Ping the Workstation's IP Address

Next, ping the workstation's IP address. If you don't know what it is, look at the output of the winipcfg (Windows 9x family) or ipconfig command (Windows NT, 2000, and XP). (This command might tell you something else as well: Are you running out of leases on your DHCP scope? Is the DHCP server down? See Hour 19, "Internet and Intranet Troubleshooting: TCP/IP at Work," for more on DHCP.)

You might get a hardware error during either of these local pings, which means you've got a hardware problem. You'll need to run the network card diagnostics that came with your network card.

> If you can't ping the workstation's own IP address, perhaps when Windows started up, the user ignored an error message stating that a conflict existed with the IP address and Windows was going to disable the protocol—meaning no TCP/IP for you! Try rebooting to see if you get such a message. (See Hour 19, "Internet and Intranet Troubleshooting: TCP/IP at Work," as well as Hour 21, "Protocol Analyzers" for tips on hunting down a duplicate IP address with a network analyzer.)

17

Step 3: Ping the IP Address of Another Workstation on the Same Segment

If you *can* ping the workstation, see if you can get to another workstation on the same local network (VLAN). If you can, it means that the workstations involved are functioning correctly on the data link level; that is, they're able to make local calls. If not, you might be dealing with a data link problem.

Don't know the address of a station on the same segment? Try pinging the *broadcast address* (a special address that tells all stations on the segment to respond).

> The broadcast address is typically your IP network number with a 255 tacked on for the node number. Therefore, if your IP address is 192.168.10.5, with a net mask of 255.255.255.0, your node address of 5 would be replaced with 255, giving you 192.168.10.255 as a broadcast address.
>
> Some routers or UNIX workstations allow you to ping 255.255.255.255 and figure out the broadcast address for you, but Windows will not.
>
> The broadcast address is not always 255. If you have a netmask other than 255.255.255.0 (like you probably do with the outside network with your

home router), the broadcast address will be something different. If you have any doubt, and don't want to get into the nasty binary arithmetic involved, check out the free IP calculator at `http://jodies.de/ipcalc`. Just enter your network number and your netmask, and voila, instant answers, including what your broadcast address is. (If this site is down, just Google for "ipcalc.pl".)

Once you ping the broadcast address, display the Address Resolution Protocol (ARP) table (this gives you information about IP-to-MAC address resolution) by typing

`arp -a`

If you see the following message, it means that the ping of the broadcast has failed, and you've probably got a data link problem:

`No ARP Entries Found`

If other folks on this segment are working okay, check this workstation's cable and the card.

A successful ping of the broadcast address looks something like this:

```
C:\>ping 167.195.163.255

Pinging 167.195.163.255 with 32 bytes of dat    A

Reply from 167.195.163.255: bytes=32 time<10ms TTL=128
Reply from 167.195.163.255: bytes=32 time<10ms TTL=128
Reply from 167.195.163.255: bytes=32 time<10ms TTL=128
Reply from 167.195.163.255: bytes=32 time<10ms TTL=128


C:\> arp -a

Interface: 167.195.163.7 on Interface 1
Internet Address   Physical Address    Type
167.195.163.3      00-00-c9-0b-ec-7f   dynamic
167.195.163.9      00-00-c9-14-93-17   dynamic
167.195.163.15     00-00-c9-1e-30-97   dynamic
167.195.163.17     00-05-24-dd-79-ea   dynamic
```

This technique does two things for you: It gives you a handy list of MAC-to-IP addresses, and it tells you that this network card, in conjunction with the TCP/IP stack, is working fine.

Take notes about what works and what doesn't. You'll begin to see how the picture starts to come together.

Step 4: Ping the Local Router

Try pinging the local router (that is, the router responsible for routing traffic for this VLAN). Chances are, if you were able to ping other stations on the segment, you'll be able to ping this, too. But if not, you've probably isolated the problem. Maybe the router's down, but maybe just the transport from your segment to the router is down. For example, some routers aren't truly "local" to a VLAN; they might be connected by fiber-optic cable. So, perhaps the router is up, but the fiber-optic transceiver connecting the router to that VLAN is down.

Step 5: Ping the Server by Name and IP Address

Ping the server by IP address and then try to ping it by name. The important thing to remember is that you want to troubleshoot by IP number *before* bringing name services into the picture; otherwise, you might confuse an already complex issue.

If pinging the IP address works but pinging the name doesn't, you should investigate the DNS configuration of the workstation or check the DNS server itself.

You can check the DNS configuration with the nslookup tool in NT or UNIX. (More discussion on DNS can be found in Hour 19.)

If pinging the IP address doesn't work, you'll definitely want to traceroute the address. Note that the traceroute command on most routers and UNIX systems is actually spelled out (traceroute), whereas Windows' traceroute command is typed as **tracert**. Here's an example of a healthy traceroute from a good workstation to a server:

```
C:\>tracert 167.195.165.15

Tracing route to mail2.blibdoolpoolp.com [167.195.165.15]
over a maximum of 30 hops:

1 10 ms 10 ms 10 ms 167.195.163.1
2 60 ms 70 ms 61 ms 167.195.174.2
3 60 ms 71 ms 60 ms mail2.blibdoolpoolp.com [167.195.165.15]

Trace complete.
```

Now, let's follow this through Figure 17.2. Point A is where you start the `traceroute`, and point B is the address that you have requested the `traceroute` for. `traceroute` knows nothing about switches, so you won't see anything about them. Line 1 of the `traceroute` tells you that the `traceroute` has successfully entered Router 2 on the diagram. The second line tells you that you've successfully entered Router 1 on the diagram. The mail server is local to Router 1, so no further routers are displayed, and line 3 shows successful entry to `mail.blibdoolpoolp.com`.

FIGURE 17.2

Using the `traceroute` *command is helpful when you're troubleshooting routing problems.*

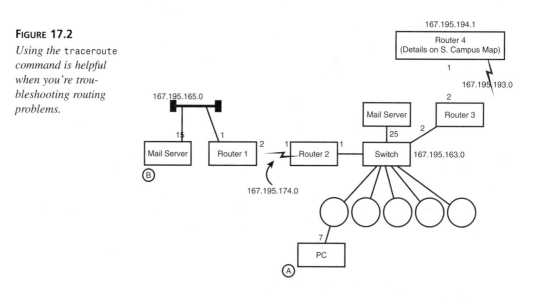

If the only router serving a subnet is down, you might get a `destination unreachable` message, depending on your routing setup. Some implementations of traceroute show this as `!N`.

This happens because the router isn't alive; therefore, it can't generate the routing protocols that advertise the network to other routers. If no router knows about it and no default route passes it off to another better informed router, the destination probably doesn't exist.

Also, be aware that on the Internet, some ISPs or organizations filter at their firewalls, and block `traceroute`.

Each and every router involved is shown in the `traceroute` output. It goes without saying that if you see the `traceroute` just stop, you've discovered the most likely point of failure. For example, if the preceding `traceroute` example had stopped at `167.195.163.1` and never made it to the next hop (`167.195.174.2`), it's likely that there's a problem with the wide-area link (maybe the telephone company) or Router 1 is down. A successful ping of 167.195.174.1 and an unsuccessful ping of 167.195.174.2 would verify this. (It would also show that Router 2 was doing its job but was unable to contact the other side of the wide-area link.)

> Bear in mind that only *one* interface from each router is shown in a traceroute. Notice that there's no record of the packet passing through 167.195.165.1 or 167.195.174.1.

You can also spot misconfigurations with the traceroute command. For example, if you try to traceroute the mail server and get the following output, Router 3 is seriously confused, either by bad configuration information or incorrect information from a routing protocol:

```
C:\>tracert 167.195.165.15

Tracing route to mail2.traceroute.com [167.195.165.15]
over a maximum of 30 hops

1 <10 ms <10 ms <10 ms 167.195.163.2
2 <10 ms 10 ms 10 ms 167.195.194.1
3 <10 ms 10 ms 10 ms 167.195.163.2
4 10 ms 10 ms 10 ms 167.195.194.1
5 10 ms 10 ms 20 ms 167.195.163.2
6 10 ms 20 ms 20 ms 167.195.194.1
7 10 ms 20 ms 20 ms 167.195.163.2
^C
```

Here, Router 4 says, "Hey, this isn't a packet for *me*, take it back!" Then Router 3 says, "Duh, no, George, this is a packet for you!" In this case, you'd have to look at several routers' routing tables to figure out what the deal was. (This problem is called a *routing loop*, which typically comes about when a router is configured with an incorrect static route.)

Summary

It would be nice if you could simply concentrate on improving your network neighborhood each day. And, indeed, doing so goes a long way toward preventing outages. Unfortunately, grim reality dictates that in addition to taking proactive measures to avoid or ameliorate trouble, you also need to know how to react. Fine-tuning your reaction habits every day is a good way to lower your stress level and make you a more effective troubleshooter.

Telephone and trouble-call skills play a large part in determining whether a problem is systemic or local. Sometimes, however, you need to go take a look for yourself, use a remote control program, or let the user guide you to re-create the problem on your workstation.

If you discover a connectivity problem, TCP/IP tools such as `ping`, `traceroute`, `arp`, and `nslookup`, in conjunction with the TCP/IP loopback mechanism, can show you where on the network a problem lies. As you make your way from the local loopback device to the ultimate destination, you continue to gather good information about what the problem is—and what it is not. Always troubleshoot by IP number before bringing name services into the picture so as not to confuse an issue that might already be quite complex.

Q&A

Q Under Windows, what happens if I ping the loopback address and it fails?

A You might want to remove and reinstall the TCP/IP protocol from your Network Control Panel. This could fix corrupt TCP/IP stack files. This isn't too common, though, and might be symptomatic of major problems on the workstation.

Q Hey, can you tell me more about this `nslookup` tool, please?

A This is a really great tool, but is more appropriately discussed in Hour 19 than here. I mention it here because as you get more sophisticated with DNS—particularly if you build an Internet site or deploy Microsoft's Active Directory—it might become part of your initial rote troubleshooting.

Q I can't ping a server on the Internet, even when it's up! What gives?

A As with the UDP datagrams behind `traceroute`, some corporate and ISP firewalls block the IP protocol that's responsible for ping: ICMP. There's really nothing you can do about this, except make a note in your documentation that it's never reachable by ping.

Workshop

Golly, is it workshop time already? My, how time flies. Here's a brief quiz and some activities to help you make the most out of this hour's lesson.

Quiz

1. True or False: Proactive troubleshooting is what you do when you get a call saying that the network is down.

2. Reactive troubleshooting habits include which of the following?

   a. User interviews

   b. Rote connectivity checking

   c. Neither A nor B

   d. Both A and B

3. True or False: Finding out whether a problem has occurred in the past can help resolve the current problem faster.

4. A user has called and said that he can't get into the network at all. You can't get much more out of him. You're able to ping his workstation from your desk just fine, and you see his login on the file server connection list. What do you need to do?

   a. Sever his connection from the file server.

   b. Ping him again.

   c. Call him a jerk and hang up.

   d. Go visit him and see for yourself.

5. True or False: You cannot ping a user's workstation, but you can use a remote control program to view his configuration and fix it.

6. What's the TCP/IP loopback address?

   a. 127.0.0.1

   b. 1.0.0.127

   c. 128.0.0.1

   d. None of the above

7. One user can't get into the server SpaceMonkey; a ping to SpaceMonkey from that user's workstation fails. What's your next step?

   a. Ping another server to make sure SpaceMonkey isn't down.

   b. Ping SpaceMonkey's loopback address.

   c. Look up the numeric IP address for SpaceMonkey and try pinging that.

   d. All of the above.

17

8. My TCP/IP address is `200.1.1.55`, and my netmask is `255.255.255.0`. What's my broadcast address?

   a. `200.1.255.255`

   b. `200.1.1.255`

   c. `200.1.1.0`

   d. `200.1.0.0`

9. My TCP/IP address is `167.195.160.5`, and my netmask is `255.255.255.224`. What's my broadcast address? (Hint: Use the IP calculator referenced earlier in this hour.) (Another hint: this address/netmask combo is also represented as `167.195.160.0/27`.)

   a. `167.195.161.255`

   b. `167.195.160.255`

   c. `167.195.160.31`

   d. `167.195.161.31`

10. After pinging the broadcast address, what do you type to see a table of MAC-to-IP address correlations?

    a. `netstat -a`

    b. `traceroute -a`

    c. `arp -a`

    d. `ping -a`

11. A traceroute reveals that a workstation can't get beyond the third hop. Where might the problem be?

    a. The router at the third hop

    b. The router at the fourth hop

    c. The router at the fifth hop

    d. The router at the second hop

Answers to Quiz Questions

1. False
2. D
3. True
4. D
5. False
6. A
7. C
8. B
9. C
10. C
11. B

17

Activities

1. Browse the Web and find a remote control package that offers a free demo. Run the demo and see how well it works. If possible, run it over a dial-up connection to get a sense of how fast or slow this can be.

2. Using your PC, ping `127.0.0.5`. Then ping `127.5.2.3`. Do you get a response? Why do you think this is? (Hint: Check the routing table on your PC.)

HOUR 18

Managing Change: Establishing Consistency and Standards

The art of progress is to preserve order amid change and to preserve change amid order.

—Alfred North

Network components that are configured consistently—identically, when possible—are a godsend to busy network troubleshooters. In particular, I'll discuss two techniques in this hour that will help you build and maintain as consistent (*homogenous* in geek speak) a network as possible:

- Manual consistency methods (which rely mostly on personal organization skills combined with the use of operating system features)

- The use of automated deployment tools

Apart from the obvious benefits of planning once and deploying many times, these consistency techniques are going to make your troubleshooting life a lot less complex.

In addition, here are four network components that, if kept standardized, can contribute to an easy life as a troubleshooter:

- Hard drive configuration
- Network scripts and policies issued on a group basis
- Network user templates
- Network application configuration

Having identically configured components means that if one component works in one place, it should work in others as well, unless a hardware problem exists. (Hardware problems become more obvious if everybody is on the same operating system page.) It also means that you don't have to understand many problems in order to troubleshoot them. Instead of having to understand the nuts and bolts behind a complex network configuration, you can compare simple items to *known good items* (for example, login scripts or user attributes) or quickly redo more complex items.

For example, once you discover that a workstation (that is *supposed* to be identical to other workstations) is having an operating system or application problem (and you've ruled out the entire user object, user attributes, and network application configuration), you can simply clone its hard drive. This operation takes 15 minutes (versus the hours that you might spend troubleshooting it otherwise). What's more, if the hard drives are indeed all configured the same, cloning the workstation couldn't hurt—that is, at least it won't hurt the configuration that's *supposed* to be on the drive.

If you're an experienced PC technician, you're probably nodding your head at this point, thinking, "Holy cow, how many hours of my life have I wasted tracking down some stupid obscure registry or driver conflict?" Yeah. Me, too. In a multi-workstation environment, tracking down obscure stuff usually isn't what you want to be working on. Workstation cloning is one way to reduce this—but to minimize the hassle of workstation re-setup, you also want to use other management tools. Read on.

To keep from upsetting your users, you need to communicate before you leap. That is, you need to let your users know that keeping data files on their hard drives is a really, really bad idea. Apart from the fact that their data will be lost in the event of a hard drive failure—c'mon, how many people actually back up their hard drives every single day?—the cloning of a given hard drive completely overwrites any information stored there. The organization that I work for deals with this in a low-tech but effective way: Each PC, at delivery, comes with a "hard drive policy" statement tacked on it.

Here's the bottom line: Troubleshooting starts with identifying whether the problem is local or systemic. If it's a local problem, you can often treat it via homogenization of the workstation or user object. This means that, typically, all you need to spend your brain power on are the *systemic* problems. If you apply the techniques in this hour, local problems will become no-brainers.

Manual Standardization

You don't really need automated deployment tools in order to get organized. (On the other hand, they do make tasks go a lot quicker and easier.) Regardless of whether you choose to use power tools or a hand drill to automate your network rollouts, in order to be successful, you definitely need a well-defined work plan. (It's an old saw in the automation game: How can you automate anything that has yet to be done manually?)

Let's look at the parts of your work plan that need to be addressed whether you automate or deploy manually:

- Divide tasks into workstation-oriented tasks and user setup–oriented tasks
- Make checklists of tasks that must be completed
- Keep good records
- Write down a detailed rollout plan, shoot holes in it, and refine the plan
- Resist the temptation to deviate from the plan

In short, the characteristics of a good network rollout—big or small—are basically your good work habits translated to the computing arena. Try to think of any network rollout as a factory job or as a cookie-cutting session: Anything done to one network object must be done to the next network object.

Here's the problem with doing things manually. Unless you and everyone in your department do things in *exactly* the same machine-like manner *all* the time, there's no guarantee that each object will be exactly the same. Accordingly, many folks prefer to use power tools to standardize their networks.

18

Power Tool Time

Between your network operating system, the directory services, and third-party software, some serious tools are available to help you in your consistency quest:

- **Hard-drive duplication (cloning) tools** As mentioned previously, these help you to standardize your user's PCs and start fresh if you need to.

- **User templates** These enable you to create large numbers of users who are identical in all properties except for their unique identifiers (username).

- **User-level login scripts** Login scripts exist to perform various startup configurations, such as adding a PATH to a user's environment, showing a message of the day, and so on. User-level login scripts are run when an individual user logs in.

- **Organizational or group-level login scripts** Organizational or group scripts run when anybody from that group or organization logs in.

- **Group policies** Group policies ensure both that certain aspects of user workstations are consistent. (For example, you can make sure that everyone is configured with the correct proxy for Internet Explorer.) Group policies also prevent users from changing certain attributes of the workstation. (For example, you can lock users out of the Network Control Panel.)

- **User network profiles** Network profiles are network-stored configuration information, such as your Windows desktop, Start menu, preferences, and so on.

- **Application deployment and update tools** Once a basic standard image is on the PC, these tools automate the process of mass deployment to a group: sending down new applications and tweaking existing ones.

Send in the Clones: Disk Duplication Details

Disk duplication has been one of the innovations that has made using complex desktop operating systems such as Windows a survivable experience for network administrators. It has allowed administrators to treat the whole Windows kettle of DLLs, VXDs, configuration files, and so on as one manageable container. Disk duplication isn't a panacea for all your standardization woes, but it sure helps. The idea behind a disk-duplication rollout is that you get it right once for each functional group and then roll it out many times.

Instead of doing an hour-or-so-long Windows install from CD-ROM for each workstation—to the tune of 40 or so hours for 40 workstations—you can perform a 10-minute disk duplication of a hard drive that already has Windows on it, which translates into a mere six-plus hours for those same workstations. This disk duplication is also called *cloning*, and we'll discuss it in more depth in a little while.

Yes, Microsoft supports automated setup scripts for Windows, which allow you to run unattended setup sessions for large numbers of computers, usually from the network. However, writing unattended setup scripts requires a reasonable amount of "inside knowledge" and customization for your site. Here's the bottom line: It's not as easy and quick as disk duplication. Even Microsoft has backed off of this unattended install script thing somewhat.

What's more, in addition to the time consideration, you *know* that each workstation is the same. You don't have to write anything down—even those small tweaks you do to optimize your system—to ensure that all installs have the correct settings.

You'll want to make sure that all the workstations' hardware is pretty much the same before you duplicate drives between them; otherwise, you run the risk of intermittent or hard-to-find problems. This typically isn't a big deal—if you're buying 10 to 20 PCs, it's highly unlikely that you're going to purchase them all from different sources. This sanity check comes more into play when you're upgrading folks rather than doing new installs.

Yes, Windows is really good at detecting when the hardware changes—but why risk *any* problems? We're looking at using duplication to avoid trouble, not cause it.

18

Every so often, no matter how sure you are that the duplication is a known good one, you should verify that the duplication image is still what you want to be rolling out. For example, if your Lotus Notes software gets updated, you probably want to update your drive image.

Also, make sure that your image is "clean" from a scandisk perspective. Trust me, it's pretty depressing to roll out a whole department, only to find out that you've rolled out a defective File Allocation Table along with the operating system. Spend a lot of time verifying that all applications and options run correctly. It will pay off in the long run.

A duplication session in its simplest form is basically a DOS or character-mode UNIX session, loaded off of boot disk or from the network. Once the session is loaded, you can use software such as Symantec's "Ghost" to copy the entire contents of the current hard drive to a file on the network (with or without compression) or download the contents of the network file to the workstation's hard drive.

To boot from the network (as opposed to a floppy), you will have to enable the *PXE (preboot execution environment)* feature of your PCs' BIOS. In a nutshell, PXE enables a PC to download a small boot image from the network, and then to load the hard drive with another downloaded image. Of course, to be able to download PXE images, you need a PXE server to download from. (Altiris's RapiDeploy and Novell's ZenWorks for Desktops are two examples of products that include a PXE server.) If you want to keep it simple, a boot disk is always an option.

You have other options, too. Many duplication software packages (again, Symantec's Ghost is a good example) can duplicate disk to disk, to a tape drive, or to a writeable CD-ROM.

After you duplicate, you have to change the individual parameters on the new workstation—for example, the machine name and the TCP/IP address (if you're not using DHCP). Software that has advanced duplication features, such as Altiris's RapiDeploy or Novell's ZenWorks, has the capability to do this for you. Cool!

User Templates

User templates are awesome, but they're really just a takeoff of what network administrators have been doing for years: creating a "Joe User," testing him out, and then duplicating all his attributes for the other users.

If you don't use a directory service that allows for user templates (like Windows 2000's Active Directory or Novell's NDS), you will have to pull the "Joe User" trick.

Joe User

If your operating system doesn't provide user templates, meet Joe User. He's the guy who will let you standardize your user population. (In fact, you might have to create several Joes for different departments.) You create his login, his group associations, and his home directory, and you populate his home directory with the various configuration files he might need. For example, different groups of UNIX users might need certain startup files, including but not limited to .xdefaults, .xinitrc, .pinerc, and so on. Similarly, some Windows applications also need user-specific files for terminal emulation settings, Lotus 1-2-3 settings, and so on.

You can copy Joe every time you need to create a new user. Copy his home directory contents to the new user's home directory, and you can rest assured that the new user has everything she needs to get her job done. Think of this as making a boilerplate document in your word processor for a letter you send out every week or so—all you need to do is copy the document, change a few specifics, and you've saved yourself a good deal of time and energy.

For example, if you still use Windows NT Domains, Figure 18.1 shows the copy user feature for Windows NT.

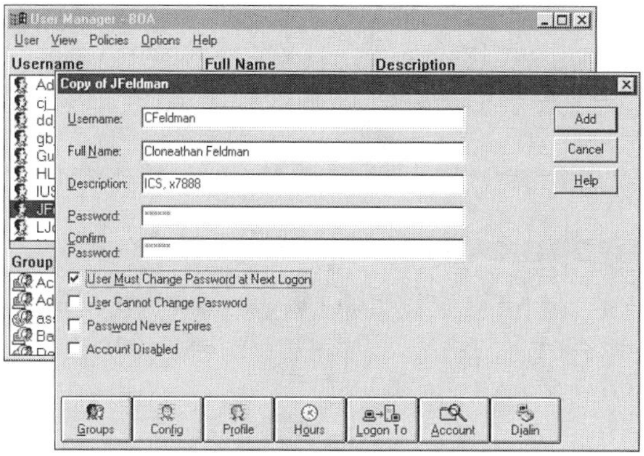

FIGURE 18.1

You can use NT's User Manager for Domains to copy a domain user.

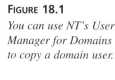

User-Level Login Scripts

Every server has the capability to run login scripts for all users. These login scripts perform common tasks for all users. Here are a few examples:

- Show a message of the day
- Set environment variables needed by application programs
- Update workstation software
- Synchronize workstation time to the network
- Set up dumb terminal environments or run "startup" software

You should avoid user-specific login scripts as much as possible because it's time-consuming to configure every workstation one at a time. Instead, do as much as you possibly can in the system login script and the group-oriented login scripts.

Group or Departmental Scripts

Systemwide login scripts include /etc/profile in UNIX, for example. These allow administrators to have certain things happen for everyone in the system, which is neat. Of course, you might want certain other things to happen on a departmental level—not on a systemwide basis.

Until the advent of modern directory services, administrators didn't have the ability to write a script for users on a departmental basis. Nowadays, it's pretty common to write a script for everyone in an OU (organizational unit department). This, of course, increases the number of scripts to keep track of, although it also separates and organizes your scripts pretty nicely.

So, are departmental or group-level scripts a blessing or a curse? Well, it depends on whether you need them. If everybody at your company uses the same applications and requires the exact same settings, system-level scripts are your best bet. However, if certain departments in your organization need different settings from others, group-level scripts are almost a necessity.

Faking Group or Departmental Scripts

Group scripts are all well and good for users of ADS or NDS, but what about those without a directory service? Fret not—there are tricks that allow you to specify group-level operations from your system login script.

 Windows NT's logon scripts are usually .BAT or .CMD files—which, of course, are regular old batch files.

For example, under Windows NT, for each user in your finance department, a workaround to enable group-level logon scripts would be to specify each user's logon script as FINANCE.BAT, which will run all the commands needed for the Finance department.

But what about users who really do need their own stuff? If certain users really do need their own login scripts (and you should think long and hard about this because it's much harder to maintain), you can have a line such as the following as the last line of FINANCE.BAT:

```
if exist %USERNAME%.bat %USERNAME%.bat
```

This will run a user-oriented script if such a file exists in the login directory (so, the user SMonkey would run SMONKEY.BAT).

In Linux or UNIX, if you use the standard ksh or bash shell, you can perform a group test in the /etc/profile script and then execute a particular set of instructions if a person turns out to be in that group:

```
groups | grep -q -w finance && {
  echo "You're in the Finance group, no party for you!"
  cat /finance/message-of-the-day
  PARTY="false"
}
```

```
groups | grep -q -w network && {
    echo "Hello network person, party on!"
    cat /network/message-of-the-day
    PARTY="true"
}
```

The potential "gotcha" behind group-level scripts is that some single users might be in multiple groups. For example, let's consider a user in the previous example who's both in the Finance group *and* the Network group. She would end up with a PARTY variable of "true". Is this what you want? If it isn't, you'll need to change this so that the Network group is tested for first.

> Don't get overly excited about the ability to affect large numbers of users at once. When treating mass quantities, a slip of your electronic knife has the potential of making a lot of people very unhappy all at once.
>
> You should always test pilot as far away from spectators as possible. If you have a test server, use it; in any event, you should use a test group and a test user when testing out a new script or a new way of doing something.

Windows Profiles

All currently supported Windows products have the capability to store user-specific information on the network, rather than storing it on the local hard drive (although the hard drive has a copy of the information, too). This information consists of the following items:

- The Start menu (shortcuts)
- The Desktop (shortcuts)
- Recently used files (shortcuts)
- The User Registry (a roaming version of the Registry with user-specific settings— it's a system, hidden, read-only file called USER.DAT)

Profiles are a wonderful standardization tool, as well as a good network-troubleshooting tool. Because the user settings are easily separated from the user's workstation, having the user try something at another workstation is easy and painless—you sometimes don't even have to reinstall applications to have the application settings move with you.

If you're still using Windows 9x, be aware that it ships with profiles turned off by default (so that every user has the same settings): You'll want to make sure that you turn them on. To do this, click the Start button; choose Settings, Control Panel; and select Passwords. Click the User Profiles tab in the Passwords Properties dialog box, and then make the appropriate changes (see Figure 18.2). (You can also set this with Windows policies, which we'll discuss in a moment.)

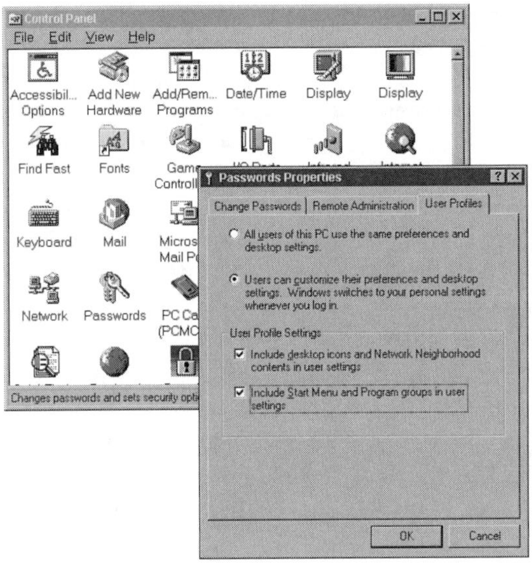

FIGURE **18.2**

The Windows 9x Control Panel allows you to turn profiles on or off for a given machine. Many corporate networks use the settings shown in this figure.

Where do the user profiles live? On a Windows network, as well as on a NetWare network, they live in the users' home directories. The Windows NT family (which includes NT, 2000, and XP) uses a special subdirectory of the user home directory; the Windows 9x family just plops them in the root of the home directory so that there's a Desktop, Start Menu, and other familiar folders at the root.

If you're going to add or replace something in the user's *network* profile files, make sure that you do it while the user is logged out because Windows writes a user's profile to the network as she logs out of the network. If you don't enact changes while the user is logged out, your changes will be overwritten at the point when she logs out.

Windows Policies: Saving Users from Themselves

"Save the users from themselves!" is the cry heard from many a network administrator. I'm sure you've at least thought it. Consider the case of the lady who learned how to change her screen colors—and changed them to yellow, her favorite color. This would have been fine, only she changed *all* the colors to yellow—foreground and background—leaving her with a yellow-on-yellow Windows installation, which was kind of hard to read!

To avoid this type of situation, Microsoft introduced a special administrative tool called a *policy file*. If you're using Windows NT 4.0 or Windows 9x, a policy file, when in the SYS:PUBLIC directory of a NetWare server or the NETLOGON directory of an NT server, will enforce certain Registry settings for either default users or specific ones. This makes it sort of tough for users to shoot themselves in the foot, and it keeps you from wanting to shoot them elsewhere.

A policy file can be as restrictive or as permissive as you like. You can lock down the Control Panel in part or in full, restrict application installation, and so on. In short, you can make yourself really, really unpopular with the users. It's a tough call—how much restriction is fair protection versus how much restriction makes a network a fascist police state. This pretty much depends on your corporate culture.

Windows policies make it possible for you to ensure that certain Windows attributes stay the same between PCs on your network.

Microsoft's latest take on policies, Group Policies (supported in Windows 2000 and above), are great. As with everything else, you will be better off if you plan your Group Policy rollout rather than winging it. Some good tips can be found at http://www.microsoft.com/windows2000/techinfo/planning/management/groupsteps.asp.

In a nutshell, whether you use the old-style policies (POLEDIT), or the new MMC snap-in (GPEDIT.MSC), you can assign a policy to a *system* or a *user*. If you assign a policy to a system, any login to that system enables that policy in the system registry (HKEY_LOCAL_MACHINE). If you assign a policy to a user, only the user portion of the registry is affected (HKEY_CURRENT_USER).

How do the clicks that you do in GPEDIT or POLEDIT get translated into registry modifications on the workstation?

Microsoft provides special script files that tell the policy editors how to build the policies, and what keys in the registry will be affected. These files are called *administrative templates*, and they all have the file extension ADM. To add a custom ADM file in the Group Policy Editor, go to Computer Configuration, and right-click on Administrative Templates. Select Add/Remove Templates. If you want to create your own template, check out the Windows 2000 Resource Kit—or simply plunder an existing ADM file for your own purposes.

Stuck with POLEDIT? Ouch! The basic old-style policies were a lot harder to use, and you couldn't do much unless you snagged additional administrative templates. Although things like the Control Panel were covered, as in Figure 18.3, you couldn't do much with Internet Explorer until you added an ADM file.

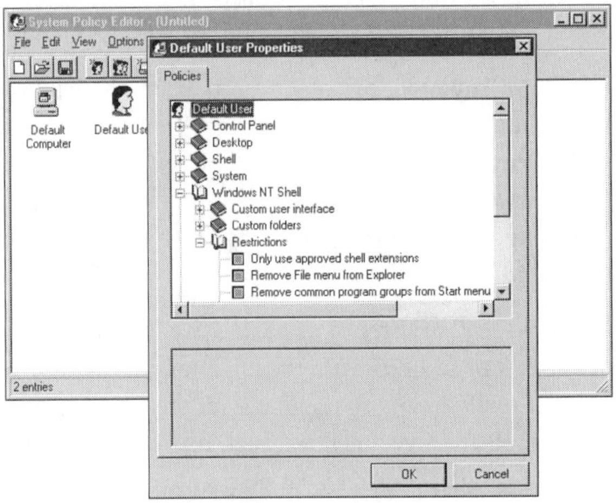

FIGURE 18.3

The Windows Policy Editor can restrict your users, but keeping track of ADM *files gets ugly.*

By comparison, GPEDIT (see Figure 18.4) is much nicer; it provides granular control over just about every feature. Figure 18.4 shows how to "lock down" Internet Explorer proxy settings for users.

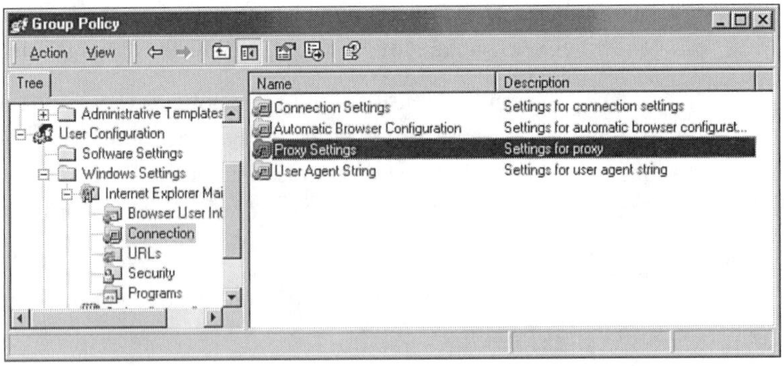

FIGURE 18.4

The Microsoft Management Console (MMC) snap-in GPEDIT.MSC *(with its window titled Group Policy) showing proxy policy.*

I'll leave you with one important concept about policies that many folks (including me) have a hard time getting past. There are three possible *states* for a given policy item:

Enabled (checkbox checked)

Disabled (checkbox cleared)

Not Configured (checkbox gray)

If a policy is enabled by user A, and it is not explicitly disabled by user B (that is, user B has that policy in the "not configured" state), user B will receive that system policy.

Here's one example: Joe is supposed to be able to run the *MMC (Microsoft Management Console)*, but Mary has it explicitly disabled. Mary logs in to Joe's PC to do some work, and then Joe comes back from lunch, and finds that he can no longer pull up the MMC. Why? Mary's policy explicitly disabled the MMC, and Joe didn't have a policy one way or another. (One tip: To display the "current" group policies for a user, use GPRESULT.EXE from the Windows resource kit.)

A good rule of thumb is, if you create a policy that enables something, make sure to modify your other policies to disable it, if appropriate.

App in a Snap: Application Rollout Tools

It used to be that all you needed to do to deploy a network application was give a user a menu option or a shortcut. Modern Windows applications are a lot more complex; some install a lot of workstation files, make changes to the user's Registry, and can, frankly, drive network administrators nuts.

18

Using Shared Network Directories

Some (but not most) Windows applications are easy to standardize, simply by installing the application into a shared network directory that many people can access. This way, you can configure the application from this central location.

For example, both NetTerm, a Telnet application, as well as PuTTY, an SSH client, allow many users to use the same network directory to run the application without running the setup program on each workstation. Here's how I'd do this for NetTerm (I'd do PuTTY similarly).

1. Run NetTerm's setup program.

2. Specify a network location for the program (for example, G:\NetTerm).

3. Create an icon for NetTerm on each user's desktop that points to G:\netterm\ netterm.exe, either by visiting the user (perish the thought!) or by modifying the user's profile on the network.

You'll have to check your manufacturer's documentation or experiment to determine whether you've got an application that will support this.

For complex applications, application deployment tools are almost as cool as disk dupli-cation. They come in two styles: script-based and snapshot-based.

Script-Based Application Deployment

You probably use script-based application deployment tools every day. The two best-known script-based application deployment tools are InstallShield and Microsoft's Windows Installer. Both of these tools tightly couple their scripts with the SETUP.EXE installation utility. Learning how to bend these tools to your mighty whim is not only gratifying, but incredibly useful. Here's how.

InstallShield is a script-based application deployment tool; it customizes its install based on user queries, and generates a *script file* that you can then use again and again to do unattended installs. This way, you don't have to repeatedly answer "which directory do you want the software installed in" and other inane questions. The best part is that this allows you to install the software *silently*, without allowing a user to either see what's going on or interrupt. Cool, eh?

In order to record a script file for an InstallShield-bundled app (you can identify these because you'll see a wizard that mentions InstallShield), run setup.exe with the -r flag. Run the install the way you want it done for all users. Then, snag the setup.iss file out of the Windows directory. (Caution: Make sure that it's dated today's date—if it's not, you might be looking at the wrong setup.iss file.)

You'll then use either a login script or provide the users with an icon to click to install the package. The command line (for either the icon or the login script) should say setup -s—but make sure that the working directory contains the setup.iss.

Here's one word of caution: The setup.iss script will look different depending on the platform; you can't use a script generated on Windows 98 to install an app on Windows 2000. Accordingly, you'll probably want to create separate .iss scripts depending on the platform you're dealing with. Table 18.1 shows the command line switches that allow this.

TABLE 18.1 Useful InstallShield Command Line Switches

Switch	Function
-r	Record setup to setup.iss
-s	Do silent install using setup.iss
-f1*file*.iss	Use *file*.iss instead of setup.iss, for example, G:\myapp\setup2k.iss. There must be no space between the f1 switch and *issfile*.

TABLE 18.1   continued

Switch	Function
`-f2logfile`	Log the results of the install to `logfile`. I suggest using `%WINDIR%\myapp.log`, or, if you're brave, you can write this to the user's home directory, such as `H:\myapp.log` or even `G:\myapp\userlog\%username%.log`. (If you take this last option, make sure that users can write to the `userlog` directory.) Again, there should be no space between the `f2` and the `logfile` name.

Now let's discuss my favorite script-based installer, Microsoft's Windows Installer. The Installer is loads of fun, allowing you to both add and remove products with impunity.

Script files are, predictably, called *MSI (MS Installer)* files. Although you can simply double-click on an MSI file to install it (at least, if you're running Win2K or better), running the `setup.exe` will install the product and give you better control.

There's good news and bad news here. The good news is that most MSI-compliant packages use the same set of command-line switches. For example, for every MSI-packaged application that I've run into, you can specify `/qb+` for a non-verbose install that allows the user to cancel the install. The `/qn+` option makes the install run silently and doesn't allow the user to cancel, only reporting success or failure at the end. You can see the supported command-line switches for Office 2000 (and thus for MSI in general) at `http://support.microsoft.com/default.aspx?scid=kb;EN-US;q202946`.

The bad news is that certain properties vary widely among MSI packages. For example, if you wanted McAfee VirusScan 4.5 to scan at startup as part of your `setup.exe` command line, you would also indicate `SCANATSTARTUP=true`. (You know this by reading the McAfee installation manual.)

Although some manufacturers provide a tool to further customize MSI scripts, some don't; and some don't provide a lot of flexibility in their tools. What's a system admin to do?

Well, here comes Orca to the rescue. The Orca tool allows you to customize MSI scripts, even down to the registry level (see Figure 18.5). You'll have to download the *SDK (Software Developer's Kit)* from Microsoft. Don't worry, you won't have to start programming; just install ORCA from the `tools` subdirectory after you've installed the SDK. Snag the SDK from `http://msdn.microsoft.com/msdn-files/027/001/457/IntelSDK.msi`.

18

For example, if you wanted to change the FTP directory for virus pattern updates, you could use Orca on McAfee's VSCAN45.MSI file to find a registry entry with FTP in it. Sure enough, you'd find what you see in Figure 18.5. You can change many other values in this way. That's very snazzy!

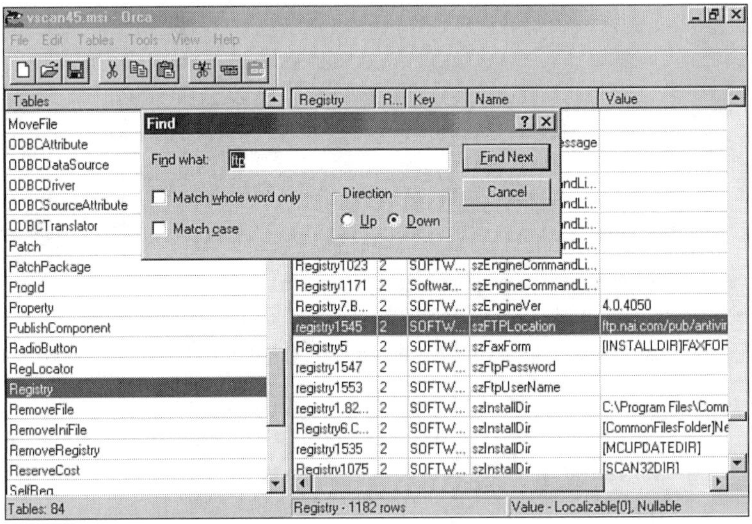

FIGURE **18.5**

ORCA can edit any MSI file, letting you search for "known content" to find the field you need—and then modify it— whether or not the developer has provided you access to them with an app-specific tool.

Snapshot-Based Application Deployment

Snapshot-based deployment tools basically take a look at a PC *before* a given application is installed and then take one again *after* the application is installed. The differences—whether in the Registry, in the files on the C:\ drive, or wherever—are calculated and stored on the network. These differences can be applied to any PC. You have an instant application with minimum user interaction, and all from the network. This is a great method for standardizing user workstations in conjunction with disk duplication.

The only thing to bear in mind when using one of the snapshot-style deployment tools—for example, Microsoft's SYSDIFF, Novell's SnAPPshot, or LANovation's Picture Taker—is that you need to make sure that you're using a perfectly clean workstation when taking the "before" snapshot. That is, the workstation should *never* have had the application installed on it (ditto for shared components that the application wants). My preference is to keep the *dupe* for that department around as a disk duplication file; I reload a hard drive with this right before taking a snapshot. This ensures that each app has a chance to perform a totally fresh install.

Are there problems with snapshot-style application deployment? There can be, particularly if you don't test before deploying (making sure to test on a workstation that is just like the ones that you will be deploying to).

The key, again, to *any* successful application deployment, is to test, test, and test some more before you deploy. This up-front work—for any of the standardization techniques we've discussed in this hour—will pay off as you experience easy troubleshooting operations for hours, days, and weeks in the future.

Summary

Using network components that are similar means that you don't have to undertake deep troubleshooting in order to solve many local (not systemic) problems. Besides, heterogeneous components tend to behave the same—which, if they have a known good configuration, is a wonderful thing.

Apart from using common-sense work habits while creating users and workstations, you'll also want to check out the built-in cookie-cutter functions of your network operating system, such as user templates and Joe User user copies. Although a little bit of scripting knowledge can be a dangerous thing, it can also be a huge help in streamlining user login setups.

User profiles and disk duplication are simple and easy ways to ensure uniformity among your users, as well as to guide workstation setups or user setups back in line when they stray. What's more, Windows policies can really help as well. Add application deployment to the recipe, and you've got a mix of strong tools that will help your network stay as consistent as possible.

Q&A

Q I just rolled out a hundred workstations and I didn't test thoroughly enough, and I only now realize that I forgot to set an important registry setting on all of them. What do I do?

A Well, you could read up on creating your own Administrative Template file, but here's a simpler trick. Create the registry setting in REGEDIT. Export the settings into a REG file. Then, from the group login script, execute the REGEDIT tool with the /s (silent) flag:

```
REGEDIT /s filename.REG
```

Q Which third-party management software is right for me?

A Here are a few options; if you are looking for an all-in-one solution, I'd look hard at Altiris or ZenWorks because they include everything but the kitchen sink.

- Altiris (RapiDeploy & Client Mgmt Suite) `www.altiris.com`
- Intel (LANDesk) `www.intel.com`
- InstallShield (InstallShield AdminStudio) `www.installshield.com/isas/`
- PowerQuest (DriveImage) `www.powerquest.com`
- Phoenix Technologies (ImageCast) `www.imagecast.com`
- Novell (ZenWorks) `www.zenworks.com`
- Symantec (Ghost) `www.ghost.com`

Workshop

Workshop time! Here's a brief quiz to help you make the most out of this hour's lesson, and some activities for you to try on your own.

Quiz

1. You discover, halfway through a departmental rollout of workstations, that although the SQL server client you've been using is working fine, it's not the latest and greatest. A prudent consistency technique would dictate that you do what?

   a. You start using the latest and greatest client on the rest of the machines.

   b. You start using the latest and greatest client on power users' machines.

   c. You keep rolling out the same client on power users' machines and the latest and greatest on others.

   d. You keep rolling out the same client on the rest of the machines.

2. True or False: It's a good idea, whether or not you opt to use disk duplication, to advise users *not* to rely on their hard drive as a permanent storage medium.

3. Which of the following statements is true concerning user templates?

   a. They're available on all operating systems, making user copies undesirable.

   b. They're not available on any operating systems, making user copies mandatory.

   c. They're not available on some operating systems, but user copies are possible.

   d. None of the above.

4. For consistency's sake, it's best to _____.

    a. use as many individual login scripts as possible

    b. use system-oriented or group-oriented login scripts

    c. Both A and B

    d. Neither A nor B

5. When copying a Joe User, what should you remember to do?

    a. Copy the user object, the system login script, and home directory files.

    b. Copy the user object, home directory files, and login script if necessary.

    c. Copy the home template.

    d. Copy the login template.

6. True or False: There are tricks that allow you to perform group-oriented login scripts, even if the operating system does not directly support login scripts for groups.

7. True or False: Disk duplication is appropriate for every workstation installation.

8. A user of yours keeps accidentally changing her display driver settings, leading you to repeatedly troubleshoot a terminal emulation problem. Which action should you take to stop this nonsense?

    a. Edit her Registry.

    b. Create a policy file.

    c. Neither A nor B.

    d. Both A and B.

9. When creating an application deployment snapshot, you should be certain to do what?

    a. Use a workstation that already has the application installed on it.

    b. Use a user's workstation.

    c. Use a clean workstation image that is just like those deployed in the department, without any additional installed components already on it.

    d. None of the above.

Answers to Quiz Questions

1. D

2. True

3. C

4. B

5. B

6. True

7. False. It's only appropriate for the installation of groups of similar hardware.

8. B

9. C

Activities

1. See whether you have roaming profiles enabled on your workstation. Where are the profiles stored? Are files there that you didn't expect to be there? What about non-shortcut desktop items?

2. Do a File Find on the policy administrative templates (*.adm) on your hard drive. Open one of them in Notepad. Do you think it would be really hard to create your own .adm? Check out the Windows 2000 resource kit if the .adm file looks like chicken tracks to you.

   For extra credit, and to prove to yourself that this .adm stuff isn't *that* big a deal, try writing your own with something trivial, like creating a policy called MyDog, which affects the registry setting HKEY_LOCAL_MACHINE\MyDog\Type.

HOUR 19

Internet and Intranet Troubleshooting: TCP/IP at Work

We've all heard that a million monkeys banging on a million typewriters will eventually reproduce the entire works of Shakespeare. Now, thanks to the Internet, we know this is not true.

—Robert Wilensky

Although the Internet, in the minds of many business folks at the time, began as a huge waste of time, business as we know it in this century could not exist without the Internet and private intranets. Moreover, it's all driven by the same humble protocol that began it all in the 1970s: TCP/IP.

The basic idea behind this hour is that the same backhoes and steamrollers used to fix the information superhighway at large are also used to troubleshoot your local streets and byways. We'll start off by defining the Internet versus intranets and quickly get into troubleshooting techniques both for TCP/IP infrastructure as well as client/server applications.

Nobody needs to define the Internet for you. The source of life, the Mecca of computer civilization, the wellspring from which information flows, the fount of all packets good and ill, is the Internet. In the space of one kid's college career, the Internet has gone from being a pretty nice resource for computer geeks, to being indispensable for geeks, to being indispensable for everyone. Many folks used to call the Internet a "noncritical, but important resource," but that's no longer the case, particularly if your business relies on email or a Web page to keep in touch with customers. Nowadays, it is a critical resource; if it's down, oftentimes folks can't do their work. This book was edited largely over the Internet. Had I been unable to use the Internet—ouch! I don't want to think about it. I would have taken much longer to write this (and that's saying a lot).

Whether you use Internet or the intranet, when you use your workstation to browse, here's what happens:

- Your browser checks to see if a proxy is configured (see Hour 16, "Firewall and Proxy Server Basics"). We'll assume for the purposes of simplicity that one isn't configured, so we'll continue normally.

- Your workstation extracts the host name from the URL (that is, the host name for `http://www.Microsoft.com/support` is `www.Microsoft.com`) and then uses DNS to resolve this into a usable IP number (say, Microsoft.com).

- Your browser asks your workstation's IP stack to form a TCP socket between itself and the IP address, port 80 (which is the HTTP service). This part can involve anywhere from zero to a dozen routers.

- Your browser then uses the HTTP protocol to ask the foreign server for the page.

Should troubleshooting your Internet connection differ from the TCP/IP troubleshooting that you've already learned? Not fundamentally; the problem is that various security devices (such as proxies) and speed-up devices (such as caches) change the rules a bit. Accordingly, let's start with basic TCP/IP communication and troubleshooting techniques, and then get fancier.

Typical TCP/IP Troubleshooting

The applications that make an intranet run are similar in nature to the applications that you'll run on the Internet, so you can apply the techniques discussed in the following sections to your Internet servers as well. Here's a good rule of thumb: The Internet is your intranet writ large.

It goes without saying, but I'll say it anyway: Do not start troubleshooting at a TCP/IP level (layer 3 of the OSI model) until you have verified that layer 1 (physical) and layer

2 (data link) are okay. There's no sense in chasing after a TCP/IP problem if your connectivity problem has been caused by your Ethernet switch blowing a fuse! (See Hour 17, "Where Do You Start?" for more info on problem triage, including basic TCP/IP problem triage.)

IP Addresses, DHCP, and DNS

When I first wrote this chapter, just about everyone in the universe was using statically-allocated (manual) IP addresses. What a pain! Fortunately, it seems like nowadays everyone in the universe is using dynamically-allocated IP addresses via DHCP, the Dynamic Host Configuration Protocol.

So, probably the first thing you want to do with a given problematic host (given that you've used other troubleshooting techniques to pinpoint *this* host) is to verify its address configuration. Should it be configured dynamically or statically? Does it have the correct configuration, or has someone fat-fingered it?

If the answer is "Well, it's dynamically configured, but I don't have an IP address," you have either a client or a server DHCP problem. (Under Windows, you can try `ipconfig /release` followed by an `ipconfig /renew` to manually initiate the DHCP client process. Under Linux, you can manually run the DHCP client by invoking `dhcpcd`.) I've definitely seen DHCP client problems on Windows that were only solvable by removing TCP/IP and re-installing it. Yuck! Usually, though, a simple release/renew works out pretty well.

Before you go blaming the client, though, (and feeling foolish when you remove and reinstall TCP/IP with no result) it pays to check out the DHCP server. What, exactly, can be wrong?

19

 Figure 15.2 in Hour 15, "Home and Office Routers," shows how routers can sometimes be the culprit in DHCP problems.

For starters, I'd investigate whether you have a messed up DHCP database. Look up the workstation's MAC address in the database. See anything funny (strange characters in the IP address, or unlikely IP addresses)? You might need to explicitly delete this record or repair the database. (Under Linux and many other UNIX systems, it's a flat text file called `/etc/dhcp.leases`.)

When troubleshooting a DHCP server, bear in mind that DHCP is a timed animal. What do I mean by this? Well, because DHCP typically issues IP addresses for a fixed period of time (called a *lease*), consider this scenario. Mary comes in to do some extra work at

6:00 a.m. on Sunday. Because this site is under maintenance a lot, the administrators of this site have purposely set a lease time of two days so that *most* leases expire over the weekend. (This is actually a fairly common practice.) Simply by booting her workstation, she renews her lease, due now to run out on Tuesday at 6:00 a.m. Other folks don't come in until Monday at 8:00 a.m., so their leases don't run out until Wednesday at 8:00 a.m.

If there was a problem with the DHCP server on Tuesday morning, *only* Mary would notice. Everybody else is good to go until Wednesday. So you could be troubleshooting Mary's workstation until you're blue in the face—except the problem is really with the DHCP server. Right? So, how do you deal with this? It's easy—just release and renew a lease at a *different* station. If the server is okay, this will work fine. If it's not, well, you might have a problem with the server. The cool thing is that you can *typically* restart a DHCP server without disrupting client operations because DHCP servers are only contacted at the time that the client renews its IP address. The lease information typically survives a server restart.

However, sometimes it's not the database. For example, in the problem we discussed in Hour 3 (the Telnet disconnect that happened in the middle of the day for all users in a department), we ultimately discovered "what had changed" was that a tech had reduced the lease to four hours in anticipation of future maintenance. It so happened that these were older workstations using an older DHCP server, and the lease renegotiation wasn't happening perfectly—the DHCP request would be denied, but then immediately would be renewed. It was really bizarre, but ultimately we had two options: upgrade/patch the DHCP server or crank the lease way up. We did the latter until the former was possible.

What happens if the lease information goes away? Well, let's start with the word "ouch" and go from there with an example. If workstation A has lease 192.168.1.100, and the lease information goes away, A *keeps* the IP address. But, the next time the server starts, it *thinks* that 192.168.1.100 is available, and it will merrily dole it out to workstation B (instant IP address conflict). Now multiply this by 10 or 100 workstations. It's not pretty.

As a practical matter, what can you do about this, or, for that matter, someone who evilly sets his static IP address smack in the middle of your DHCP range? Well, as a practical matter, exclude that person's address from the DHCP range. It's not pretty, but it will let your users work until you track down the offending workstation.

> How do you generally track down an IP conflict? Well, it depends. My favorite method, nowadays, is to get into the local VLAN switch and search through the MAC addresses until I track down the rogue MAC address. (If you've ever gotten an IP conflict message, you know that the *only* address that appears in the message is the MAC.)

For example, on a Cisco 3500-series switch, I would start searching for MAC address `00-10-a4-9f-9b-2a` by typing **show mac address 0010.a49f.9b2a**, which would result in output like this:

```
Non-static Address Table:

Destination Address  Address Type  VLAN  Destination Port
-------------------  ------------  ----  --------------------
0010.a49f.9b2a       Dynamic       188   FastEthernet0/5
```

Checking your switch tables is certainly the easiest and quickest way to correlate a MAC address back to an actual workstation. But if you don't have a switch (or if your switch is "dumb," and won't let you go through its tables), don't lose hope. Disconnect the workstation that's doing the complaining; it's not the one you have to find, right? Then, start checking your application logs (email, Telnet login using 'who', and so forth) and hunt for the offending IP address. Many times, you'll find it a correlation between the IP address and the username, and then it's just a hop, skip, and a jump to finding the workstation.

Finally, why am I talking about DNS in the same breath that I'm discussing DHCP and IP addressing? Well, mostly to point out that DHCP can do more than just configure your IP address info: It also can and should provide name resolution configuration, specifically, DNS and WINS. WINS is outside of our scope here because it's Windows-specific (see Chapter 12, "Windows Networking Basics," for details). DNS, on the other hand, is the standard TCP/IP naming service, and in fact is the primary name service on Windows 2000's Active Directory.

Unless you have reason to the contrary, make sure that any particular workstation using DHCP to obtain its address is also configured to use DHCP for its DNS.

Although I urge you to address DNS problems centrally (for example, fix the server or fix the DNS client), for troubleshooting purposes, it might be illuminating to temporarily assign an IP address to an entry in a hosts file. (Windows NT Family; `%SYSTEMROOT%\system32\drivers\etc\hosts`; Windows 9x, `%WINDIR%\hosts`; and Linux, `/etc/hosts`.) I urge you to *not* permanently assign IP addresses in this manner and to *remove* your entries when you are done. Otherwise, down the road, when the server name changes, that workstation won't know about it because it will still be using the static hosts file.

I'll talk more about big picture DNS in a little while. If you've got an IP address, name resolution, and routers—see Hour 15 for more on that—we're ready to start dealing with specific TCP/IP applications, most of which are client-server.

19

TCP/IP Application Troubleshooting

Remember how we discussed in Hour 1, "Understanding Networking: The Telephone Analogy," that a *socket pair* is the combined IP address and port number of *both* sides of a network connection? Well, this is how applications talk to each other.

As we discussed in Hour 13, "UNIX and Linux Troubleshooting," client/server systems can answer specific questions about a database of items, for example. Rather than shoving a catalog in your face the way a file and print server might do, a client/server system would listen politely to your inquiry about widget pricing, perform a lookup on its local database, and then send the response back to you, as illustrated in Figure 19.1. (Microsoft's SQL server is a great example of this: It listens on TCP/1433 for queries).

FIGURE 19.1

Think of client/server computing as two people on two ends of the phone. The client asks the questions, and the server provides the answers.

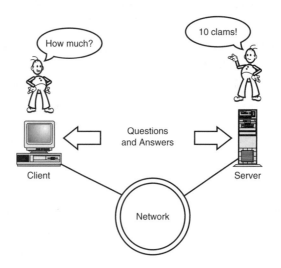

What else can a client/server system do? Well, take your Web browser for starters. It's the client of a client/server relationship. Your client says, "Hey, give me your default Web page," and the server spits it out at the client. (We'll look at how this works in a moment.)

That said, sometimes it's a bit more complicated than that. Life is not just about client/server. For example, Microsoft file and print networking (SMB) uses three separate ports for what is a fairly complex protocol. But don't sweat it—more protocols are simple than not simple, and more of them approach the client-server model than don't.

Whether you call it "client/server" or simply boil it down to "TCP/IP services," troubleshooting of TCP/IP apps basically entails verifying that the server program is "answering the phone" on the other end—that is, the correct port is listening at the server end and giving out the correct type of response. If you do this *outside* the client program, you will have a good sense that the server is okay—then you can concentrate your efforts on the client.

Again, before you even start investigating application-level TCP/IP issues, you will want to make sure that you've done the following:

1. Ping by name: Is the name resolvable?

2. Ping by IP address: Is the server reachable at all?

3. Use `traceroute`: Why can't you get there? Where does the packet stop?

State of the Socket

Okay, you've checked the basics. Now it's time to dive in and see what the deal is. Get used to typing the `netstat -a` command—it is *the* tool for troubleshooting client/server application problems. Let's quickly go over what the output of `netstat -a` shows you:

```
Proto Local Address    Foreign Address   State
```

- `Proto`   This refers to the TCP/IP sub-protocol (either TCP or UDP).

- `Local Address`   This refers to the socket pair that the workstation is using to speak.

- `Foreign Address`   This shows the remote socket pair that you're speaking to.

- `State`   This describes the state of the socket pair.

> Does the *client* socket pair matter? No. Just like with a phone call, you can use just about any free extension to dial out—and your computer will do so automatically. The socket pair only matters if the computer that you're sitting on is a *server*. In that case, it must be listening at the correct port number on the correct IP interface; otherwise, nobody will be able to talk to it. (Certain servers only "listen" at specific interfaces.)

Depending on the operating system, you'll see something that looks like one of the following TCP socket states in the `State` column (why not UDP? you'll see why in a moment):

19

State	Description
LISTENING	"I'm a server, and I'm ready to talk to someone."
ESTABLISHED	"I'm having a conversation; things are groovy."
SYN_SENT	"I'm trying to synchronize the call with someone by establishing a TCP handshake, but no luck so far."
SYN_RECV	"I'm in the process of synching up a TCP connection with someone."
CLOSE_WAIT	"The other end just hung up; I'm waiting for the dial tone."
TIME_WAIT	"I hung up; I'll get rid of this entry shortly. Chill, will you?"
LAST_ACK	"The other end said goodbye and will shut down shortly."
FIN_WAIT1	"The socket is closed. I'll get rid of this shortly."
FIN_WAIT2	"The socket was closed by other end. I'll get rid of this shortly."

Services with a Smile

For any client/server service, you'll want to be able to objectively check to see if the server is listening. This usually means trying to connect to it from a client machine. In order to try to connect—or verify a service on the server end—you'll want to know the numeric value of the well-known services, as well as their names.

> A list of services mapping service name to port number is available in
> C:\Windows\Services under Windows, /etc/services under UNIX, and
> SYS:ETC\Services under NetWare. You can also check out a really good ser-
> vices list at http://www.neohapsis.com/neolabs/neo-ports/neo-ports.html.

Table 19.1 shows the numeric values of some of the services I work with a lot (and there are many more).

TABLE 19.1 Numeric Port Values of Common Services

Service Name	Number	Comment
FTP	21	File Transfer Protocol (Internet)
SSH	22	Secure Shell services (TCP)
Telnet	23	Login service for UNIX (sometimes NT or Novell)
SMTP	25	Internet-style server-to-server email

TABLE 19.1   continued

Service Name	Number	Comment
Domain	53	DNS services (UDP and TCP)
Gopher	70	Internet Gopher
HTTP	80	Hypertext Transfer Protocol (the Web)
POP2	109	Post Office Protocol version 2 (user email)
POP3	110	Post Office Protocol version 3 (user email)
NNTP	119	USENET news
netbios-ns	137	NetBIOS (MS Windows sharing) Name Service
netbios-dgm	138	NetBIOS (MS Windows sharing) datagram service (actual data)
netbios-ssn	139	NetBIOS (MS Windows sharing) session service (Hi, how are you?)
https	443	HTTP protocol over SSL (Secure Socket Layer)
shell	514	Rlogin socket (UNIX or NT)
printer	515	Line Printer Daemon (network printing for UNIX)
socks	1080	Socks proxy server (Socks 4 and Socks 5)
http-proxy	8080	Proxy for the HTTP protocol

What if you don't know the port number (or numbers) of a client/server program that you're using? Simple—stop the server program and run `netstat -an`. Print it out or save it to a file:

```
netstat -an > socklist.txt
```

Then start the server program and run `netstat -an` again:

```
netstat -an > socklist2.txt
```

Finally, compare the two lists. If you're using UNIX, type

```
diff socklist.txt socklist2.txt
```

If you're using Windows, type

```
fc socklist.txt socklist2.txt
```

`fc` and `diff` compare two files; the difference will show you the new socket (or sockets), and therefore the port number (or numbers) for your client/server program.

19

Connection-Oriented Versus Connectionless

As we discussed in Hour 16, there are two types of TCP/IP ports: UDP and TCP. When a program sends out a UDP packet, it has no way of knowing that the packet got there because it's *connectionless*, rather like a message in a bottle. For our troubleshooting purposes, we hate UDP. It's a very irresponsible child. We like TCP best because a connection is set up even before the application starts to communicate. Because there's overhead, we can leverage this to understand whether the application itself can communicate once the circuit is set up. Because TCP is a connection-oriented socket, we *can* initiate a call on our own to see whether the connection gets set up right—even without knowing anything about the application level protocol. Remember, many important protocols do use UDP, such as DNS.

One way to check whether the socket pair is being established is to use the client program itself and then check the workstation's socket list. For example, here's how you can connect with an FTP service in one window and run `netstat -an` in another window:

```
C:\WINDOWS>netstat -an | find ":21"
TCP 192.168.10.5:1025   192.168.5.1:21   ESTABLISHED
```

Here you have an ESTABLISHED connection, so no matter how much your FTP client is complaining, you do have a *bona fide* socket. In this case, you might want to look at client configuration if you're experiencing problems.

Another way to check whether a remote socket is listening is to telnet to that socket. For example, let's perform a control experiment. You can run an FTP server on a PC and then use Telnet to go to it to see if it's listening. Just so you don't even go to the outside network, use your loopback address. (The loopback address in TCP/IP is always 127.0.0.1.) You can see the results just by typing (see Figure 19.2):

```
telnet 127.0.0.1 21
```

As shown in Figure 19.2, the screen indicates that the FTP server is running. This is a really neat trick, and you can do it with any sane TCP service. (For example, try to Telnet to port 1494 on a Citrix server: You'll see the text "ICA".) But will you *always* get a reasonable response? No. Sometimes there's no prompt. However, the trick is whether or not you get an immediate CONNECT FAILED from the Telnet program. If you do, odds are that nothing is listening on the other end.

Because the version of Telnet provided with Windows is not very verbose about *why* a connection failed, I really prefer to use a better Telnet program, like putty. Get it at www.chiark.greenend.org.uk/~sgtatham/putty.

FIGURE 19.2

You can run a local FTP server on your PC and connect to it with Telnet by asking for a connection to the loopback address at port 21.

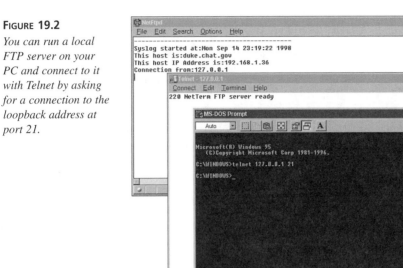

No matter what operating system you're running, the service number will be the same. For example, any Novell or NT server that gets a print job from a UNIX server is usually listening to the print socket (TCP/515). If you telnet to the server at port 515 and get a `Connection refused` message, it's time to check the server program.

> Not all UNIX printing uses TCP/IP directly. There's a method of printing, called *pass-through printing*, that has *nothing* directly to do with the network. It's entirely dependent on your terminal program to react properly to certain invisible codes that are sent with the text. For instance, if your application on a UNIX host sends the `Control-T` code to your Wyse-60 terminal, your terminal—or terminal emulator—will start printing the text that's sent immediately following the code, rather than showing it on your screen. Another code—for example, `Control-R`—will make things go back to normal. Just be aware of this; you might just save yourself some aggravating running around.

19

"I Can't Print!"

I once had to troubleshoot a problem where certain print jobs would just sit there for long periods of time before printing. This happened with wide area–connected printers, as well as printers that were connected to dedicated print servers.

Also, only one printer at a time was printing on any given standalone print server. Our host vendor claimed that it had to be our network, whereas our print server vendor said it had to be the host.

After sending print jobs to multiple queues from the host to one of our standalone print servers, I went to the host and typed the following:

netstat -an | grep 515

I only saw *one* socket pair being opened to the print server (even though the print server served multiple queues). That was enough evidence for me, although I did a network trace to make sure—apparently, the print services on this vendor's version of UNIX didn't support more than one printer on a given network host, and it was only sending one job at a time, which became worse at WAN speeds.

The vendor claimed that this aberrant behavior was "as designed," and declined to fix it. So we worked with our reseller to swap it for something that actually worked correctly.

Content Checker

For certain services, such as HTTP, you can actually check content. For instance, here's a troubleshooting session with a Web server:

```
mori    A    ~$ telnet 167.195.160.6 80
Trying 167.195.160.6...
Connected to 167.195.160.6.
Escape character is '^]'.
GET /
<title>Neato Geeky Stuff(tm)</title>
<B>Neato Geeky Stuff(tm)</B><P>
<img src="jonny/smguru.gif">
<B>Leo sez:</B>
<p> Check it out. <I>Lotsa</I> neato geeky stuff.
...
```

Whoa—it's the whole HTML page. This definitely tells you more than a ping—it tells you that your Web server is up and serving HTML. In other words, who cares if your Web server is responding to pings? You don't have it there to respond to pings; you have it there to serve Web pages. If it's responding to pings but not serving Web pages, it is for all intents and purposes "down." By checking the content like this, you *know* that it's functioning properly.

Mail Fail

If you can Telnet to a port but are still having application problems, it can be time to point the finger at the app.

I saw a proprietary mail system that was failing at a remote site—the users were connecting but then getting hung up for long periods of time while they were trying to access their mail. We put in a mail server to serve them locally (and get the wide area out of the picture), and the users were then fine. However, when the new mail server tried to talk to the main server, we got lots of disconnected sockets—a lot of sockets in the TIME_WAIT state. By *a lot*, I mean, 30 to 50 in a space of several seconds. This was *way* above par, and indicated that there were many successful connections, followed by disconnections.

This was really bizarre: Usually, when a connection is established, the server program sits there and does its work merrily. Disconnects are usually caused by network problems—not the application. However, I could stay connected to the main server port using Telnet as long as I liked—unlike the new app server. This really, really pointed to the app.

A search of the vendor's Web site on the socket state revealed that, with certain router configurations, this problem would occur. The vendor recommended fixing the router but also provided a patch and a workaround applicable to the server and client software, which fixed the problem. (For what it's worth, we ended up having to decrease the TCP/IP maximum transmission unit to 512 for all servers.)

Your Web Server

Okay, that's cool. So I can Telnet to socket 80 of a Web server and see whether I can use the GET HTTP command. What else? Other than layer 1-3 problems, you'll want to treat Web server problems the way that you would any server application (and check out Hour 20, "In-depth Application Troubleshooting," for more application troubleshooting tips). It's all about reliability (caused by the manufacturer and standard configurations) and resources (influenced by load).

Verify load by checking your server log files. Are the hits that you're getting "official" hits? Or has one of your users posted a non–work-related (but very popular) Web page? Overload is really unlikely on a non–Internet-connected server. Most Web servers can handle hundreds, if not thousands, of users without a problem. It's when you start to get hundreds of hits per second that you really have a problem.

If you really want to be that popular, you'll have to collect your log files and involve your server vendor and ISP, and you'll probably have to upgrade two things: your Web server and your Internet connection. Based on the amount of Web data shown to be transferred in your logs, these two vendors will make recommendations about how you can upgrade.

19

Many reliability problems are related to revisions or to other software on the server. Make sure to get the latest version or patches for whatever Web server you use, as well as to use divide-and-conquer and rule-out methods on other services that run on the server. Dig into the operating-system specific chapters in this book, flex your black box troubleshooting techniques, and don't forget to check the various Internet knowledge bases.

Finally, Web servers deserve special mention for their "tiered" nature—that is, when a Web server consults an external application or server to generate dynamic content.

It's a good idea to have or generate documentation of how these applications interact with each other. It doesn't have to be complicated—it could be that several Web servers access your human resources database, and thus need that database to be up and functional in order for Web applications to be working.

The key to tiered applications is this: Although your Web server might be functioning, its nonstatic content probably depends on one or more other content (usually database) servers. Document your dependencies, and you'll know what to check when things bollux up.

Email Checking Examples

Proprietary email is basically a client/server application or, in some cases, a specialized file-sharing application. When trouble arises with your proprietary email system (such as GroupWise, Lotus Notes, or Exchange), you're best off approaching them using the TCP/IP techniques just discussed (for example, checking their ports using Telnet, checking the netstat—a output on the server), and the techniques that we'll discuss in Hour 20.

Each one of these proprietary email systems does support standard email gateways, usually to hook up to the Internet at large, but these can also be used internally. These typically have three components:

- SMTP—Simple Mail Transfer Protocol (server-to-server communication)
- POP—Post Office Protocol (client-to-server communication)
- IMAP—Internet Mail Application Protocol (client-to-server communication)

Email is so important to most organizations that I want you to see what normal Telnet sessions to these services look like. Check them out. We'll do SMTP (TCP/25) first.

```
$ telnet wpo 25

Trying 167.195.160.7...
Connected to wpo.co.chatham.ga.us.
Escape character is '^]'.
```

```
220 wpo.co.chatham.ga.us GroupWise SMTP/MIME Daemon 4.11 Ready
1993, 1996 Novell, Inc.
```

Here's IMAP (TCP/143):

```
$ telnet moria 143
Trying 167.195.160.6...
Connected to moria.co.chatham.ga.us.
Escape character is '^]'.
* OK moria.co.chatham.ga.us IMAP4rev1 v10.170 server ready
```

And finally, here's POP3(TCP/110):

```
$ telnet feldmonster.com 110
Trying 208.60.153.82
Connected to shrek.feldmonster.com.
Escape character is '^]'.
+OK POP3 shrek.feldmonster.com v7.59 server ready
```

Troubleshooting Out on the Internet

With all the fancy terms surrounding the Internet, it can be easy to lose sight of the fact that it's just one big TCP/IP network. Let's look at some specific TCP/IP troubleshooting techniques that can pinpoint Internet problems in your shop.

To start with, we'll need to identify what kind of Internet connection your shop has. Once you know what type of Internet connection you have, you'll be better able to identify which of the following techniques are right for you.

Unless you work for a huge multinational company with fault-tolerant Internet connections all over the place, you probably have just one firewall and one domain name (company.com).

19

Types of ISP Connections and Firewalls

More than likely, you have one of the following types of Internet access:

- Method 1: Workstation dial-up connections only
- Method 2: Firewall or proxy to ISP
- Method 3: ISP router only, no firewall
- Method 4: Firewall or proxy, DMZ (demilitarized zone) network to ISP router

It's important to identify what type of connection you have. How do you find out? Well, method 1 (see Figure 19.3) is pretty easy—if you use Windows Dial-Up Networking to connect to the Internet, you usually hear a modem dial and you see the Dial-Up

Networking dialog box before you connect. A dial-up connection makes you a "connec-tion unto yourself," and you're actually classified as method 3 (a direct connection to your ISP with no firewall).

FIGURE 19.3

A workstation dialing up to a typical Internet service provider.

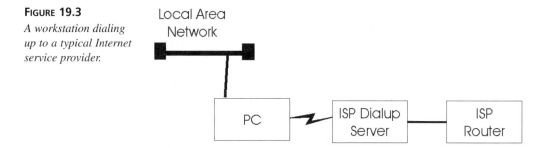

You're using Microsoft's *ICS (Internet Connection Sharing)*, you say? Without getting into a rant here, I really don't recommend using it—a typical Windows box is just too dynamic of an environment to trust as a firewall and a workstation. Snag a cheap hard-ware router instead. (See Hour 15 for more on this.)

In general, the first steps for troubleshooting dial-up connectivity are pretty easy—you either make the connection or you don't. In most cases, being "down" is because of the ISP's equipment or the telephone company.

In contrast, if you use methods 2 through 4, you don't usually do anything more than boot up your workstation; the local area network is used as the onramp to the Internet access device.

Method 2 (see Figure 19.4) is one of the more common configurations, particularly if your ISP hosts your Web pages (that is, it runs a server that your Web pages live on, without you needing to run your own Web server). This is a particularly easy way to do things for a small-to-medium sized shop; you only need a wide-area connection (dial-up or leased) from the firewall or proxy to your ISP.

Method 3 (see Figure 19.5) is sort of unusual. It implies that the user either doesn't care about security—possible, I suppose—or that security is taken care of in the ISP's shop. Although there are still some folks in the United States who don't lock their doors, their numbers are dwindling; so, too, are those who don't have their own firewall.

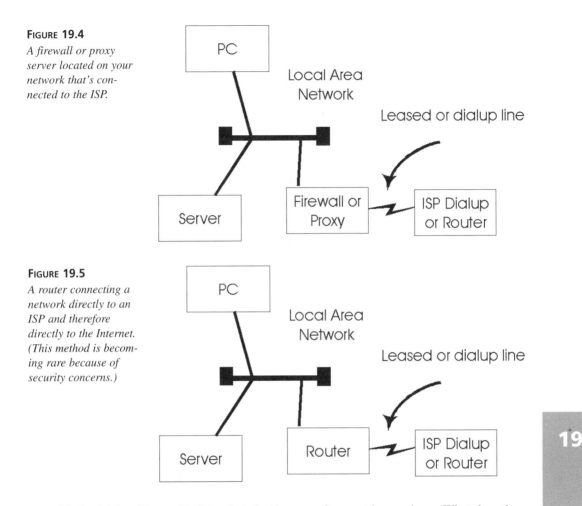

FIGURE 19.4

A firewall or proxy server located on your network that's connected to the ISP.

FIGURE 19.5

A router connecting a network directly to an ISP and therefore directly to the Internet. (This method is becoming rare because of security concerns.)

19

Method 4 (see Figure 19.6) tends to be the norm for most larger shops. What does the presence of an intermediate network, or *demilitarized zone (DMZ)*, mean? Machines that don't have to be absolutely and totally secure machines can be placed on the outside network and made available for outside Internet users. The fact that they're "in front" of or "on the side" of the firewall means that they're treated separately from the production network.

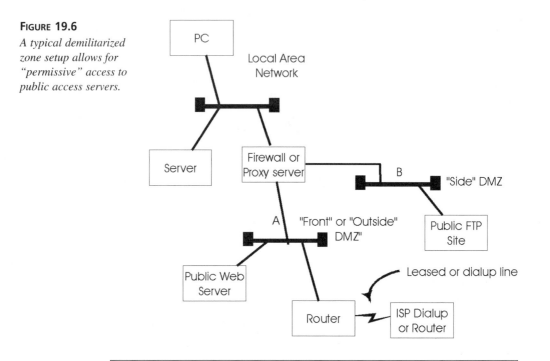

FIGURE 19.6

A typical demilitarized zone setup allows for "permissive" access to public access servers.

If an outside machine is "on the side" of the firewall, it means that you need outside users to get to the server, but you also want those users to be restricted in some way. Instead of having to configure many servers, you just need to configure the firewall to only allow certain traffic. For example, you might allow FTP sessions from the outside world to get to the FTP server at point B in Figure 19.6 but not allow anything else from the outside.

When a server is "in front" of the firewall, it means that the firewall is *not* protecting the server at all. Sometimes this is done because the firewall would impede the function of the server. For example, because a proxy server requires a proxy client, it would be impractical in this case to use a "side" DMZ for machines meant for public access. In this case, a front DMZ would mean that Internet traffic could reach public access machines without being hindered by the proxy server.

An outside DMZ is cool because you can walk up to the hub that it's on and monitor your traffic, as well as check or use intruder detection software to see if unwanted folks are probing your network. More importantly for our purposes, you can hook a network analyzer or a regular old Windows laptop to it and troubleshoot unhindered by possible firewall restrictions. (Refer to point A in Figure 19.6.)

Even if you have a proxy server that will not pass ping packets, `traceroutes`, or DNS lookups, you can plug into your DMZ segment and troubleshoot your little heart out because you're bypassing the firewall.

What Normal Behavior Looks Like

Once you've identified your firewall type, it's really important—before trouble strikes—to try the troubleshooting techniques presented earlier in this hour so that you can know what works and what doesn't work during a "normal" period. (Of course, when firewall "rules" change, so will your methods of troubleshooting—if you're troubleshooting Internet problems on a regular basis, establishing good lines of communication with the firewall admin is a really good idea.)

If you don't figure out what's normal for your shop, how will you know when it's broken? In other words, if you have a proxy server that doesn't permit pings past it—you're not going to ever be able to ping, so attempting to ping during an outage will gain you no knowledge. However, if you know that ping typically does work through your firewall, during an outage, if you're not able to ping through your firewall, you might suspect that either the firewall is down or that the link (Ethernet or leased line) to your provider's router is down. You can then investigate appropriately.

You should *definitely* baseline what type of transfer rates you can expect from your ISP; this way, you can authoritatively tell them when you are getting slower-than-expected traffic. One interesting site that will run an informal benchmark for you is `dslreports.com`; see Hour 23 for more formal ways of benchmarking.

Checking Normal IP Connectivity

You'll start off your Internet connection adventure by doing the same kinds of things you'd normally do internally. The easy part of Internet troubleshooting is that because you more than likely only have one router or firewall, it's pretty easy to point the finger at what's down if you cannot get to the Internet at all.

This router or firewall is called the *choke point* because it's the point at which all traffic could get choked off if it malfunctions.

If you cannot ping an address right outside your firewall, router, or proxy server, you have a pretty good idea that your choke point is down. Remember to ping by IP address rather than DNS name—you always want to make sure that IP connections work before dragging name resolution into the picture. (If IP connections aren't working, you can bet your bottom dollar that DNS resolution isn't working either.)

How do you know what address to ping? That's a good question! You can ask your provider for the far side address of its router. That's the router interface farthest from you—the end that isn't connected to your system. You could also simply keep the IP addresses of several reliable Internet hosts handy. A ping usually resolves a DNS name to an IP address, so just ping a couple of your favorite WWW addresses and write them down.

> You can also use `traceroute` to trace your path to your favorite WWW address while everything is working and then write down the second hop that `traceroute` reports. This is probably the far side address of your ISP's router.

My preference tends to be to ping my ISP first and then ping an outside address. If your ISP link is up but you can't get to anything else, your link to your ISP could be fine but the ISP's link to the outside world might be having problems. Although your ISP probably already knows that it's having problems with its link to the outside world, it couldn't hurt to call and report this.

Let's say that you can't ping because TCP/IP's ICMP sub-protocol (which ping uses) is explicitly blocked (as is more and more common these days). Can you use Telnet to check various services, as outlined earlier? Sure. I can Telnet to port 80 of a foreign Web server just as easily as I can Telnet to a local one. Although this certainly isn't as convenient as ping or `traceroute`, it's at least something that establishes the level of your connectivity.

DNS Problems

Suppose that your IP connectivity is okay. However, although you can ping by IP addresses all day, the second you bring a domain name into the picture, your ping command barfs. No problem! Let's take a look at the types of DNS problems you're likely to see:

- Inside-to-outside problems—You can't see others' DNS names.
- Outside-to-inside problems—Others can't see your DNS names.

For either type of problem, the tool of choice is `nslookup`, although the `dig` tool (only available on Windows if you've installed the ISC's BIND name server package) is also popular. Here, we'll talk about `nslookup` because it is there by default on all Windows family machines.

The `nslookup` tool allows you to connect to a given DNS server and find out what that DNS server thinks about things. In other words, when you ping, you're forced to use the DNS server configured into your TCP/IP stack (usually the local DNS server), but `nslookup` allows you to bypass this and choose which server to talk to—giving you some perspective. You can specify servers by IP address (when name resolution isn't working at all) or by name (when you're trying to track down a strange problem) and tell `nslookup` what type of information to give back to you.

> Using Windows 9x? That's a bummer, dude. Although Microsoft has an exact UNIX-like version of `nslookup` for Windows NT, 2K, and XP, for some reason, it didn't supply this program with Windows 95/98. Fret not. You can find reasonable equivalents by searching your local shareware site (`www.shareware.com`, `www.tucows.com`, and so on) for "nslookup." Or, you can just say, "To heck with it," and download Sam Spade at `www.samspade.org`. It's a GUI front end for all sorts of TCP/IP tools, and it's free.

The DNS Hierarchy

To be able to use the `nslookup` tool effectively, you need to know the basics of the DNS hierarchy. Like your hard drive, the DNS has so many individual records that it's separated into many different levels (folders on your hard drive; zones in the DNS world). Take a look at Figure 19.7. It's drawn as a tree, and you read it from the top down (dots separate the zones). That's not too bad, right? That's the way the entire DNS is organized.

Now let's consider how this is implemented in real life. Each zone is usually handled by one primary server and several secondary servers. How does everybody know which server is responsible for which zone? That's easy. Each zone has a special record called the SOA, which stands for start of authority. Each zone's SOA record details which servers are responsible for that zone, and, among other administrative records, contains contact information for the party responsible for that zone.

Secondary servers get their information from the primary server for the zone; they otherwise act exactly like a primary server for the zone. Furthermore, the secondary servers can live at any IP address—they do not have to be geographically or physically close to the primary server. The zone is a logical concept and has no physical restraints.

FIGURE 19.7

DNS zones, like the folders on your hard drive, are arranged in a tree structure.

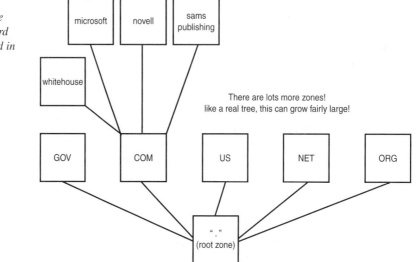

There are lots more zones! like a real tree, this can grow fairly large!

Finally, because DNS is hierarchical, if the DNS server that you use does not know the answer for a DNS query, it must kick the query "up the tree" to the zone server above it to see if it can get an answer. If it does get an answer, it stores the answer in its cache. That way, if it gets asked for the same hostname again, it can give an answer back to the DNS client without having to query the zone above it.

Each zone also has a several attributes associated with it, including the following:

- Serial number: Indicates which "version" of zone it is. Zones only get transferred when their serial numbers go up. By convention, serial numbers are usually in *YYYYMMDDVV* format, so the first zone file modification on August 22, 2003, would be written as `2003082201`.

- Refresh: How often secondary servers check with the primary to see whether changes have been made (measured in seconds).

- Retry: How long (in seconds) a secondary server should wait after a failed transfer to retry the primary.

- Expire: If no master is available, how long (in seconds) to wait before discarding the zone records.

Each record also has a TTL associated with it, which is defined as the amount of time, in seconds, that a record should be kept in a foreign name-server's cache before it is looked up again. TTL is important to you if you change IP addresses on your servers: If a foreign DNS server has cached your DNS records and it hasn't been long enough for the TTL to expire, the foreign DNS server will point the user at the *old* IP address.

> Do not ever make your serial number go down. If you do, an outside cache will assume that what it has (a higher number) is the valid one, and will ignore the entire zone.

With this information in mind, let's look at a real-world, inside-to-outside DNS problem.

Inside-to-Outside DNS Problems

Once upon a time, I was at a site that was having intermittent problems with DNS lookups. Sometimes the DNS lookup was fine; other times, not so good because users at Windows workstations would complain that they got an error stating that there's no DNS entry for *www.company.com*. (I'll be using fictional addressing in this example.) Assuming that the site's DNS server at 200.1.1.6 was responsible for the ci.monkey. ny.us zone (standing for Monkey City in the state of New York), our immediate tasks were as follows:

- Make sure that the Internet at large knew that 200.1.1.6 was authoritative for ci.monkey.ny.us. I didn't suspect a problem here, but on first blush, this is *always* a good thing to check.

- Find out "who" the zone server above us was (ci.ny.us). I suspected that this was where the problem was. (Any query that your own DNS server can't handle gets kicked to the next zone above it.)

We dug out nslookup and proceeded to check out the first task:

```
> server a.root-servers.net
Default Server: a.root-servers.net
Address: 198.41.0.4

> set type=soa
> ci.monkey.ny.us
Server: a.root-servers.net
Address: 198.41.0.4

Authoritative answers can be found from:
     US   nameserver = NS.ISI.EDU
     US   nameserver = RS0.INTERNIC.NET
     US   nameserver = NS.UU.NET
     US   nameserver = ADMII.ARL.MIL
     US   nameserver = VENERA.ISI.EDU
     US   nameserver = EXCALIBUR.USC.EDU
```

19

```
       NS.ISI.EDU  internet address = 128.9.128.127
       RS0.INTERNIC.NET  internet address = 198.41.0.5
       NS.UU.NET  internet address = 137.39.1.3
       VENERA.ISI.EDU  internet address = 128.9.176.32
       VENERA.ISI.EDU  internet address = 128.9.0.32
        EXCALIBUR.USC.EDU  internet address = 128.125.51.11
> server ns.isi.edu
Default Server: ns.isi.edu
Address: 128.9.128.127

> ci.monkey.ny.us
Server: ns.isi.edu
Address: 128.9.128.127

ci.monkey.ny.us
origin = ns.ci.monkey.ny.us
mail addr = hostmaster.ci.monkey.ny.us
     serial = 29981
   refresh = 3600 (1 hour)
   retry = 600 (10 mins)
   expire = 86400 (1 day)
   minimum ttl = 3600 (1 hour)
```

Okay, that's cool. We went directly to a root server—that is, a server that has the authority for all the root zones (.com, .us, .gov, and so on)—and asked it what it knew about our little Monkey City. It responded that we needed to go to another server—one that knew all about the .us domain. We then asked that server about the same thing, and it responded appropriately, so we were in good shape.

> All root servers, in addition to being in the "dot" or "root" zone, are also in the root-servers.net zone. Each server is designated with a letter, so you can go to b.root-servers.net, c.root-server.net, and so on.

Our next task was to find out what the zone above us was:

```
> monkey.ny.us
Server: ns.isi.edu
Address: 128.9.128.127

Non-authoritative answer:
monkey.ny.us
   origin = Buggy.net
   mail addr = postmaster@Buggy.net.savannah.ga.us
   serial = 1998080901
   refresh = 3600 (1 hour)
   retry = 1200 (20 mins)
```

```
    expire = 12096000 (140 days)
    minimum ttl = 14400 (4 hours)

Authoritative answers can be found from:
monkey.ny.us nameserver = dns2.Buggy.net
monkey.ny.us nameserver = dns1.Buggy.net
    dns2.Buggy.net  internet address = 128.6.1.9
    dns1.Buggy.net  internet address = 128.6.1.10
```

Okay, apparently the servers that are authoritative for monkey.ny.us are called dns.buggy.net and have IP addresses of 128.6.1.9 and 128.6.1.10, respectively. Because these servers are on the same subnet, we took a look at how far away they were and how long it took to get a packet from here to there.

Using ping and traceroute revealed that, in fact, certain packets were taking anywhere from 800ms (an eighth of a second) to 1,500ms (a second and a half). Whoa! A second and a half is an eternity in networking. Could, perhaps, the slow connection to the zone server next up in the tree pose a problem? It sure could! DNS only waits for so long before it decides that no answer is in the offing and returns an error to the client. So how did we resolve this?

There were two answers here. The folks in question needed to upgrade their line to the Internet because their own traffic was killing them. (One person's download was cramming the line so full that DNS traffic wasn't responding fast enough.) What's more, the traceroute revealed that the ns.ultra-monkey.net server was 16 hops away. Sixteen hops is, well, a lot. Asking their ISP to take responsibility for the monkey.ny.us zone also helped with this problem because this meant that there was only one hop between the users and their parent zone.

Sometimes, someone else's DNS servers are down. This generally means that you can't look up DNS names for one domain only. Most sites have multiple DNS servers, so this shouldn't happen, but it does. This probably means that you'll just have to sit tight and wait for the zone in question to have its problem resolved.

In a nutshell, here are the things that typically cause you to be unable to look up outside addresses (an inside-to-outside lookup problem):

- Too much lag between you and your upstream zone.
- Upstream DNS servers are unreachable.
- The DNS server is down or unreachable for a particular zone.

Outside-to-Inside DNS Problems

Let's say that you stop getting email—even "junk" email. You pick up the phone and call your friend Space Monkey, who tells you that his email is getting bounced back to him.

He's terribly busy being a successful businessman, so he hangs up before you can get details. However, he does mention that he can't get to your Web pages either. You suspect that there's probably an outside-to-inside DNS problem because you can ping everybody in the world and can resolve their DNS addresses inside to outside.

So, how do you check out how the outside world looks you up? The first thing you do is (you guessed it) fire up nslookup. Let's start off by checking your DNS server, which is the most likely culprit:

```
$ nslookup - dns.frob.com
Default Server: dns.frob.com
Address: 167.195.160.6

> www
Server: dns.frob.com
Address: 127.0.0.1

Name: wizard.frob.com
Address: 167.195.160.10
Aliases: www.frob.com

> mail
Server: dns.frob.com
Address: 127.0.0.1

Name: dragon.frob.com
Address: 167.195.160.8
Aliases: mail.frob.com
```

Hmm...Everything looks okay from a local standpoint.

> Many (but not all) DNS servers on the Internet are called dns or ns to designate whether they're domain name servers or just name servers in general.

Well, your DNS server is, in fact, dealing with the world—when it gets queries about your domain, it answers just fine. If this wasn't the case, you would troubleshoot it further: Is it down? Have its data files been corrupted? (If so, you should restore from a backup.)

The DNS server is okay, so we'll move on to other possible problems. Using nslookup again, let's find out how the root servers are telling others to look up your server. In other words, we need to look at the SOA record for your domain, starting from the beginning:

```
$ nslookup - moria.co.chatham.ga.us
Default Server: moria.co.chatham.ga.us
Address: 167.195.160.6

> set type=soa
> server a.root-servers.net
Default Server: a.root-servers.net
Address: 198.41.0.4

> frob.com.
Server: a.root-servers.net
Address: 198.41.0.4

Authoritative answers can be found from:
frob.com nameserver = NS4.frob.com
frob.com nameserver = NS2.frob.com
NS4.frob.com internet address = 167.195.160.15
NS2.frob.com internet address = 167.195.160.6
```

Whoa! What's going on? There's an IP address listed here for a server you don't know about. Actually, you do know about it, but it's a server that's due to be rolled out next month, not this month. Apparently, one of your co-workers has jumped the gun and told the powers-that-be on the Internet that your name server has moved to this new address. Unfortunately, your current name server isn't listed because of a paperwork foul-up. A quick visit to the www.internic.net page (the clearinghouse for most domain names, which will likely point you in the right direction for this domain's registrar) and a discussion with your co-worker fixes this.

This scenario is unlikely (although I've seen it happen). However, it gives you an idea of the type of havoc that can go on in the world of DNS. There are also scenarios in which someone changes *one* record for a host (because it gets moved to a different subnet, or he's changing ISPs, or whatever) and forgets to check the TTL, which often defaults to a week or more. Again, if you move a server and the TTL hasn't expired, you are asking for trouble. To check the TTL for a record, you can once again use nslookup, but this time, turn on debugging level 1.

```
> set d1
> shrek.feldmonster.com
...
    QUESTIONS:
        shrek.feldmonster.com, type = A, class = IN
    ANSWERS:
    -> shrek.feldmonster.com
        internet address = 192.168.1.19
        ttl = 595885 (6 days 21 hours 31 mins 25 secs)
```

19

```
 ->   shrek.feldmonster.com
      internet address = 208.60.153.82
      ttl = 595885 (6 days 21 hours 31 mins 25 secs)
...
```

As you can see, the TTL here is 6 days, 21 hours, 31 minutes, and 25 seconds. Not a great "change window." If you were going to do a weekend change for shrek.feldmonster.com, you'd want to change the TTL for this record to 2 days, wait 6 days to make sure that the original TTL expired, and *then* do the move.

Finally I've seen companies in which a disgruntled system administrator has stolen the domain name after having left the company, leaving the company unable to get email or Web visits from the outside.

Eek! Can this happen? Unfortunately, yes. Two contacts are listed on a DNS entry: the administrative contact and the technical contact. If a system administrator lists himself as both, he can do an address change to his home address and then, after leaving the company, change the SOA record to something else. There's not a lot you can do about this (from a technical standpoint). Your best bet is to pursue this from a business standpoint: check out the UDRP, or *Uniform Domain Name Dispute Resolution Policy* at www.internic.net/faqs/udrp.html. There's at least a chance that you'll be able to get your domain name back without having to get a legal eagle involved.

Checking MX Records

An MX record is a special record denoting the *mail exchanger* for a zone, with a number that indicates preference. The lower number gets tried first. If you're having trouble getting outside mail from the Internet to your intranet, you'll want to use nslookup to check your MX record for your zone. Here's an example—this time using the dig tool rather than nslookup:

```
[root@shrek /root]# dig +short -t mx chathamcounty.org
5 apoc.chathamcounty.org.
10 gw-smtp.chathamcounty.org.
```

In this example, "Apoc" is the preferred server for chathamcounty.org. If you don't see the right server, if the preferred server is wrong, or if you don't even see an MX record, you'll need to deal with this on your DNS server or ask your ISP to do it for you. Similarly, if you're having trouble emailing someone at a certain domain, check their MX records for the mail host *before* you start verifying whether the host is up.

Tracking Down Responsible Parties

What do you do when you find a problem you need to report, but you have no idea where to get started?

For example, one time, our library system was having trouble reaching a certain Web address. I used traceroute on the IP address and found that my traceroute packet was being repeatedly chucked back and forth between two routers. This routing loop definitely indicated a routing problem, but it was hard to know who was responsible for it.

I reported the problem to the library's ISP, but also wanted to let the folks who were responsible for the routers know about it. How do you know who's responsible for a router? You can do this in two ways—reverse DNS mappings and netblock lookups.

Each IP address on the Internet should (but does not always) have a corresponding DNS name in a special zone called in-addr.arpa. This is so you can quickly resolve an IP address to a DNS name using a special kind of record called a *pointer*, or *PTR*. If you check the SOA for the DNS name—or for the network number—you can frequently find out the responsible party for the address. The only catch is that you need to enter the address in reverse. This is to make it convenient for the DNS zones. However, don't worry too much about it—the important part is that you need to enter the addresses backward. For example, let's say that the two routers that were looping were 192.168.1.10 and 192.168.2.5. During my troubleshooting session, I fired up nslookup, as follows:

```
$ nslookup
> set type=PTR
> 10.1.168.192.in-addr.arpa
Server: dns.frob.com
Address: 209.52.182.122

10.1.168.192.in-addr.arpa    name = router10.foo.net

> 5.2.168.192.in-addr.arpa
Server: dns.frob.com
Address: 209.52.182.122

5.2.168.192.in-addr.arpa    name = router5.foo.net

> (Ctrl-D)
$ whois foo.net
[rs.internic.net]

   Registrant:
John E. Monster (FOONET-DOM)
P.O. Box 4242
Indianapolis, IN 46219

Domain Name: FOO.NET

Administrative Contact:
Monster, John E. (JEM12) monster@FOO.NET
317-555-1400 ext. 5066 (FAX) 317-555-1800
```

19

```
Technical Contact, Zone Contact:
Monster, Joey (JM48) joey@FOO.NET
317-555-1400 ext. 5067
Billing Contact:
Monster, John E. (JEM12) monster@FOO.NET
317-555-1400 ext. 5066 (FAX) 317-555-1800

Record last updated on 07-Aug-98.
Record created on 25-Sep-97.
Database last updated on 29-Sep-98 08:19:55 EDT.
```

Okay! I've got all the information I need to report these shenanigans! Foo.net owns both of these routers, and the whois for foo.net provides an email address for the technical person responsible for this zone. I emailed both my ISP and joey@foo.net, gave them the traceroute output, told them what IP address I had done the traceroute from, and the problem cleared up in a matter of hours. Sometimes, you'll get a friendly letter back telling you what the problem was—other times, you'll be greeted with stony silence. I've had it go both ways, but at least I could tell the folks at the library what the problem was and that I had reported it.

When tracking down spammers or other evil ilk, you'll find that there are sometimes no reverse mappings. In this case, check out the whois at http://www.arin.net—the Internet is divided into *netblocks*, and you'll be able to discover at least who the ISP is. Sam Spade, the tool that I've already mentioned, has netblock lookup functionality as well. Finally, www.abuse.net also has some pretty good responsible party tracking resources.

Summary

Your intranet operates pretty much the same as the Internet at large—just on a smaller scale. Accordingly, troubleshooting strategies that work on one will also work on the other.

After you're done establishing basic layer 1-3 connectivity, you'll want to focus on infrastructure like DHCP, DNS, and the like. Moving on, you'll establish basic TCP reachability by using Telnet to service ports. Applications like Web servers and databases require the same kinds of resources and maintenance (such as patching) that all other applications do.

Part of getting ready to troubleshoot your Internet connection is identifying what type of Internet connection you have. After you've done so, you'll want to practice troubleshooting measures using nslookup, ping, and traceroute to see if these tools will work through your firewall. To be able to rule out IP connectivity issues versus DNS problems, you'll want to keep a few IP numbers of reliable hosts on the Net handy.

If you have a DMZ (demilitarized zone) segment "in front" of your firewall, you can plug a laptop or other workstation into it for the purposes of troubleshooting, even if the firewall will not allow diagnostic tools to work through it.

A little DNS knowledge goes a long way when troubleshooting Internet problems—whether you're having trouble resolving a hostname or others are having trouble seeing your hosts. The nslookup tool will give you a lot of help when troubleshooting DNS issues.

Various Internet problems require that you discover the responsible party for an IP address. You can try the DNS or check the netblock if DNS is of no help.

Q&A

Q I've read that the Internet at large uses routing protocols different from a typical local area network, so how can troubleshooting techniques on my intranet apply to Internet troubleshooting?

A True, the routers on the Internet are major beefcake. (I hear that some of them use steroids.) But although they might use different routing protocols, they're still routers. A packet that comes in on one interface must be routed to another interface and passed off to the "next hop" or dropped if the destination is unreachable. Seriously, the routing protocols are merely methods of routing table updates—as such, they don't matter to us because we're not ISPs. We just care about pointing to the trouble and reporting it. If a packet isn't doing what it's supposed to be doing according to a `traceroute`, we have a reportable problem, and that's where our responsibility ends. Here's the bottom line: Let the ISPs worry about the routing protocols, just so long as they route our packets properly.

Q My proxy server connects straight to my ISP via a leased line, and I cannot use ping, `traceroute`, and `nslookup` through it. I'd like to be able to troubleshoot my own problems, but I have no DMZ and my firewall's getting in the way! Any suggestions?

A Get a dial-up account from your ISP (you might even be able to get a discount if you have a big and expensive leased line for the main part of your business) and troubleshoot using that. The dial-up account will allow you to be on the ISP's DMZ, and you should be able to use standard troubleshooting procedures from there.

19

Workshop

Workshop time! Here's a brief quiz to help you make the most out of this hour's lesson as well as an activity for you to try on your own.

Quiz

1. What does ISP stand for?

    a. Internet supplier partner

    b. Internet service provider

    c. Internal stud professional

    d. Interior service provider

2. Which of the following is a legitimate way of connecting to an ISP?

    a. Workstation dial-up connections

    b. Firewall or proxy direct to ISP

    c. Neither A nor B

    d. Both A and B

3. What does DMZ stand for?

    a. DNS main zone

    b. Demilitarized zone

    c. Demilitarized zebras

    d. DNS mystical zodiac

4. What's the main tool for resolving DNS problems?

    a. `dnslookup`

    b. `nslookup`

    c. `ping`

    d. `traceroute`

5. If the DNS server you've queried doesn't know the answer to your question, what must it do?

    a. Scream and cry.

    b. Ask one of your internal file servers.

    c. Ask its parent zone server.

    d. Ask the ISP.

6. True or False: An SOA contains information about a zone's name servers and point of contact.

7. To look up the hostname for the host 167.195.160.6, you would fire up nslookup and type

    set type=ptr

    and then type what?

    a. 167.195.160.6.in-addr.arpa

    b. 6.160.195.167.in-addr.arpa

    c. 6.160.195.167.in-reverse.arpa

    d. 167.195.160.6.in-address.arpa

8. When a DHCP lease expires, the client must

    a. Use a static IP address.

    b. Renew its lease with the DHCP server.

    c. Unload TCP/IP.

    d. Change subnets.

9. You're trying to get a user's Web browser to work. You pull up a DOS prompt in another window and type **netstat -a** right after you try the browser. You see a connection in TIME_WAIT, but it's to the wrong server and has the wrong socket number. What is most likely happening here?

    a. The browser is suffering from latent network errors.

    b. The TCP/IP stack is hosed.

    c. The browser is misconfigured.

    d. The user needs to update the browser.

Answers to Quiz Questions

1. B

2. D

3. B

4. B

5. C

6. True

7. B

8. B

9. C

19

Activities

1. Go to www.arin.net. Enter your IP number in the text field at the top of the page and click SEARCH WHOIS. Is the ISP returned the correct ISP? If not, is it possible that the ISP returned is the "big fish" ISP, providing IP services to your ISP?

2. Go to www.internettrafficreport.com. This is a really cool site that keeps track of the state of the Internet at large. Print out the report for the area that is most pertinent to you (in my case, North America). The next time your users are reporting Internet delays that don't seem attributable to your ISP or to your own network, print out the report again. Is there a significant difference?

HOUR 20

In-depth Application Troubleshooting

I have yet to see a problem, however complicated, which, when looked at in the right way, did not become still more complicated.

—Paul Anderson

Sadly, most problems won't be reported to you as "I can't update my customer database due to insufficient file permissions" or "A network checksum error due to bad router code is making my print file garbled." (I only wish!) Most times, in addition to the generic troubleshooting mechanisms we discussed in Part II and the initial problem triage techniques we discussed in Hour 17, "Where Do You Start?" you're going to have to do some specific application-level investigation.

This hour, you're going to grab a backhoe and do some digging in your network neighborhood to aid you in specifically determining where an application's network problem is coming from. We'll start with file and print networking, define its difference from the client/server networking that we've talked about thus far, and finish up this hour by discussing common problems and diagnostic techniques that are pertinent to application servers.

File and Print Services

When most folks think about the common ways that people network and share files, they're thinking of file and print services. Apart from things like Gnutella and other peer-to-peer file sharing services, this is the typical way users share a hard drive folder with other users, allowing them to map a drive letter to that folder and even modify files if the permissions allow.

File and print networking offers a simple basic file transfer service. Unlike the peer-to-peer programs, normal file and print usually offers

- A reasonably complete security model, usually tied to some sort of directory service
- File "seeking," which allows programs to access slices of a file (called *records*) rather than an entire file
- File and record *locking,* which keeps track of who has what file open and denies access on a *mandatory* or an *advisory* basis

All application programs that can be run from the network using file and print services require that the application files themselves be transferred to your computer's memory. (For example, if I run Solitaire from my friend's network share, the entire Solitaire executable, SOL.EXE, gets transferred.)

On an end user basis, you can't usually take advantage of file seeking to access specific records. That is, if you want to search the contents of a file while using file and print networking, you must load the entire file over the network and then use a program at your end to do the actual search. Sort of inefficient, huh?

If you're using a database program, it can identify and ask for slices of files (or *records*) over the network, but it will still need to comb through these slices—no matter how much of an index the program has—in order to find data for you. As a point of information, databases based on file-and-print (like Microsoft Access or the venerable DBase) tend to be less reliable and slower than their client/server equivalents (like SQL server, Oracle, and the like).

The File and Print Blues

The underpinning of a file and print client is, of course, the vendor-supplied client you load on the workstation. The dominant file and print client is, of course, the "Client for Microsoft Networks," which is included with every copy of Windows, and uses the *SMB (Server Message Block)* file and print protocol. There are other clients, the most common of which deal with either native Novell file and print (*Novell Core Protocol*, or *NCP*), or native UNIX file and print (*Network File System*, or *NFS*).

How do clients work? Even though the clients might *look* simple, they are, of course, complex internally. In order to make your file sharing and print sharing effortless for *you*, here are some of the things that any given client must deal with:

- Establishing your login, or *authentication*, to the network
- Locating a server on the network
- Connecting to a server share and then reading and writing files and directories to and from that share
- Connecting to a server and then transferring files to a printer queue on that server
- Magically making a drive letter, a UNC, or a printer port appear on your workstation and act as if it were the real thing, even though the files reside on the server (the *redirector*)

Troubleshooting these pieces and parts on an individual basis is usually more trouble than it's worth—just realize that the client is more complex than it seems.

> File and print client software is complex enough that it's pretty vulnerable to domino-effect problems from other workstation software. Verifying good workstation configurations—and more importantly, *consistent* workstation configurations—is also really important for file and print troubleshooting. And, of course, don't forget to verify basic network infrastructure with ping and other tools!

20

Naturally, file and print problems can be broken down into two major categories: file access problems and printing problems. Let's start with printing.

I Can't Print!

If you surveyed the entire country and asked administrators which network problem they found most aggravating, my bet is that one of the top answers would be network print problems. You want to get good at dispatching these problems quickly. Read on for what I've found to be a highly effective five-step process to diagnosing most print problems.

> Unfortunately, many delayed resolutions to printer problems are because of insufficient network printer documentation. When Cassie and friends refer to the broken printer as "Cassie's printer," that means something to *them*, but to you as a network troubleshooter, it means zero (unless it's followed by "Oh, yeah, that's the finance-10 printer on the PENELOPE server").
>
> Having a table of departments and printers works, and is necessary, to be sure, but I find it even more convenient when the printer installer slaps a label on it with server/directory/queue name information. That way, you can ask the user, particularly at a remote location, "What does the printer label say?" and be able to immediately start looking in the right place. (You still need to have off-site documentation, realizing that users love to rip labels off things.)

Let's take a look at what network printing usually entails. You connect to a network printer queue by browsing servers or the directory services tree, and you install drivers appropriate to that printer. So far, this is just like installing a printer that lives on your PC's LPT1 port, right? The only difference is that you're specifying some spooky network location rather than a local port.

What happens when you try to print? To answer that, check out the flow chart in Figure 20.1, and follow through these steps:

1. Your application either generates a print file that the printer can understand (usually PostScript if you're using Linux), or (if you're using Windows) it generates a print metafile that it sends to the print driver. *Metafile* is a term for a "common ground" graphics file that both applications and printer drivers know how to read.

2. In the UNIX world, there is a separate enqueuing process (depending on your operating system, either `lp`, `lpr`, or `enq`.) I mention the enqueing process because it is a potential cause of failure; as such, it can be illuminating to perform manually.

3. The print driver processes the metafile and ends up with a printer-specific spool file. A *spool file* is where a print job is kept until it's printed by the printer. What's a spool? Think of a spool of thread, all of which will eventually get used, with the thread nearest to the top getting used first.

4. The *spooler,* the program on your computer that deals with spool files, works with the file and print client to transmit the spool file to the appropriate server's printer queue. (In Linux/UNIX, this is usually `lpd`; for the Windows NT family, it's the Print Spooler Service, which runs `SPOOLSV.EXE`.)

5. The server places the spool file in the appropriate holding directory if the printer is busy. Each spool file is treated on a "first come, first serve" basis.

6. The spool file is transmitted to the physical printer (or a network print server) when the printer is free (after other jobs have printed).

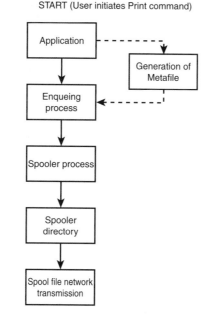

START (User initiates Print command)

FIGURE 20.1

Consider the print system as a flow between these components, and your troubleshooting will become more targeted and efficient.

With six potential points of failure (more, in some cases), it's no wonder that print problems can be a big deal. Thankfully, most printer problems can be handled by divide-and-conquer techniques and the *Sesame Street* method. That is, you'll want to determine whether other users can connect to the printer, as well as whether the user who reported the problem can print to another printer. So, this is the part where we divide and conquer this entire process for you by breaking it down into five easy troubleshooting steps.

Step 1: Check the Application

Your first step when facing a printing problem will be to check the application. Although this sounds rather obvious, I see a lot of printing problems where, say, a database is

20

producing no output for the spooler to process. One would *think* that the database manu-facturer might clue the user in that his report parameters produced no output, but that's not always the case.

> One good trick to see if a job is being generated: disable the queue and print again, and then check the queue.
>
> Also, if a user is still in the Windows 9x world, check to make sure that the user has logged in to the network before you do *any* of these steps. (Windows 9x, in its default configuration, allows a user to bypass the login window by pressing Esc; therefore, a user might be trying to print to a network printer without being logged in to the network!)

More complex problems can occur when an application is either improperly configured or has DLL problems that do not manifest themselves in other ways. For example, I have seen an application that needed special DLLs to print a file; when these DLLs were cor-rupted, either by another application installing its own versions of these DLLs or by sim-ple hard drive problems, the application stopped printing, even though it otherwise behaved flawlessly.

You can find out whether the printing problem stems from the application by printing from another application—for example, Notepad or WordPad. In UNIX, type the follow-ing to check printing outside of a given application:

```
lp -dprintername /etc/services
```

Step 2: Check the Driver

If two programs on a given workstation are not printing, I like to introduce another printer into the picture. In particular, I set up a local printer with a destination of LPT1. If the workstation has no printer attached to LPT1, don't despair—just set it up with a desti-nation of FILE, which will simply direct the output to the hard drive. You can then view that file to make sure that the output is being generated.

> To make sure that the print file is actually okay, you can transfer it to another workstation that does have a printer directly attached and then type something such as this:
>
> ```
> copy /b PRINTFILE LPT1:
> ```

To rule out driver problems, make sure to use a different driver for your test printer. I like to use the Windows Generic/Text only printer driver for some things, but, of course, this won't work too well if your application is graphical. Because you're ruling out the driver, it doesn't really matter which print driver you use, as long as you're fairly confident that it's a good driver.

> Sometimes, even though you have a good driver, your workstation might be running out of gas while the driver is processing the metafile. (One clue that it might be running out of gas would be that it prints after you reboot.) Check the resources as we discussed in Hour 9, "Overcoming Hardware Phobia."

Step 3: Check the Spooler

First, I want to make it clear that (especially in the Windows world) there is usually *more than one* spooler involved. (Huh?) Well, if you are printing from Windows 2000 Professional to a UNIX server, two spoolers are involved: your local Win2K spooler and then your UNIX spooler. Bear this in mind when you are investigating. Simplify, simplify, simplify! Check the server spooler first! (Try printing something while sitting at the server console.)

So, can someone else spool to the server queue? If so, your first guess might be that the problem lies with the workstation. In this case, I want to make darn sure that the printer, as set up on the workstation, is going to a valid queue and has not lost its mind. Also, is the spooler even running on the workstation? If SPOOLSVC.EXE is not running on a Windows NT family workstation, *no* printers will show up at all.

To check queues, I usually go ahead and set up another printer on this workstation—pointing to the correct server queue—just to make sure. If that doesn't work, I set up another queue to a different server, just to prove that queuing is messed up on this workstation. If this works, it means that the problem might not lie with the workstation; you've probably got some sort of communication or security problem between this workstation and the original server queue.

Check whether you can see the server in any other way: Can you log in to it? Ping it? Check your security rights to this queue, or, even better, try to spool to it as someone else.

Step 4: Check the Server Queue

The server might show that it's getting the spool file just fine—whereupon the output just disappears into thin air. A couple things might cause this that aren't limited to

20

communication errors between the workstation and the server. In this case, you might want to rule out a communications problem.

One way you can verify that the server is getting passed a good spool file is by taking a look at it at the moment the server gets it. You can do this by putting the printer in question offline because the server will delete the spool file after it thinks the printer has processed it. Because you're blocking the printer, spool files will be left alone. You can then take a gander at the spool file that's being passed to the server. Where does the spool file live? Table 20.1 gives you an idea.

TABLE 20.1   Spool File Locations

Operating System	Spool Files Kept In
Windows 9x family	`%WINSYSDIR%\spool\printers\`*`jobnum`*`.spl`
Windows NT family	`%SYSTEMROOT%\system32\spool\printers\`*`job num`*`.spl`
(Intra)NetWare	`QueueVol:SYSTEM\QUEUENUM.QDR`
UNIX	`/usr/spool/lp/temp` (actual queue files)
	`/usr/spool/lp/requests` (control files)

Spool File Locations

Here's where spool files for various operating systems live:

Windows: Usually, the `%WINSYSDIR%` variable (you can show it by typing **set** at a command prompt) is `C:\WINDOWS`, but it could be something else, such as `C:\winME`. Similarly, under NT, `%SYSTEMROOT%` is typically `WINNT`, but it might be something else, such as `WTSRV` for Windows Terminal Server 4.0. *jobnum* is a system-assigned number, and it could be anything—you'll want to troubleshoot on a fairly quiet system so that you don't have to wade through thousands of spool files trying to find yours.

NetWare: Each queue needs a place to store its files; NWAdmin will let you choose a place, such as `SPACEMONKEY_SYS`. *QueueVol* is usually one of the `SYS:` volumes on one of your servers, but you should check NWAdmin details of the queue for where it really lives.

Each queue in NetWare also has a unique eight-digit hexadecimal value that's also listed in the properties in ConsoleOne. Just fill in the hex number in place of *QUEUENUM*. For example, my queue might live in `SPACEMONKEY_SYS:\system\f00d160d.qdr`.

UNIX: `/var/spool/lpd` is one other possible spooler location out of many. UNIX printing has changed a good bit, and not all distributions use the ancient and crusty `lpd` spooling system anymore. For a good overview of the various UNIX spooling systems out there, check out `www.linuxprinting.org/howto`.

Once you find the file, what do you do with it? First, you can always look at it with a regular text file editor. It will probably look like vomit if you're dealing with a laser or inkjet printer. In this case, you might want to temporarily change the driver at the workstation to "Generic/Text Only," unless you speak "laser printer" fluently. This way, you can read the spool file once you find it.

In addition to reading the spool file on the server end and seeing that it does not contain `Paul is dead` over and over again—or some other such gibberish that might be caused by network communication problems—you'll also want to check the size of the file against the source. Just compare the file size to that of the file on the workstation. (To capture this on the workstation, just set the printer to work offline before printing.)

Step 5: Check the Printer

The last step between your server and your output is the link between the server and the printer. In most cases, if this link is having problems, *everybody* is going to be having problems printing. It's very rare that this is a user- or workstation-associated problem. (I've been burned enough that I never say *never*, particularly when strange print problems are involved.)

So, let's assume that Penelope the Bug is sharing her PC's printer with Space Monkey's entire office. Space Monkey can't print, and neither can Quincy. First, you should determine whether Penelope can print. It turns out that she can't.

She's connected to her printer directly via her parallel port and a parallel cable. You've rebooted her workstation, and determined that the cable to her printer is good. (You determine this by swapping it out with someone else's printer.)

Next, try to print directly to the printer, avoiding Windows entirely, by getting to a command prompt and typing this:

```
dir > lpt1:
```

This doesn't work, either, even after you reset her computer. You're pretty sure that her LPT1 port has been fried. Penelope is sad. Fortunately, you brought a spare parallel card. You swap it in, and this solves the problem. Penelope is happy.

20

Hardware print servers, obviously, won't let you type `dir` or anything else because they're not running DOS or Windows. You'll want to check your documentation to see if there is a "print self test page" button or administrative option. Usually, there is, and you can use this to verify the integrity of the server-to-printer link.

> If the "self test" is kicked off by some sort of administrative program that
> you run on your workstation, make *sure* (ask your manufacturer) that the
> print is generated at the hardware server—not at your workstation.
> Obviously, if the print is generated at your workstation, you're not exclu-
> sively testing the server-to-printer link.

That Problematic File Pile

File problems can be classified into several categories:

- Inability to use a file (read, write, delete).
- Resource problems (out of disk space).
- Files are corrupted.

Several techniques can be used to name your pain for these troubles; because there's
more than one problem, there's more than one shooting iron you can use.

Access Denied

A file access problem usually manifests itself in a user saying that he can't write or read
a file. Alternatively, a user might see the following message:

```
This file is already open, and can only be opened read-only
```

This can be caused by a few things:

- Someone has set the file to be read-only to protect it from casual overwriting.
- The user lacks the proper security permissions to access the file.
- Someone else has the file open, and because that person is busy with it, the file is
  locked.
- The user's server connection was dropped by a network error (or whatever), and
  the client is confused.

Read-Only

A read-only file is easy enough to check. If you're using Windows, right-click the file, go
to Properties, and see whether the Read-Only check box is checked. If it is, somebody
has set it this way. You'll have to go find out why. (You can find out who owns the file in
the same dialog box.) One reason might be that someone copied files from a CD-ROM.
Because a CD is a read-only device, doing a blanket copy of files from that device can
flag the files as read-only on the network.

Blanket Security

You'll want to check pertinent files and directories to see that the user can, in fact, access the files in question.

In UNIX, look at the full properties of the file and make sure that the file is readable or writable by the user in question. Here's an example of a file's full properties:

```
ls -la mysecretfile
-rwxrwx—- 1 monkey root   140 Nov 14 1997 mysecretfile
```

UNIX file properties are usually the same, even between versions of UNIX. There are three potential clusters of rwx along the left side, each meaning "read, write, or execute permission" for the cluster. The first cluster means "user permission," the second means "group permission," and the third means "world" permission.

In this example, the mysecretfile file is owned by the user monkey, and it belongs to the group root. It's 140 bytes long and was last modified on November 14, 1997. monkey has full read, write, and execute permissions and anybody in the root group can read, write, or execute this file, but the rest of the world cannot do *anything* to this file.

Using a Windows desktop, you can check the file properties for various information, including security permissions. (Add-on clients, such as NetWare or NFS, will add a tab to the window.) Simply right-click any file and select Properties from the menu that appears: The results will look like those shown in Figure 20.2.

FIGURE 20.2

File properties, as viewed from a Windows client's perspective on a Windows 2000 server.

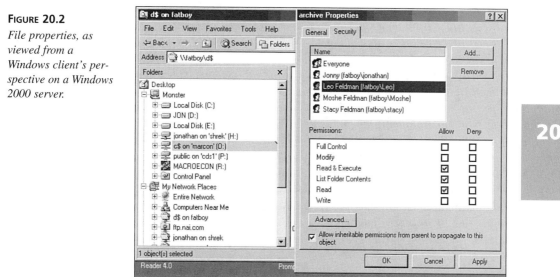

20

If you know that one user can get to the file but another user can't, you should compare the groups to which the users belong. It's not a common practice to assign user-level permissions to files that *groups* of people need to get to (which works to your advantage).

When all else fails (and you're starting to tear your hair out), one cool trick to rule out security issues is to *temporarily* make the user into an administrator equivalent and try again. (You can do this under NetWare by assigning Admin to the user's Security Equivalences; Windows users can be added to the Domain Administrators group as well as the Administrators group.) If the operation succeeds after you've done this, you *know* that you have a security-related issue and can then pursue it further.

> Every security person on the face of the earth is going to have conniptions over me telling you to do this. There *is* danger here, Will Robinson. I'm *not* advocating the practice of normal users running as a supervisor or administrator equivalent—that would be nuts, and it would cause you more problems than you'd know what to do with. (Can you imagine Traci in HR with the power to delete your server's hard drive? I'm shuddering.)
>
> I *am* saying that you can rule out security-related problems this way. If you temporarily allow a user these rights—and then take them away when you're done—this is a powerful method for ruling out (or ruling in) security problems.
>
> Here's the bottom line: As long as you don't forget to take away the security rights when you're done, and you do this for a short, controlled period of time for a known and relatively trusted user, you should be okay. Remember, use this as a *last resort*.

File Locking Issues

File locks can cause all sorts of wondrous problems. For example, some backup programs can't deal with a user who has a file open—which causes all sorts of backup problems. Some email programs or database engines keep their files open even while not in use—which causes backup programs to skip them while backing up. Come again? Wouldn't you rather have *any* backup—even risking that the file changed in the middle—than *no* backup of a file? The solution to this is to purchase a backup program with an open file manager, which avoids this sort of thing. (A problem found in Novell and Windows, but not UNIX.)

Many problems, though, are caused by users being in files. For example, suppose that I'm trying to update a terminal emulation program early in the morning, say, at 5:30 or 6:00. I attempt to install the update, only I get a Can't write to file error in the install program. The install program is helpful enough to tell me that it thinks someone else might be using the file, but that's about it. Alternatively, I might get a call from a user who is trying to update a file, and Microsoft Word is telling her that she can only open it as a read-only file. In both of these cases, if I know the name of the file, I can use server utilities to find out who has the file locked.

Under NetWare, go to the Monitor's File Open, Lock Activity menu, navigate the volumes and directories, and pick the file, which would show you the server connections that have locks on the files. Then go to Connection Information and scroll down to that connection number, which tells you the username.

For NT, use the Server Manager to show the files in use (see Figure 20.3) by following these steps:

1. Click the Start menu and then choose Programs, Administrative Tools, Server Manager.

2. Right-click the server you're interested in.

3. Choose Properties.

4. Click the In Use button.

FIGURE 20.3

The Server Manager can show files (and other resources) that are in use on an NT server.

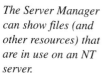

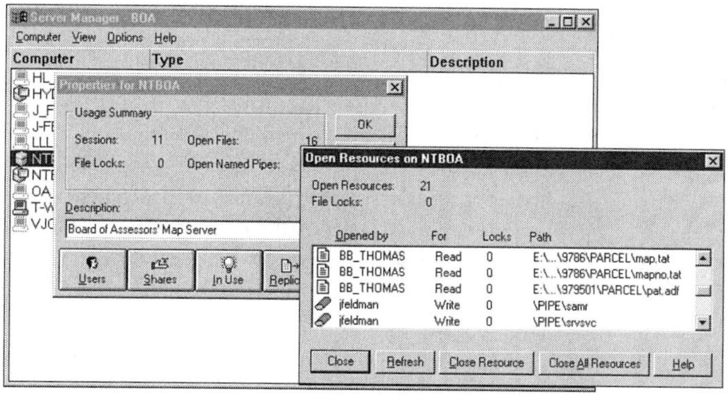

For Windows 2000, you'll see something like Figure 20.4 once you open up the MMC's Computer Management snap-in. Here's how:

1. Right-click on My Computer, choose Manage.

2. Click on Open Files.

If you're using Linux or UNIX, use the `fuser` command on a given file, which shows the process number that has the given file open. (Then, check the process table using `ps` to see which user has it.) If your distribution comes with `lsof`, that works, too.

20

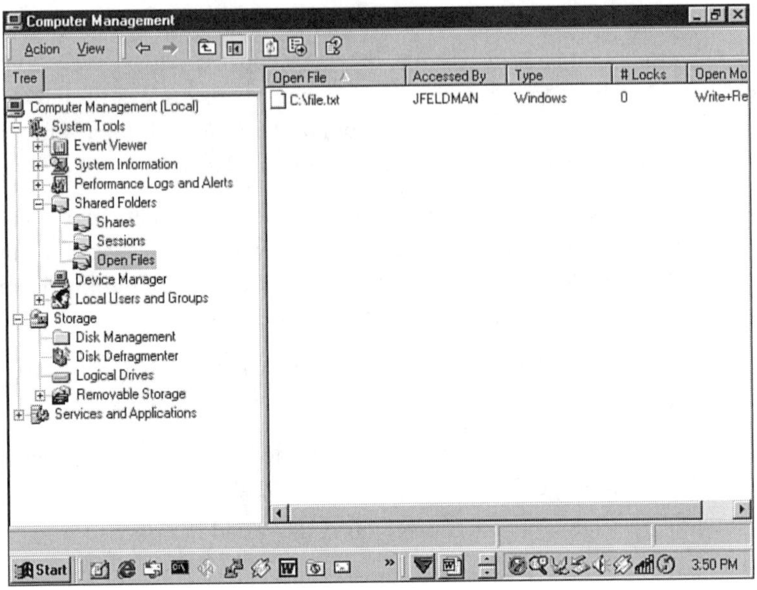

FIGURE 20.4

Deal with Win2K open files using the MMC's Computer Management snap-in.

Because file locking is aggravating when updating a program, my favorite thing to do when I'm updating a program is to *not* update it. Let's say that I'm updating the NETTERM program, which lives in my \\myserver\apps\ netterm folder. I need to put the new version out there for users. One of the methods I like to use (which doesn't apply to all cases, but this is a simple application in this case) is to rename the old folder, which means that I'm not updating the old program. Rather, I'm installing the new program in the same location. To keep the older version, I pull up a Windows Explorer window on the \\myserver\apps share, and then rename netterm to netterm.old.

If something goes wrong, and I need to quickly put the old stuff back, I can always delete the netterm folder, and then rename netterm.old back to netterm.

The benefit in this case is that the file locks don't apply—I'm not updating the old app; I'm installing a new app into an empty folder.

The only caution here is that you need to assign the new folder the same security attributes as the old folder; otherwise, none of your users will be able to see it, much less use it.

Slow Database File Access

Applications that are built using file-sharing databases rather than client/server drive me crazy. (For example, many small industry-targeted applications use Access because it's *much* cheaper to use than SQL server.) These types of databases are common in general workgroup applications. However, the enterprise-class databases (Oracle, Sybase, and so on) will tend not to have these types of issues.

Sometimes these developers do things correctly: They have their program *seek* (skip) to the correct location in the file for a given record. But sometimes, for whatever reason, the developer doesn't use a *seek*, but rather a *sequential read*. A sequential read is a really, really bad thing. It means, to get to record 10,000, start at record 1, and then read and discard each sequential record until you get to record 10,000. This makes things *really* slow. A seek would simply specify a file offset and read just that record.

The hilarious part is that developers who use a small test database to test their application *will not* have the same problem as you do with your large production database.

To add insult to injury, using logic to convince developers that they have done this is close to impossible. After all, they reason, you don't have access to their source code; how can you possibly know how they have coded their application. Well, uh, if it takes 1 second to look up record #1000, and it takes 10 seconds to look up record #10000, um, we seem to be taking a tenth of a second per record. Logic says that they are doing a sequential read because the time increments proportionally as the record number increments.

But they're not going to believe you. Trust me on this, I've been down this road a few times. The best thing to do in this case is to fire up your trusty protocol analyzer (see Hour 21), and capture a small, discrete event that proves the fact. For example, do a trace recording you jumping from record #10 to record #20. The trace will show that every record from 10 to 20 is read by the workstation: You'll send this to the developer, who will then be shamed into fixing the problem.

The Case of the Missing Space

20

No matter how much disk space you have, it's never enough, is it? Even though hard drive sizes have gone up considerably in recent years, the amount of multimedia being stored online has gone way up, apps have grown in size, and so have their data files. Particularly if you run an enlightened system without file quotas, users can quickly eat up any disk space you throw their way.

In general, when you have acute "diskitis," work tends to grind to a halt. It's important to be able to identify the blockage and excise it quickly.

> I know system administrators who always hedge their bets—they either
> keep a hidden file out there that's a couple hundred megabytes (which they
> can quickly delete if they get into a full disk situation), or they simply don't
> dole out all the disk space at once.
>
> Check your operating system manuals; there are ways to add disk space
> where it doesn't show up immediately. You can also add space on-the-fly. In
> a nutshell, you can allocate the storage and add bits of it later. That's very
> cool. (Under AIX, see the Logical Volume Manager; under NetWare, see
> NWCONFIG.)

On a day that starts out *without* a disk space problem, it's likely that your remaining disk space has been eaten by any of the following items:

- Large files created that day.
- Large numbers of smaller files accumulated over a couple of days.
- Large files created in the last couple of days, recently pushed over the edge by normal user activity.
- A persistent application error has filled up a log file or created a lot of small files.

How do you find these? If your organization is like most, you have thousands of files and hundreds of directories and subdirectories—wading through these unaided is nuts. Fortunately, you have automation tools—file finders—to assist you.

Your Friends, the File Finders

The find command in UNIX is my best friend. When faced with a space problem, I might type the following:

```
cd /full filesystem
find . -mtime -1 -print | xargs ls -lad | more
```

This means "find everything with a modification date within one day and print out its name with the size, a screen at a time."

Alternatively, I might type this:

```
find . -size +2048 -print | xargs ls -lad | more
```

This finds everything that's more than 2048 512-byte blocks (1,048,576 bytes, or 1MB).

If nothing turns up, I try the first command with mtime (modification time) set to 3 (three days) instead of 1. Something will usually turn up.

If you like using the command prompt and you're a Windows user, you can get the `find` command in Cygwin (www.cygwin.com) or the MKS Toolkit (www.mks.com). I happen to like it because you can redirect the output to a text file, which comes in handy.

However, the graphical Find tool in Windows is also pretty cool (see Figure 20.5). It also allows you to search by date and size.

Does finding files take a long time? Yes. This is why keeping a little bit of hard drive space on the side is probably a good idea.

If you find yourself doing this a lot on your servers, there are a bunch of commercial/shareware "find" applications that can help. I like Space Watch Pro pretty well: It supports the "big three" operating systems, and deals with the "time to search factor" by allowing you to keep a file database.

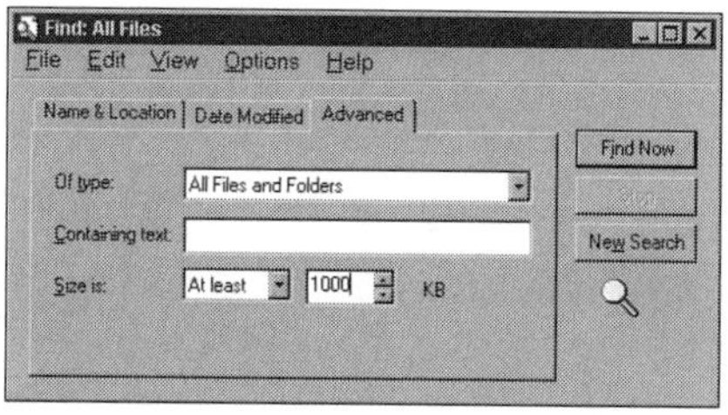

FIGURE 20.5

The Windows Find tool's advanced settings can help you track down large files (and, thus, disk space hogs).

Hey! Jane! Stop This Crazy Thing!

Sometimes finding the individual files doesn't do you any good. For example, our UNIX system administrator and I came in one Monday morning to find the /usr file system full on the main UNIX system. We saw that most of the files that had been generated over the weekend were print spool files, so we stopped the spooler, deleted the queue jobs, chalked it up to a crazy user, and restarted the spooler. Fifteen minutes later, the file system was full again.

We looked at the spooler control files and saw that they all belonged to one particular user. We did a process list for her:

```
ps -fu jane
```

We killed the lp process that she had been running, stopped the spooler, deleted the queue files, chalked it up to a crazy spool job, and restarted the spooler. Fifteen minutes later...

20

Apparently, the application she had been using to run a report had lost its mind, and it kept repeatedly printing the report over and over again. Once we killed all her processes, we were okay, but that was a pretty fun half hour.

Here's the lesson: Just finding the files isn't always enough; sometimes you need to find out *why* they're being generated.

Application Celebration

Some applications are pretty complicated. For example, email and scheduling applications can be insanely complex with a lot of configuration files; incoming, outgoing, administrative, and extra queue directories; and so on. It can be hard to identify a corrupt file—or any other cause—that's the monkey wrench in the works.

Here are some strategies that work with file and print application problems:

- Check server and application logs.
- Change the rules. (Can you simplify them? Can you move the app?)
- Restore from a known good point in time.

App Logs

A log file typically tells the tale pretty well. You'll want to make sure that your application is configured for verbose- or debug-level logging if you're experiencing problems. (For example, most email post office agents run "error only" logging, which is cool, but sometimes you miss the steps *leading up to* the error.) You don't necessarily need to be an expert to take action after looking at the logs—you can always search an error message on the Web, or sometimes the log file will suggest an action, like so:

```
file.idx is corrupt--run rebuild process
```

Lying Error Messages

Are error messages or log messages always the straight skinny? No. Sometimes the application didn't trap the error message correctly, and you end up getting a totally unrelated error message. When you're lucky, though, the error message that you get points in the general direction of the root cause.

For example, I was configuring some desktop management software to deploy Adobe Acrobat 5 across about 800 desktops, and I kept getting `executable path not found` errors. But the executable path was perfectly fine! I compared it over and over again, and went so far as to cut and paste the path from the desktop management console into the Explorer, and indeed, the path was fine.

I finally broke down and showed a co-worker what was going on, and when I brought up the management console to show him, he immediately said, "Jonathan, you've got a typo in the current working directory field." Lesson: Check *related* configuration information, and don't get boxed in by an error message—it might be lying to you.

Checking File Dates

It can be useful to check file dates to discover where exactly in the process something is bailing. For example, I once kicked off a virus protection update from the network, and when I went to verify a couple of workstations (manual checks are *very* important, folks, in any type of automation scenario), it turned out that the update hadn't happened.

Well, gosh. Had my update even run? Did I have a problem with the virus protection installation process, or was there a problem with the desktop management package? I quickly looked at the virus protection installation executable's *access time* (the last time the file was accessed, as opposed to when it was created or modified), and discovered that it hadn't been accessed since I manually ran it. This pointed me toward a problem with the desktop management execution mechanism, and sure enough, I found the problem.

Note that file systems like FAT32 do *not* keep track of access time, and file systems like NTFS keep track of access time in one-hour increments, so if I access the file at 13:20, it's the same as accessing it at 13:50.

You can check file modification times to ensure that files that should not be modified haven't been. In other words, if you see that a file executable or DLL has a modification time that is way off that of other application files, you should be suspicious of it, and it couldn't hurt to copy it from the distribution media.

Virus Protection and Databases

20

Speaking of virus protection, I find that, as useful a beast as virus protection is, it sometimes is the root of a problem with databases. As a general rule of thumb, you should configure your virus protection to *exclude* any directories that are being used by a database application. First, scanning database files is typically pretty useless; viruses don't live in database records. Second, scanning these files at the server slows you down. Third, I've seen cases in which excluding virus protection from database files made some weird problems go away. Should you turn it off altogether? No! But you might want to turn it off while you rule out a problem.

General Environment

Changing the environment is pretty case-specific. For example, you might be able to move the application from one server to another to rule out server problems—but I wouldn't do this unless you had reason to believe that the problem was server related. If you're having problems that seem capacity related, can you move some users to a different application server?

Restoring from a Known Good Point

If you're not an expert in the application, and no troubleshooting seems to be pointing out where the problem is, you might want to consider restoring the application executables and data from backup. You'll still need to know where the application lives in order to restore it, but if you installed it, or if you have the manual, this should be trivial to find out.

> Complex applications sometimes have more than one location—an app that exchanges state information with another location *should not* be restored on its own. A distributed app might get really, really, confused if all of a sudden half of its brain gets restored. Case in point: directory services. If one replica says one thing, and another replica says another thing, this can create *huge* problems.

Expert's Inaction

I've been in a shop where nobody had been trained on the email system; that is, although everybody had been trained on how to *use* the system, nobody had been trained in how to *administer* it. So when the mail system stopped talking one fine morning, nobody really knew how to deal with it.

Log files showed nothing in particular. A search of the Web revealed nothing. Technical support hold times were in excess of an hour, with the promise of a callback later that afternoon—maybe.

All the IT personnel in this shop were highly trained professionals—but not having been trained on the administration of this application, they were just as useless as anybody else in diagnosing this problem. But waiting all day for tech support was not a popular option.

After restoring the system from backup, everything worked—nobody even lost any mail, since the problem had occurred during the night, after the backup ran. To this day, nobody knows what the specific problem was—and nobody cares. Moral of the story is good backups win.

Summary

File and print networking tends to be the underlying mechanism of many applications, so many troubleshooting sessions will have you digging through file permissions, locks, queues, spoolers, and so on.

Printing is one of the most important and aggravating functions on your network. Understanding the print process can help you to quickly pinpoint where a problem is. Printer-oriented documentation helps tremendously, particularly when it's slapped on a label on the physical printer. Knowing how to trace a print problem is really helpful for complex problems.

File errors aren't always necessarily accurate—someone who opens a read-only file might be opening a file that's only read-only to *him* because of security attributes on that file. Knowing how to navigate your particular server's security is really important here. You can rule out security-related problems by trying the same operation after assigning administrator rights to a user—and then quickly removing them.

Disk space problems can bring your entire operation to a halt. Apart from finding the culprit, you can alleviate the problem by keeping some spare disk space on the side.

Checking application server logs, being suspicious of the ultimate origin of error messages, making sure that a file server excludes database directories from its virus protection, and changing the server location of an application all can help you to troubleshoot server-based applications.

Q&A

Q What in blazes is a queue?

A *Queue* is the British-English word for a *line*, such as the line at a bank. It was adopted for use with computing, and it refers to any situation in which something is dealt with on a "first-in, first-out" basis. In a file and print context, a queue is an imaginary line that print jobs wait in to get serviced.

Q I can't print from one particular station, and I've traced it down to something to do with the server because the queue file is not the same on the server as it is on the workstation. What's the next step in tracking this down?

A If other folks are successfully printing to this server queue, it might be something to do with the workstation. However, this workstation might be on a different network segment from the others that print successfully. Try putting the workstation to another switch or VLAN. That might point to a failing router or switch port.

20

Q Is there any way to clear somebody's locks on a file without disconnecting them from the server?

A Sure. Use NT's server manager, or NT can clear someone's lock on a file; NetWare can as well, if you've got OnSite (see Hour 14). Use the `fuser -k` command under UNIX to clear file locks. Bear in mind that when you clear someone's locks under UNIX, this means that you are killing the process that has the file locked. If that's what you want, great.

Workshop

Workshop time! Here's a brief quiz to help you make the most out of this hour's lesson as well as a couple activities for you to try on your own.

Quiz

1. A Windows 9x user says that she can't print to your NetWare file server. What might be the trouble?

   a. Her router.

   b. Her switch.

   c. TCP fragmentation.

   d. She hasn't logged in.

2. You are called in to troubleshoot "network slowdown" for your garage's fleet management system. The company that made the system claims that there is something wrong with your network. "Sure," says the garage mechanic, "the more cars I enter, the slower this thing seems to search!" What might be a good first diagnosis of this?

   a. No incremental reads being used.

   b. No seeking being used.

   c. TCP/IP router has the wrong MTU.

   d. Server is running out of hard drive space.

3. During a print troubleshooting session, you've verified that the application is producing output and that the printer driver is working correctly. What would be the next thing to look at in your troubleshooting efforts?

   a. The transfer of the spool file to the server

   b. The transfer of the spool file to the workstation

   c. The transfer of the spool file to the physical printer

   d. The transfer of the spool file to a new department

4. Where does the Windows NT family (Windows NT, 2000 and XP) store its spool files?

   a. `WINDOWS\Printers`

   b. `%SYSTEMROOT%\System32\Printers`

   c. `%SYSTEMROOT%\Printers`

   d. `WINDOWS\System32`

5. True or False: It's a good idea to allow someone to run with supervisor, root, admin, or administrator privileges for a long period of time.

6. In order to find out who has eaten up all of your disk space on a given day, what should you look for?

   a. Files starting with n

   b. Files created that day

   c. Files modified in the last week

   d. Files particular to the most popular application

7. True or False: You can use the Windows Find utility to find files that are at least a specific size.

8. True or False: Restoring all application files from a known good point in time should be a last-resort method of fixing them.

9. What commands can you use to check the status of file locking under UNIX?

   a. `ls, du`

   b. `fsck, ls`

   c. `fuser, lsof`

   d. `ldd, fgrep`

Answers to Quiz Questions

1. D
2. B
3. A
4. B
5. False
6. B
7. True
8. True
9. C

20

Activities

1. Find a Windows 2000 computer, and share a folder on your network. Go to another computer and map a drive to that folder. Then go to the Win2K machine and pull up the Computer Management MMC snap-in. Can you tell what the IP address of the other workstation is? If not, how might you determine that?

2. Disable your printer, and then print a job. Can you edit the spool file in Notepad? Do you think that putting another file into the spool directory would print that file once you re-enabled the printer? How come?

HOUR **21**

Protocol Analyzers

All are lunatics, but he who can analyze his delusion is called a
philosopher.

—Ambrose Bierce

Tell me about your network....

Many network troubleshooting cases that you'll encounter will be "elementary, my dear Watson," that is, solvable by deductive reasoning alone.
However, to solve the most hard-boiled network crimes, you'll need to get a
wiretap to give you the hard data that you need. Protocol analyzers provide a
type of "wiretap" that allows you to gather objective data about a networking problem.

Like a wiretap, protocol analyzers shouldn't be used indiscriminately; you
definitely want to use your noodle before you use your analyzer. You should
always formulate a theory before breaking out the analyzer—otherwise,
what are you looking for? (After all, it's a big network out there.) To wit:
Only use protocol analyzers when you've exhausted other means; there are a
lot of bits and bytes out there, and digging through them can be tough.

Still, when you run into a problem that needs an analyzer, it can be the difference between a stone wall and a breakthrough. After you've formulated a theory, analyzers can *prove* your theory by providing you tangible evidence to either sift through yourself or to give to a vendor for analysis.

What the Heck Is a Protocol Analyzer?

Every time I talk about protocol analyzers, I think about a piece of network gear reclined on a couch, with some Freudian white-bearded psychoanalyst listening to it babble on about its problems. As silly as that seems, this picture isn't far off—a protocol analyzer's primary job is to listen while other network gear talks.

Protocol analyzers, while they have a physical and data-link connection, operate primarily on the network layer. Although some have special hardware to detect data link or physical problems, most are simply software operating on a PC with a network card that is able to run in "promiscuous" mode—that is, a NIC that is physically able to listen for frames that are destined for MAC addresses *other* than its own.

So, one caveat here is to not rely 100% on typical protocol analyzers to analyze data link information—typically, the network interfaces, unless they are special purpose (just being promiscuous isn't enough), aren't beefy enough to give you good data link detail.

Here are the two basic kinds of protocol analysis tools:

- Packet analyzers—Capture the actual packets on the wire and *store* them for later analysis, do a certain amount of statistical analysis, but this is not the primary function.

- Statistical analyzers—Primary function is to gather quantitative data to be able to later report on various statistical trends, but typically don't store packets for later analysis.

A packet analyzer can be either standalone or *distributed*. Statistical analyzers are typically distributed. Like it sounds, a distributed analyzer is one that has several points of capture, with a centralized console (see Figure 21.1). Network Observer is a good example of a distributed packet analyzer. CompuWare's EcoScope is a good example of a distributed statistical analyzer. We'll discuss statistical analyzers in Hour 23, "Network Management Tools," because they are really network management tools.

Figure 21.1

A distributed analyzer setup.

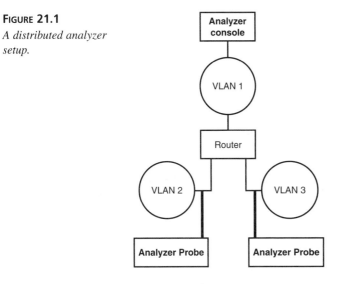

If you don't own a commercial packet analyzer, but would like to get up to speed on the concepts discussed in this chapter, check out the Network Monitor that comes with Windows NT Server and Windows 2000 server. It lives in `C:\WINNT\SYSTEM32\NetMon` and works either with NT Server or NT Workstation. It only captures packets to or from the station that you use it on, and it has other limitations. A full-featured version of Microsoft's Network Monitor is only available if you purchase Microsoft's SMS (Systems Management Server). Still, the free version is a good way for you to get familiar with how this stuff works.

Perhaps even better than Network Monitor is Ethereal, a freeware packet analyzer that is available for various distributions of Unix. It does not have the limitations of the standalone Network Monitor, and if you have a PC running Linux, downloading this and running it is as easy as browsing `www.ethereal.com`. Although it doesn't have some of the bells and whistles of the commercial analyzers, it's got some serious meat and potatoes: it decodes most of the major protocols out there, plus, it reads just about every major packet analyzer file format there is. For example, although I don't use Network Associates' Sniffer anymore, Ethereal is more than capable of reading my old Sniffer traces.

21

Packet Analyzers

Because packet analyzers capture entire data link frames from the wire, you can use their sophisticated software modules to *decode* these frames and the encapsulated packets, enabling you to examine them for protocol and application problems. (See Figure 21.2 for a sample decode window.) The fact that software analyzers are not hard-coded into chips makes them extremely flexible; you can evaluate and purchase different ones as you need them, install them on a laptop, and use the one that seems to best suit the problem at hand.

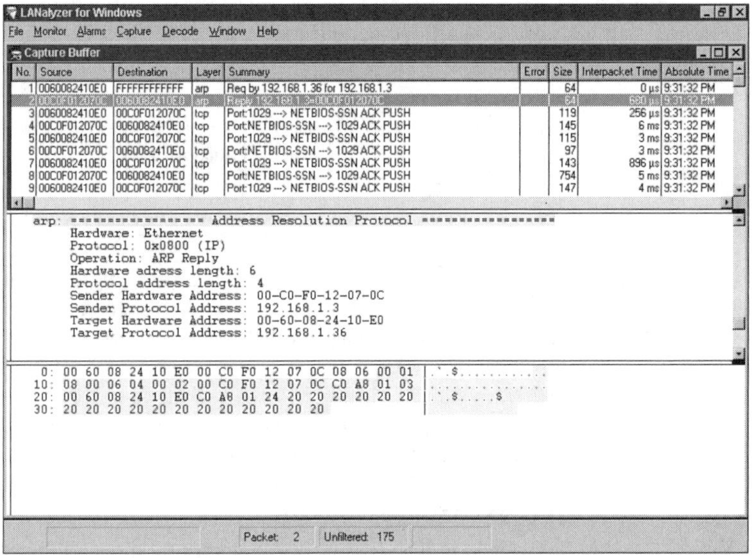

FIGURE 21.2

Decoding the reply packet for an ARP (Address Resolution Protocol) exchange.

Packet Analyzers, Typical Operation

Most packet analyzers have two modes of operation:

- Capture/Monitor mode
- Decode

During the capture phase, the analyzer can perform some statistic gathering, including number of errors per station, number of packets transmitted/received by each station, network utilization (how congested the network is), and so on. The really cool analyzers will show you graphs, let you sort by "most talkative station," and so on during the capture phase. The decode phase allows you to sift through the specific data that the analyzer captured (the equivalent of reading the transcript of a party-line wiretap).

Captive Packet: Capturing

Capturing *everything* on a shared network is possible—although it's resource intensive on your analyzer! Consider a busy 100Mbps network: At a conservative estimate of 6MBps, that would mean you would need 360MB of physical memory (virtual memory simply isn't fast enough to keep up) to capture a minute's worth of data. Gigabit Ethernet? Sorry, you need specialized hardware to even *capture* the data on a gigabit link, at least as of this writing. (A PCI bus can't keep up with a full-bore gigabit pipe.)

10Mbps Ethernet isn't bad, roughly only requiring 90MB and 36MB, respectively, of physical memory to keep up with a minute's worth of data. Still, that's a lot of stuff to sift through and store. How do analyzers deal with this?

Most analyzers have a certain "buffer space" they allocate to capture data. When the buffer is full, you have an option to stop capturing or you can simply discard data at the "end" of the buffer to make room for new data (see Figure 21.3).

FIGURE 21.3

An analyzer can either discard the oldest data once the buffer is full or stop capturing altogether.

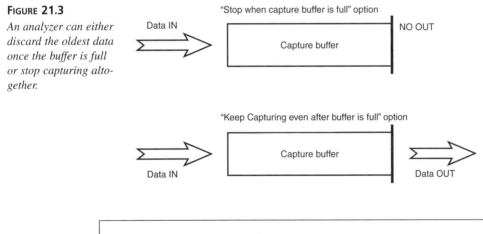

Check with the provider of your software analyzer to see what kind of network interface you need to keep up with the network that you're analyzing. Some hardware is more supported than other hardware; some cheapie drivers and/or hardware won't be able to keep up with full 100Mbps Ethernet and will end up missing some traffic.

How do *you* deal with this? In other words, are network troubleshooters expected to pore over hundreds of megabytes worth of data to find the problem? No, certainly not. Just as police aren't expected to listen to 50 random wiretaps at once, an effective network troubleshooter should only be expected to scan through a limited number of network conversations at a time.

21

You usually won't be capturing *all* the data on the wire. When you are, you're probably concerned with statistic gathering, and you're not really interested in looking at the specifics of what each packet contains—that is, packet analysis. So, for packet analysis, depending on the scenario, you'll tell your analyzer that you're only interested in capturing traffic specific to the following items:

- Network or data link protocols
- Workstation identification (data link or network)
- Service protocols
- Miscellaneous packet or frame data

This way, you *seriously* cut down the amount of data you need to sift through. This is a very important function of any analyzer. The ability to ignore irrelevant data allows you to target the problem and solve it much quicker. Another interesting and useful function is the trigger function; this allows you to tell your analyzer to only start capturing when it sees a certain event on the network (for example, when a certain traffic threshold gets reached).

Secret Decoder Ring: Decodes

After a capture, the analyzer enables you to look at the data you've captured. The analyzer uses software modules called "decodes" to translate the bits and bytes from within the frame into human-readable form. Will *all* the bits and bytes be translated? Well, maybe not. If not, why not? Well, there are three types of translations that your analyzer has to accomplish before you can view data:

- MAC (data link)
- Network (network protocol)
- Service (server or application oriented)

The MAC layer is sort of simple: There aren't that many ways that you can put data on the wire, and the specifications for this are fairly well laid out. It gets a little more complicated with the network protocol layer because network protocols are more complex, and therefore have more "fields" to interpret. It gets *very* complicated when you get into services. There are hundreds and hundreds of services, and it's just not possible for every analyzer to be great at decoding each one. Think of it as expecting your translator in another country to also be a good golfer, electrician, doctor, technician, dancer, and architect. Sure, you *might* find such a translator—but you'd probably have better luck finding several translators with those skills.

Here's the bottom line: Not every analyzer can handle every service. Although the common ones, such as Telnet, DNS, and Microsoft file and print, are pretty well covered, others are covered scantily, and still others are not available at all. Typically, the more proprietary a service protocol is, the less likely that there will be a widely available decode for it. For example, although every protocol analyzer in the universe deals with HTTP (see Figure 21.4 for an Ethereal decode of an HTTP session), there is no decode that I know of for WiredRed's E/Pop, a multiuser chat and remote control program.

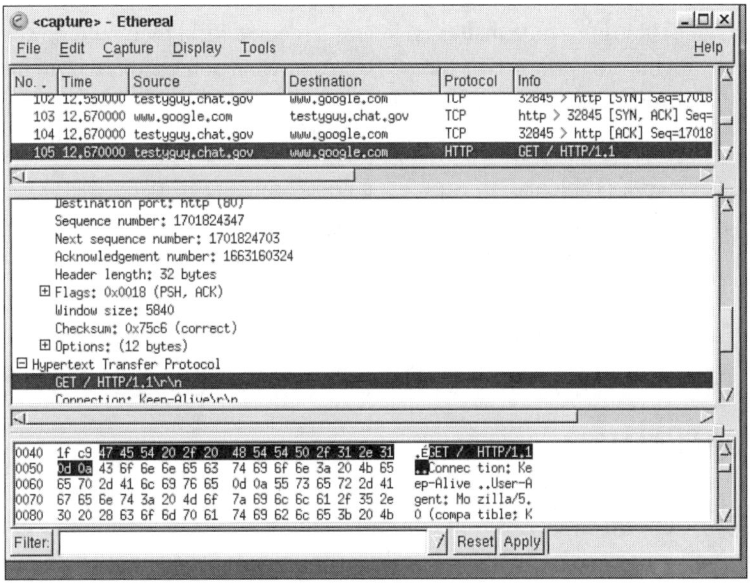

FIGURE 21.4

Ethereal, a Unix-based analyzer, showing the decode for packet containing HTTP data.

Is this a disaster? Not really. Even though the analyzer can't *decode* the service so that you can read it, it's still *capturing* what's going on. If you're working with tech support for a proprietary service, you can bet that they'll be able to read your trace using in-house decoders. After all, for our purposes, one of the primary reasons to use a protocol analyzer is to capture evidence to submit to a vendor, and if the vendor can't decode its own service, we're all in trouble.

Experts: Dave, I'm Afraid I Can't Analyze That

Some packet analyzers have an "expert" mode, which, during packet capture, makes a guess at what could be wrong with your network. In theory, this is wonderful. You and I can't sort through hundreds of conversations at once; this is the sort of job that's well suited to a computer.

21

In practice? Well, my experience with "expert" analyzers has convinced me that they're somewhat less than *expert*. Sure, they pick up on workstations that are running slowly—they're very good at seeing that a workstation has a significant delay in responding to a request. They're also good at seeing duplicate IP addresses and other simple problems. But *expert*? Not really. Teaching a computer how to solve complex network issues would probably be just as hard as teaching a computer how to think. They have no idea how to differentiate the little things that might be wrong with your network from the big thing that is preventing payroll from running.

The truth of the matter is, in any large network, there *will* be some problems. How do you start prioritizing them? Based on what some expert system tells you, or your users? Sure, you'll go with "user pain."

The bottom line is don't think of an expert analyzer as a panacea for all your hard network problems. An expert is a good tool, and is really useful for identifying a limited set of problems that it has been "taught" about. In combination with your own situation analysis, expert analyzers can be very powerful allies in your troubleshooting wars; in some cases they might actually point to the root cause of a given problem.

Net Therapy 101: Techniques for Using Your Analyzer

Each analyzer is different; choosing your weapon appropriately is one of the first steps toward success with a protocol analyzer. If you have an old and crusty FDDI network, for example, do not use an Ethernet-specific analyzer that "happens" to work with FDDI as well: use an analyzer made for FDDI.

Your scenario always dictates which tool you need. There's more than one tool out there because there's more than one problem out there. Because you can't buy *all* the tools available, it pays to know your network environment thoroughly before you invest so that you can buy the most appropriate tools for you.

Filtering: Cold-Filtered, Ice-Brewed Packets

As I mentioned earlier, knowing how and when to filter your capture data is one of the most important skills you can have when using a protocol analyzer to capture network traffic. Otherwise, you'll likely be searching for a very small needle in a very large haystack! Even a veteran packet analyst would get discouraged without filtered data.

Several types of filters are available both during capture and display:

- MAC address filtering.

- Network protocol filters—TCP/IP, IPX/SPX, AppleTalk…

- Service protocol filters—Either filter by service or by service attribute (for example, DNS queries only, but not other DNS traffic).

- Generic filters—Hexadecimal values within a packet.

- Station filters—Usually based on some attribute that is at least temporarily assigned to a network name. Use with care because these can be quite dynamic. For example, say that I choose "JFPC" as a NetBIOS station to filter on. Ultimately, this is based on a pairing between network protocol and service naming, and if the "name discovery" is run earlier than the trace, you might find that you are capturing data for the wrong station (bearing in mind that address assignment protocols like DHCP do not guarantee that you receive the same address day after day).

Not every kind of filter is available on all analyzers; for instance, some analyzers won't filter every kind of service—at least by name. You can get around this by using a generic filter based on some portion of the decode window.

Let's look at how to make one analyzer filter by TCP port number. For example, Wild Packets' EtherPeek doesn't specifically have a filter for Gnutella sessions, but it *does* allow you to filter based on a right-click in the decode window. In our case, we're interested in a Gnutella session, TCP port 6346, which translates to hexadecimal 18CA (see Figure 21.5).

Notice how several bytes (18 CA) are highlighted; these are the bytes in the packet that are the *hex codes* that identify this packet as TCP port 6346. Right-clicking will bring up a menu with a choice to apply a filter based on these values. You can apply this to other fields in the decode as well. Very cool!

Here are the two ways an analyzer can filter:

- Precapture—This is useful when you don't want your buffer to overflow with needless data.

- Postcapture—This is good for when you've already captured the general data in question and want to refine your search.

Why would you *not* filter while capturing? After all, we want to avoid the needle-in-a-haystack problem, right? Well, *if* it's possible to take a small trace by sticking to a very small time window, sometimes the additional information in that trace can be useful. Or, if you know that the problem lies in one protocol family, but not another, sometimes it's possible to only capture one protocol family. This can be pretty illuminating because a service can fail based on lower-level protocols failing. Read on.

21

FIGURE 21.5

FIGURE 21.5

*Typically, packet ana-
lyzers let you filter on
just about any decode
field; for example,
when using Wild
Packets' EtherPeek,
simply right-click and
choose "Make Filter."*

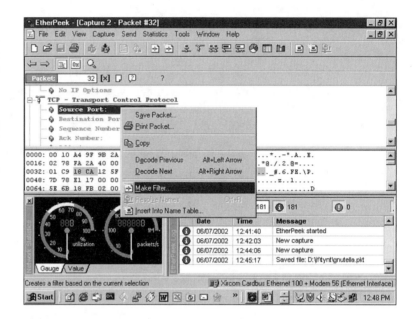

Limited Filtering Scenario

Here's a case in point for how limited filtering can help in troubleshooting a busy server.

I once had to deal with a problem in which one server started to have trouble sending print jobs to a print server. The print server would all of a sudden, and at seemingly random times, generate socket errors in its log stop processing. Only a restart of the server would make it start processing print again. Our first question was, "Who changed something on the print server?" The answer was…nobody. Nothing had changed on the print server. No interrogation or torture was spared to verify this; we were absolutely certain (ha, ha) that nobody had changed anything in the time frame that we were talking about.

This was a really tough problem to troubleshoot: A search on the print server support site for the particular error message revealed nothing, and the problem was still popping up intermittently. We needed an answer relatively quickly because this print gateway was responsible for processing print for a time-sensitive function. Because we were relatively certain that nothing had changed on either the print server or the application server (in fact, the app server was printing fine to other print servers), we decided to see what was happening on the network. Maybe some errant evil packet was causing the print server some mental illness.

We connected a protocol analyzer to the print server's segment (because we suspected something bad was happening to the server) and considered what we wanted to filter on:

- Because we knew something was happening to the print server, we would only capture packets destined for the print server's MAC address.

- Because we knew that this was a very busy file and print server, it wasn't feasible to capture *all* packets destined for this server.

- Because we knew that the problem was with Unix type printing (LPD), we would only accept TCP/IP packets. This eliminated most of the packets destined for this server; the file services didn't use TCP/IP, but used a different protocol. This left us with a test setup that looked something like what's shown in Figure 21.6.

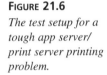

FIGURE 21.6

The test setup for a tough app server/ print server printing problem.

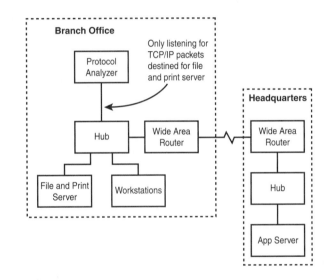

As soon as the problem occurred again, we looked at the packet capture. There are two important concepts here: First, we ran the analyzer until we received the report, and then stopped the analyzer immediately. Second, we synchronized the clock on the protocol analyzer to the network time before we started capturing, and we asked the user who reported the problem to also report the time of the problem. Because this was a pretty busy print service, we were sure that the problem report was within plus or minus two or three minutes, so we now only had to consider packets around the time of the report (plus and minus a minute), thus limiting how much junk we had to wade through.

Skipping to the end of the trace, we first filtered on the LPD port number, TCP/515. We did see a problem: The server stopped responding to the LPD requests from the UNIX host at the end. Well, we knew *that* without taking a trace. Doh!

21

Still, this was useful: It let us know *where* in the packet list the problem occurred. Therefore, we got rid of the LPD filter, jumped to the packet where the problem occurred, and looked at the packets right *before* the problem.

Apparently, right before the problem occurred, there was an ARP request (TCP/IP's Address Resolution Protocol). Remember, each TCP/IP address must have a corresponding MAC address in order for two network cards to talk. The ARP request I saw was responding with the *wrong* MAC address. An ARP packet with the wrong MAC address typically means that someone else has used a TCP/IP address that's the same as yours, thus interrupting communications—but that was *not* the case here.

We tried to find the MAC address reported by the ARP request, but there was no such network card on our network. Not only that, but I couldn't find the OUI of the MAC address in my OUI table, which was also suspicious. Furthermore, this was a network where only one or two well-known vendors' cards were in use.

Because there was no such device on the network, we next looked at the switch configuration. Because there was a MAC-level problem, we naturally suspected the switch. We asked the person responsible for switch configuration if anything had changed in the last couple of days—and, in fact, something had (so much for being "absolutely certain"). He therefore changed the configuration back to the way it used to be, and the problem went away. Tough problem solved!

Two things still bothered me, though. Why could I ping the print server *at all* if the ARP was incorrect? Well, because ARP is "redone" every couple of minutes, by the time I was on the scene troubleshooting, the ARP was correct again; therefore, I could ping the server without a problem. The switch was only *sometimes* messing up the ARP; usually, it was just fine. Second, why did a bad ARP hang the LPD server? That was a tougher question, and one I wasn't going to find the answer to, mostly because it didn't really matter. (Would the customer keep paying me to troubleshoot it further once the problem was fixed? Ah, no.)

For what it's worth, the print server program (and for that matter, the whole server in question) was somewhat old, and an interruption in the data stream was apparently driving it berserk. After the switch configuration was fixed and the ARP problem went away, everything was okay once more (and that, after all, is what's really important).

Decode View Options

When viewing specific packet traces, you'll want to explore your view options. Most analyzers have many options that allow you to be flexible about which attributes of the trace you're viewing at one time. Some of these attributes include the following:

- Hexadecimal representation of packet
- Capture time
- MAC and/or protocol and/or service decodes
- Protocol or MAC address
- Network name (DNS and NetBIOS)

> Many protocol analyzers have a name-gathering feature; that is, they "read" the packets as they go by and see whether there's a name identifier in any of them. If there is, the analyzer will make an entry in its name table, which enables you to *later* specify a capture filter or view based on a network name. This, of course, is a much more "user friendly" way to specify a filter or view data.
>
> Be aware that some analyzers do *not* capture names automatically; they offer it as a manual operation on data that you've already captured during the viewing portion of your analysis.
>
> Be further aware that in a DHCP environment, viewing by station names can be dicey—what if you name-gather when MOSHEPC has IP 10.50.1.30, but later start analysis, capturing on MOSHEPC, not realizing that LEOPC now has IP 10.50.1.30. All of a sudden, you'll be capturing data for the wrong station! Be careful out there.

Even with a good analysis tool, your brain can only process so much input at one time; being able to specify view options lets you "keep it simple" so as not to overwhelm yourself with too much information. Accordingly, you can view strip charts that summarize certain aspects of your data, as shown in Figure 21.7, which divides network traffic by application.

You can also change your packet decode display options—in particular, how time and network names are displayed. Because a network is a timing-sensitive animal, the time-related options are particularly important. Your *relative* or *interpacket* time is important because it's the delay in between two packets. A value that looks way out of line with other packets indicates a delay caused by network glue such as routers or switches—or, more likely, a delay caused by processing at the other end of the conversation (by a busy server, for example).

21

FIGURE 21.7

Finisar Surveyor and other analyzers can graph "top talkers" and other statistics, thus helping you to interpret raw data.

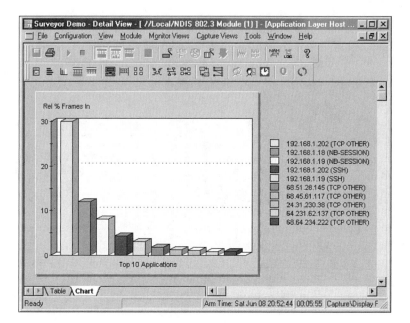

High Level Packet Analysis: "Poor Man's" Statistical Analyzer

As helpful as capturing specific packets can be toward finding a solution to a specific problem, there are times when you'll want to run your analyzer "wide open" in order to get a general overview of your network segment. Some analyzers call this *monitor mode*; others simply bundle this mode into capture mode. Although this isn't a total substitute for statistical analysis (which we'll discuss in Hour 23), it *can* be helpful in identifying "big picture" issues on the network.

For example, when everybody on a given segment is complaining that they're running slowly, and you don't have any network management tools running, you might want to break out an analyzer that will statistically analyze the segment while it's capturing. The packet analyzer will likely keep a running total on several things:

- Errors per station
- Frames received per station
- Frames transmitted per station
- Total utilization of the network
- Total errors on the network

On the slow segment, you might see that the total utilization of the network was running high, say, 65 percent. (Ethernet tends to degrade after 35 percent, so this is really high.) You would probably want to know why the utilization was high: Is it because of many users, all of whom are using a fair portion of the pipe, or a couple of users hogging up the pipe? A good way to find this out would be to sort your statistic list. For example, if you used WildPackets' EtherPeek, you might choose Node Statistics, choose All Sent, and sort by bytes, and you'd immediately find out that Fatboy seems to be a top transmitter on this pipe (see Figure 21.8). If that's what you expect (and in this case, it is because Fatboy is in fact a big fat server, and bunches of folks request stuff from him), then great. But if it's not, seeing this type of disproportionate utilization is an indicator to investigate this station further.

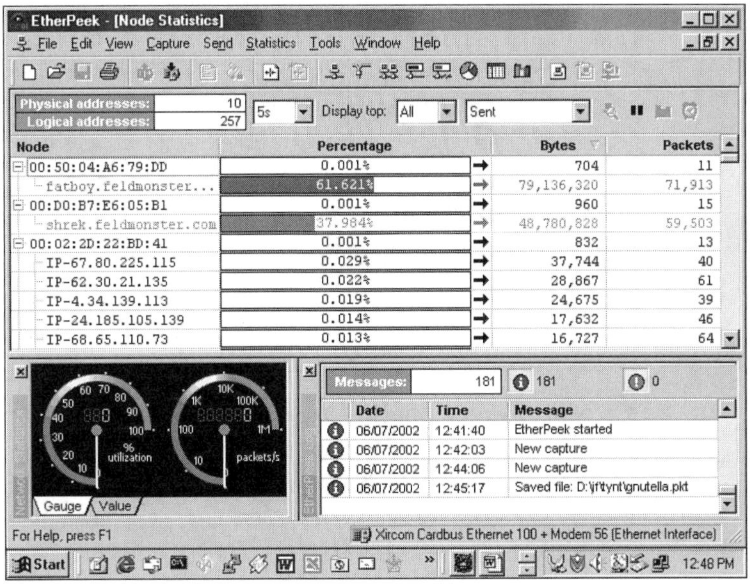

FIGURE 21.8

Packet analyzers such as EtherPeek can usually display a helpful list of network nodes sorted by various statistics, including byte count.

You might want to capture specific data from this station to find out just what type of traffic was being generated—even quicker, check your documentation and make a phone call to determine what the user in question is doing. In this case, let's say that Fatboy is a workstation, and your phone call reveals that the Fatboy user was doing a backup of his hard drive to the network. You'd probably want to politely ask him to stop doing this during peak hours and suggest other methods for hard drive backup, such as a tape drive.

Just to make sure that the network is otherwise healthy, you can also sort your node list by errors. A couple of errors here or there is fine—you just want to make sure that there isn't one station that's jamming up the freeway by behaving badly.

21

Appropriate Analysis: Some Analyzer Scenarios

Let's take a look at a couple scenarios in which analyzer use helped me out. In all cases, I was confronted by problems where we arrived at a theory, which then was *proven* through the use of the packet analyzer. This is how all of your analysis sessions should go.

I Can't Print, Again

Let's travel back to a problem we've discussed previously in Hour 19, "Internet and Intranet Troubleshooting: TCP/IP at Work." Remember how I found a UNIX host that would not spool more than one print job to a given network print server at one time, even if that print server had multiple printers attached to it? In other words, the host assumed that each print server only had one printer—a seriously wrong assumption! In this scenario, even though I had proved to myself that the host was at fault by using black box troubleshooting, I wanted evidence to submit to the vendor to prove that its stuff worked differently (wrongly) from other vendors' implementations of UNIX printing in order to try to force the vendor to fix it.

It was fairly easy to take a trace of this by specifying a capture filter of the print server's MAC address or TCP/IP address. Why not the UNIX host? Because the UNIX host had hundreds and hundreds of users, all accessing it via TCP/IP—had I specified the UNIX host, I would have had a little more data than I could handle.

I set up two test queues (queue1 and queue2) on the suspect host—one for each printer on the print server. As a "control experiment," I set up the same two queues on another host. I started the analyzer capture, went back to my desk, and quickly printed two jobs to the two test queues. I went back to the analyzer, stopped the capture, and saved it to disk, giving it the filename problem.

Then I did the exact same procedure, but used another host to print to the queues. I called this trace file good because this capture illustrated what happens with a UNIX host that's not brain dead. (Although the vendor didn't immediately act, our salesperson saw that we acted on this objective data and bought something else, which had good long-term effects on our leverage with this vendor—so it was worth doing. In fact, when we started having more problems with the machine and implementation of UNIX, we were given a new machine in reparation.)

Here are the important points to remember when submitting analyzer traces to a vendor:

- Traces should be small. Filter as much as you can. If you have extraneous "stuff" during the initial capture, do a post-capture filter to remove everything but pertinent data.

- Traces should be discrete. In particular, it is very useful to submit traces showing a "good" event versus a "bad" event.

- Traces should be backed up with an objective and succinct description of the problem, describing what troubleshooting measures were taken.

Slow Databases 'R Us

Remember when we discussed file sharing databases in Hour 20, "In-depth Application Troubleshooting?" Unfortunately, these are still widely in use, and running into problems with these is pretty common. Let's take a look at the packet trace that I did in one case to prove that sequential record searching (rather than indexed) was in use on one database file. Again, this wasn't a problem in the vendor's 100-record database, but it was a huge problem once they sold it to my customer—who had tens of thousands of records.

The symptom of the problem was pressing Next Record on the work order system. Remember that databases are usually composed of more than one table, and more than one database file. To go to the "next record" in this work order database, another database was first consulted (to gather customer information to show on the screen). Because a sequential, rather than seeking (index-based) search was in use, this meant that finding the customer data could be quite a lengthy process!

How'd I prove this? Simply by capturing the network traffic generated at the workstation when the Next Record button was pressed. Then, I scrolled through the capture, and indeed, I found that sequential record reads were being used.

Here's how. Check out Figure 21.9. It shows the information that you'll need to start doing *any* type of file-and-print analysis. (This happens to be of an NCP session, but the basics are the same whether you're doing SMB or NFS.) First, you want to establish "where does the file get opened?" So, in packet #108, you see the OPEN (the details in the decode are what differentiate an OPEN from a CREATE) requested by the workstation. In packet #109, you see an important piece of data returned by the server: the *file handle*. A file handle is simply a number that refers back to the file. In subsequent file operations, you will not see the filename, just the handle.

21

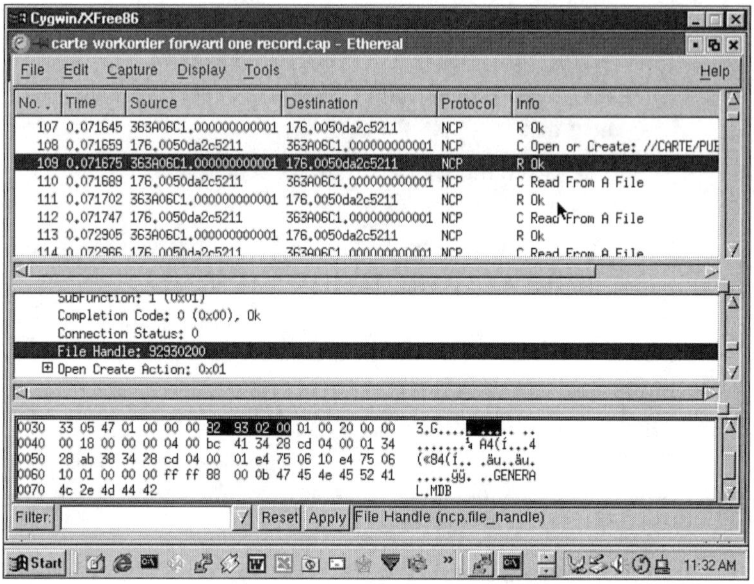

FIGURE **21.9**

When dealing with file-oriented captures, discovering the file handle that the server allocates is a good first step.

Now look at Figure 21.10. Packet #110 is the initial read request. Notice two things about the decode—the first of which is that this packet uses the same file handle as in Figure 21.9, that is, file handle `000092930200`. (One analysis trick, whether you're dealing with SYN numbers, file handles, or any other long number: just remember the last four numbers when you're bouncing between packets. If there's a question, sure, compare the whole thing, but for quick reads, using the last four digits usually works out fine.) If a different file handle was displayed, you know you're dealing with the wrong file.

Second, note that you're starting at file offset 0. This *could* be an index file, being checked from the beginning, but it's not. (The decode of Figure 21.9 shows that the file name is not an index.) What if it was an index? In this case, you would expect that the file seeking would start jumping around, as indexes are sorted, and typically use a binary search, a concept that we discussed in Hour 5, "The Napoleon Method: Divide and Conquer."

Scanning through the next couple of transactions tells the tale. Each one of the subsequent transactions looks similar to the one shown in Figure 21.11: It increments the offset by a small amount, which is basically the definition of what a sequential read sequence is. Again, this is a totally crazy and irresponsible thing to do if you are designing a fast database: Any field that gets searched needs some sort of index, which, when used, avoids sequential reads through binary search.

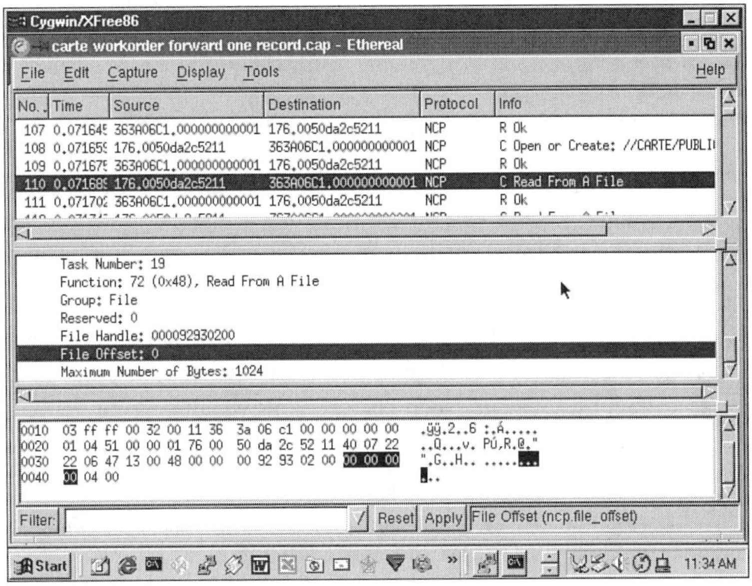

FIGURE 21.10

*The initial read request
for this problem starts
at file offset 0—the
beginning of the file.*

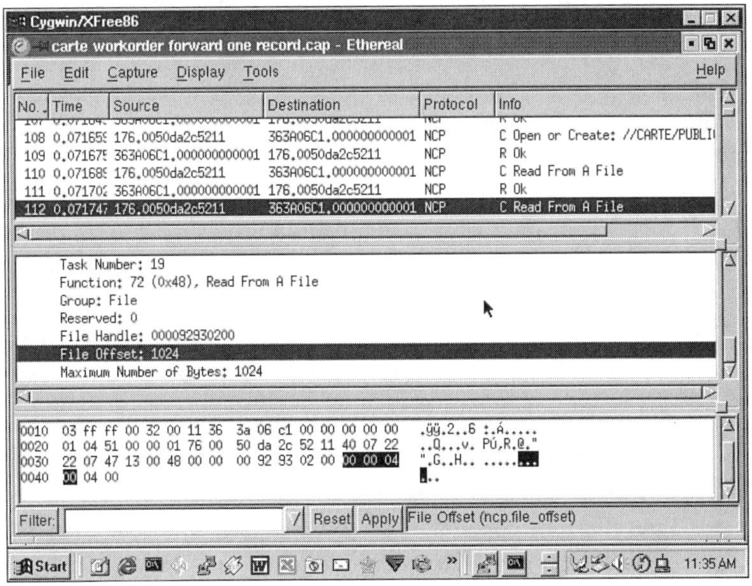

FIGURE 21.11

*Future offsets in this
problem show that
sequential reads are
occurring because file
offsets keep increment-
ing in a predictable,
sequential way.*

21

At this point, you'd filter this trace to start at packet 108, and progress through perhaps
10–20 sequential reads. That should be enough for your vendor to get the idea. And, in
our case, it was. We received fixed code within 30 days of reporting this. That's not bad.

Identifying a Station

In addition to analyzing and reporting bad network events, another use of an analyzer can be to identify workstations by MAC address using application data.

We've all been at sites where the MAC addresses weren't terribly well documented, so any MAC-related error was difficult to run down. For example, suppose Windows exclaims that there's a duplicate TCP/IP address on MAC address `00:00:C9:05:89:62`. If you don't have switches and can't use the port-to-MAC table as we discussed in Hour 19, you might think that you're totally stuck.

Undocumented MAC addresses can be a nightmare. If your analyzer doesn't automatically identify network names for you, you might think that you're out of luck. The same goes for when your expert analyzer tells you that `00:08:02:55:29:2A` is probably a bad network card and is causing many network errors.

But, no problem—you've got a wiretap, right? You can listen to all the traffic generated by this workstation, and it's likely that you'll get *something* that will identify the user. By taking a look at the data in the hexadecimal or character-oriented decode window, you can see various data that might lead you to identify the workstation's user (or department).

This is something that takes a little practice, but use your head and you'll get good at it in no time. For example, filtering on Telnet sessions will give you the entirety of a user's Telnet. Find the Password: prompt sent by the server, as in Figure 20.12, and you'll get the login name. The only problem is that you will likely have to assemble the password manually: As you go backward, the username data will present itself. To add to the fun, it's likely that the username will be "character-by-character," rather than the whole thing in one data packet. So, if the user name was "joe," you would see an "e" in packet #40's Telnet data section, and then an "o" in #37, with "j" coming right before that. The astute reader will point out that there are packets sent by the workstation (`192.168.1.202`) in between #45 and #40—what's up with that? Do the experiment: You'll see that they don't contain character data.

Too much of a pain? Check out some of the Telnet data itself. You might see a report or a menu screen that only a particular user or department uses. This sort of use of an analyzer is a good opportunity to get good at reading your protocol decodes. But clearly, documenting your MAC addresses is the real solution.

FIGURE 21.12

*Telnet session user-
names can be found in
the packets immedi-
ately preceding the
Password prompt.*

| File | Edit | Capture | Display | Tools | | | Help |

No.	Time	Source	Destination	Protocol	Info
40	1.406026	shrek	192.168.1.202	TELNET	Telnet Data ...
41	1.526678	192.168.1.202	shrek	TCP	3618 > 23 [ACK] Seq=238840739
42	2.217132	192.168.1.202	shrek	TELNET	Telnet Data ...
43	2.217364	shrek	192.168.1.202	TELNET	Telnet Data ...
44	2.329227	192.168.1.202	shrek	TCP	3618 > 23 [ACK] Seq=238840739
45	2.329460	shrek	192.168.1.202	TELNET	Telnet Data ...
46	2.529875	192.168.1.202	shrek	TCP	3618 > 23 [ACK] Seq=238840739
47	6.483319	Agere_22:bd:41	ff:ff:ff:ff:ff:ff	ARP	Who has 192.168.1.200? Tell
48	7.767204	Agere_22:bd:41	ff:ff:ff:ff:ff:ff	ARP	Who has 192.168.1.200? Tell
49	8.767173	Agere_22:bd:41	ff:ff:ff:ff:ff:ff	ARP	Who has 192.168.1.200? Tell

```
⊞ Flags: 0x0018 (PSH, ACK)
   Window size: 5840
   Checksum: 0x7466 (correct)
⊟ Telnet
   Data: Password:
```

```
0000  00 10 d4 51 3b 2d 00 d0  bf c8 03 b1 08 00 45 10   ...Q;-..  ......E.
0010  00 32 04 c9 40 00 40 06  b1 bf c0 a8 01 13 c0 a8   .2.É@.@.  ±¿À..À
0020  01 ca 00 17 0e 22 f3 bc  f3 e2 8e 5c 34 60 50 18   .Ê..."ó¼  óâ.\4`P.
0030  16 d0 74 66 00 00 50 61  73 73 77 6f 72 64 3a 20   .Ðtf..Pa  ssword:
0040  6c 8b 29 dd                                        l.)Ý
```

| Filter: | | / | Reset | Apply |

When looking for the start of any TCP-based session, go down in the TCP decode and filter on `synchronize=1`. This will get you to the beginning of the session. It's the equivalent of saying "hello?" when you first pick up the telephone—the next steps, like "may I speak to Ms. So-and-so?" are likely in a nearby packet. Of course, encrypted authentications are going to make this a lot harder.

Packet Analyzer Limitations and Solutions

Using an analyzer can be as much of a time sink as you're willing to let it be. If you were the kid in elementary school who had a good time reading the dictionary, you'll have a great time pouring over protocol decodes. If, however, you need to get a lot of work done, you might have to sigh and save the protocol decodes for a less busy time—and employ your black box troubleshooting skills to isolate if and where you need to use your analyzer.

Now it's time for the physical limitations: Remember that an analyzer can only listen in on a "party line." You cannot listen to a station that has a point-to-point connection to a switch because there's no hub to connect to and listen in on. What do you do?

21

If you are using switches, look in your switch documentation for a feature called *port mirroring*. (Cisco calls it SPAN, for Switched Port Analysis) This allows you to specify which port of the switch you want to listen in to. Just plug in your analyzer on another switch port, and the switch will do its own wiretap on the port and tell your analyzer all about it. Cool!

If your switch doesn't support port mirroring, you can always "roll your own" wiretap, as illustrated in Figure 21.13. Simply do the following:

1. Obtain a mini-hub.
2. Unplug the network cable from the station you want to "wire tap."
3. Plug that station's cable into the mini-hub's cascade port.
4. Connect a network cable from the mini-hub to your analyzer.
5. Connect a network cable from the mini-hub to the target station.

This has the effect of creating a shared segment on the switch port, and you can now listen in.

Here's the bad part: If you are doing a lot of analysis, you might be tempted to leave the hub in place where it might be most useful—as in the uplink between your user switches and your server switches. But, if your $50 hub fails, your $50,000 worth of servers are all of a sudden unavailable. For uses like this, you probably want to get something called a "passive tap." (Finisar, at `www.finisar.com`, makes good ones.) Because of its passive nature, even if it fails, the link between devices stays up, as opposed to a hub.

Here's the bottom line: Any type of *ongoing* probe (such as those required for statistical analysis) should be passive, not hub-based.

FIGURE 21.13

You can roll your own wiretap for a switch port simply by getting a "mini-hub" and creating a segment between the switch and the end station.

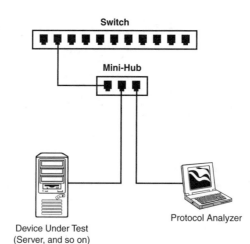

Summary

A protocol analyzer is a tool that listens to network packets on a *shared* segment and decodes them into human-readable format. There are two types of protocol analyzers: packet analyzers and statistical analyzers. Freeware and commercial packet analyzers are available. The neat thing about packet analyzers is that they run on most PCs if you have the right type of network card—that is, a "promiscuous" network card, which is able to listen to all network packets.

Depending on the analyzer, you can expect to see many functions that will help you analyze the raw data that the analyzer captures. Some of these functions include capture filtering, sortable statistical displays, "expert" analysis of data, and customizable views.

There's more than one analyzer available on the market because there's more than one problem out there. Different analyzers are good for various things, and some analyzers have better decodes of certain protocols.

Knowing what and when to filter is a really important part of learning how to use an analyzer. After you learn how to take small manageable trace files, you'll be able to quickly go through them and find what you need in order to vanquish your problems—or to entice your vendor to help out.

Analyzers, like any tool, have limitations, such as the need to use a passive tap, hub, or switch port mirroring when switching is in the picture. Still, if you have your wits about you, they're a powerful addition to your troubleshooting arsenal.

Q&A

Q **C'mon, Jonathan! Network analysts spend years learning how to sift through protocol data. How do you expect me to learn this in an hour?**

A The key here is to limit the *scope* of what you're learning. Although you're perfectly capable of learning the various protocols and service nuances that underlie the everyday programs and services that you know and love, why would you want to? (That is, unless you need to.) Remember that protocol analyzers are simply an effective way for you to verify that which your black box troubleshooting skills have already shown you. Don't get discouraged if you don't understand everything you see on the decode screen—just remember: "Which of these things is not like the other?" and use a little common sense, and you'll do very well. If you feel you need or want to dig deeper, grab a protocol book and have fun. But in many cases, that won't be necessary.

21

Q Where can I download a free analyzer?

A Check out `www.ethereal.com/download.html`. It's awesome. If you're looking for Win32 analyzers, free demos are about all you can expect. Check out Finisar, at `www.finisar.com/virtual/virtual.php?virtual_id=download`, for a trial version of Surveyor.

Workshop

Workshop time! Here's a brief quiz to help you make the most out of this hour's lesson as well as some activities for you to try on your own.

Quiz

1. A "distributed" analyzer is one that has the

    a. Ability to get into trouble

    b. Ability to capture frames on several different segments

    c. Ability to decode more than one network protocol

    d. Ability to produce charts and graphs

2. Most analyzers have which two functions?

    a. Capture the flag and a secret decoder ring

    b. Packet capture and packet decode

    c. Capture of data and decode of Ethernet

    d. Drill and fill

3. A protocol analyzer requires a computer and a _____ network card.

    a. promiscuous

    b. promethean

    c. amorous

    d. packetized

4. True or False: Identifying how and when to filter is a highly important part of learning how to use an analyzer.

5. A filter can be _____.

    a. Workstation related

    b. Protocol related

    c. Both A and B

    d. Neither A nor B

6. True or False: If your analyzer does not gather network names (such as DNS or NetBIOS), it's impossible for you to identify whose computer corresponds to a particular MAC address.

7. You're about to connect an analyzer to a network segment. For best results, what should you have done first?

   a. Sniffed packets

   b. Formed an option

   c. Come up with a theory

   d. Decided not to use a filter

8. A SYN packet is

   a. The beginning of an IBM SNA session

   b. The beginning of a TCP session

   c. A folder containing misdeeds

   d. The beginning of a Telnet session

Answers to Quiz Questions

1. B
2. B
3. A
4. True
5. B
6. False
7. C
8. B

Activities

1. Capture a session where you log in via Telnet to a Linux server. (You'll need, of course, to have a Linux server connected to a hub, with the Telnet service on. In RedHat 7.2 and above, try `service telnet start`.) Practice finding the username. What else can you see? (Hint: Can you say "security problem?") Make sure to turn off the Telnet service if it wasn't on at the beginning of your test.

2. Build a filter to capture all SMB packets. Then, copy a large file; in the middle of the copy, remove the workstation's network cable. Then, plug it back in. Look at the trace: does it tell you anything?

HOUR 22

Network Troubleshooters Just Wanna Have Fun

O, it is excellent
to have a giant's strength; but it is tyrannous
to use it like a giant.

—William Shakespeare, *Measure for Measure*, II, 2

Let's say that you've been tasked by your boss to get good at network troubleshooting. So far, things are wonderful: You've gotten permission to buy this book, to go to a class or two, and things are just great. The only problem is that nothing's broken in almost forever. It's as if the network gremlins *know* that you're prepared for them and are waiting until your guard is down—they're waiting until you forget the stuff you've learned before they pounce.

Well, you can foil their crafty little plans by plying your troubleshooting trade to help the masses have a little bit of fun. This hour deals with stuff you'll need to know in order to play various games and use non–work-related toys through your firewall or proxy server. And why not? You've worked hard; you deserve it.

For those of you who've paged directly to this hour—please don't! In this hour, I assume that you've already engaged in the skull-sweat involved in the past 21 hours and that you have a basic grasp of TCP/IP troubleshooting, particularly the concepts involved in Hour 19, "Internet and Intranet Troubleshooting: TCP/IP at Work," Hour 16, "Firewall and Proxy Server Basics" and Hour 20, "In-depth Application Troubleshooting."

Seriously, learning how to use games (during your *own* time, of course) and toys on the Internet is a great incentive to practice your Internet and client/server troubleshooting. It teaches you how to perform these types of troubleshooting techniques on a noncritical basis—in other words, you're unlikely to get stressed out helping somebody do something that's strictly optional. Additionally, you're then more of an expert at this type of troubleshooting technique when *real* trouble arises. Let's face it, network troubleshooters and IT (information technology) people, in general, have a bum rap for being sociopaths. Helping people do fun things has the following benefits:

- It's enjoyable.
- It's a good learning experience.
- It's helpful in establishing a rapport with users.
- It's a way to avoid a Dilbert-like work environment.

As you'll see, configuring toys (games, chat programs, and so forth) for use on your network combines a knowledge of your network, the ability to dig into the network sockets in use on your PC, and the ability to use dialog boxes.

Here's the down side (why does there always have to be a down side?):

- Your organization's acceptable-use policy might forbid fun, either specifically or implicitly.
- Using certain toys on your corporate network might in fact be a network security hazard. (For example, one version of a popular multiplayer game had a vulnerability in it that allowed remote attackers to execute arbitrary code on your PC if you were hooked up to a game server.)
- Certain toys might actually explicitly (by design) violate privacy or security by installing malware like viruses or Trojans, or spyware such as Gator.

Still, nothing says that you need to do this stuff at work. In the four-person, five-computer family, there are plenty of firewalls and ISP issues. As far as the security issues go, although keeping current on your virus patterns and only downloading from trusted sources aren't totally foolproof, they're good steps in the right direction. For privacy concerns, using spyware-catchers like Ad-Aware (www.lavasoftusa.com) can help out a great deal.

With that said, let's do it. If you're caught, or killed, the secretary will deny all knowledge of your actions.

Finding Your Firewall

If you know every detail about your firewall, skip this section.

Still here? Great. There are really two major issues here. First, you have to figure out whether you're using a proxy server or a packet-filtering firewall. Second, you need to figure out whether user authentication is in use.

Assuming that you have a working browser, finding your firewall type should be no problem. Fire up your browser and load a fairly complex page off the Internet (one that takes more than a second or two to load). While that's happening, get into a DOS prompt and type the following:

```
netstat -a > before.txt
```

After that's done, type this, but don't press Enter yet:

```
netstat -a > after.txt
```

Now switch to the browser and refresh the page. Then *quickly* switch back to the DOS prompt and press Enter. After you do this, you'll have two files: before.txt and after.txt. The difference between these files shows what additional sockets open when you refresh the browser screen—and whether you're using a proxy server or a packet-filtering firewall. Let's say that you do this for a Web page at www.quizro.com:

```
C:\windows> fc before.txt after.txt
Comparing files before.txt and after.txt
****** before.txt
  TCP   duke:1071      frotz.frob.com:23  ESTABLISHED
****** after.txt
  TCP   duke:1572      socks.frob.com:1080 ESTABLISHED
  TCP   duke:1071      frotz.frob.com:23   ESTABLISHED
```

Here's the rule of thumb: If you see a hostname that's *different* from the hostname you were going to on the Net, you're using a proxy server. (In the preceding example, you don't see a socket established to port 80 of www.quizro.com. Instead, you see a socket to socks.frob.com; therefore, you're using a proxy server.) The hostname you see is the name of the proxy server; the socket number is the proxy port number. This is an essential bit of knowledge to have to start configuring your toys.

If you see a connection directly to the outside Web site, you likely have a packet-filtering firewall. A packet-filtering firewall acts similarly to a router; it automatically routes your request for a connection to the outside, so you don't need to know the name or location.

However, you do need to know the name of a proxy server in order to configure your browser or any toys. Common names for proxy servers are "proxy," "socks," "http," and "firewall," among others. You can, of course, perform an `nslookup` to scan through your DNS names to see probable names for proxy servers:

```
$ nslookup
Default server: 192.168.1.6
> ls -d mycompany.com
 [ns.mycompany.com]
 mycompany.com.          SOA     ns.mycompany.com postmaster.mycompany.com.
 (1017 10800 3600 604800 86400)
 mycompany.com.          NS      ns.mycompany.com
 ns                      A       192.168.1.6
 ns                      A       192.168.3.6
 ntserver                A       192.168.1.10
 mailserver              CNAME   ntserver.mycompany.com
 cotton                  A       192.168.3.7
 socks                   CNAME   cotton.mycompany.com
```

In this output, you can see that `cotton` is the real name of the `socks` server, which is at `192.168.3.7`. However, it's probably less effort to pick up the telephone, call corporate IT, and *ask*.

If *you're* responsible for all the networking at your shop, and you've been handed a totally undocumented network, know that you are not alone—this happens more often than most network pros want to admit—and see Hour 24, "Reverse Engineering, Discovery Tools, and Other Black Magic," for more tips on how to explore services on your network.

Troubleshooting Port Access Using Proxies and Port Forwarding

If you're having trouble using a certain port through your firewall, you might want to test whether this port is specifically being blocked—not necessarily at your site, but perhaps somewhere upstream from your site. Let's say, for example, that you cannot use Gnutella—the popular file-sharing program doesn't seem to be able to contact any of the "host discovery" services. Although Gnutella runs on many ports, the most popular "discovery" port is TCP/6346, and it's a common port blocked by firewall administrators; that is, many folks make this an explicitly forbidden port to traverse the firewall.

What if your AUP (acceptable use policy) says "Don't do file sharing"? Okay, leave it alone. Don't do it. It's not worth your job, right? And besides, as troubleshooters, we want to be part of the solution, not part of *any* problem.

But, you might well be the system administrator for a branch office, and there might be a perfectly reasonable user who wants to use, not abuse Gnutella. It might well be in your province to help out here. For example, I've had to deal with upstream blockages for one client who was trying to use RealPlayer: He needed it for training, yet it was being blocked upstream. Calls to the upstream help desk were fruitless until we proved that things worked fine if we bypassed their all-too-helpful port block. Argh!

There are two ways that you can work around a blocked application: use a proxy, or use port forwarding.

If you're using an app that can transport itself over HTTP proxy (like AOL Instant Messenger), you're in good shape. But if you're not, you'll need to use a circuit proxy like Socks.

Remember, there's nothing about *any* proxy protocol that says you have to use a proxy that is on site. You can, in fact, use any proxy server on the Internet, given that you have permission, a password, at least *one* open port, and so forth. So, find a friendly administrator and get temporary access to a proxy server. Or, run one at your home site: For Windows users, there's WinGate; for Linux users, there's the NEC Socks software or Dante. Proxy ports like TCP/8080 (http-proxy) or TCP/1080 (Socks) blocked? Try running the proxy on an allowed port, like TCP/80.

Lest I get a barrage of emails pointing out that "there are plenty of open servers on the Internet," let me say this: It is a really poor practice to use proxy servers that allow anonymous, or open access. The popular idea behind "open" servers is that they are run by libertarians who want to provide others with anonymous access, free from tracking by whomever. This might be true in a small number of cases. But in most cases, open proxies are simply *misconfigured* proxies: proxies that allow folks from the outside, as well as the inside, to use the proxy service. Avoid them. These lists of open proxy servers are a bit like cracker-generated lists of "free" calling card numbers: In reality, they belong to someone, and you should not be using them without consent.

Access Via Socks Proxy

Whether you run your own Socks server or are using someone else's to test with, Socks requires a bit of configuration. (Hour 16 includes more down-and-dirty details on Socks.)

The bummer about any generic circuit proxy server is that unless a given application has built-in support for it, you need to use a separate client to enable the proxy. In the Socks world, two companies distribute free client software that will "socksify" various programs, including games or other fun toys:

- NEC SocksCap (`http://www.socks.nec.com`)   This is the least intrusive client; that is, it runs as a "launcher," without the need to modify system files. You use dialog boxes to configure it with the name of your socks server, the socks port (by default, TCP/1080), and the names and locations of the program files that you want to use the socks server. See Figure 22.1 for a sample configuration—it's pretty simple.

- Hummingbird Communications (`http://www.hummingbird.com`)   This client gets "underneath" your TCP/IP DLL files and intercepts all TCP/IP requests. The Hummingbird client is a lot more intrusive to your PC because it replaces Windows system files with its own files. Another thing about the Hummingbird client is that it's not obvious when a workstation is using it; that is, there's no icon that appears on your desktop. Therefore, troubleshooting in general gets tougher because you might not realize that the client is running on the workstation. I recommend that you do something to indicate to yourself that this PC has the Hummingbird client on it (big flaming letters on the monitor, that kind of thing).

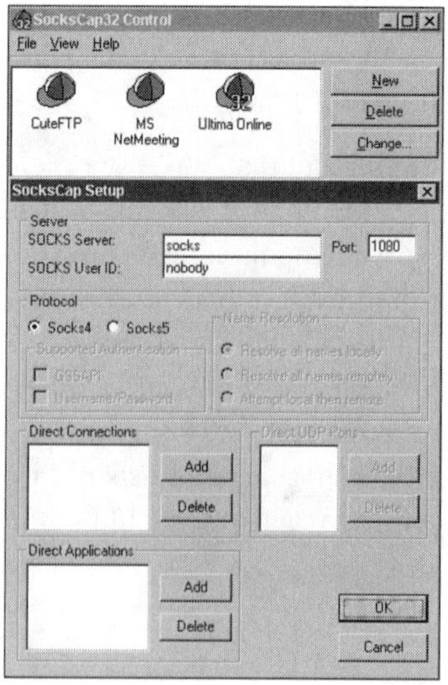

FIGURE 22.1

SocksCap32 is really easy to configure and use.

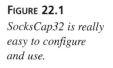

Hummingbird also doesn't sport a graphical setup. You must configure the client by editing the SOCKS.CNF file in your Windows system directory. (Different versions of this software store it in different places, so do a hard-drive search for the file if you're unsure.) Here's an example of how I might set up a Hummingbird configuration file for a simple two-segment network:

```
Direct 192.168.1.0 255.255.255.0
Direct 192.168.2.0 255.255.255.0
@SockD = 192.168.2.10 0.0.0.0 0.0.0.0
```

This file means that you're directly connected to 192.168.1.0 and 192.168.2.0. Traffic to those segments will not use the Socks server. All other traffic will be passed to the Socks server at 192.168.2.10.

In a nutshell, Hummingbird's client is extremely configurable yet hard to configure, and it adopts a "grab everything that goes on in the network and deal with it according to my configuration file" policy. Although this client works with more applications than does the NEC client, it affects *all* rather than *some* applications you run. The NEC client, on the other hand, is less intrusive, more friendly to configure, requires a separate configuration for each application, and sometimes doesn't work for certain applications because it *is* less intrusive.

NEC's client doesn't always work. But how do you know that a given app doesn't work with the NEC client?

Try this. Run the app through the NEC socks client, and while it tries to connect, run netstat -a in a DOS window. If the app is trying to directly contact the host on the Internet, you will see a foreign IP address (*not* the proxy) and a SYN_SENT socket state. (See Hour 18, "Managing Change: Establishing Consistency and Standards," for socket state details.) If it talks properly to the NEC client, you'll see a socket to the socks server in the ESTABLISHED state, or at worst, CLOSE_WAIT or TIME_WAIT.

If you see a CLOSE_WAIT or TIME_WAIT, this tells you that your problem is *not* with NEC software.

In short, these clients don't work *all* of the time for all programs, but at least one of these Socks clients will work for the majority of software out there.

Port Forwarding

What's port forwarding, and how does it differ from proxying? Basically, it's when you establish a connection to a port forwarding server using an allowed port, and then perform two operations:

1. Listen on the "localhost" (the PC that the port forwarding software is running on) for the *disallowed* port.

2. When a connection is made to the localhost, use the established connection as a data channel and tell the port forwarding server to actually go ahead and make the connection to the *real* server and *real* port that you're trying to get to.

Clear as mud? Check out Figure 22.2. It might also help if you think of this as "tunneling," rather than port forwarding, though calling it port forwarding is more precise.

FIGURE 22.2

Port forwarding "tunnels" a request through an allowed port.

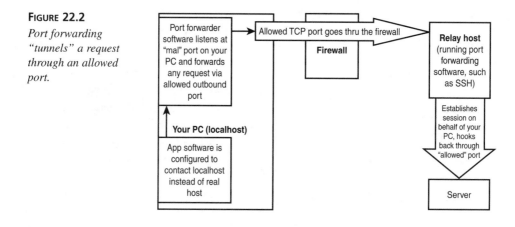

Let's say that you want to play a MUD game that runs on a server (say, mud.mygame. com) TCP/3333, and TCP/3333 is not on the "allowed" list on your firewall. (Everything is denied except what is expressly permitted.) If you have access to an SSH server and TCP/22 is allowed through the firewall, you could use a multipurpose terminal emulation/SSH tunneling package, such as F-Secure, or I could use Tunnelier, software that specifically is made for port forwarding. (A good Web page about various SSH clients for the Windows world is `www.jfitz.com/tips/ssh_for_windows_doc_version2.html`.)

If TCP/22 isn't allowed, you can run your SSH server on TCP/80. Nothing says that you have to use the application's default port.

Once you SSH through the firewall on an allowed port, your SSH *client* listens for the MUD connection on your local PC, on TCP/3333. If a connection is made to your PC at localhost:3333, the SSH client tells the SSH server to initiate a connection to the MUD game; the client then forwards your local connection to the actual server at mud. mygame.com:3333. Figure 22.3 shows the configuration you'd use with F-Secure's SSH client.

FIGURE 22.3

F-Secure SSH, config-ured to tunnel port 3333 on localhost to mud.mygame.com: 3333.

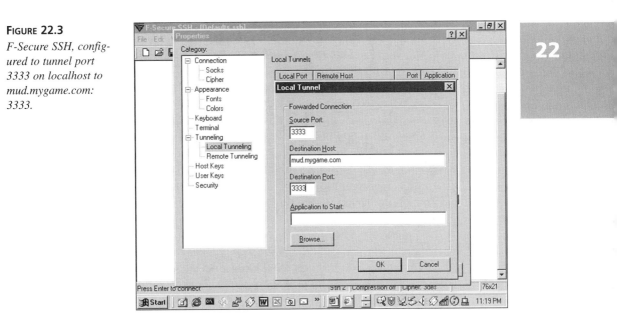

NAT Problems

NAT can be a major bummer if you're trying to play multiplayer games. Sometimes, this is because the games embed your IP address inside the application payload. There's nothing that a NAT firewall can do about this at layer 3; you would need an application-aware firewall.

What happens when NAT gets embedded in an app payload? Well, the application ignores layer 3 information in the packet and decides to try to contact the network address within the payload. Clearly, this isn't happening if you are using private (RFC 1918) addresses—the Internet will refuse to route them (see Figure 22.4).

What else might happen? If you have *two* workstations using the same game, only one might be able to play. Why? This is probably because the game isn't too flexible about *which* TCP or UDP ports can be used. Remember that a *socket* is a *unique* pairing of address plus port. Can you and your spouse use the same *socket* using the same external address? Ah, no. Sockets must be unique on a host.

Most NAT firewalls with one external address use what Cisco calls PAT, or port address translation. That is, if more than one person tries to use a port, PAT *changes* that port (much like NAT changes the address) to be unique. Simple. But many games aren't quite flexible enough to deal with this. (Of course, if you have more than one external address, you're in good shape—and most corporate firewalls do have more than one external address to map to internal addresses—but at home, most of us don't have more than one.)

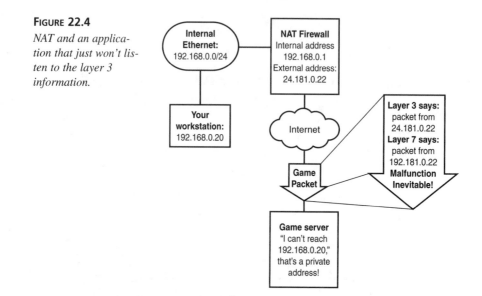

FIGURE 22.4
NAT and an application that just won't listen to the layer 3 information.

Some NAT Solutions

Some cheery news to start with: Microsoft's new DirectPlay system is pretty NAT friendly. The bad news: Games that either don't use DirectPlay or use a version of DirectX before version 8 typically exhibit the problems previously described.

Some application-aware firewalls are available; for example, Linux's IPMasq function has modules to deal with some quirky applications. (See `www.e-infomax.com/ipmasq/` for details.) Don't forget to check game-specific sites as well for configuration help with commercial firewalls. (`www.planetbaldursgate.com/bg/help/multiplayer/proxy` is one good example.)

One interesting thing that you can do to blow away all NAT issues is to simply throw up a VPN between you and interested gaming friends. (All of a sudden, everybody is on the same local network with no NAT issues or port blocks. Pretty cool.) I've done this, and it works pretty well. (For example, when I was having trouble playing *Icewind Dale* with my brother Joe, I'd went to Google, searched on "firewall Icewind Dale," and, indeed, found out that not only did I need TCP/47624-49672 and both TCP and UDP 2300-2400, but that NAT wasn't supported. This was such a hassle that VPN was a natural way to go.) Obviously, this is something that you should do *only* if you totally trust the other parties; doing this with people you meet in a chat room is a bit like having a face-to-face in an isolated location with someone you met in a chat room.

Finally, bear in mind that there are more things than firewall issues that might keep your network toys from working; don't forget basic black box troubleshooting strategies. In particular, you'll want to monitor system resources (most games and toys are resource hogs) and check whether the server on the other side of the Internet is "listening" for connections.

If you're able to telnet to the TCP port that a particular toy uses (and TCP is the only thing it's trying to use), it's extremely unlikely that your firewall is interfering with the operation. Also, bear in mind that certain toys, like Yahoo! and AOL Messenger, are port adaptive—that is, if one port won't work through your firewall, you can use a common port like 80, which is unlikely to be blocked.

Summary

You can practice your network troubleshooting skills, create goodwill with your network users, and satiate your desire to blow away aliens all at the same time. Network toys, such as streaming video and audio, and games are loads of fun to use on your network, but they are usually designed for home use or for a specific corporate customer. To successfully use these, you'll either need to enable their built-in proxy support, use a client for proxy support, use a client for port forwarding, or fix your firewall to allow their port numbers to pass through unmolested.

NAT can be tough with some games, but DirectX 8 promises to make NAT (and even PAT) less of an issue. Don't forget to check game sites for tips, as well as check for non-firewall related issues.

Q&A

Q How do I figure out which port a specific game or toy uses?

A I'd be very surprised if the vendor didn't tell you. Still, some don't. You'll want to do the "difference" trick again to find out which port your Net toy uses. Dial in to an Internet account that you know works, and type the following:

```
netstat -a > before.txt
```

Then run the game, stay connected, get back to a DOS prompt, and type this:

```
netstat -a > after.txt
fc before.txt after.txt
```

You'll be rewarded with the socket number(s) that your game uses. This method has two drawbacks: UDP ports won't show up this way because there is no "connection." Also, you have no idea whether there's a different TCP connection used at login versus during game play.

If you *must* know exactly which ports your game uses—check out Hour 21, "Protocol Analyzers," and use a network analyzer to capture the packets of a game session. You'll have to do this from your DMZ, unless you have a serial (dial-up) analyzer. At this point, you should ask yourself whether you really want to play *that* badly. Well, sure!

Workshop

Workshop time! Here's a brief quiz to help you make the most out of this hour's lesson as well as some activities for you to try on your own.

Quiz

1. You can find the address of your proxy server by checking the _____ while using a functional browser.

    a. socket pocket

    b. socket list

    c. route list

    d. route rocket

2. True or False: The Hummingbird socks client (versus the NEC socks client) applies to *all* applications that are run on the workstation on which it is installed.

3. We used an `nslookup` command to list all entries in a company's DNS zone. What was that command?

    a. `netstat -rn company.com`

    b. `ls -la company.com`

    c. `ls -d company.com`

    d. `netstat -d company.com`

4. Port forwarding supports

    a. `TCP connections only

    b. UDP connections only

    c. Both UDP and TCP connections

    d. Neither UDP nor TCP connections

5. True or False: NAT, using one external IP address, will likely not support a game that requires specific, static port numbers.

6. True or False: Open proxies are usually run by folks who want to support free and open access on the Internet.

Answers to Quiz Questions

1. B
2. True
3. C
4. A
5. True
6. False

Activities

1. Call up your IT coordinator, or, if you work for the IT department, have a discussion about what the acceptable-use policy says about having fun on the organization's equipment during your free time. Is this any different from calling your sister after working hours, understanding that this will cost your organization no more in toll charges?

2. If you have a home firewall (or if you have permission and knowledge to configure the one at work), using port blocks, try to block AOL's Instant Messenger from phoning home. Can you? Tricky little devil, isn't it?

HOUR 23

Network Management Tools

If you do what you always did, you're gonna get what you always got.
—Yogi Berra

"Network management" is a fairly amorphous phrase that changes depending on the context in which you use it. When you're talking about a person practicing good network management, you're talking about someone who is good at change management, staffing practices, and so on.

Network management *tools*, as we discuss them in this chapter, are tools that allow you to perform both short- and long-term monitoring of network infrastructure gear, applications, and servers; and for some tools, to also perform simple configuration of these devices. (If you're looking for more complex remote configuration of user workstations, see Hour 18, "Managing Change: Establishing Consistency and Standards.")

What's the practical use of these tools? Well, first of all, proactive monitoring is always a good thing: When something goes out of whack, you can fix it before it becomes a big problem. Second, to the network troubleshooter, more information is always good; and graphical trend data is an excellent way of usefully summarizing lots of mind-numbing statistics, as we'll see in this hour.

Now, let's get to work. First, a discussion of the various types of tools is in order; then, we'll examine how to use these tools to address a common user complaint: "The network is slow!" Having a handle on device statistics go hand in glove with being able to address this sort of complaint because, ultimately, well-thought-out network management not only allows you to know whether devices are functioning at all, but also what kind of device statistics are "normal." Like a physician with vital signs in hand, you can rule in or rule out various problems by comparing what is "normal" to what is currently being experienced.

Monitoring

The germane function of network management is, in fact, the monitoring of key services and infrastructures. As network troubleshooters, we are interested in seeing when things are about to fail, as well as when they fail. When we monitor, we're interested in the following items:

- Performance—Is the resource running out of steam? What's it running out of? How close to capacity is it running?
- Uptime—How long has the device been up? Should we restart it as a preventative measure?
- Availability—Is the resource available, or is it down?

Because you could monitor literally hundreds of individual resources via the network—for example, the power supplies in your server, each hard drive, the internal temperature of the CPU, its network card buffers, and so on—network management packages have introduced the concepts of thresholds and alerts.

When a resource goes outside the thresholds you or the manufacturer set up, an alert to the network is generated, and you are notified (either by email, by pager, or via a network console) about it. This is the basic concept behind network monitoring.

Depending on which network management package you choose, this can be more or less automatic. Some management packages use proprietary methods of monitoring (which is not a terrible thing if it works and is easy to use), and some use standards-based monitoring. Which one is right for you? It really depends on how large your shop is, what tools your vendor provides when you buy your network gear, and how well they fit into a management solution. As you'll see in a little while, you can "roll your own" monitoring script and have this feed into a freeware package, and this works perfectly well. We'll explore this further, but first, let's look at SNMP, the protocol upon which many monitoring systems are built.

SNMP

Network management, like all networking, is full of crazy acronyms. Three of the most important acronyms (which also double as important TCP/IP standards) are SNMP, MIB (not to be confused with *Men in Black*), and RMON.

SNMP stands for *Simple Network Management Protocol* and is a standard way of providing certain network information to nodes that request it, while allowing privileged nodes to change that information. How is this accomplished?

SNMP is just another TCP/IP service, a service that lives on UDP/161. A workstation, server, router, switch, or other network device that has the SNMP service running on it is called an *SNMP agent*. Any SNMP agent provides certain variables to requesting management stations. Two types of access are allowed: read-only and read/write. The passwords used to gain this access are known as *communities*. So, when someone asks for the SNMP read/write community, he's actually asking for the password. The default read-only community is public, the default read/write string is private. Obviously, when you set up SNMP devices, you really want to use a good password—it just doesn't do to have others snooping around or modifying your devices! In particular, you will want to use *long* community names because there are plenty of "brute force" SNMP crackers out there. Although some SNMP implementations limit your community strings to 25 or so characters, longer community names would not be out of order.

MIBs

A common set of well-defined variables is known as a MIB (pronounced as a whole, as in "Mihb," not "M-I-B."). MIBs organize information available through SNMP much like folders organize files. Figure 23.1 shows a MIB browser from MG-Soft (www.mg-soft.com).

Whoa! What's a MIB? MIB stands for *managed information base*, and is a shorthand way of referring to all the resource variables that exist in one group, mapping numerical OIDs (Object IDs) to human-readable symbols. For instance, just about all SNMP agents respond to MIB-I and MIB-II variables, such as SysContact, SysName, SysLocation for record keeping, and ifOutOctets and ifInOctets, referring to the number of bytes received or transmitted by an interface (if).

23

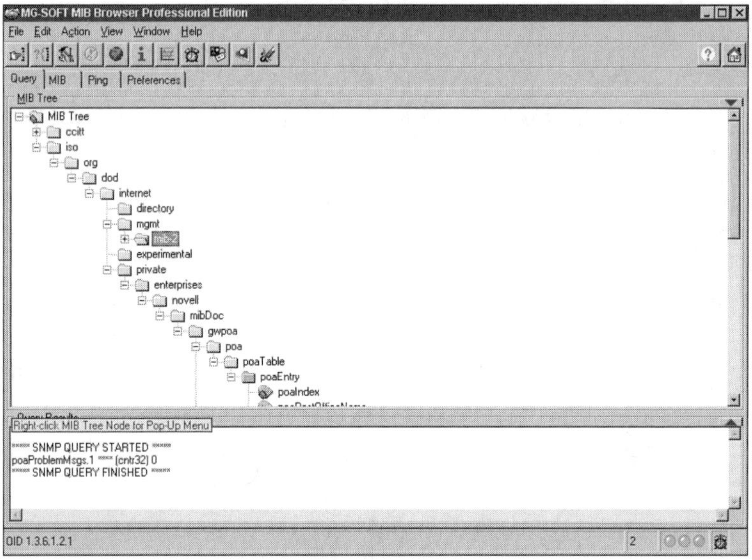

FIGURE 23.1

The MG-Soft MIB browser is a good way to start getting familiar with SNMP and MIBs.

Many manufacturers provide their own MIBs because they have specific information that isn't contained in the general MIBs. These are sometimes called *enterprise* MIBs. For example, my GroupWise system has a couple of specific variables in its MIBs that wouldn't be useful for any other system (for example, poaUndeliverableMsgs, which stands for *Post Office Agent's Undeliverable Messages*). The agent that lives on the device or software already knows about its MIB; however, a MIB file exists that allows you to "export" the MIB to a network console that doesn't know about it. In a nutshell, a MIB file correlates a numeric value, such as 1.3.6.1.2.1.1.4, with a symbolic meaning—in this case, iso(1).org(3).dod(6).internet(1).mgmt(2).mib-2(1).system(1).sysContact(4). A MIB file also specifies whether a variable is read-only, such as ifOutOctets, or read/write, such as sysContact.

> The MIB browser shown in Figure 23.1 provides a good way for you to tool around the MIB and SNMP world, called "walking the SNMP tree." Cool!

Okay, so having SNMP enabled on a device allows you to keep track of kazillions of resources at once. This is neat, but what about alerts? That is, when something bad happens, how does SNMP tell you about it?

Each SNMP agent can be configured to broadcast a trap to the network (*trap* is just another word for an alert). Traps can be broadcasts (literally sent to the broadcast address of the subnet), or they can be targeted to a management station. Because many routers are configured to *not* forward broadcasts, generally, on a large network, you will want to specify a specific management station by IP address.

If your network management station is listening for traps, it pages you, sends you an email, plays the *Star Trek* "Red Alert" sound—whatever you want—when something bad happens. This sort of alerting system provides an excellent way of letting you know that something is wrong with your network.

However, in real life, a trap can also be a silly extravaganza. For example, the print servers that we use in my office all send an SNMP trap out when their printers are offline. Argh! Give me a break. We've got hundreds of printers out there on the network: many of which are purposely offline at any given time (to change paper, add forms, and so on). There's no way I want all of them sending traps to my network management station every time this happens. Fortunately, when I configured the print server, I had the option to turn off this trap (see Figure 23.2).

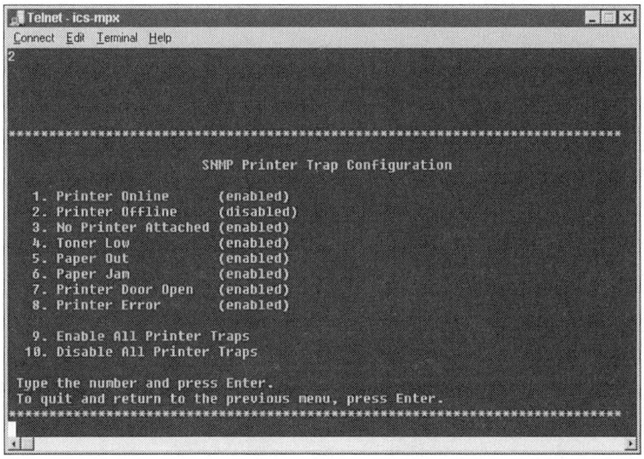

FIGURE 23.2

A dedicated print server with an SNMP configuration via a Telnet session.

Some SNMP agents can be configured to send several different levels of traps to your network manager. This way, you don't get paged for silly stuff. For example, my GroupWise MIB defines certain traps as *informational* (for instance, when the post office first starts up) and others as *critical* (for instance, when the post office must go down). Obviously, I'd like to be paged for critical issues but not necessarily for informational ones.

RMON

The Internet MIBs (MIB-I and MIB-II) are a set of variables that allow individual devices to keep track of their internal status, that is, "How much memory do I have left?" and so on. But what about the status of the VLAN that the devices are on? That's where

RMON comes in. *RMON (Remote Monitoring)* is a MIB whose variables are designed to keep track of network traffic statistics. Is this much like a protocol analyzer? Well, yes and no. Each RMON device does keep track of network *statistics* much like your analyzer does when it's capturing packets. However, RMON doesn't continually capture packets; instead, it continually gathers statistical data about the network and other network stations.

A package that supports RMON in combination with RMON probes also allows you to perform short- and long-term statistical analysis on multiple segments, as well as create a baseline of how your network runs when it is healthy. This is really important when trying to figure out why the network is slow *today* when it wasn't *yesterday*; as you'll see in a little while, it is incredibly useful to compare today's stats with yesterday's stats. Here are some examples of SNMP management packages, meant for small-to-medium-sized networks (as in, packages that don't cost $50,000 and require a staff of 20 to implement). All of them have the option to automatically "discover" your network from the public community name, but don't expect the discovery process to be totally painless; you'll have to manually tweak whatever network map the software discovers.

- WhatsUp Gold (www.ipswitch.com)
- SNMPc (www.castlerock.com)
- NetInspector (www.mg-soft.com)
- SolarWinds Network Management and Discovery Tools (www.solarwinds.net)

Taking a Poll

In addition to using SNMP monitoring tools for particular pieces of gear, you can also use third-party monitoring tools that actually check for the real application-level availability of any service or server that you choose. These tools generally

1. Get a list of IP numbers and services (port numbers) that the user wants to monitor.
2. Try to *poll* the services (check them using the appropriate protocol) every so often.
3. Request content as if an actual user were requesting it (and therefore can evaluate how an actual user perceives this service).
4. Evaluate the response: Did the services respond at all? Did they respond correctly? How fast did they respond?
5. Sound the alarm (via pager, email, and so on) if something doesn't respond correctly.

This is actually a pretty cool way of monitoring your services; after all, SNMP might be working, but in the final analysis, you want to know that your *service* is working. Who cares if SNMP thinks that your Web server is up? If it's not actually responding to the service when a network station tries it, it might as well be a boat anchor! Many third-party packages are available; some monitor whether generic TCP ports are "alive and listening," and others are complex utilities designed to monitor specific applications such as email or network databases.

Here are some examples of service monitoring packages, listed from the primitive to the sublime:

- NetSaint (`www.netsaint.org` or `www.nagios.org`)—UNIX-based, Web-page oriented, and free.
- Big Brother (`bb4.com`)—UNIX- or Win2K-based, and free for non-commercial use.
- IPSentry (`www.ipsentry.com`)—Runs under Windows; has a per-plugin fee.
- WhatsUp Gold (`www.ipswitch.com`)—Polling, uptime statistic collection, SNMP features (including trap management and enterprise MIB support).

Pollers are typically inexpensive compared to the costs of deploying even a modest SNMP installation, and they're very easy to configure and use. Without SNMP, you won't have all the detail that MIBs provide, but you might not need it. In short, a polling package is a one-stop application in which you can monitor many services easily. These packages are easily the most practical of all network management tools.

Baseliners

Baselining, the practice of keeping long-term statistics, is a very important part of problem determination when, as they say, "The network is slow!" After all, if you don't have a sense of how things typically are, how can you tell when something is out of range? Long-term, service-level record keeping is also a way to know—and a way to show your boss—that everything is operating efficiently and is working properly.

The point of baselining is that if you don't know what things look like when times are *good*, you'll have no idea what you're looking for when things go bad. Accordingly, you really want to expend a little effort and create a picture of what your network infrastructure looks like when things are running pretty well.

A couple of words about the length of a baseline: Any good statistical picture must entail a large enough sample to make the data valid. In other words, the American Medical Association doesn't set normal lab values from a population sample of young, anemic computer geeks—they take large samples from healthy people from all walks of life and figure out what the normal range (highs and lows) for cholesterol, iron, white blood cells, and so on should be for most folks. If the doctor finds out that *your* blood has abnormal ranges, she'll likely investigate what's causing them.

The same is true of your baseline. You can't expect to take samples during your busiest time of the year and get normal values. Nor can you take a day's worth of data and consider it to be gospel. Instead, you need to take at least a week's worth of data at a time of year when it's business as usual. You can graph this data and keep it for when you have problems. When you do, you take the same measurements and see which statistics jibe with your baseline numbers and which do *not*. For example, suppose that your network utilization on segment 3 never exceeds 15 percent and never has an error rate of more than 2 percent when things are normal. If you find out that its utilization is 65 percent with an error rate of 12 percent, you would probably investigate the segment some more. This is the magic of baselining.

Possibly the best known baseliner is MRTG, the Multi-Router Traffic Grapher (www.mrtg.org). In its simplest form, MRTG keeps both long- and short-range statistics for router and switch ports by reading SNMP ifOctets variables. For example, Figure 23.3 shows a daily trend graph for one port on a data center switch. The cool thing is patterns definitely develop; you can tell that the monthly traffic (Figure 23.4) is pretty much the same, but that the yearly trend (Figure 23.5) is getting higher and higher on a gradual basis.

FIGURE 23.3

A daily trend for a router port, showing the hour of day on the bottom.

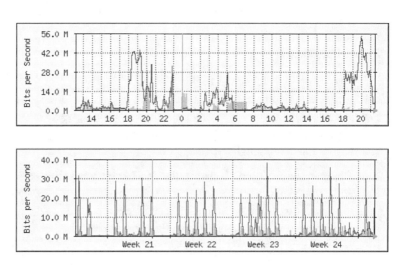

FIGURE 23.4

A monthly trend for a router port, showing week numbers.

FIGURE 23.5

A yearly trend for a router port; you can tell that traffic is gradually increasing over time.

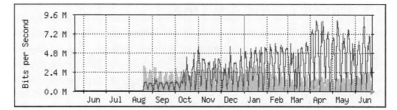

By following the directions given on the MRTG Web site, you can pretty easily craft your own statistic-providing scripts. For example, my site uses MRTG to keep track of email trends (see Figure 23.6). One time, when viewing the monthly graph, we discovered what looked to be a really strange anomaly (see Figure 23.7): 8,000 messages per day when our normal was in the low 2,000s. Whoa! We investigated, and sure enough, discovered a user who was, um, experimenting with automated email, and his experiment had gotten out of control. Plenty of sample configurations are built by folks just like you and me—to monitor things like CPU utilization, free memory, free disk space, and so on—so go to the site and check out the "Companion Sites."

FIGURE 23.6

Email trends provided through MRTG and a custom script shows spam versus real messages. (Thursday was spam attack day.)

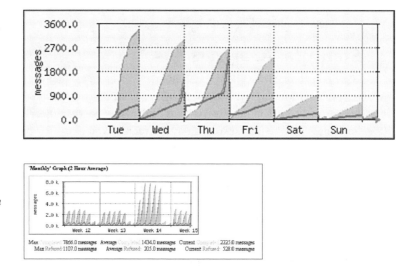

FIGURE 23.7

Anomalies, like the email delivery spike in week 14, need to be investigated.

If you want to get more complicated than graphing two pieces of data, you'll have to check out Cricket (`cricket.sourceforge.net`), or RRDTool (`rrdtool.com`). These are also pretty cool, and they work pretty similarly to MRTG. In fact, RRDTool was written by the fellow who wrote MRTG; and Cricket is basically an MRTG-ish front end to RRDTool. (See `www.ircache.net/Statistics/mrtg` for some good examples of how one site changed over from MRTG to RRDTool.)

Baseline Bottom Line

When you are baselining critical server and network statistics, and a user reports a problem such as slowness on the network, it's a simple matter to compare values that you're *currently* getting to what they *should be* on your baseline graph. This allows you to know whether these stats are out of line for your network. Here's a list of common stats and appropriate actions to take when they look out of spec:

- Network utilization too high—Seek and destroy the "top talker" using a protocol analyzer, check your MAC address documentation, or check your switch MAC-to-port tables.

- Network errors too high—Seek and destroy the top error producer using an analyzer. Also check the cabling.

- Server paging too high—Decrease the number of users or apps on the server or add more memory.

- Server waiting for I/O too high—Upgrade the disk cache or consider a new high-performance disk upgrade.

- Server CPU utilization too high—Decrease the number of users or apps on the server, add CPUs, or replace the server.

Statistical Analyzers

Baseliners typically work by querying devices or hosts; they do *not* sniff the network the way that a packet analyzer does. *Statistical analyzers* are the cross between standard packet analyzers and baseliners. They sniff the network, collect data about it, and create baselines. They're cool, except that they require you to deploy probes throughout your network (much like the diagram in Figure 21.1 in Hour 21, "Protocol Analyzers"), which in practice becomes a pain in the neck. Two statistical analyzers are CompuWare's EcoSCOPE (www.compuware.com) and Network Instruments' Link Analyst (www.networkobserver.com). These tools have output similar to the baseliner traffic indicated previously, but they're (obviously) more centered on network traffic statistics than things like CPU utilization, and so on.

Although I think that baseliners that query hosts tend to be more useful than statistical analyzers, there are definitely uses for these. For example, if you're trying to keep track of what percentage of bandwidth is being used by various applications over, say, a WAN link (whose bandwidth is usually pretty limited), statistical analyzers are a good fit. Can you say, "Geez, guys, stop surfing already and let your Telnet traffic come through"? In all seriousness, though, I've used this type of analyzer to investigate a trouble report at a certain time during a period when it was pretty obvious that Telnet traffic was being slowed down by excessive ESPN surfing.

Speaking of Internet traffic, although this isn't necessarily a network management topic, it's worth mentioning that end-user traffic monitoring and control software and devices, such as SuperScout and Websense, can and do produce traffic graphs. This is cool, but they're not generic tools for network management, and they don't always keep track of *all* Internet traffic—just end-user stuff. Typically, servers aren't configured to use the end-user monitoring devices, so what the end-user monitoring device does not reveal is the true state of the entire Internet pipe. Caveat emptor.

23

Measuring Actual Data Rates

One final note about what you can do to measure the true state of the Internet pipe (or any other pipe) without installing a baselining infrastructure.

One option is to use sites like `dslreports.com` to generate a guesstimate of how much bandwidth is possible through your Internet pipe, but because the good folks at `dslreports.com` don't live in your ISP's data center, it's hard to tell where any given slowdown might be. After all, a slowdown between your ISP and `dslreports.com` will translate as a Net slowdown for you, even if there is no slowdown between your ISP and other Internet sites.

The other option is to use local tools that transmit data, time the transmission, and then come up with a per-second data rate. One tool that I like quite a bit is `ttcp`. Although it is not a Cisco tool, Cisco has a nice write-up about it at `www.cisco.com/warp/public/471/ttcp.html`. Put this one in your tool belt, for sure.

Here's how it works. You run it on two workstations—one at your end, and one at the remote end. If you want to test download speed, do a *transmit* from the remote end and do a *receive* at the local end. If you want to test upload speed, reverse the receive and transmit.

Here's an example to go along with Cisco's write-up. Let's say that I'm using a wireless adapter while I'm sitting in my kitchen. To verify the upload speed from my laptop in the kitchen to my Linux server in the living room (that is, the rate at which I can save files to the server), I'd type the following at the server end:

```
ttcp -r -s
```

If it was a Windows server, I'd use `ttcpw` instead of `ttcp`. The `-r` means "act as a receiver," and the `-s` means "don't display the test data." (If you don't do this, you'll see the test pattern show up on the receiver end, which looks kind of like the screens in *The Matrix*.) Although this might not slow things down, it certainly can't speed things up, so I feel it's the better part of valor to use the `-s` option.

At my laptop end, I would then initiate a transmit (-t), using a test pattern (-s) for 1,000 test buffers (-n1000):

```
ttcp -t -s -n1000 myserver
```

The output looks like this, and shows that I'm getting about 400 kilobytes per second out of my wireless LAN because of range issues:

```
ttcp-t: buflen=8192, nbuf=1000, align=16384/0, port=5001  tcp  -> myserver
ttcp-t: socket
ttcp-t: connect
ttcp-t: 8192000 bytes in 18.99 seconds = 421.34 KB/sec +++
ttcp-t: 1000 I/O calls, msec/call = 19.44, calls/sec = 52.67
```

If you wanted to do this with your ISP, you would just have to find a friendly soul at your ISP willing to run ttcp for you. I find it pretty easy to find someone at the ISP who will do this because most of the time you're trying to *rule out* the ISP connection as the source of a slowdown, which is what they're interested in doing.

Summary

"Network management" can be a slippery phrase; it's used to refer to everything but the kitchen sink. In its most helpful form, network management involves remote network monitoring and configuration, which allows you to assess the health of your network, as well as to tweak things from a distance.

Tools can be broken down into several categories: SNMP management consoles, which can auto-discover your network, track critical SNMP statistics, receive SNMP traps, and page you when things are out of spec. Pollers, unlike SNMP management stations, actually attempt to contact services the way that end users do; the good ones also keep track of response time and page you when things are "down" or simply slow. Packages like WhatsUp combine SNMP console functionality with polling. SNMP traps can be annoying or they can be a blessing, depending on whether they're waking you up in the middle of the night for a printer jam or to alert you that a public safety system is down.

Baselining tools such as MRTG, Cricket, and RRDTool are really good and inexpensive ways to keep long-term track of critical statistics such as server CPU utilization, network utilization on switches, ports, and servers, and even "custom" statistics, such as email received. Baseliners use either SNMP or custom host-based scripts to extract pertinent data. Statistical analyzers, on the other hand, are basically distributed protocol analyzers with the heart of a baseliner; they naturally concentrate on what is happening on the wire, rather than what is happening with a given host. Although this is powerful, probe deployment makes this an expensive proposition.

However you do it, baselining your network is an important step in being able to quickly rule out what is *not* causing a problem; they're important because if you don't know how things are when life is great, you have no reference to troubleshoot by. With a baseline, you can compare current stats to "normal" stats—just as a doctor does when diagnosing your blood chemistry—and quickly take action to fix it.

Q&A

23

Q **How do I configure my SNMP agents to send traps to my SNMP management station?**

A Each SNMP-enabled device is different. Some devices use a GUI to specify a SNMP manager that accepts the IP number of the trap destination; others only broadcast SNMP traps. Some routers can be configured to catch these broadcasts and forward them to the real trap manager. Check your documentation for specifics.

Q **I've got three file and print servers, one intranet server, forty workstations, an Internet firewall, a DMZ, and a Web server on the outside. What type of network monitoring is right for me?**

A You said "monitoring," without saying "predict" or "resource," so my bet is that you're probably just interested in whether things are up or down, not in baselining or resource management. In particular, Web monitoring is accomplished just fine by polling. I'd invest a small amount of money in a polling solution and then plan to investigate an SNMP solution if polling isn't enough for your needs. From the size of your network, however, I'd guess that the polling will suit you just fine.

Workshop

Is it workshop time already? Wow! Time does pass so quickly when you're having fun. Well, here we go with the quiz and a couple of activities.

Quiz

1. When you monitor a network, you're typically interested in what?

   a. Resource utilization

   b. Availability

   c. Neither A nor B

   d. Both A and B

2. True or False: Network polling packages, unlike SNMP solutions, typically provide you with a detailed picture of resource utilization and device statistics.

3. What is an SNMP trap?

    a. When a vendor entices you to spend too much money on an SNMP solution

    b. An alert issued by an SNMP agent intended for a management station

    c. A point-to-point communication between two management stations

    d. An event that occurs after a server's power goes off

4. What is RMON?

    a. An SNMP MIB

    b. A standard for the types of information a probe can supply to a management station

    c. Both A and B

    d. Neither A nor B

5. Good SNMP management stations and good polling software will allow you to what?

    a. Broadcast

    b. Baseline

    c. Babble

    d. None of the above

6. What are the advantages to using polling software?

    a. Lets you know when actual services are down or slow from a user point of view

    b. Allows you to configure end stations

    c. SNMP compliant

    d. All of the above

7. What does a statistical analyzer do that typical baseline software does not do?

    a. Uses SNMP

    b. Monitors network traffic by using probes

    c. Uses custom scripts to collect data from hosts

    d. Uses Excel to present a spreadsheet of data

8. True or False: Internet traffic monitors that are geared toward browsing, such as SuperScout, typically sift through all traffic going through your Internet pipe.

Answers to Quiz Questions

1. D

2. False (it's the other way around)

3. B (it uses UDP port 162, by the way)

4. C

5. B

6. A

7. B

8. False (they *typically* just examine user-initiated traffic from workstations)

23

Activities

1. Check out how people are using MRTG; you can start with www.menet.umn.edu/stats. Then, go to www.somix.com/software/mrtg and download a custom template that is useful to your site.

2. Download the MIB browser from MG-Soft (www.mg-soft.com) and start to browse through SNMP-enabled devices on your network. To see manufacturer-specific MIB variables, download MIBs either from your manufacturer or from www.somix.com/software/mibs.

HOUR **24**

Reverse Engineering, Discovery Tools, and Other Black Magic

The beginning and end of all human endeavors are untidy.

—John Galsworthy

Congratulations! You've been following along, and have a good grasp on the skills in Hours 1–23. Armed with these skills, you now know enough to reverse-engineer *anybody* else's undocumented network, no matter how much it's snarled up. Hoo-ah!

You've probably noticed that documentation has been a major theme of this book. And why? If you've turned ahead to this hour out of desperation, you might well be the victim of somebody else's undocumented network, and you have a good idea of how frustrating it can be. Fret not. This is where we're going to comb the tangles out of that undocumented network and make it into a reliable, manageable beast. It's going to be humming along by the time you get through.

Grab a sharp pencil and take a deep breath: You're about to chart uncharted territory, using both your street smarts as well as some interesting discovery tools. We'll start with OSI layer 1, and talk about physical cable tracing and infrastructure identification; we'll then move straight on to layer 3, the network layer. Finally, we'll chat about how to use SNMP to identify network infrastructure, and how to use port scanners to document where various application services on your network live.

We're going to assume that you've come into possession of a *working* network; it's too tough to reverse-engineer a network that's broken. That said, let's hurry and document it before it goes down. The network is up now, so today's the day.

Cable Tracing

An unlabeled cable is a troubleshooter's nightmare. After all, it's in the wall, making it just a little hard to know where the heck it's going. Fortunately, most sites only have a certain number of electrical closets, which narrows the number of locations that you'll need to search. (There is, of course, the apocryphal story about the server and hub that gets accidentally plastered behind a wall with nobody being able to find it, but I've never believed that, have you?)

One tool is an absolute must if you're trying to trace (and label) unlabeled cables—for less than $100, you can get an *inductive tone generator* and an *inductive tone tracer*. (Jensen Tools, at www.jensentools.com, is one supplier, but there are others.) The theory behind these tools is that the generator creates a strong and "known" electromagnetic signal on the wire that the tracer can then find along the length of the wire using inductive principles—that is, even without touching the wire. Very cool! This allows you to quickly and easily trace a wire from one end to another.

The operation of the generator/tracer pair is pretty simple. Follow these steps:

1. Identify the wall jack or cable end that you want to start with. (I start with "far end" stuff, for reasons you'll see in a minute.)

2. Hook the tone *generator* to the cable, following the wiring directions that come with it. The generator usually has alligator clips that can be hooked either to bare wire or to a network plug adapter (see Figure 24.1) for existing sockets.

3. Switch the generator to "continuity," rather than "tone." Make *sure* that you do *not* have continuity (the continuity light should not come on) or the tone generation will not work well. (If you do have continuity, use different combinations of wires until you do not.) Switch the generator back to "tone" and continue.

FIGURE 24.1

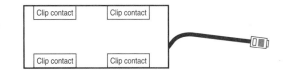

You can clip your tone generator to a plug adapter to trace wires that already have sockets.

4. Take the tone *tracer* and do a quick test to make sure that everything is working: Follow the wire a couple of feet down, and make sure that you can hear a tone—remember that you shouldn't have to touch the cable to hear the tone. Notice how the tone gets stronger as you move toward the cable.

5. Take the tone tracer to a site where most cables seem to "terminate" and wave the tracer near all the cables. If you hear a tone, you're in the right area. Play "hot and cold." (As the tone gets louder, you're closer to the right cable; as it gets softer, you're getting away from the cable.)

6. Repeat this at different closets, hubs, and so on until you find the cable.

7. Label both ends, including patch panels, wall boxes, and the cable itself.

You now see why you put the generator at the workstation end: You want to limit the number of places you have to visit with the tracer.

If you only have a couple of ports to deal with, or if you don't have an inductive tracer, you can always have a friend turn off a computer while you're looking at the hub. The hub port light that goes out belongs to the PC that just got turned off. Turn the PC back on and check the hub light to make sure that this wasn't a coincidence; now you can label the wire appropriately.

I usually find tracing large groups of cables to be too mind-numbing of an exercise to do all at once; but if I do it in small lots mixed in with other more interesting work, it's pretty tolerable. The end goal is a noble one: Remember, if for any given problem you have to spend 10 minutes finding the toner and then another 10 minutes tracing the cable, that's 20 more minutes of downtime per problem. Multiply this over the course of a year, and the time spent becomes pretty scary to contemplate. It's always better to have cables pre-labeled.

Network Infrastructure Discovery

Your first task in discovering how a TCP/IP network is laid out is to identify the "glue" of the network—the routers! The easiest way to discover the routers on your network is to go to a functional workstation and server and check the TCP/IP configuration. Go to several in different locations, particularly if you're not sure whether you have multiple VLANs or other data link segmenting mechanisms.

Router Configuration

Can you use Telnet or SSH to access the router? Or, does it have a Web interface? Being able to access the router's native configuration interface is totally ideal; you can gather whatever information you need.

Oh, no! It's asking for a password. Hopefully, because you own this router, you have the password. (Check inside the manual's front and back covers; some folks write it in one of those places.) If not, call the manufacturer for technical support. If the manufacturer won't help you, don't despair. Although you *definitely* should have the password in case you need to troubleshoot or reconfigure this router, you still can discover your network without it—it'll just take a little more sleuthing. (I'll talk about this in a little while.)

Here are some good passwords to try:

- `manager`
- `security`
- `supervisor`
- `admin`
- `administrator`
- `root`
- Press the Enter key
- The name of the company that makes the device, such as `Linksys`.
- 12345 (and variations on that, like 54321, 1234, 4321, and so forth)
- Your company or product name (or one word of your company name)

You'd be amazed at how many folks (particularly the people who don't document the networks they build) leave the "default" passwords on devices or simply pick "bad" passwords.

If you still can't get into the router or switch, it might be time for surgery. Better now than in an emergency, right? Check out vendor pages for ways to reset the password on a router. Of course, you'll need physical access to the router, and you'll have some downtime, but this shouldn't be a problem because you own the router, right?

Of course, you shouldn't simply shoot from the hip. First, check out alternative means of access, like SNMP, which is discussed in a moment. Next, if you are totally stumped, first gather all the configuration information you can (in case the router configuration gets blown away), and schedule the password reset for a block of time when nobody needs the network. (Most businesses usually identify a window for scheduled downtime. That would be the time to reset the password on the router if necessary.)

At any rate, being able to access the router's *CLI (Command Line Interface)* means that you can also create a status report on which interfaces are which network numbers. Write 'em down! Don't know how to show the addresses on the router? Check the manual.

> Many routers will show you which router commands are available if you type **?** or **help**.
>
> If you can't find the manual in your shop, check the manufacturer's Web site; most manufacturers keep the manuals on the Web as a service to their customers.

Another cool and highly informative task you can perform while in the router is to dump the routing table. As nasty as that sounds, it just means that you're going to list all the known routes to that router. All the routes that apply to your organization are going to be in the route table—be sure to write down the list of network numbers (even if the router is not connected to them) with their next hops. The next hop will be a router that knows something more about that network, and it's more than likely only a hop or two away from the network. Repeat this process until you have all the networks written down with a corresponding router identification. (Naturally, doing this on software routers and hardware routers is a good idea.)

24

> By convention, most routers for a given network segment have either node numbers starting at the first possible number and working up to as many routers as there are on that segment, or starting at the top of the range and working down. For example, for 24-bit network mask (255.255.255.0), you'd start with 1 or 254. See www.cisco.com/univercd/cc/td/doc/product/iaabu/pix/pix_v50/config/subnets.htm for some typical IP address ranges.

Once you have an idea of which routers have which IP numbers, you should be able to start drawing a map. Start with the router, draw the network segments off of it, and then play "connect the dots." That is, make correlations between which routers have common network numbers and then connect them (see Figure 24.2).

FIGURE 24.2

Once you've laid out your network pieces, like LEGOs, you can then snap them together using common networks to reveal the entire picture.

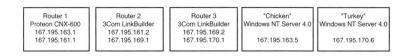

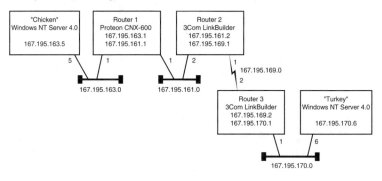

Servers

If you have an idea of what the server names are, you're one step further in the right direction. If not, you'll have to perform name discovery. From an operational workstation, look at the DNS configuration. No DNS configuration? That's *possible*—some sites don't use DNS—but *very* unlikely if the Internet is in the picture. If you're *sure* that no DNS is available, you have two options for gathering hostnames and IP addresses of servers:

- Check the `C:\Windows\HOSTS` file on several functional workstations.
- Check the client configuration of several functional workstations.

For the second option, you'll have to be familiar with the client (for example, the Telnet client). Many Telnet clients allow you to put a hostname or IP address in the command line that invokes the program, so check the properties of a working icon to glean hostnames or IP addresses. One example of this is shown in Figure 24.3, where the word `assessor` is used as a command line parameter to the executable, `"c:\program files\netterm\netterm.exe"`. It's entirely possible that someone has set up an entire office using just IP addresses—in which case, you'd see an IP address (such as `192.168.2.303`) rather than `assessor`). This is totally crazy, but I've seen it happen.

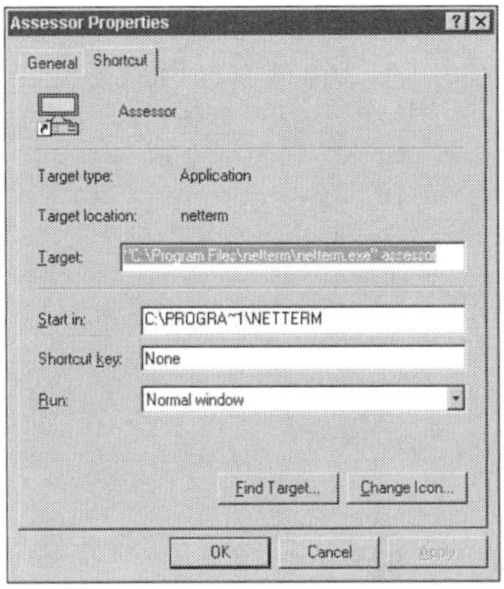

FIGURE 24.3

The Assessor icon points to the program NETTERM, *but is also configured with the command-line parameter of* assessor, *a hostname.*

If DNS *is* in the picture, you can usually dump the name table using nslookup, as discussed in Hour 22, "Network Troubleshooters Just Wanna Have Fun." Remember, nslookup doesn't work for Windows 9x; you'll have to use a tool with nslookup functionality. Some of the "network discovery" tools listed in the next section dump any given name table (see Figure 24.4).

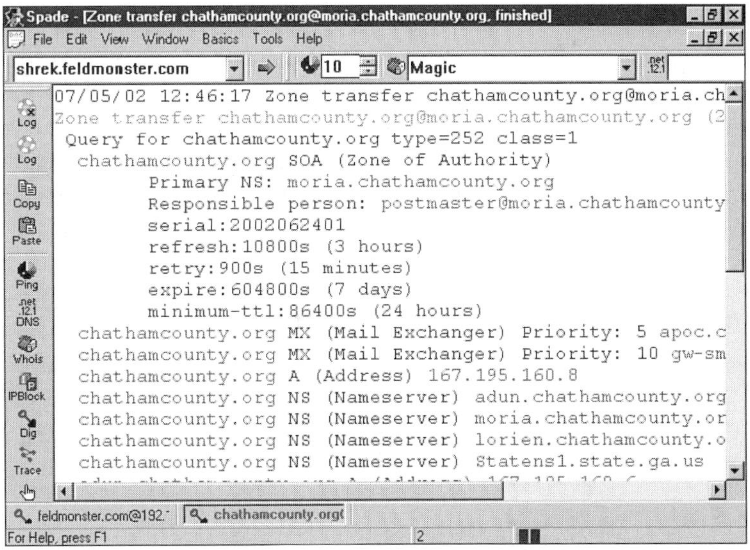

FIGURE 24.4

Because nslookup *isn't an option for Windows 9x users, you'll have to use a third-party utility. Sam Spade is one utility that can dump a zone.*

Some people configure their name servers to disallow a name dump from an arbitrary workstation. This is a good security practice but a pain in the neck for network discovery. You'll have to log in to the primary or secondary server and print out the DNS configuration file. On UNIX, you can usually take a look at the `/etc/named.conf` file:

```
options {
        directory "/usr/local/named";
};

zone "feldmonster.com" IN {
        type master;
        file "feldmonster.com";
        allow-update { none; };
};
```

This points you to the data files. (In this case, this is a primary name server; it keeps its database for the zone in the `feldmonster.com` file. Because there's a `directory` keyword in the boot file, you'll specifically find the `feldmonster.com` data file in `/usr/local/named` rather than in the default directory.)

Once you have either server names and IP addresses for your important servers, connect them to the appropriate segments laid out when you performed router discovery. If the servers are on a segment that you don't know about, perform a `traceroute` to the server, which will show you the segments that it passes through. You can Telnet to each hop (assuming that the router has Telnet capability), gather configuration information along the way, and flesh out your map. Alternatively, use an SNMP tool to check out the router's routing table (discussed in a moment).

Application Discovery

Discovering applications on your network is just as essential as discovering the wires and the basic network infrastructure. After all, if you figure out that DNS at your organization is completely hosed up, it might be nice to know exactly which servers on your network offer DNS.

SNMP: Application and Network Tool

SNMP has a sort of dual existence. On one hand, it's a very important part of your network infrastructure. On the other hand, it *is* a TCP/IP application—it's just embedded on your hardware platforms.

No matter what device you're attempting to find—routers, switches, servers—the wonderful thing about SNMP, if you're arriving at a new job where your predecessor hasn't documented anything, is that its community strings (remember, these are passwords) are very easily guessed. For our purposes, we're mainly interested in the read-only community string. The likelihood is that your predecessor, not caring enough to document, probably didn't care enough to change the default community string. Try `public`. If this doesn't work, try `private`. Still not working? This is not that common a problem, but it does happen. In this case, check out these community string discovery utilities:

- In the Windows world, you can't go wrong with SolarWinds SNMP Brute Force Attack, part of the SolarWinds network tools arsenal (`www.solarwinds.net`).
- If you're running Unix, snag ADMsnmp from any one of various security-oriented sites—for example, `www.softpanorama.org/Security/port_scanners.shtml`.

Once you have the community string, SNMP is really, really useful. You can use a MIB browser or console to display the routing table of any managed device, as shown in Figure 24.5, or you can simply tell SNMP network management software (see Hour 23, "Network Management Tools") to auto-discover the entire network—and presumably, if it has MIBs loaded for each and every piece of server software you're running, it will correctly identify the apps on the servers. In practice, this rarely happens. It's pretty common for devices to be misrepresented after an auto-discovery. "Totally automatic" discovery, with SNMP, basically means "trust, but verify."

24

FIGURE 24.5

Routing tables are easy to display if you're using SNMP software and you have the correct community string.

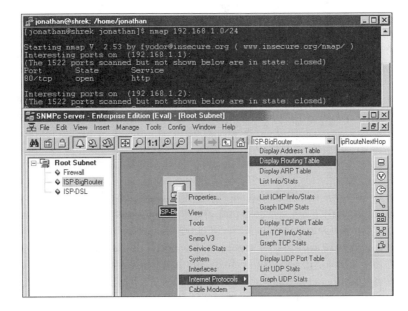

Here's one other point about SNMP: Even if you don't have the community string, a device that runs SNMP responds to an SNMP query from your MIB browser or management console. Those that respond (as opposed to those that aren't running SNMP at all) are likely to be a server, router, switch, or other infrastructure device. Further application-level investigation of devices that respond to SNMP (and the discovery of the community string) is definitely in order.

Application Discovery Using Port Scanners

The security community has blessed network troubleshooters by creating *port scanners*: software that thoroughly checks for "listening" ports on a range of IP addresses—and thus identifies the application software that is likely running on a given IP address.

These are either free, or cost less than $100, making them, in my opinion, quite a bargain for what they enable you to accomplish. From a TCP standpoint, they work by doing what you or I would do if we were attempting to troubleshoot a TCP service: They attempt to establish a TCP connection, not worrying about the application specifics, and record which ports allow a connection. Some of these port scanners (for example, nmap) also support UDP.

Whoa, you say, UDP is connectionless. How can you attempt to form a connection with a UDP server? Wouldn't you have to "speak the lingo" of the service to get a response?

Well, you're right. But here's the interesting thing: UDP is discovered not by positive response, but by negative response. *Most* hosts, when you attempt to send a message to an invalid UDP port, send an administrative message back to your TCP/IP stack via ICMP (Internet Control Message Protocol, the same protocol that is used for ping) indicating that your machine has attempted to reach a port that doesn't exist (to get technical, it generates a ICMP_PORT_UNREACH message). By keeping track of which ports *do not* generate this message, tools like nmap are able to, by process of elimination, keep track of which ports are open.

This is hugely useful because you can run a quick scan on your IP address range and receive a list of which ports on which IP addresses are in a listening state. Check out the nmap scan in Figure 24.6—it shows a scan of the network 192.168.1.0/24, which, of course, can also be written as 192.168.1.0 / 255.255.255.0. This network was scanned in 63 seconds, found six hosts up, and scanned several thousand ports per host, finding common services on each. As you can see, this is a pretty quick method for obtaining information about services that are running on all network devices.

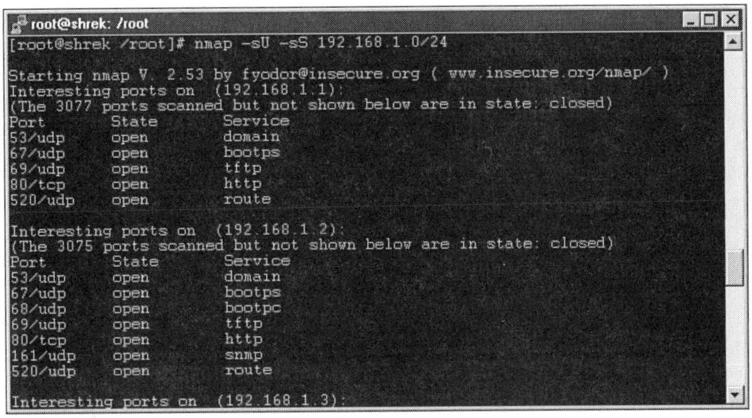

24

FIGURE 24.6

The nmap *utility is quite configurable, scans TCP and UDP, and provides quick output.*

```
root@shrek: /root
[root@shrek /root]# nmap -sU -sS 192.168.1.0/24

Starting nmap V. 2.53 by fyodor@insecure.org ( www.insecure.org/nmap/ )
Interesting ports on  (192.168.1.1):
(The 3077 ports scanned but not shown below are in state: closed)
Port        State        Service
53/udp      open         domain
67/udp      open         bootps
69/udp      open         tftp
80/tcp      open         http
520/udp     open         route

Interesting ports on  (192.168.1.2):
(The 3075 ports scanned but not shown below are in state: closed)
Port        State        Service
53/udp      open         domain
67/udp      open         bootps
68/udp      open         bootpc
69/udp      open         tftp
80/tcp      open         http
161/udp     open         snmp
520/udp     open         route

Interesting ports on  (192.168.1.3):
```

What about proprietary, high port numbers for services such as Lotus Notes or GroupWise? Well, you can certainly specify to your tool that these port numbers should be included in the wide-ranging scan (for example, you could specify TCP/1677 and TCP/7100 for GroupWise), but my advice is to not worry about these initially. Once you identify that a server is running at a certain IP address, you can do a more thorough port scan later.

Software with port scanner functionality includes

- nmap—www.insecure.org/nmap (Unix and Windows)
- Internet Anywhere Toolkit—www.tnsoft.com/toolkit.htm (Windows)
- Sam Spade—www.samspade.org (Windows)

Summary

Once you understand the underlying technology of a network, reverse-engineering it isn't hard—just tedious. However, getting an inductive toner set is a must if you have a lot of unlabeled cables.

From a network perspective, on a functioning network (that is, if servers are talking to each other and to workstations), there's always a trail that you can follow, starting with the routing tables and the DNS. Don't forget, application configuration can be very helpful.

SNMP is very useful if you have the community strings, but if you don't, discovery tools are available. Although SNMP consoles' network discovery agents can be a good starting point, rest assured that you will be doing manual verification. Finally, a good port scanner is your best friend when it comes to identifying which applications live on which hosts on your network.

Q&A

Q **Some of this network discovery stuff looks like cracker-type espionage. Are you sure I should be doing this?**

A If the network that you're performing a discovery on isn't a network that you're responsible for, definitely not. It's considered antisocial and possibly illegal to gather this type of information without authorization. However, if you're the person responsible for this network, you've *got* to know this information. If someone has not left you a paper trail, you must create one. Just as in the movies, the good guys use some of the same tools as the bad guys—it just depends what your motives and responsibilities are.

Q **Any more tips for TCP/IP discovery without automation tools?**

A Sure, but isn't it worth $15 or a 10-minute download to save a couple of hours of your time? I highly recommend the automated discovery tools. Back in the bad old days, I lost hours of my life manually discovering networks that I could have otherwise spent doing something fun or productive.

One interesting thing you can do to discover routing tables is to go to a server that you *do* have access to, add RIP, and *then* dump the routing table using `netstat -rn`. (For example, if you have a Linux box; just add the gated package to it, have it listen for RIP, and see if you discover anything. This seems like a lot of work compared to downloading a cheap or free utility, though, doesn't it?)

Workshop

Hey! Lucky you! It's workshop time again! The quiz and activities will help you make the most of this hour.

Quiz

1. The generator part of an inductive tone generator/tracer pair should be put where?

   a. At the far end, away from where most cables terminate

   b. At the concentrator end, where most cables terminate

   c. In the middle of the cable

   d. None of the above

2. The first thing to find when performing network discovery is the address of a what?

   a. Server

   b. Novell file and print service

    c. Web server

    d. Router

3. True or False: Once you discover all the routers on your network, it's a simple matter to map all the servers to where they belong.

4. True or False: All TCP/IP networks use DNS.

5. You can't find a DNS server for a network that you've been hired to reverse-engineer. A sensible way to find host addresses would be to check the _____ of a functional PC.

    a. network card

    b. router entry

    c. client application configuration

    d. destination hop

6. After you perform an auto-discovery of your network using SNMP, _____.

    a. your job is done.

    b. it is likely that your job is done.

    c. it is likely that you will have to verify that the discovered network is in fact accurate.

    d. None of the above.

7. True or False: Because UDP is not connection-oriented like TCP is, it is impossible to scan a server for open UDP ports.

Answers to Quiz Questions

1. A

2. D

3. True

4. False

5. C

6. C

7. False. Certain packages, like nmap, will do this.

24

Activities

1. Using a cable that is *not* in a wall, trace it using an inductive toner. What happens to the signal strength if you short out a wire pair (that is, hook wire #1 to wire #2 at the far end) and then try to trace it?

2. Download `nmap` from `www.insecure.org` and experiment with the OS "fingerprinting" feature. (Hint: Use the `-O` flag.) How useful might this be in documenting an undocumented network?

INDEX

How can we make this index more useful? Email us at indexes@samspublishing.com.

How can we make this index more useful? Email us at indexes@samspublishing.com.

How can we make this index more useful? Email us at indexes@samspublishing.com.